Production in the UK of the high speed trains for the Intercity Express will commence in 2016.

A CHALLENGE FOR THE FUTURE

Looking back at the events in the rail industry over the past year, I find it very striking that we have had another outstanding year, with much to celebrate. 2014 has seen the celebration of the rail industry's 175-year-history in Derby, a heritage that Britain can be very proud of. This exhibited the many faces of the rail industry and how UK companies are ready to invest, innovate and continue going strong into the future.

The year also saw the much-awaited contract award for rolling stock for Crossrail, with massive tunnelling and infrastructure works continuing, as well as the presentation of the first Thameslink train to the public, all of which were tangible proof of significant progress in these two major projects.

It is also very encouraging to see that politicians across all parties have expressed their support for ongoing investment into rail, a commitment to expanding the rail network and to electrification. The celebration of 50 years of high-speed 'shinkansen' bullet trains in Japan was a great reminder of the economic benefits a well-performing high-speed rail network can bring to a country. It is therefore encouraging to see that HS2 is now firmly rooted in the future agenda and discussions on HS3 and Crossrail 2 are taking shape. This helps to reinforce the view of rail being an industry of the future – not the past. However, this future can only be safeguarded when real action is taken to tackle the problems of an ageing workforce that cannot sustain itself. Announcements such as the establishment of a high-speed college were therefore welcome news to the rail industry, as attracting young people to the rail industry is just as important as keeping them, and nurturing and developing their skills.

2014 has also seen great progress on the construction of the first train factory to be built in the UK in over 100 years. Work at the Hitachi Rail Vehicle Manufacturing Facility is ongoing and the production of the high speed trains for the Intercity Express will commence in 2016. Keeping the manufacturing tradition in Britain alive through the production of rolling stock and the promotion of a vibrant supply chain will continue to be vital to the UK economy.

Already in 2014, we have seen great steps by government and the private sector to further develop and secure the rail supply chain for years to come. Ongoing investment into electrification, new signalling and Traffic Management Systems guarantees that the industry has the opportunity to move forward with confidence into 2015 and the future. With the government and Network Rail dedicated to improving the infrastructure and performance of the network across the country, 2015 will be a busy year for us as an industry.

In all areas, we are making great strides to focus more and more on increasing capacity and becoming more cost effective. And that for me is a great indication of a change in thinking. While high-speed rail travel is of course a desirable goal, we are moving to a focus on network capacity and ensuring that existing lines are being used to their best potential. ETCS technology and Traffic Management Systems are major steps to a Digital Railway offering 21st century technology, delivering increased capacity on our railway lines, reducing headway between trains, while ensuring a safer service, and enabling integrated systems solutions to be implemented simultaneously.

At the same time, the transport industry needs to move even more to a whole-systems approach, where we no longer see ourselves as a number of separate entities, but a fully integrated industry, delivering a better travel solution to the public. Improving the end-to end journey experience for passengers will increase our ability to get new passengers onto the railway. As our industry is maturing, and technology moves ever onwards, this whole-system approach is becoming increasingly important and passengers will greatly benefit from this focus on a reliable, smooth, efficient and customer-focused rail operation.

To maintain the current healthy growth in rail travel, we must recognise that our passengers' expectations are for a 21st century service with 21st century technology, and this is our challenge for the future.

We have big tasks ahead of us, but visionary thinking will help us to deliver these expectations.

Keith Jordan,
Managing Director,
Hitachi Rail Europe

CONTENTS

3 Foreword by Keith Jordan, MD of Hitachi Rail Europe

SECTION 1 - SETTING THE AGENDA - INDUSTRY STRUCTURE

9 Innovation – Key Enabler for the Future: Jeremy Candfield, Director General, the Railway Industry Association
10 Rail Freight on Track for 2015: Maggie Simpson, Executive Director, the Rail Freight Group
11 2015 - Year of Uncertainty. Business review by Roger Ford, Industry & Technology Editor of Modern Railways
15 Across the industry
- Department for Transport
- Scotland and Wales
- Network Rail
- Office of Rail Regulation
- Rail Delivery Group
- Passenger Focus
- The privatised rail industry

SECTION 2 - FINANCE AND LEASING

28 Angel Trains
30 Eversholt Rail Group
31 Porterbrook Leasing
33 Britain's rolling stock - who owns it?
- The ROSCO fleets

SECTION 3 - TRAIN FLEET MANUFACTURE AND MAINTENANCE

40 Knorr-Bremse RailServices
41 Direct awards revive Rolling Stock market - review by Roger Ford
46 Hitachi
48 Bombardier
50 Siemens
52 GE Transportation Electro-Motive Diesel
54 Alstom
56 Vossloh
    CAF
58 Wabtec Group

SECTION 4 - PASSENGER TRAIN OPERATORS

60 ESG
61 Train operating company index
62 Passenger operator finances: review by TAS's Chris Cheek
68 First Group:
69 First Great Western
70 First TransPennine Express
71 First Hull Trains
72 ScotRail
74 Serco and Abellio:
74 Northern
76 Merseyrail
77 Greater Anglia
79 Govia:
79 GTR (Govia Thameslink Railway)
80 Southern
82 Southeastern
85 London Midland
87 Arriva:
87 Chiltern Railways
88 Arriva Trains Wales
89 CrossCountry
91 Grand Central
92 Stagecoach:
92 South West Trains
93 East Midlands Trains
95 Virgin Trains
96 c2c
97 East Coast
98 Eurostar
99 Eurotunnel
100 Heathrow Express

SECTION 5 - FREIGHT AND HAULAGE

104 Railfreight looks to the future - we analyse the freight market
- Freight company accounts
107 Finning UK
108 DB Schenker UK
109 GB Railfreight
110 Freightliner

111	Colas Rail Freight
	Direct Rail Services
114	BARS, Riviera Trains, West Coast Railway

SECTION 6 - INNOVATION AND ENVIRONMENT

114	Knorr-Bremse
115	New boost for Community Rail? Modern Railways columnist Alan Williams reviews progress and prospects
118	The Railway Industry Innovation Awards
■	Golden Spanners focus on reliable trains
■	The Golden Whistles awards
■	The Fourth Friday Club
120	Industry exhibitions update

SECTION 7 - KEY PROJECTS AND CONSULTANTS

122	Delta Rail
123	Electrification at the Crossroads – Roger Ford on a crucial year for electrification
127	Thales
128	Atkins
129	Key projects
■	London Crossrail
■	Intercity Express Programme
■	Thameslink Programme
■	High Speed 2
■	Scotland's rail projects
■	Great Western modernisation
■	Consultant files – supporting rail developments

SECTION 8 - INFRASTRUCTURE MAINTENANCE AND RENEWAL

136	Lloyd's Register
137	NR drives towards reliable assets
■	Infrastructure review
■	The main infrastructure contractors

SECTION 9 - SIGNALLING AND CONTROL

144	Siemens Rail Automation
146	Signalling review
■	Traffic Management develops
■	ERTMS infrastructure, ETCS cab fitment

SECTION 10 - LIGHT RAIL AND METRO

154	Light rail spreads its wings
■	GB light rail systems reviewed
158	Thales
159	Transport for London
■	London Underground
■	London Overground

SECTION 11 - INTO EUROPE

164	Bombardier
165	Into Europe - developments in European rail

169 - THE MODERN RAILWAY DIRECTORY

A compendium of 2,250 UK Rail businesses, suppliers and industry bodies

For the Fallen: loco No 91111 running through Morpeth with a King's Cross to Edinburgh express on 24 October 2014. **BILL WALSH**

The Modern Railway

Editor:	Ken Cordner
Production Editor:	David Lane
Contributors:	Roger Ford
	Alan Williams
	John Glover
	Chris Shilling
	Ken Harris
	Tony Miles
	Chris Cheek
	Keith Fender
Advertisement Manager:	Chris Shilling
Advertising Production:	Cheryl Thornburn
Graphic Design:	Matt Chapman
	Jack Taylor
Managing Director and Publisher:	Adrian Cox
Commercial Director:	Ann Saundry
Project Manager:	David Lane
Executive Chairman:	Richard Cox

The Modern Railway is published by:
Key Publishing Limited, PO Box 100,
Stamford, Lincs PE9 1XP

Printing:
Printed in England by Berforts Information Press Ltd,
Southfield Road, Eynsham, Oxford, OX29 4JB

Purchasing additional copies of *The Modern Railway*:
Please contact our Martin Steele on 01780 755 131
or by email at martin.steele@keypublishing.com
Corporate and bulk purchase discounts are available on request.

Thank you!
We are very grateful to the many individuals from businesses in all sectors of the railway who have kindly provided help in compiling The Modern Railway. Information contained in The Modern Railway was believed correct at the time of going to press in November 2014. We would be glad to receive corrections and updates for the next edition.

© Key Publishing Ltd 2014

All rights reserved. No part of this publication may be reproduced or transmitted in any form by any means, electronic or mechanical, including photocopying, recording or by any information storage and retrieval system, without prior permission in writing from the copyright owner. Multiple copying of the contents of the publication without prior written approval is not permitted.

Cover photos: Hitachi, Network Rail, Tony Miles, Stewart Armstrong and Brian Morrison
ISBN 978-0-946219-71-1

National Rail Enquiries
08457 48 49 50
www.nationalrail.co.uk

SETTING THE AGENDA

IN ASSOCIATION WITH
HITACHI
Inspire the Next

vossloh
KIEPE

Vossloh Kiepe UK

Perfection in integration

With the introduction of ERTMS and greater demands for technical enhancements, our engineers are keeping relentlessly busy, finding new ways to fit more equipment into less space.

We combine longstanding UK experience with our parent group's expertise, gathered from further afield. Relying on Vossloh Kiepe UK for your next contract, you can ensure that challenges are overcome, projects are delivered... and your success is sweet.

Vossloh Kiepe UK Ltd 2 Priestley Wharf, Holt St, Aston, Birmingham B7 4BN
T +44 (0)121 359 7777   E enquiries@vkb.vossloh.com

Innovative tunnelling techniques have enabled Crossrail's impressive tunnelling achievements, with just a 'final push' from Whitechapel towards Farringdon to be completed in 2015. During the second half of 2014, whilst tunnelling continued, the project's focus began to shift to the substantial job of fitting out the stations and tunnels. In the photo, tunnelling machine Victoria breaks through into Whitechapel station in April 2014. **COPYRIGHT CROSSRAIL**

INNOVATION
KEY ENABLER FOR THE FUTURE

As usual, The Modern Railway 2015 provides a valuable insight into the diversity of the rail industry. The many examples of projects and developments covered show increasing evidence of the march of new technologies, essential if the industry is to continue to grow and thrive, as it has been doing so successfully since the mid-1990s.

There is widespread recognition that innovation is a key enabler for the future of the industry, to reduce costs, to improve network capacity, to improve the commercial environment and, not least, to attract the best talent. Much work is going on behind the scenes to develop new technology and facilitate innovation, with the active involvement of cross-industry bodies including the Future Railway Group, the Rail Delivery Group and the recently-formed Rail Supply Group.

At the Railway Industry Association, we ourselves have been heavily involved in promoting and assisting innovation, not least through the 'Unlocking Innovation Scheme' that we run under the Future Railway umbrella, working with and on behalf of the industry's Technical Strategy Leadership Group.

The scheme is a collaboration of rail industry clients and innovation-enabling organisations, including Network Rail, London Underground, UKTram, the Association of Train Operating Companies (ATOC), Future Railway, RSSB, Innovate UK and the Knowledge Transfer Network.

Based on day workshops, the scheme seeks to foster innovation across the industry by bringing together suppliers and clients to share challenges, solutions and best practice. Helping companies to develop a spirit of innovation, facilitating access to the considerable support available, and promoting the transfer of technologies from other industries are all of vital importance.

Companies themselves of course will continue to develop their own products and services, but are receiving increasing encouragement from key players. Network Rail in particular is strongly promoting the concept of 'The Digital Railway'. Use of new technologies is already starting to transform ticketing and commercial systems, which should develop faster, with cardboard tickets being anachronistic in an era of Smartphones. But 'The Digital Railway' is much more than that; digital technology has a much wider role to play, in train control systems, in testing of new installations, in monitoring and maintenance systems and many other functions.

Academia also has a role to play, with a number of leading Universities with strong rail expertise forming partnerships with the commercial sector, principally under the auspices of the Rail Research UK Association (RRUKA). This opens up access to a much wider scope of knowledge, research, development and testing facilities than most companies could expect to have themselves.

One important aspect is that research and innovation is not just in the domain of the larger companies. Some of the most exciting and potentially important developments come from smaller companies, which emphasises the need for properly-focused support to help them get through to successful implementation, bridging the notorious 'Innovation Valley of Death' between concept and delivery.

Some of the companies listed in The Modern Railway already have exciting technologies with the potential to aid the transformation of the sector. We look forward to seeing many more in the future. ■

Jeremy Candfield,
Director General,
Railway Industry Association

SETTING THE AGENDA

West Coast main line capacity and its port access routes are key issues for rail freight. Freightliner's No 90016 heads the 09.32 Felixstowe to Crewe Basford Hall container train, approaching Stafford on 22 July 2014. **STEWART ARMSTRONG**

RAIL FREIGHT ON TRACK FOR 2015

For the rail freight operators and their customers there have been many positives in 2014. The memories of the downturn are fading and business is strong in many rail freight sectors, particularly construction materials. Intermodal is showing signs of returning to growth, although there are still network limitations such as on the Felixstowe branch line which affect the ability to run additional services during the week.

There has been continued investment by Network Rail with a number of important projects completed, and development work on others continuing, and there has been private sector investment in terminals, ports and in rail equipment such as wagons. The freight operators have invested heavily in new locomotives, particularly GB Railfreight, Colas and DRS, and the benefits of this new equipment should be seen over the year ahead.

The General Election in May will set the tone for emerging Government rail policy. On the face of it, the parties have quite different policies, although there is perhaps more in common than might first appear between the current arrangements at DfT and the Labour Party plans for a new 'Guiding Mind' for rail. For rail freight, it is often the case that the direct and immediate impacts of such changes are limited, but the second order effects can be significant, and we need to ensure support in pursuit of growth and business confidence. We have been, and will continue to be, in dialogue with all parties as they develop their proposals.

With a fair wind, HS2 should conclude its parliamentary stage for Phase 1 during the year. We are pressing for satisfactory safeguards for freight in the programme and in particular in respect of the existing network and the use of released capacity. There is a great deal of analysis yet to be concluded, and the demands for investment to support HS2 must be clarified along with other network needs. The work for Phase 2 is also expected to progress, which is particularly important for freight traffic wishing to serve the north west and north east conurbations.

Network Rail, now part of Government, has a challenging year ahead as it seeks to get the enhancement programme on track. A number of rail freight schemes are in the portfolio, not least Felixstowe to Nuneaton, and it is imperative that the delivery of these important projects is not allowed to slip back. We also need to start making a firm case for investment in the next Control Period as new Ministers start to consider their future transport priorities.

An important part of investment for freight is in helping to improve the efficiency of the sector. There have already been significant gains, but there is much more to do. Longer and heavier trains, which deliver more goods in fewer train paths, are critical, as are better equipped and modern terminals. We expect to see progress in developing modern 'strategic rail freight interchanges' over the year, with a number of projects in the planning stage and others due to move into construction.

The 'digital railway' also has much to offer, through modern train control, and also in smaller programmes which seek to improve journey times, fuel efficiency and safety. Pilot schemes are already underway in some areas, and it is a key area for unlocking incremental progress. Such measures also help with the perception of rail freight amongst its customers and potential customers who are often used to a fast moving road haulage sector and despair at some aspects of the railways!

Efficiency of international traffic is also critical to making economic flows, and with charges for the Channel Tunnel reduced, there are prospects of more business on this route. HS1 is of interest to many for its superior gauge, and the ability to serve London through the hub at Barking. For the conventional routes, there is early development to see whether there is the case for gauge enhancement above the current 'W9' gauge. The UK Government has now formally signed its participation in the European Rail Freight Corridor 2 which extends to the bottom of the West Coast main line, and the necessary work to formalise this into the UK framework is now being led by Network Rail and ORR ahead of the 'go live' date of November 2017.

So a busy agenda for 2015, and we look forward to reporting progress in our *Modern Railways* column over the year.

Maggie Simpson,
Executive Director,
Rail Freight Group

HITACHI
Inspire the Next

IN ASSOCIATION WITH **HITACHI** Inspire the Next

2015 – YEAR OF UNCERTAINTY

ROGER FORD, INDUSTRY & TECHNOLOGY EDITOR OF *MODERN RAILWAYS*, AND CILT TRANSPORT JOURNALIST OF THE YEAR, SUGGESTS THAT IN A YEAR OF POLITICAL UNCERTAINTY, A PRAGMATIC APPROACH TO FRANCHISING WILL BE ESSENTIAL

For the railway industry, the General Election in May 2015 is likely to be of more than usual significance. For the first time in nearly two decades, the main opposition party is expected to propose radical changes to the structure of the franchised passenger railway established by the Conservative Government between 1992 and 1997.

Prime Minister John Major's aim had been to make rail privatisation irreversible in one Parliamentary term. And despite the Labour leadership giving a commitment at the 1995 Labour Party conference to restoring a 'publicly-owned, publicly-accountable' railway, after the 1997 election victory Tony Blair's government accepted the status quo. This was despite Shadow Transport Secretary Clare Short's blood curdling threats of re-nationalisation in the run up to that election – in the process knocking millions from the prices obtained from the on-going sale of British Rail's assets.

RADICAL

Nearly two decades on, in 2014, came an action replay of 1997, with the current Shadow Transport Secretary Mary Creagh MP. According to Ms Creagh, the choice passengers would face on 7 May 2015 was between the Coalition Government's 'inaction on fares and chaos over rail franchising' and Labour's proposal for 'the most radical package of reforms since privatisation'.

Central to Labour's proposals is the creation of a 'guiding mind' – defined as a single organisation which plans investment in the railway and integrates track and trains.

Ms Creagh claimed that whichever party wins the May election it will face 'big decisions' over the future of the railway and her proposed changes will ensure that these decisions are taken in

One of Network Rail's major current projects. Next to the Shard in this impression is the new London Bridge station, as it will appear on completion in 2018. **NETWORK RAIL**

SETTING THE AGENDA

the interest of passengers.

Labour's 'guiding mind' would combine Network Rail with a 'representative passenger rail organisation'. This new body will: 'contract routes; co-ordinate services; oversee stations, fares and ticketing; plan new rolling stock; raise skills and be accountable for customer satisfaction'. In effect, Ms Creagh is looking to revive the Strategic Rail Authority, created by Deputy Prime Minister John Prescott (see box), but with the addition of direct responsibility for Network Rail.

Also on the Labour agenda was a review of the franchising process. This would include legislation to allow a public sector operator to take on new lines and bid for franchises against the private transport operators 'on a level playing field', with the aim of obtaining better value for money 'for both passengers and taxpayers'.

Weighting of franchise bids on quality has made new and re-engineered rolling stock affordable in franchise bids, and new trains for Gatwick Express are now planned. One of the existing Class 442 trains approaches East Croydon. **TONY MILES**

RE-NATIONALISATION

Compounding the political uncertainty in 2015 will be the emerging impact of the reclassification of Network Rail as a Government body. This change took effect on 1 September 2014 and the implications were explained in a Framework Agreement between the Department for Transport (DfT) and Network Rail.

DfT claimed that the framework agreement provided 'appropriate accountability to Parliament and the taxpayer while preserving Network Rail's operational independence'. It added that Network Rail's accountability for its performance was unaffected, and that the regulatory process managed by the Office of Rail Regulation, which gives industry the confidence to plan for the long term, was maintained.

But in reality the renationalised Network Rail will be under even tighter Government control than British Rail. This is made clear in the Memorandum of Understanding between the Department and the Scottish Ministers, setting out how they will be involved in future decisions on Network Rail's governance and financial management.

In addition to the extensive powers over the governance of Network Rail (see box), the change in status means that DfT's Permanent Secretary becomes the Principal Accounting Officer (PAO), accountable to Parliament for the issue and stewardship of any grant-in-aid, government loans or other resources provided to the company. The PAO also appoints the Accounting Officer (AO) for Network Rail who will usually be the company's Chief Executive.

As a result, Network Rail will subject to a wide range of new financial controls and associated auditing and reporting. In particular, the Framework agreement reveals that 'The AO will receive and act in accordance with a budget delegation each year from the Department and operate within that delegation'. This indicates a return to annual budgeting.

In an interview with *Modern Railways* in September 2014, Transport Minister Claire Perry expected that the new status would make Network Rail 'more aware of the cost/benefit of an investment, because they are in a tougher category' where 'they can't go on borrowing and you have to justify every investment'. From the 'taxpayer's viewpoint' this new relationship could result in an 'even more commercial focus' on investment in capacity and how overcrowding is priced into the business case.

KNOWN UNKNOWNS

Further uncertainty is likely to emerge as the costs of major infrastructure schemes emerge from the Office of Rail Regulation's (ORR's) Enhancements Cost Adjustment Mechanism (ECAM). While ORR's Final Determination for Control Period 5 (CP5), 2014-19, included enhancements worth a notional £12.5 billion, firm costs had been agreed for only £6 billion of this total.

In the case of the remaining schemes, the cost was uncertain because they were late additions to DfT's CP5 High Level Output Specification (HLOS) and Network Rail had been unable to develop them to the required detail by the time the Final Determination was published. As a result ORR excluded these projects from its Determination and introduced ECAM, under which as Network Rail develops each scheme under its project management process, GRIP, to Stage 3 (single option), then it is

GOVERNMENT'S NEW POWERS OVER NETWORK RAIL

The Secretary of State will ensure that Network Rail is guided and monitored in the public and taxpayer interest. In particular, the Secretary of State will:
- Appoint the Chairman and have the power to dismiss the Chairman;
- Have the right to approve the Board's suggested candidate for Chief Executive;
- Have the right to appoint a Special Director.
- Be consulted on non-executive Board appointment:
- Hold regular meetings with the Chairman, to discuss corporate strategy and raise any strategic concerns;
- Approve the three-yearly Remuneration Policy for executive directors;
- Set pay for the Chairman and non-executive directors;
- Agree the Membership Policy with the Board, which will cover the process for selecting members and the competencies they will be required to possess;
- Select the Membership Selection Panel;
- Have the right both to approve the appointment of Members, based on the recommendations of the Membership Selection Panel, and remove all of the Members.

BACK TO THE FUTURE

In its manifesto for the 1997 General Election, Labour proposed the creation of a new rail authority combining the functions of the Office of Passenger Rail Franchising and the Department of Transport. Pending the legislation required to transfer powers to this new Strategic Rail Authority (SRA), the organisation began operating in 'shadow' form in the summer of 1999 and became effective on 15 January 2001.

But only two years later, with the cost of the railway rising, the then Chancellor Gordon Brown made the extra funding conditional on a 'credible rail reform package'.

Ministers also wanted a 'single point at which the key decisions on rail funding and strategy would come together' arguing that such decisions should be taken by the Secretary of State and not by Non Departmental Government Bodies.

Faced with the choice between the Secretary of State and a 'super SRA' as the 'national specifier', the SRA was abolished, with most of its responsibilities reverting to the DfT. The transfer was completed by mid-2005.

IN ASSOCIATION WITH **HITACHI** Inspire the Next

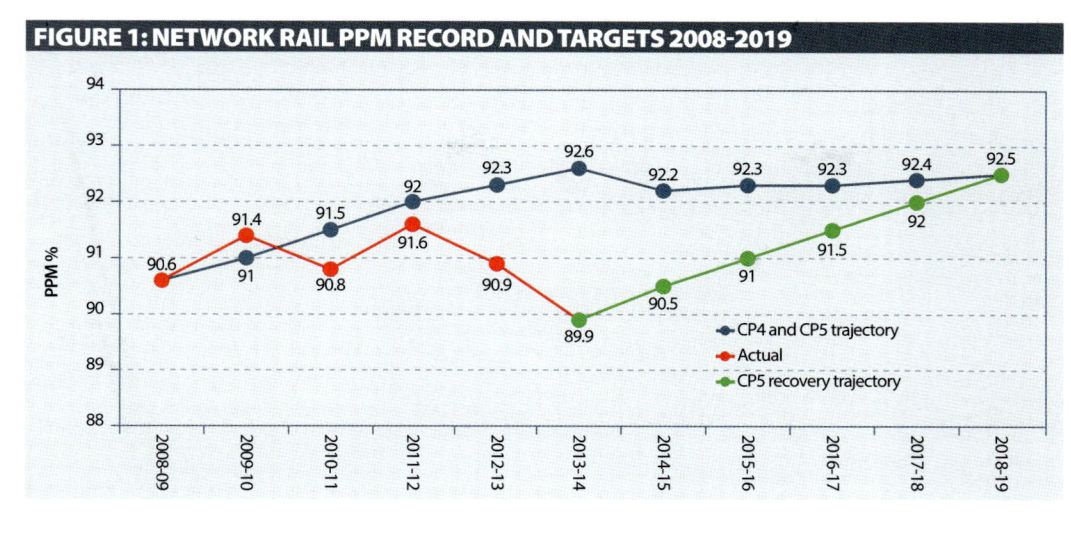

FIGURE 1: NETWORK RAIL PPM RECORD AND TARGETS 2008-2019

[Chart showing PPM % from 2008-09 to 2018-19 with three series: CP4 and CP5 trajectory, Actual, and CP5 recovery trajectory. Values: 2008-09: 90.6; 2009-10: 91/91.4; 2010-11: 91.5/90.8; 2011-12: 92/91.6; 2012-13: 92.3/90.9; 2013-14: 92.6/89.9; 2014-15: 92.2/90.5; 2015-16: 92.3/91; 2016-17: 92.3/91.5; 2017-18: 92.4/92; 2018-19: 92.5]

submitted to ORR for assessment and, if accepted, added to the CP5 funding. (GRIP = Governance for Railway Investment Projects.)

As a result, in June 2014, when challenged by the House of Commons Transport Committee on reports that the Great Western Route Modernisation (GWRM) was over budget by 50%, Network Rail Chief Executive Mark Carne had to admit 'We don't have a fully defined cost for GWML'.

All but £300 million worth of the GWRM electrification work was still in the GRIP/ECAM process. Similarly, as this issue of The Modern Railway went to press, the Welsh Assembly Government and Whitehall were still arguing over who would pay for electrification of the Cardiff Valleys.

DEADLINE

ORR has set March 2015 as the deadline for Network Rail to submit its costings for the outstanding CP5 enhancements. The Regulator has told *Modern Railways* that any scheme which has not been signed off at GRIP stage 3 by this date is likely to struggle for completion in CP5.

Under ECAM, ORR has to consider whether the proposed cost of a scheme represents efficient spending. If a project does not pass this test, ORR can set the efficient cost lower than Network Rail's proposal: this has already happened.

ORR expects Network Rail to manage such individual cost increases within the overall £12.5 billion enhancement funding. However, if this is not possible, and planned expenditure exceeds the total funding available, then, warns ORR, 'government will need to consider on the way forward'.

This could see projects sliding back into CP6. But both Conservative and Labour are warning of greater austerity ahead when it comes to public spending. This is one reason why delivering all the schemes funded in CP5 on time is critical.

Ministers have often stated that the Government is 'investing £38 billion in rail' in CP5. Although only a third is actual investment, if schemes are de-scoped, deferred to CP6 or run over-budget, this failure to deliver value for money could dissuade further investment in CP6.

PERFORMANCE

Of more immediate political importance in 2015 will be punctuality. Where once Members of Parliament relied on their postbag for feedback from constituents, today they can be contacted in near real time through social media and e-mail.

As Figure 1 shows, after a promising start to CP4 (2009-2014), the final two years saw punctuality, as recorded by the Public Performance Measure (PPM), fall away rapidly, ending up 2.7 percentage points below the Regulatory target of 92.6%. This was despite the ORR making available a £150 million performance fund to be spent on improving punctuality and reliability. Even worse, in 2014 NR was fined £53.1 million for failing to improve the punctuality of Long Distance Services.

For CP5, ORR cut back the opening PPM requirement to 92.2%. In addition, instead of the steep improvement trajectory set for CP4, from 90.6% PPM to 92.6%, the ORR requirement for CP5 is a 0.3 percentage point gain over the five years.

This apparent generosity reflects the fact that, with NR ending CP4 at 89.9%, the effective improvement trajectory for CP5 is even more demanding than that for CP4. Network Rail's response is a two part approach. For the first three years, the emphasis will be on detailed improvements to operations and timetabling, dealing with what are termed 'sub threshold' delays.

While these delays are below the nominal 3min cut off, they are recorded by the TRUST system and are categorised as 'unexplained loss in running'. While not attributed to the train operating company or Network Rail, their accumulated effect can show up in lateness on which PPM is based.

A typical example of a sub-threshold delay is an extended station dwell time. At Clapham Junction one train taking 25 seconds longer in the platform in the morning peak can affect following services for the next half hour and extend average journey times by nearly 3min.

Some sub-threshold delays are built into the timetable. Changes to infrastructure or traction may have affected a Sectional Running Time (SRT) for example. NR has begun reviewing 250,000 train planning moves looking for such anomalies.

For the last two years of CP5, Network Rail is planning to bring technology to bear on performance, with rollout of the first phase of the Traffic Management System (TMS). However, as Fig 2 shows, for 2015 the task will be to reverse the current decline in punctuality. Failure to do so will add to the post-election uncertainty.

FRANCHISING

But amidst all the uncertainty, the return to both stability and predictability in the franchised passenger railway, forecast in last year's edition of The Modern Railway, is likely to be consolidated in 2015. On 1 November 2015, the Office of

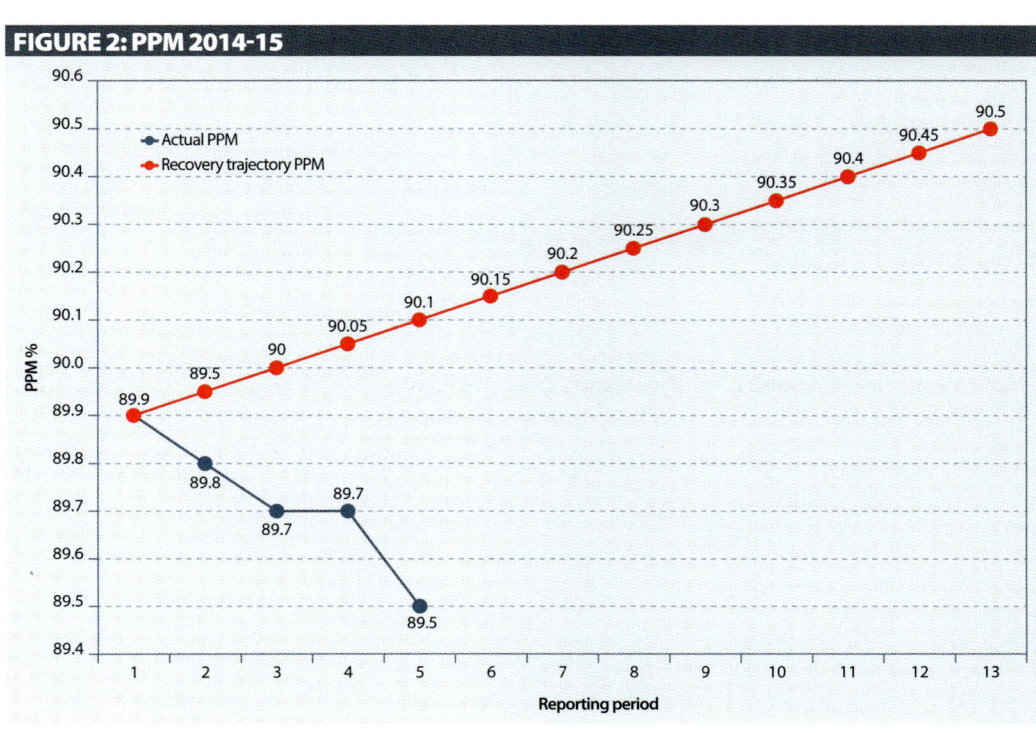

FIGURE 2: PPM 2014-15

[Chart showing PPM % across reporting periods 1-13 with Actual PPM and Recovery trajectory PPM. Actual: 1: 89.9; 2: 89.8; 3: 89.7; 4: 89.7; 5: 89.5. Recovery trajectory: 1: 89.9; 2: 89.95; 3: 90; 4: 90.05; 5: 90.1; 6: 90.15; 7: 90.2; 8: 90.25; 9: 90.3; 10: 90.35; 11: 90.4; 12: 90.45; 13: 90.5]

13

SETTING THE AGENDA

Rail Passenger Services (ORPS) was established formally as a separate section within the DfT's Rail Executive with responsibility for letting and managing franchises.

Managing Director of ORPS is Peter Wilkinson who joined DfT as Interim Franchise Director in January 2013. Having re-launched the franchise replacement programme following the collapse of the Intercity West Coast competition, Mr Wilkinson has been responsible for two innovations.

QUALITY COUNTS

In the case of franchise replacement, he has added a quality factor in the assessment of franchise bids. As before, offers are scored on the Net Present Value (NPV) of the subsidy or premium over the life of the franchise. However, this now represents only 65% of the total score.

Proposals to improve the quality of service represent the other 35% of the offer. This score is given a financial weighting and the resulting value added to the premium or subtracted from the subsidy.

As reported in the 'Train fleet manufacturing and maintenance' section of this edition of The Modern Railway, this approach has made new and re-engineered rolling stock affordable in franchise bids. In the case of the Thameslink Southern & Great Northern franchise, it will fund replacement of the Great Northern Class 313 fleet, plus new trains for Gatwick Express. Transport Scotland has used the same template for the ScotRail franchise with similar dramatic effect, including 80 new EMUs from Hitachi.

The DfT concluded that it would be a massive distraction to let a replacement Greater Western franchise during a major route upgrade. The new Reading station is a key part of the upgrading. **NETWORK RAIL**

DIRECT AWARDS

Richard Brown's review of franchising policy highlighted the importance of matching the franchise bidding programme to the resources of the train operators and the DfT. Brown considered that the industry could handle no more than two or three franchise competitions at any one time. This has been reflected in DfT's Rail Franchise Schedule, now in its third iteration.

Smoothing the franchise replacement programme required some franchises to be extended. Mr Wilkinson has achieved this with Direct Awards which are new Franchise Agreements negotiated with the incumbent operators.

However, a Direct Award is not necessarily a holding operation. In the case of Abellio Greater Anglia, for example, the new franchise agreement includes extensive rolling stock upgrades which need to be in place or underway before the replacement franchise is let. The Northern Direct Award also includes significant new expenditure.

First Great Western's initial Direct Award was limited to 23 months because of European procurement rules. But as The Modern Railway went to press, a follow-on three and a half year agreement was expected.

This highlights the flexibility of the Direct Award concept. With the Great Western Route Modernisation involving electrification, resignalling and new trains, DfT concluded that it would be a massive distraction for management if a replacement franchise was let during a route upgrade which dwarfs that that on the West Coast main line. The management must keep the service running while working as Network Rail's delivery partner on the work programme.

A Direct Award, with an option to extend for a further year, will ensure continuity of senior management through this intensive period. It will also enable DfT to specify and fund associated activities, such as procuring rolling stock for the electrified Paddington commuter services.

Similar considerations influenced the structure of the TSGN replacement franchise which will be responsible for managing the railway through the major disruption of the Thameslink Programme. With this franchise DfT takes the revenue and then reimburses Govia Thameslink Railway for the cost of running the franchise.

In a year of political uncertainty, this pragmatic approach to franchising will be essential. Should Labour come to power and implement the Creagh proposals, ORPS will be well placed to provide the 'guiding mind'. But whatever the outcome, it is likely that 2015 will see further developments in franchising policy – but driven by ORPS rather than party politics. ■

TABLE 3: DIRECT AWARDS AS AT NOVEMBER 2014

FRANCHISE	INCUMBENT	START (SCHEDULE)	START (ACTUAL/REVISED)	END DATE (SCHEDULED)	NOMINAL LENGTH (MONTHS)	END DATE (ACTUAL)	NEW FRANCHISEE
Essex Thameside	National Express	May 2013	26 May 2013	Sept 2014	16	Nov 9 2014	National Express
TSGN	First Group	Sept 2013	Apr 2014	Sept 2014		Sept 14 2014	Govia
Great Western (1)	**First Group**	**Oct 2013**		**July 2016**	23	July 2016	
Great Western (2)	First Group	Sept 2015		Mar 2019 (3)			
Northern	**Serco/Abellio**	**Apr 2014**	**No change**	**Feb 2016**	22		
South Eastern	**Govia**	**Apr 2014**	**Oct 12 2014**	**Jun 2018**	45	**Jun 24 2018**	
Greater Anglia	**Abellio**	**July 2014**	**No change**	**Oct 2016**	27	**Oct 2016**	
West Coast	**Virgin/Stagecoach**	**Nov 2014**	**Jun 22 2014**	**Mar 31 2017**	33	**Mar 31 2017**	
TransPennine	First Group	Apr 2015	No change	Feb 2016			
East Midlands	Stagecoach	Apr 2015	Oct 2015	Oct 2017			
London Midland	Govia	Sept 2015	Apr 2016	Jun 2017			
Cross Country	Arriva	Apr 2016	Oct 2016	Nov 2019			
South West	Stagecoach	Feb 2017		Apr 2019			
South West (4)	Stagecoach		Jan 2015	Apr 2019			

Notes

Bold type award made

1 Initial DA length limited by EU regulations
2 Proposed Direct Award to cover Great Western Route Modernisation
3 Optional 12-month extension as a precaution against GWRM running late
4 Proposed early extension to include Waterloo Plan C funding shelved ahead of 2015 election

ACROSS THE INDUSTRY

The government has announced the creation of a new body called Transport for the North (TfN) made up of the main northern city regions, to deal with big decisions for the North of England. A Class 333 train operated by Northern for West Yorkshire Passenger Transport Executive (Metro) at Saltaire. **PTEG**

DEPARTMENT FOR TRANSPORT

The Department for Transport is the Government body responsible for rail transport, 'responsible for setting the strategic direction for the rail industry in England and Wales – funding investment in infrastructure through Network Rail, awarding and managing franchises, and regulating rail fares'. The Department also encourages the use of new technology such as smart ticketing and the maintenance of high standards of transport safety and security.

At the top of the list of priorities is continuing to develop and lead the preparations for a high speed rail network, followed by improving the existing rail network and creating new capacity to improve services for passengers.

Following the failed attempt to let the West Coast main line franchise in 2012, and subsequent enquiry and review, the governance of the franchising programme has been redesigned to establish clear roles for individuals. All rail activity is now overseen by a single Director General, and the franchising programme has a single responsible Director.

The Department has created an Office of Rail Passenger Services, responsible for the Department's rail delivery functions, including franchising and major projects such as Crossrail and the Intercity Express trains programme.

The conditions attached to individual franchises vary, but in general invitations to bidders specify frequency levels and carrying capacity to be provided, punctuality and reliability standards, and the control of some fares levels.

The train operating companies also commit themselves to financial regimes. Typically, these require less subsidy as time progresses, or paying an increased premium. They may also undertake specific enhancements, such as train fleet renewals. The evaluation of replacement franchise bids now includes a form of quality weighting as well as financial factors,

The Department works with local and regional bodies, the rail industry and Passenger Transport Executives for major urban areas. Transport Scotland and to some extent the Welsh Assembly Government have devolved rail responsibilities. The DfT also sponsors the British Transport Police.

DIRECTOR GENERAL, RAIL GROUP: Clare Moriarty
MANAGING DIRECTOR, OFFICE OF RAIL PASSENGER SERVICES: Peter Wilkinson

TRANSPORT SCOTLAND

Transport Scotland is an agency of the Scottish Government, whose purpose is to increase sustainable economic growth through the development of national transport projects and policies. It is accountable to Parliament and the public through Scottish Ministers.

The Glasgow area is the largest commuter operation outside London and its users account for about 60% of railway passengers in Scotland.

Transport Scotland's Rail Directorate is responsible for managing the ScotRail and new Caledonian Sleeper franchises; relationships with Network Rail and the Office of Rail Regulation; sponsoring major rail projects, including the Edinburgh-Glasgow Improvement Programme (EGIP) and the Borders Railway; advising Ministers on investment priorities; working with the UK Government on Scotland's interests in Cross-Border services, including high speed rail north of Manchester/Leeds; and leading policy development.

Aims included in the Scottish High Level Output Statement for 2014-19 include hourly services between Aberdeen and Inverness taking around two hours; Highland main line development to provide an hourly service between Inverness and Perth with extensions to either Glasgow or Edinburgh; and Network Rail to electrify further parts of the network at a rate of 100 single track km per annum when EGIP work is finished.

There are funding schemes for stations, freight, network improvements and level crossings, while passenger and train handling capacity at the main Edinburgh and Glasgow stations is clearly a concern.

Transport Scotland also coordinates the National Transport Strategy and is responsible for the national concessionary travel scheme.

DIRECTOR OF RAIL: Aidan Grisewood

TRANSPORT WALES

The Transport (Wales) Act 2006 conferred a general duty on the Welsh Assembly Government to promote and encourage integrated transport

SETTING THE AGENDA

The Office of Rail Regulation's (ORR's) assessment of Network Rail's performance during Control Period 4 (CP4), 2009-14, commends its success in dealing with exceptionally challenging weather conditions over the winter of 2013-14. This is Datchet on the Staines-Windsor & Eton line in February 2014. **NETWORK RAIL**

in Wales. The Assembly now has full responsibility for the Wales & Borders rail franchise operated by Arriva Trains (Wales) and which continues until 2018. The Assembly Government can specify services and regulate fares, and is responsible for the franchise's financial performance and for enhancements.

The Assembly is able to develop and fund infrastructure enhancement schemes, develop new passenger rail services, and invest in improving the journey experience for rail users. Revenue support is given to the Cardiff-Holyhead rail link.

The Welsh Government wishes to be responsible for specifying and procuring the next franchise. A 14-point plan of matters to be addressed was set out in December 2013.

£62million was allocated in autumn 2013 for new capital projects in south Wales, including rail improvements, and to progress future 'Metro' transport priorities including Newport-Ebbw Vale trains, and light rail and tram-train options, such as links with Cardiff Bay.

DIRECTOR GENERAL, ECONOMY, SCIENCE AND TRANSPORT:
James Price

LOCAL TRANSPORT AUTHORITIES

Passenger Transport Executives (PTEs) are statutory bodies, responsible for setting out policy and expenditure plans for public transport in the former metropolitan areas. They are funded by a combination of local council tax and grants from national government. That in the West Midlands is in effect part of the Integrated Transport Authority (WMITA), made up of elected representatives of the local councils.

The other five PTEs are now responsible to, or have become an executive body of, the five Combined Authorities. The position varies according to the Statutory Instrument concerned. The Combined Authorities are based on the former metropolitan areas though some have a wider geographical coverage. That for Greater Manchester was established in 2011, to be followed by West Yorkshire, Liverpool City Region and Sheffield City Region on 1 April 2014 and the North East on 14 April 2014.

Combined Authorities are responsible for setting out transport policy and public transport expenditure plans in their regions, but they also have wider economic development responsibilities. They plan and manage local rail services in the PTE areas in conjunction with the Department for Transport. They have the power to secure additional passenger rail services, contracting with the local franchised TOC and funded by themselves.

They may invest in local networks, including new stations. They can also develop and promote new schemes, notably light rail. They are neither bus nor rail operators themselves, but they are providers of local transport information.

Merseytravel itself lets and manages the concession (not franchise) for Merseyrail Electrics. The Northern and TransPennine franchises (new franchises for both due in 2016) provide local rail services in all the PTE areas other than the West Midlands.

The government in October 2014 announced the creation of a new body called Transport for the North (TfN) made up of the main northern city regions. This body was to 'work together with other authorities and stakeholders and allow the north to speak with one voice on the big decisions to benefit the region as a whole'. The government, working with TfN, set out to produce a comprehensive transport strategy for the region, including options, costs and a delivery timetable for a High Speed 3 east west rail connection.

The DfT has already been working together with Rail North, a consortium of 30 local transport authorities, on collaborative development of the new Northern and TransPennine Express franchises, proposing that a more formally constituted Rail North would later be capable of managing the franchises.

Increased powers over transport for Greater Manchester, with a devolved and consolidated transport budget, were announced by the government in November 2014. In the West Midlands, 14 Metropolitan District, Shire and Unitary local transport authorities have proposed devolution of the region's rail network as West Midlands Rail.

In other areas of England, Local Enterprise Partnerships, business-led bodies designed to promote local economic growth, have produced Strategic Economic Plans in collaboration with local authorities, which set out, among other things, priorities for transport investment, and bid for funding from the Local Growth Fund.

The Passenger Transport Executive Group, PTEG, is a non-statutory body bringing together and promoting PTE and related interests.

EUROPEAN UNION

In the last 20 years, the European Commission has been active in restructuring the rail transport market and strengthening the position of railways. Efforts have been concentrated on: opening the rail transport market to competition; improving interoperability and safety of national networks; and developing rail transport infrastructure.

Four railway 'packages' aimed to open up the international rail freight market, provide a legally and

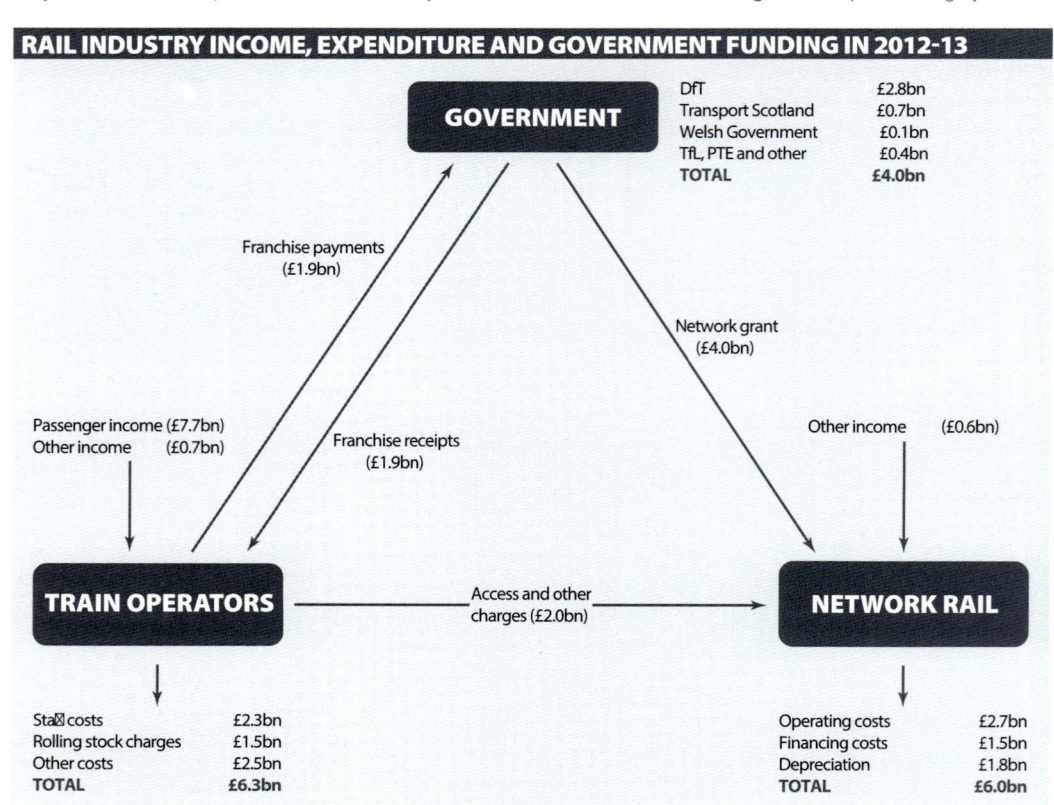

RAIL INDUSTRY INCOME, EXPENDITURE AND GOVERNMENT FUNDING IN 2012-13

GOVERNMENT
DfT	£2.8bn
Transport Scotland	£0.7bn
Welsh Government	£0.1bn
TfL, PTE and other	£0.4bn
TOTAL	**£4.0bn**

Franchise payments (£1.9bn)
Network grant (£4.0bn)

Passenger income (£7.7bn)
Other income (£0.7bn)
Franchise receipts (£1.9bn)
Other income (£0.6bn)

TRAIN OPERATORS — Access and other charges (£2.0bn) → **NETWORK RAIL**

Train Operators	
Staff costs	£2.3bn
Rolling stock charges	£1.5bn
Other costs	£2.5bn
TOTAL	**£6.3bn**

Network Rail	
Operating costs	£2.7bn
Financing costs	£1.5bn
Depreciation	£1.8bn
TOTAL	**£6.0bn**

Creative Systems

GLOBAL EXPERIENCE AND LOCAL EXPERTISE...

...combined with continuous innovation means that Knorr-Bremse can offer customers project-specific systems solutions. | www.knorr-bremse.co.uk |

KNORR-BREMSE

SETTING THE AGENDA

The Glasgow Subway improvement project is under way, and is planned to include new automated trains and signalling; and refurbished stations with platform edge doors and improved accessibility. These are the refurbished platforms at Hillhead. **STRATHCLYDE PTE**

technically integrated railway, and revitalise international passenger services by extending competition and interoperability. They also introduced standards and authorisation for rolling stock and independent management of infrastructure.

COMMONS TRANSPORT COMMITTEE

The Transport Committee is appointed by the House of Commons to examine the expenditure, administration and policy of the Department for Transport and its associated public bodies.

During the course of a year, the Committee will consider around 20 topics on which they will call formally for written evidence from interested parties. Formal reports are made to the House, which are published together with a verbatim report of the evidence sessions and the main written submissions.
CHAIR: Louise Ellman

NETWORK RAIL

Network Rail (NR) is the not for dividend owner and operator of Britain's railway infrastructure, and aims to deliver a safe, reliable and efficient railway for freight and passenger trains. From 1 September 2014 Network Rail was reclassified from the private sector to the public sector. As an arm's length body, it retains the commercial and operational freedom to manage Britain's railway infrastructure.

That infrastructure consists of the track, signals, bridges, viaducts, tunnels, level crossings and electrification systems, of which it is the monopoly owner. Network Rail also operates 19 major stations. With minor exceptions the others are owned by the company, but day-to-day operations are under the control of the franchised train operating company which has the most train calls.

Network Rail Ltd is licenced by the Secretary of State for Transport and regulated by the Office of Rail Regulation. The company board is responsible to its members and government, and other stakeholders for the overall leadership and long term success of the company. In addition, it will continue to run Network Rail to the standards required of a company with shares listed on the Stock Exchange.

Network Rail's revenue comes from grants by the Department for Transport and Transport Scotland; commercial property income; and track access payments from train and freight operating companies.

In future, the company will be borrowing direct from government via a £30.5bn loan facility designed to cover its CP5 funding requirements.

One of the company's most important responsibilities is to improve the railway continually, so that as the system operator it delivers good value for taxpayers and users alike. That includes timetabling trains to make the best possible use of the network. In conjunction with stakeholders the company's Long Term Planning Process predicts future demand, agrees priority uses for the capacity available and assesses value for money options for investment.

CHAIRMAN: Richard Parry-Jones
CHIEF EXECUTIVE: Mark Carne

OFFICE OF RAIL REGULATION (ORR)

The Office of Rail Regulation (ORR) is the independent health and safety regulator for the railway industry, covering the safety of the travelling public and industry workers. The ORR has concurrent jurisdiction with the Office of Fair Trading to investigate potential breaches of the Competition Act 1998 in relation to railways.

HM Railway Inspectorate (HMRI) is part of ORR and its inspectors and policy advisors develop and deliver the safety strategy. ORR is the enforcement authority for the Health & Safety at Work Act 1974 and various railway specific legislation. ORR is led by a Board appointed by the Secretary of State for Transport.

The principal economic regulatory functions are to regulate Network Rail's stewardship of the national rail network, to licence train and other operators of railway assets, and to approve track, station and light maintenance depot access arrangements. ORR also regulates High Speed 1.

ORR holds Network Rail to account for delivery of the regulatory outcomes for the five years 2014-19 (Control Period 5). These identified the scope for further efficiency gains and performance improvements, and reflected the need for investment in more capacity.
CHAIR: Anna Walker
CHIEF EXECUTIVE: Richard Price

RAIL DELIVERY GROUP (RDG)

The Rail Delivery Group was set up in 2011 to bring together the owners of Britain's passenger train operating companies, freight operators and Network Rail to provide leadership to Britain's rail industry. The intention is to promote greater cooperation by working together with government, the supply chain and stakeholders. It is committed equally to the long term health of the industry and short term improvements. The RDG develops industry strategies and proposes solutions for policy makers. Some of these functions were undertaken prior to 2013 by ATOC.

The Rail Delivery Group is a company limited by guarantee, whose Articles of Association define its objects. It aims to be the leadership body and collective voice of the rail industry on cross-industry issues; develop and issue policies, strategies and plans for the rail industry, and promote their adoption by industry participants; and promote a better alignment of conflicting interests between and among train operators and between train and network operators.

The RDG aims to lead the industry with a view to advancing the provision of a safe, efficient, high quality rail service for both users and for taxpayers.

The RDG has a number of areas of work. These cover Asset, programme and supply chain management, Contractual and regulatory reform, Communications, Franchising, Freight, Health & safety, Information and ticketing, People, Performance, Planning, Stations, Technology and operations, Transparency and EU policy.
DIRECTOR GENERAL:
Michael Roberts

ASSOCIATION OF TRAIN OPERATING COMPANIES (ATOC)

The Association of Train Operating Companies acts as a clearing house for passenger train operators through the Rail Settlement Plan. This allows passengers to buy tickets to travel on any part of the network from any station.

It also provides the National Rail Enquiry Service (NRES).

ATOC runs a range of discounted and promotional Railcards for the public and also staff travel facilities.

There is also an operations, engineering and major projects team that supports Scheme members in delivering a safe, punctual and economic railway.
CHIEF EXECUTIVE:
Michael Roberts

Proven Ability

INNOVATIVE AND COMPETITIVE SOLUTIONS...

...from RailServices include customised service packages for the maintenance, overhaul, refurbishment and modernisation of systems across all types of rail vehicles. | www.knorr-bremse.co.uk |

RAILSERVICES
always on track

KNORR-BREMSE

SETTING THE AGENDA

RAIL FREIGHT GROUP

The Rail Freight Group is a representative body for rail freight in the UK, with a membership which includes some of the biggest names in logistics along with many smaller companies, all of whom contribute to the success of rail freight. Its members include ports, terminal operators, property developers, equipment suppliers and support services.

Since 1991, the RFG has been working to increase the amount of goods conveyed by rail. It seeks to achieve this in three ways: by campaigning for a policy environment that supports rail freight; promoting the rail freight sector, and supporting members as they grow their businesses.
CHAIRMAN: Lord Berkeley
EXECUTIVE DIRECTOR:
Maggie Simpson

FREIGHT ON RAIL

Freight on Rail, a partnership between the rail trade unions, the rail freight industry and Campaign for Better Transport, works to promote the economic, social and environmental benefits of rail freight, both nationally and locally. It advocates policy changes that support the shift to rail and provides information and help on freight related issues.

HIGH SPEED 1

HS1 Ltd is the long term concession holder of HS1, the 109km high speed rail line connecting London St Pancras International with the Eurotunnel boundary. The 30 year concession to operate, maintain and renew the railway continues until 31 December 2040, when asset ownership reverts to the government. The concession may then be relet.

The delivery of operations and maintenance responsibilities is achieved principally through contracts with Network Rail (High Speed) Ltd.

HS1 stations are London St Pancras International, Stratford International, Ebbsfleet International, and Ashford International. All have both domestic and international platforms, but international platforms at Stratford have yet to be used for that purpose.

Present operators are Eurostar for international services under an open access arrangement, and Southeastern TOC for domestic operations as part of its franchise agreement. Vehicles operating on HS1 must be specifically authorised so to do, and their compatibility with the route (such as signalling systems) demonstrated.

Ashford Area Signalling Centre is the location of the traffic, signalling and electrical controls and the communications centre for HS1.

HS1 Ltd is policed by the Office of Rail Regulation, whose Control Period 2 (2015-2020) begins on 1 April 2015. In their review, ORR were required to approve HS1s operating, maintenance and renewal costs and the resultant Track Access charges. They approved HS1 Ltd's reductions of 12%-13% for passenger services, and 20% for freight.

Revenue earning freight traffic has been run by DB Schenker since 2011. All such movements are restricted to a six hour night time slot as conventional freight trains are limited to 140km/h.

BRITISH TRANSPORT POLICE

British Transport Police (BTP) is the specialised police service for Britain's railways. BTP provides a service to rail operators, staff and passengers throughout Britain, as well as London Underground, Eurostar, the Docklands Light Railway, Glasgow Subway, Midland Metro, London Tramlink and Emirates Air Line.

BTP is divided into seven geographical areas. There are over 2,900 Police Officers and 1,450 support staff.

The British Transport Police Authority sets the strategic targets for BTP. These are keeping the railway running, making the railway safer and more secure, delivering value for money, and promoting confidence in use of the railway. The Authority monitors BTP's performance and sets their budget. Both organisations are responsible to the Department for Transport, not the Home Office as with other forces.

The House of Commons Transport Committee report, 'Security on the Railway', was published in September 2014. It was convinced of the benefits of BT Police's risk based approach to policing the railways. They were also impressed with BTP's commitment to tackling crime, while at the same time minimising delays to the travelling public. The Committee even went as far as to suggest that airport policing could benefit from a similar approach.

Future challenges for BT Police include the increased work load represented by the growth of passenger rail travel and the amount of freight forwarded, and how to reduce unit costs over time.
CHIEF CONSTABLE: Paul Crowther

RAILWAY INDUSTRY ASSOCIATION

The Railway Industry Association (RIA) is the representative body for UK-based suppliers of equipment and services to the world-wide rail industry. It has around 170 member companies across the whole range of railway supply. RIA is an active member of UNIFE, the trade association for the European railway supply industry.

RIA members represent the greater part of the UK railway supply industry. This includes the manufacture, leasing, component supply, maintenance and refurbishment of rolling stock, the design, manufacture, installation, maintenance and component supply of infrastructure, and specialist expertise in consultancy, training, project management and safety.
DIRECTOR GENERAL:
Jeremy Candfield

RAIL SUPPLY GROUP

The new Rail Supply Group - comprising ministers, rail industry business leaders and senior representatives from the Department for Transport and the Department for Business, Innovation and Skills – agreed in June 2014 on priorities to achieve its vision of increased UK competitiveness both home and overseas, including exports and inward investment: promotion; innovation (helping UK companies develop, demonstrate and commercialise new technologies); skills (promoting rail as a career choice, raising skill levels through the National Skills Academy for Railway Engineering (NSARE); helping small and medium sized businesses access markets and funding; and developing a future pipeline of work that draws on industry best practice.

£500,000 of funding for the RSG was to be provided by the Department for Transport through the FutureRailway programme.

New points were installed at Watford South Junction as part of an £81m project which saw junction layouts improved and track renewed in the Watford Junction area over a series of bank holidays and weekends in 2014. **NETWORK RAIL**

The new train for Scotland

//AT200 COMMUTER

Inspiration delivered.

Made **Great** in **Britain**.

Hitachi Rail Europe

@HITACHIAT200 #AT200

HITACHI
Inspire the Next

SETTING THE AGENDA

Electrification of the Ormskirk-Preston line is among a wide range improvements for the Liverpool City region that have been put forward in a 30-year strategy published in 2014. A Northern Rail diesel train prepares to leave Ormskirk for Preston. **NORTHERN**

RSSB

RSSB is a not-for-profit company owned by major industry stakeholders. Its primary purpose is support its members to achieve their objectives of improving safety and performance and value for money across the industry, with a focus on: reducing safety risk so far as is reasonably practicable; and (where appropriate) increasing capacity and improving operating performance and customer satisfaction.

RSSB's activities include development of the industry's Safety Risk Model (identifying all significant risks), a Precursor Indicator Model (risk from train accidents), and the ranking methodology of risk from trains passing signals at danger).

RSSB manages the industry's research and development programme (funded by the Department for Transport). Other activities are funded by member levies. Five separate Committees manage Interfaces between Vehicles and, respectively, Structures, Track, Train Energy, Train Control & Communications, and Other Vehicles.

Safe operation is supported by the Railway Group Standards (RGS), which are managed by RSSB on behalf of the industry. These define mandatory engineering and operational matters and include the national Rule Book.

(RSSB is registered as the Rail Safety & Standards Board though it does not use the full name as its status and activities have changed over time.)

CHIEF EXECUTIVE: Chris Fenton

TECHNICAL STRATEGY LEADERSHIP GROUP

The FutureRailway programme is a collaboration between Network Rail and RSSB, working with industry and the supply chain to deliver the Rail Technical Strategy (RTS). It manages a cross industry research, development and innovation programme and incorporates the former Enabling Innovation Team.

The Technical Strategy Leadership Group (TSLG) is a cross-industry RSSB-facilitated expert body with representatives from Network Rail, train and freight operating companies, rolling stock leasing companies, suppliers, Transport Scotland, Crossrail, High Speed 2, and RSSB - as well as chairs of the systems interface committees, and the university sector through Rail Research UK Association (RRUKA).

TSLG is responsible for developing the RTS and ensuring the long-term 30 year vision for the GB railway system forms part of the rail industry's forward planning and supports the rail business.

TSLG sponsors a range of activities including research (with a dedicated fund for projects and programmes); overseeing the rail industry's Systems Interface Committees (SICs); enabling innovation; working with others in the transport sector to stimulate new ideas (including co-funding and competitions with the Technology Strategy Board, and setting up a Transport Systems 'Catapult'); and inputting technology development proposals to industry planning.

LAW COMMISSIONS

Level crossings account for one half of the non-suicide, non-trespass fatality risk on the railway. In 2013, the Law Commission and the Scottish Law Commission recommended reform of the law aimed at improving the safety regime, providing a new closure procedure and clarifying the law regarding rights of way across railways.

The response from the Department of Transport in October 2014 accepted 47 of the 74 recommendations for England and Wales, modified 18 and rejected nine, with further 12 classified as matters for the Scottish Government. An action plan was promised to outline further work and how it will be taken forward.

RAIL ACCIDENT INVESTIGATION BRANCH

The Rail Accident Investigation Branch (RAIB) is the UK's statutory but independent body for investigating accidents and incidents occurring on railways and tramways. It is part of the Department of Transport but functionally independent, and the Chief Inspector reports directly to the Secretary of State.

The RAIB's role is to find out the causes and circumstances of accidents and incidents and any other factors that contributed. Its reports contain safety recommendations, aimed at reducing the likelihood of similar events in the future and mitigating their consequences.

The RAIB is not a prosecuting body and it does not apportion blame or liability. It investigates any serious railway accident, meaning those involving a derailment or collision which has an obvious impact on railway safety regulation or the management of safety. It includes those that result in the death of at least one person, that cause serious injuries to five or more persons, or that cause extensive damage to rolling stock, the infrastructure or the environment.

The RAIB may also investigate other accidents or incidents on railway property where it believes there may be significant safety lessons.

CHIEF INSPECTOR: Carolyn Griffiths

PASSENGER FOCUS

Passenger Focus is the consumer watchdog for Britain's rail passengers and England's bus, coach and tram passengers (outside London).

Under the Infrastructure Bill, which could become law in 2015, the organisation would also represent all those who use the motorways and certain A roads in England. This relates to plans for the Highways Agency to become a government-owned company, monitored by a unit within the Office of Rail Regulation.

The organisation plans to be called Transport Focus and use the names 'Transport Focus – passengers' and 'Transport Focus – road users' to differentiate the strands of work.

Using research findings from in particular the Rail Passenger Survey and the Bus Passenger Survey, Passenger Focus seeks to drive change that will make a difference for passengers. The key issues are fares and ticketing, quality and level of services, and investment.

Passenger Focus is structured as an executive non-departmental public body. Most of its board memebers are appointed by the Secretary of State for Transport.

CHIEF EXECUTIVE: Anthony Smith

THE ASSOCIATION OF COMMUNITY RAIL PARTNERSHIPS

The Association of Community Rail Partnerships (ACoRP) is a federation of over 50 community rail partnerships and rail promotion groups. It is focused on practical initiatives, which add up to a better and more sustainable railway. Improved station facilities, better train services and improved integration with

SIEMENS

siemens.co.uk/rail

Delivering a safer railway

Working with a trusted partner

Our customers demand the highest quality in every aspect of their railway solutions. That's why they come to Siemens. Whether it's improving capacity, frequency or reliability we have the advanced technology to make it happen, safely and seamlessly.

For over 170 years we've been delivering innovative solutions to meet our customers diverse needs. Whether it be trains, signals or electrification we can provide essential local experience backed up by global knowledge and comprehensive resources. This powerful combination makes us a partner you can trust to provide the complete, safe solutions you are looking for.

Experience integrated mobility.

SETTING THE AGENDA

other forms of transport are central to the work of ACoRP and its members.

The government's Community Rail Development Strategy provides a framework in meeting social, environmental and economic objectives.

GENERAL MANAGER
Neil Buxton

DERBY & DERBYSHIRE RAIL FORUM

The Derby & Derbyshire Rail Forum (DDRF) dates from 1993 and represents over 100 businesses across the East Midlands. These employ over 25,000 people and contribute an estimated £2.6bn to the local economy. The area is thought to contain the largest cluster of rail companies in the world.

As well as providing a collective voice and promoting the area's rail industry, DDRF holds quarterly networking meetings and an annual conference. DDRF has dedicated local support from local authorities and industry groups.

THE INSTITUTION OF MECHANICAL ENGINEERS

The Railway Division of the Institution of Mechanical Engineers (IMechE) is one of eight divisions and was founded in 1969. Its scope covers research, design, development, procurement, manufacture, operation, maintenance and disposal of traction, rolling stock, fixed equipment and their components within rail, rapid transit and all forms of rail-borne guided surface transport.

CHIEF EXECUTIVE:
Stephen Tetlow

RAILWAY CIVIL ENGINEERS ASSOCIATION

The Railway Civil Engineers Association (RCEA) was founded in 1921. It is an Associated Society of the Institution of Civil Engineers, whose members are involved in the development, design, construction or maintenance of railway infrastructure. It exists to foster continuing professional development and the exchange of knowledge and experience.

Presentations, meetings and visits take place on current projects and issues and interests cover heavy rail, light rail and metro systems.

SECRETARY: Greg James

PERMANENT WAY INSTITUTION

The Permanent Way Institution (PWI) promotes and encourages the acquisition and exchange of technical and general knowledge about the design, construction and maintenance of every type of railed track.

The PWI holds local meetings in all its geographically-based Sections, as well as arranging technical conferences and visits. Its textbooks have been the industry standard works for over half a century and members receive a widely consulted Journal.

CHIEF EXECUTIVE OFFICER:
David Packer

INSTITUTION OF RAILWAY SIGNAL ENGINEERS

The Institution of Railway Signal Engineers (IRSE) was formed in 1912. Its objective was and remains the advancement of the science and practice of railway signalling, telecommunications and related matters. The IRSE is an international organisation, active throughout the world. It is the professional institution for all those engaged or interested in signalling and aims to maintain high standards of knowledge and competence within the profession.

CHIEF EXECUTIVE & SECRETARY:
Colin Porter

INSTITUTION OF RAILWAY OPERATORS

The Institution of Railway Operators (IRO) exists to advance and promote the safe, reliable and efficient operation of the railways by improving the technical and general skills, knowledge and competence of all those thus engaged.

At the heart of the IRO's educational provision is its Professional Development Programme, run in conjunction with Glasgow Caledonian University. This comprises the Certificate and Diploma of Higher Education in Railway Operational Management and the Degree in Railway Operational Management, all delivered through the combination of distance learning and direct tutorials. Through seven Area Councils, the IRO provides a full programme of local events and visits.

CHIEF EXECUTIVE:
Fiona Tordoff

INSTITUTION OF ENGINEERING AND TECHNOLOGY

The Railway Network of the Institution of Engineering and Technology (IET) covers the electrical engineering aspects of the promotion, construction, regulation, operation, safety and maintenance of railways, metros, tramways and guided transport systems.

CHIEF EXECUTIVE & SECRETARY:
Nigel Fine

CHARTERED INSTITUTE OF LOGISTICS AND TRANSPORT (UK)

The Chartered Institute of Logistics and Transport (CILT UK) is the professional body for individuals and organisations involved in all aspects of transport and logistics. As it is not a lobbying organisation, it is able to provide a considered and objective response on matters of transport policy. Through a structure of forums and regional groups, it provides a network for professionals to debate issues and disseminate good practice. There is a very active Strategic Rail Policy Group and another on Light Rail & Trams.

CHIEF EXECUTIVE: Steve Agg

YOUNG RAIL PROFESSIONALS

Young Rail Professionals (YRP) was founded in 2009 to bring together young people from across the railway industry. The YRP cover all aspects, from engineering to asset management, train operations, strategic planning, rolling stock design, maintenance, franchising, regulation and marketing.

THE PRIVATISED RAIL INDUSTRY

Until 1994, the nationalised British Railways Board (BRB) operated what became known as the vertically integrated railway. The Board itself provided the infrastructure, owned the trains and operated the services.

Under the Railways Act 1993, these and other functions were separated. The ownership of the infrastructure went to a new company, Railtrack, subsequently privatised. All operators paid Railtrack access charges for the use of the track, signalling and electrification systems.

Passenger train operations were split into what initially were 26 separate franchises. They were the subject of competitive tendering, mostly for a seven year term. Franchise awards took into account the additional services and investment commitments of each bidder, and whether that company would require a subsidy or would pay a premium to the government over the franchise term.

The passenger stations were owned by Railtrack, but all except the very largest were run by the Train Operating Companies (TOCs).

The passenger rolling stock became the property of three rolling stock companies (ROSCOs), which then leased the stock to the TOCs. The aim was to surmount the problem of relatively short franchise terms and asset lives of 30 years or more.

The freight companies were also privatised, but they owned the locomotives and any wagons which were not privately owned by customers.

Franchising was carried out by the Office of Passenger Rail Franchising (OPRAF) and various aspects of the industry including licensing were carried out by the independent Rail Regulator plus the Health & Safety Executive.

The Association of Train Operating Companies (ATOC) was created to manage passenger railway affairs such as running the National Rail Enquiry Service (NRES), Railcard schemes, and settling accounts between companies.

The last franchises were let very shortly before the 1997 General Election, which brought a change of government from Conservative to Labour. Labour said it wished to improve overall direction and planning in the industry, and created the short-lived Strategic Rail Authority (SRA). But other problems afflicted the industry, in particular the inability of some franchisees to make the financial returns they had expected, plus the level and quality of maintenance and investment by Railtrack.

Rising traffic levels and the operation of many more trains led to performance problems. These became chronic following the Hatfield derailment of 2001, caused by poor track quality. The result, according to SRA Chairman Sir Alastair Morton, was that 'the system suffered a collective nervous breakdown'. This led to huge political and media driven criticism, the downfall of Railtrack, and a strong move to centralisation.

Over time, many of the franchises, including the management buy-outs, were acquired by groups active in the bus industry. More recently, franchise ownership has extended to companies based in France, Germany, the Netherlands and Hong Kong.

The cost of the railway to the public purse rose fast, not least with the West Coast Route Modernisation. When the Rail Regulator ruled in

IN ASSOCIATION WITH HITACHI Inspire the Next

Network Rail completed a £5m project to extend platforms and improve Littlehaven station in June 2014. It is part of a programme of platform extensions and power supply upgrades to allow for longer trains on Sussex routes. **NETWORK RAIL**

For those starting out in their careers, Young Rail Professionals provides networking and professional development opportunities to enhance and inspire (as well as entertain) its members. The YRP also runs an ambassadors' programme, providing opportunities for its members to visit schools, colleges and universities to attract the next generation into a dynamic rail industry.
CHAIRMAN: Adam Stead

REF
The REF (Railway Engineers' Forum) is an informal liaison grouping of the railway interest sections of the eight professional institutions listed immediately above. As a non-political body, the REF aims to provide a common view on railway topics and a co-ordinated response to requests for professional comment. The REF also organises multi-disciplinary conferences and produces a monthly resumé of professional meetings around Britain, which is available on its own website and also those of its constituent bodies.
CHAIRMAN: Lawrie Quinn (Michael Woods from mid 2015)

RAILWAY STUDY ASSOCIATION
The Railway Study Association (RSA) provides a forum for the exchange of experience, knowledge and opinion on issues relating to all aspects of the railway industry, and the part played by railways in the total transport scene. RSA members have a wide range of backgrounds and expertise, embracing operations, engineering, business planning, project management, marketing and consultancy.

The Association's calendar of events including evening lectures in London, regional meetings in Birmingham, an Annual Dinner, a Presidential address

2003 on the level of access charges needed to fund Railtrack's successor, Network Rail, this proved too much. This became a charge funded by government, since the TOCs were protected by an indemnity clause in their contracts.

The Railways Act 2005 abolished the SRA with most of its functions transferred to an enlarged Department for Transport. Safety policy, regulatory and enforcement functions are now the responsibility of the Office of Rail Regulation (ORR). Separately, the government set out what Network Rail was expected to deliver for the public money it receives in a High Level Output Statement (HLOS) plus a Statement of Funds Available (SoFA). The access charges review process was amended, and there was some transfer of powers and budgets to Scotland, Wales and London.

Growing political and public faith in the ability of the railway to contribute to capacity shortfalls in all modes, to regional economic growth, and the wellbeing of society in general, has been credited with contributing to developments such as large scale electrification across the system, now under way.

Localism has been seen as Network Rail has pushed out more of its activities to their Route Directors, while further decentralisation of powers to Scotland, Wales and perhaps some parts of England is becoming more likely.

High Speed 2 has been pursued by the Coalition Government, though not without opposition. Potentially, this leaves the existing network with greater capacity for the traffic which it can hardly accommodate at present, but completion of Phase 1 (London to Birmingham) will not be before 2026 and Phase 2 (extensions to Manchester and separately to Leeds) in 2032.

Meanwhile, the organisation of the Department of Transport has been rethought, with the creation of the Office of Rail Passenger Services.

Who are the railway's passengers? In a nutshell, rail use is highest among young working age adults and lowest among the over-70s and under 17s, and on average, men make more rail trips than women. People in the higher household income groups make more rail trips and travel further than those in the lower income groups. On average, the largest proportion of trips are for commuting (42%), followed by leisure (27%) and business (9%).

For freight, 36% of that moved by rail was coal, the highest proportion for any commodity, 27% domestic intermodal, and 2% international.

Where are those passenger journeys made? In 2012/13, 62% of all rail journeys in Great Britain started or finished in London. Sixty six per cent of journeys in the South East and 76% of those in the East of England started or finished in London. In the north of England, the North West had the highest number of rail journeys, with 9% of all journeys in Great Britain starting or finishing in the region. Seven per cent of all rail journeys started or finished in Scotland and 2% in Wales.

Such figures certainly confirm the importance of the railway in London and the surrounding counties. Do they perhaps also indicate the scale of what might be achievable by rail in cities in the North of England? Or the larger cities anywhere in Britain? Under what circumstances could such growth conceivably become a reality in some far distant future? ■

SETTING THE AGENDA

The Victoria Place shopping centre at London Victoria station was relaunched after refurbishment in September 2014. Station retail spending has been outperforming the high street average, and growing for the nine quarters to April-June 2014. **NETWORK RAIL**

and an overseas study tour. These provide opportunities for learning, professional development and networking. The President for 2014-2015 is Michael Holden.
CHAIRMAN: Jonathan Pugh

NSARE

What are the key skills that will be required in future for those entering railway engineering as a profession? How will they be recruited? Will there be enough of them? When will they be needed and where? At what level of expertise and in which disciplines? Who will do the training and accreditation? How will this be funded? Are these general requirements for the industry as a whole, or for specific large scale projects such as Crossrail, HS2 or ETCS?

National Skills Academy for Railway Engineering (NSARE) was set up to answer these questions and propose solutions. NSARE has a strategic role in ensuring that the industry has the necessary capabilities overall. For the two broad categories of infrastructure and rolling stock, there will always be the need for maintenance, renewal and enhancement.
CHIEF EXECUTIVE: Gil Howarth

RAIL RESEARCH UK ASSOCIATION

Rail Research UK Association (RRUK-A) is a partnership between the British rail industry and UK universities. Its aims are the support and facilitation of railway research in academia; common understanding of research needs to support the rail network and its future development; identification of research, development and application opportunities in railway science and engineering; and provision of solutions to the rail industry.

The core activities of RRUK-A are funded by RSSB and Network Rail. It is managed by an executive committee.

RAILWAY RESEARCH IN BIRMINGHAM

The Birmingham Centre for Railway Research and Education brings together a multi-disciplinary team from across the University to tackle fundamental railway engineering problems. The team actively engage with industry, other Universities through RRUK-A, and international partners. Its mission statement refers to the provision of fundamental scientific research, knowledge transfer and education to the international railway community.

INSTITUTE OF TRANSPORT STUDIES, UNIVERSITY OF LEEDS

The Institute of Transport Studies at Leeds is the largest of the UK academic groups involved in transport teaching and research. For more than two decades, a principal interest has been the economics of rail transport. Key research topics include demand forecasting and travel behaviour, infrastructure cost modelling, efficiency analysis and pricing, project appraisal methodology, off-track and on-track competition, and transport safety. Fostered by close links with the successors to British Rail, some more recent projects have been undertaken for a worldwide range of clients.

THE INSTITUTE OF RAILWAY RESEARCH (IRR)

Headed by Professor Simon Iwnicki, the IRR is based at the University of Huddersfield and is one of the partners in a Euro 15 million, four-year project funded by the European Union under its Seventh Framework Programme. Named CAPACITY4RAIL, the ambitious scheme aims to ensure that railways will continue to meet Europe's transport needs over the decades to come. Low maintenance infrastructure, more resilient and easily repairable points, and higher-speed freight vehicles are among the goals. This will build on the findings of previous projects that the IRR has been closely involved with, such as the EU-backed INNOTRACK, which has investigated many of the technical challenges posed by the European Commission's goal of doubling rail passenger traffic and tripling freight traffic by 2020.

The University of Huddersfield and RSSB signed a Memorandum of Understanding in 2013, agreeing to pool resources and talent for research into system and engineering risk modelling to support informed decision making and future risk prediction.

- Investment in rail network (26p)
- Maintaining track and trains (22p)
- Industry staff costs (25p)
- Interest payments and other costs (9p)
- Leasing trains (11p)
- Fuel for trains (4p)
- Train company profits (3p)

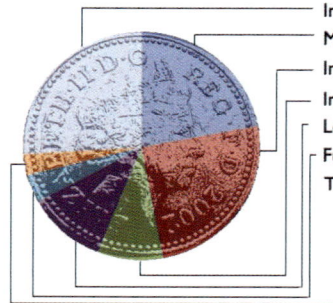

SOURCES: Network Rail and The Rail Delivery Group

The Department for Transport's January 2014 presentation of how a rail passenger's pound is spent.

FINANCE AND LEASING

IN ASSOCIATION WITH

angel Trains
Rail People
Real Expertise

FINANCE AND LEASING

Southeastern Class 465/2 Networker EMU, leased from Angel Trains, next to the Shard at London Bridge.

angel Trains

As one of the UK's leading train leasing specialists, Angel Trains is passionate about financing and delivering high quality, modern assets to its customers and is committed to providing innovative solutions to modernise and improve the UK's train fleet.

Employing around 120 professional, technical and support staff at its headquarters in Victoria, London and at a second office in Derby, Angel Trains has invested £3.5 billion in new rolling stock and refurbishment programmes since 1994. This makes the company one of the largest private investors in the UK rail industry. Angel Trains is unique in leasing to all 19 franchised operators and open access operators in the UK.

Angel Trains owns and maintains over 4,400 passenger rail vehicles in the UK, about 37% of the nation's rail stock. Angel Trains was created in 1994 as one of the three rolling stock companies in preparation for the privatisation of the UK rail industry.

In August 2008 Angel Trains was acquired by a consortium of global infrastructure and pension fund investors.

WHAT WE DO

Angel Trains bridges the worlds of finance and operations. Angel Trains attracts the necessary finance to procure, refurbish and enhance rolling stock to meet the needs of the UK's Train Operating Companies (TOCs) and provide a long term, reliable and safe asset to users of the UK railways.

Angel Trains has a diversified fleet including high-speed passenger trains, regional and commuter passenger multiple units as well as freight locomotives.

We place great importance on long-term asset stewardship, in order that the value of the asset can be consistently delivered and optimised throughout its lifecycle.

RAIL PEOPLE, REAL EXPERTISE

We employ a strong and committed team with extensive rail experience and trusted relationships within the industry. Angel Trains has strength in depth in finance, engineering, commercial and customer service.

We have assets in all stages of the lifecycle and the strength of our company lies not only in our commercial approach, but in our structured approach to the stewardship of our rolling stock from cradle to grave. Angel Trains works through the various stages in rolling stock asset life, and through its staff, provides the different skills needed throughout. The rolling stock asset life and the necessary skills that we provide are outlined below:

Specification – We have engineers who are able to write and evaluate technical and performance specifications of new rolling stock to ensure Angel Trains only invests in assets that will be desirable to lessees in the long-term (also maintenance).

IN ASSOCIATION WITH angel Trains

The new Class 350/4s for First TransPennine Express make up one of Angel Trains' newest fleets. No 350406 is seen in central Manchester.

Procurement – Our commercial and procurement experts use the specifications to negotiate formidable terms from manufacturers and maintainers (supplier development).

Project Management – Our engineers and project managers take procurement contracts and ensure timely delivery of goods and services.

Performance Growth – Our engineers and project managers work with suppliers to ensure that rolling stock is not only delivered but properly commissioned to ensure that performance grows to optimum levels and continues throughout its asset life.

Fleet Management – Our engineers ensure that a detailed understanding is retained in Angel Trains and all performance issues and changes of maintenance plans are accurately documented, so that assets can transfer from one lessee to another with comprehensive knowledge databases.

Maintenance Management – Our engineers, contract managers and planners ensure that documentation is kept up to date throughout the asset life, that vehicle maintenance is carried out in a timely manner, and that maintenance is delivered to the right quality and safety levels.

Refurbishments & Enhancements – Our team of experts ensure that any planned changes to rolling stock meet either customer or owner requirements and are carried out in a professional manner with a view to maximising asset value for the longer term.

Continuous Service Operation – Our engineers, with detailed knowledge of the assets, are able to consider future developments such as obsolescence, environmental performance, and other legislative changes.

Disposal – Our procurement specialists deal with the responsible disposal of assets when the time comes.

DIVERSITY – WOMEN IN RAIL

Angel Trains is wholly committed to supporting the diversification of the rail industry's workforce and is particularly dedicated to encouraging more women to view the UK rail sector as a long-lasting career option. As such, Angel Trains is a proud sponsor of the Women in Rail group which was founded by Adeline Ginn, General Counsel at Angel Trains, to provide networking opportunities and support for all women in the rail industry, promote rail as an attractive career choice and develop strategies for engaging young people to consider a career in rail.

TOMORROW'S TRAIN, TODAY: CLASS 707 TRAINS FOR STAGECOACH SOUTH WESTERN TRAINS

As the latest addition to its portfolio, Angel Trains is to procure 30 x 5-car Siemens Desiro City units, a second generation Electric Multiple Unit ('EMU') commuter train designed to carry more passengers and to have a significantly reduced whole life, whole system cost. This means each unit will cost less to maintain, uses less power and causes less damage to infrastructure.

Angel Trains is to provide the 150 new carriages to Stagecoach South Western Trains as part of a new lease aimed at alleviating already overloaded SWT commuter routes and rail congestion in London. The carriages will increase capacity on SSWT's busy commuter routes in and out of London Waterloo by 24,000. ■

A First Great Western High Speed Train leased from Angel Trains.

HITACHI Inspire the Next

29

FINANCE AND LEASING

Eversholt Rail Group's passenger rolling stock portfolio comprises around 3,500 passenger vehicles, of which over 3,100 are electric-powered - a UK market share of approximately one third. It is owned by the Eversholt Investment Group, a consortium of STAR Capital Partners, 3i Infrastructure plc and Morgan Stanley Infrastructure Partners, which purchased the group from HSBC at the end of 2010. The transaction valued Eversholt's gross assets at approximately £2.1 billion.

The Eversholt Rail Group brand replaced that of HSBC Rail in 2010, and the business separated its maintenance, asset management and advisory services into different legal entities. The name echoes that originally given to the business - Eversholt Leasing - when privatised.

Current major projects include the Class 334 upgrade - an investment of £37.6m for C4+ overhaul and enhancements to improve the passenger environment and performance on ScotRail's 40 Class 334 trains, starting in early 2015. The work will be carried out by Alstom and includes: time-based overhaul; overhaul and reliability works on saloon and cab doors; fitting full passenger saloon heating, ventilation and air conditioning; installation of 230V at seat sockets; preparing for future WiFi by installing an Ethernet backbone, a new Driver Only operation CCTV system; and Dellner coupler and Hall bush installation.

Upgrading of Govia Thameslink's Class 365 fleet, a £42m investment, continues. The trains are being given a new look on the inside and out with fresh seat upholstery, new flooring, refurbished finishes; plus a major engineering overhaul. Enhanced features for people with disabilities and mobility impairments include a new fully automated passenger information system with audio and visual announcements.

Eversholt Rail has also invested £11m in the Class 318 fleet. The 21 3-car units are going through a refurbishment and C6X overhaul with targeted accessibility work, Ethernet backbone and at seat power sockets. The work is being undertaken by Wabtec.

The Class 91 'Baseline' programme of works, split into three phases, is planned for completion by mid 2016 at a cost of about £5m. Indications are that the programme is having a positive effect on the reliability of the Class 91 fleet.

The Northern Rail Class 322 (5 units) and 321/9 (3 units) were halfway through a heavy overhaul at Wabtec, Doncaster, by late 2014. The work includes a C6 repair which consists of full repaint and attention to the body structure, and new floor covering; plus modifications for compliance with accessibility requirements, including fitment of a universal access toilet.

For the new Siemens Desiro City trains for Thameslink, Eversholt has signed a long-term agreement to provide project and asset management services to Cross London Trains, the consortium providing the new fleet. Services under the 22 year agreement will include project management during the build and delivery of the rolling stock, and then long-term asset management, including both technical and commercial support to Cross London Trains. Eversholt has more than 16 years' experience in procurement and through-life asset management of new rolling stock, and maintenance and enhancements of existing stock. The company believes the Cross London Trains agreement provides a significant opportunity to utilise its proven skills and expertise for the benefit of new entrants to the market.

A 4-car Class 321 demonstrator electric multiple-unit was upgraded by Wabtec in Doncaster in a £4.5m project to showcase how high-specification refurbishment of the existing fleet of Class 321 EMUs can compare favourably with the passenger experience and performance of new trains, at a significantly lower cost. Options demonstrated include both metro and suburban interior designs and revamped First class accommodation with new leather seats. A prototype traction system for the Class 321 fleet has been developed by Eversholt and Vossloh Kiepe to increase traction performance and energy efficiency of the trains.

Refurbished Class 365 train, operated by Thameslink. **EVERSHOLT/THAMESLINK**

The most recent new fleet financed by Eversholt is the Class 380 electric multiple-units for ScotRail, valued at over £185m. The company is also the funder (and project managed introduction) of the high profile Hitachi Class 395 trains for Southeastern high-speed services, under an investment programme worth some £260million. The trains' new depot at Ashford was developed by Eversholt in conjunction with its Depco partners.

SENIOR PERSONNEL
EVERSHOLT

CHIEF EXECUTIVE OFFICER Mary Kenny
CHIEF OPERATING OFFICER Andy Course
CHIEF FINANCIAL OFFICER David Stickland
HEAD OF RELATIONSHIP DEVELOPMENT Steve Timothy
HEAD OF COMMERCIAL AND BUSINESS SERVICES Clive Thomas

Porterbrook-owned Class 323 trains leased to London Midland serve the Birmingham CrossCity line. Re-tractioning this fleet is one of Porterbrook's current rolling stock investments. **PORTERBROOK**

porterbrook

Porterbrook is one of the three major Rolling Stock Companies (ROSCOs), and has owned and leased rolling stock and related equipment for over 20 years. The company has invested over £2.6 billion in new trains for the UK rail industry, including the recent announcement to finance 116 Class 387/1 vehicles for train operator Southern.

The acquisition of these new trains means that since privatisation Porterbrook has either delivered or has on order over 2,200 passenger rolling stock vehicles, giving a portfolio of more than 4,000 passenger vehicles and over 1,600 freight locomotives and wagons in use with the majority of train operators on the UK rail network.

Porterbrook has been continuously investing in its rolling stock, undertaking projects such as trialling the new ZF Ecomat transmission and re-tractioning its EMU fleets. These activities are intended to improve train sustainability, both from an environmental and performance perspective. Early results from the ZF Ecomat transmission project, currently being trialled on a South-West-Trains-leased Class 158, shows that it is achieving significant fuel consumption savings which can be considered for further application across its diesel fleet.

The re-tractioning works that are being undertaken on its Class 455 and Class 323 fleets are targeting other performance considerations. The replacement of the traction equipment on the Class 455 fleet will allow the introduction of regeneration and improved maintenance periodicities, while the Class 323 enhancement deals with both obsolescence and reliability concerns. Porterbrook will continue to identify similar opportunities.

There has also been a substantial increase in the application of Driver Advisory Systems (DAS) across the Porterbrook fleet. These systems have been applied to a number of the company's fleet and are delivering significant energy savings to operators up and down the country.

To make its fleet compliant with Passengers of Reduced Mobility Technical Specification for Interoperability (PRM TSI) regulations, Porterbrook has embarked upon a programme of work to ensure the fleet can continue to operate beyond 1 January 2020. Not only does this offer benefits to disabled passengers, it also delivers a cost effective solution to enhancing the train fleet to meet future requirements.

The company's Class 456 fleet, operated by South West Trains, is currently undergoing refurbishment work, including PRM compliance work, which will see the vehicles being modified to the same design as the Class 455 units for operation together, in multiple, lengthening the sets to 10 cars. This will provide a significant increase in capacity on one of Europe's busiest networks.

Porterbrook is committed to developing a solution for the Pacer vehicles. With this in mind early in 2015 a prototype will be produced that is PRM compliant and offers an improved passenger environment including passenger information, LED lighting, new seats and a universal access toilet.

Employing a team of 90 professional staff with expertise in areas of Finance, Engineering, and Asset Management, Porterbrook's extensive experience and knowledge of the rail industry gives the company a strong base to deliver value for money for the services they offer.

In October 2014 the company announced a change in ownership. The new owners are a global investment consortium comprised Alberta Investment Management Corporation (AIMCo), Allianz Capital Partners (ACP), EDF Invest and Hasting Funds Management. All consortium members are long term infrastructure investors with a similar strategy and have considerable experience in acquiring and managing infrastructure assets.

Over the next few years further high levels of investment are required for the UK rail industry for new train projects and on-going vehicle enhancements. Porterbrook recognises that undertaking engineering improvement work and carrying out PRM compliance modification of existing stock will offer the industry substantial value for money benefits. In this context Porterbrook's aim in the coming years is to continue to develop its existing fleet and invest in new trains where the opportunity fits with its investment strategy.

The company is also committed to its accredited graduate training scheme providing a comprehensive rail industry based training programme, which is helping bring dynamic new professionals into the UK rail industry.

Whether we're sourcing investment or new trains, our people operate at the highest levels.

For a leasing company it's rather telling that one third of our workforce are engineers.

But then, at Angel Trains we've always offered a bridge between finance and operations. Over the last 10 years, our extensive rail experience and innovative approach to financing has enabled us to invest over £3 billion in new trains and refurbishments.

See what the UK's biggest rolling stock asset managers can do for you.

www.angeltrains.co.uk

angel Trains

Rail People
Real Expertise

IN ASSOCIATION WITH **angel** Trains
Rail People Real Expertise

BRITAIN'S ROLLING STOCK
WHO OWNS IT?
ROLLING STOCK ALLOCATION ON THE NATIONAL NETWORK

Three rolling stock leasing companies (ROSCOs) own most of the passenger rolling stock on the British main-line railway network.

The three ROSCOs were established at railway privatisation in 1994 to take over ownership of this rolling stock from the nationalised British Rail, and the ROSCOs were sold to the private sector, with their initial fleet leases in place.

The aim was for each ROSCO to have a reasonably diversified portfolio, with comparable fleets allocated to each. Larger fleets of a single type were divided, but smaller fleets were allocated to a single ROSCO. This gave each a range of customers and gave most train operating companies (TOCs) a relationship with at least two ROSCOs.

Table 1 shows how different types of passenger rolling stock were allocated to the three ROSCOs.

Approximately 38% of passenger rolling stock was allocated to Eversholt, 32% to Angel and 30% to Porterbrook. By 2009, ex-British Rail rolling stock formed approximately 60% of the passenger fleet, with the rest purchased since privatisation, and Angel had a 36% share of the total rolling stock, Porterbrook 32% and HSBC (Eversholt) 29%.

By 2014, the passenger fleet had increased in size by about 25% in the 20 years since privatisation, with about 1,260 new vehicles entering service during Control Period 4 (2009-2014). Details of passenger rolling stock ordered since privatisation are shown in the opening article in the Train Fleet Manufacture and Maintenance section of The Modern Railway.

With the five-digit series for individual vehicle numbers becoming overloaded, six-digit vehicle numbers have been introduced for the new Class 387 Electrostar electric multiple-units.

OTHER OWNERS

Another substantial lessor of rolling stock to franchised TOCs is Voyager Leasing. It was established to lease a new fleet of 'Voyager' trains to Virgin CrossCountry Trains. While it is a subsidiary of the Royal Bank of Scotland Group (RBS), ownership of

TABLE 1 - ALLOCATION OF PASSENGER VEHICLES AT PRIVATISATION

ROSCO	DMU	EMU	HST VEHICLES*	TOTAL
Angel	1,039	2,010	531	3,580
Eversholt	0	2,864	1,366	4,230
Porterbrook	681	1,699	948	3,328
TOTAL	**1,720**	**6,573**	**2,845**	**11,138**

* Diesel High Speed Trains - power cars and coaches.   *Source - Competition Commission*

MAIN IMAGE: East Midlands Trains' Class 222 'Meridians' (owned by Eversholt Rail Group) are derived from the Class 220 and 221 'Voyagers' operated by CrossCountry and Virgin Trains (owned by Voyager Leasing). CrossCountry's No 221132 (right) heads north from Sheffield as East Midlands Trains' No 222006 waits in Platform 5 (left) with a train for London St Pancras. **PAUL BIGLAND**

HITACHI Inspire the Next

FINANCE AND LEASING

the trains is equally split between the Lloyds Banking group (previously Halifax Bank of Scotland) and RBS.

Voyager Leasing originated when NatWest bank was appointed to arrange funding for the new fleet of 78 Voyager trains. The operating lease was arranged by a NatWest subsidiary, Lombard Leasing Contracts Ltd, later renamed Voyager Leasing. When NatWest was acquired by RBS (at that time the parent of Angel Trains), in order to reduce RBS's exposure to Virgin Trains, the CrossCountry fleet was evenly split and half the vehicles were sold to Halifax. RBS and Halifax then entered into head lease arrangements with Voyager Leasing.

Voyager Leasing has not undertaken any other leasing business. Though it had the same parent company as Angel Trains - RBS - it remained largely separate. It contracted Angel Trains to provide technical and other support, but these arrangements ended in 2008 when Angel was sold to a consortium of investors. Most of the Voyager fleet is now leased by the new CrossCountry franchise, held by DB group company Arriva.

RBS also owns 24 Docklands Light Railway vehicles under a finance lease signed in April 2005.

QW Rail Leasing, a joint venture between Sumitomo Mitsui Banking Corporation and National Australia Bank, leases Class 378 electric multiple-units to London Overground Rail Operations Limited (LOROL) for Transport for London's London Rail Concession.

Some relatively small quantities of passenger rolling stock are owned by franchised train operating companies, most notably First Group which owns 12 HST power cars and 42 trailer vehicles, while Arriva owns Mk3 vehicles used on Chiltern Railways' London-Birmingham and Arriva Trains Wales' north-south Wales services, with others in reserve.

Connex Leasing Limited purchased rolling stock for the Southeastern / SouthCentral franchises which its parent group originally won. These vehicles were subsequently purchased and leased by HSBC (now Eversholt). Wiltshire Leasing was a subsidiary of Great Western Holdings, set up to finance new Class 175s for its North Western franchise and new Class 180s for Great Western. These vehicles were subsequently purchased and leased by Angel.

Six Class 43 HST power cars and 24 trailers used by Grand Central were purchased in 2010 by Angel Trains from Sovereign Trains, a ROSCO within the same group as Grand Central.

Heathrow Express trains were purchased by the airports company BAA, including the five 5-car Class 360/2 electric multiple-units used for Heathrow Connect services. (In October 2012, the name BAA was dropped, and Heathrow airport operates as a standalone brand.)

FREIGHT LOCOS

The three main ROSCOs lease out large fleets of freight and general purpose locomotives, as shown in the tables. Other leasers are Beacon Rail and Macquarie European Rail.

Ex-British Rail freight locomotives were transferred to the ownership of English, Welsh & Scottish Railway (now DB Schenker) or to Freightliner at privatisation. Significant numbers of freight locomotives, some ex-British Rail, are owned by freight operating companies including Colas Rail, Mendip Rail and Direct Rail Services. In 2011, Class 66 locomotives were purchased from Eversholt Rail Leasing by GB Railfreight (4 locos) and Colas (5 locos), with five more purchased from Porterbrook by GBRf. In 2013, GBRf/Eurotunnel purchased three Class 66s from the Netherlands. After a flurry of purchases in 2014, Colas Rail's fleet grew to four Class 37s, three Class 47s, ten Class 56s, ten Class 60s, five Class 66s and ten new Class 70s (though some locomotives were awaiting return to traffic).

In February 2014 GB Railfreight announced it would purchase a total of 21 new Class 66 locomotives from Electro-Motive Diesel Inc (EMD), and purchase 16 Class 92 electric locomotives from its parent company, Europorte, a subsidiary of Groupe Eurotunnel. Nine existing GBRf Class 66s were sold to and leased back from Beacon Rail. In August 2014, GBRf confirmed the purchase of a Class 59 locomotive, 'Yeoman Highlander', from German-based Heavy Haul Power International.

Several specialist companies including Harry Needle Railroad Company and UK Rail Leasing also maintain smaller fleets of locomotives which are hired to UK freight and passenger operators, and to Network Rail for infrastructure duties.

Alpha Trains - formerly Angel Trains International - manages a fleet of approximately 400 locomotives and 300 passenger trains in continental Europe. A subsidiary acquired 202 locomotive and passenger rolling stock assets from The Royal Bank of Scotland (RBS) at the end of 2013. The vehicles had been managed by Alpha Trains on behalf of RBS since a consortium of investors acquired Angel Trains from RBS in August 2008.

CROSS LONDON TRAINS

Cross London Trains is a consortium comprising Siemens Project Ventures GmbH, Innisfree Ltd and 3i Infrastructure Plc set up to finance and purchase Desiro City trains from Siemens for the Thameslink rail franchise.

Eversholt Rail was appointed to provide project and asset management services to Cross London Trains, including project management during the build and delivery of the rolling stock, and then long-term asset management, including both technical and commercial support.

MACQUARIE EUROPEAN RAIL

In November 2012, Macquarie Group announced that Macquarie Bank Limited had established a new business, Macquarie European Rail, and agreed to acquire the European rolling stock leasing business from Lloyds Banking Group.

The business comprises three separate portfolios of rolling stock. First, there are 30 four-car Class-379 EMUs operated by Greater Anglia. Second is a UK rail freight portfolio - leasing 19 Class-70s to Freightliner, 26 Class-66s to Freightliner (some of them in Poland), and 14 Class-66s to Direct Rail Services.

Third is the former CB Rail business, with locomotives, passenger trains and wagons on operating lease to operators in Europe.

Lloyds was also part of the consortium that purchased Porterbrook Leasing in 2008 but it exited from the consortium in 2010. Lloyds banking group remains the owner of DB Schenker's Class-92s and has an interest in Voyager Leasing.

BEACON RAIL

Beacon Rail Leasing Limited was established in January 2009 by BTMU Capital Corporation as a wholly-owned subsidiary, to be its business entity for freight rolling stock leasing in the European market.

In May 2014, Pamplona Capital Management announced

Class 313 No 313206, in Southern 'Coastway' livery, owned by Beacon Rail Leasing, negotiates the junction at Barnham as it leaves the Bognor Regis branch en route to Brighton on 1 July 2014. **PAUL BIGLAND**

IN ASSOCIATION WITH **angel**Trains

With Grand Central due to lease the five Class 180s currently with First Great Western, all 14 of these Angel Trains-owned 125mph diesel multiple-units are expected to be in service on the East Coast main line by 2017. Hull Trains' No 180110 (left) and Grand Central's No 180112 stand at London King's Cross on 3 September 2014. **PAUL BIGLAND**

the purchase of Beacon for a consideration of approximately $450 million.

Headquartered in London with additional offices in Boston and Rotterdam, Beacon's portfolio included (in May 2014) 77 locomotives, 632 freight wagons, and 20 passenger train units on lease in the UK, France, Belgium, Norway, Sweden and Germany.

In Britain, Beacon Rail leases ten low-emission Class 66s to Freightliner and five Class 66s to Direct Rail Services. Two Class 66s, transferred from Germany, entered service with GBRf in 2013, and a further nine GBRf Class 66s were sold to Beacon and leased back to GBRf in 2014.

Beacon Rail has worked with Direct Rail Services on the development of Vossloh Eurolight diesel locomotives for the UK: 15 of these Class 68s were ordered in January 2012 in a contract worth roughly Euro 50 million, with a further 10 ordered in September 2014. An order for ten electric/diesel dual-mode Class 88 locomotives from Vossloh was announced by Beacon and DRS in September 2013.

Beacon's first passenger trains were acquired in 2012 - twenty Class-313 dual-voltage electric multiple-units, retained by HSBC when it sold rolling stock company Eversholt Rail. The Southern train operating company leases 19 of the Class 313s, and Network Rail has leased the 20th as the resident test train for the Hertford North Integration Facility, the new test track for different manufacturers' European Train Control system equipment.

For the Caledonian Sleeper, Serco plans to use a new fleet of coaches worth more than £100m built by CAF, with funding expected to be by SMBC.

ROLLING STOCK - SIMPLIFIED GUIDE TO CLASSES

Multiple units are trains of self-propelled vehicles with their own driving cabs, usually comprised of one to five carriages. The main groups of ex- British Rail diesel multiple-unit (DMU) are:
- Class 142-144 'Pacers' - 4-wheeled bus-based trains.
- Class 150-159 'Sprinters'. Class 150 is the most basic, with Class 153 / 155 / 156 'Super Sprinters' for longer cross country services, and Class 158 / 159 Express units. Class 165 Networker Turbo and Class 166 Network Express fulfill similar roles.

Post privatisation, the main DMU designs were Class 170-172 Turbostars (and similar Class 168) built by Bombardier Transportation, and less numerous Class 175 Coradia designed by Alstom. Class 180 is an Alstom design for express services, and Class 185 a Siemens design introduced for TransPennine Express. Class 220, 221 and 222 'Voyagers' and 'Meridians', built by Bombardier, also operate InterCity services.

Electric multiple-unit (EMU) Classes 313-315, 455, 456, 465, 466, 507 and 508 are ex-British Rail inner-suburban trains; Class 317-323, 365 and 442 are outer-suburban/long-distance types.

The main post-privatisation EMUs built by Alstom are Classes 334 and 458; by Bombardier, Classes 357, 375-379, the new Class 387 and Crossrail's forthcoming Class 345; by Siemens, Classes 332, 333, 350, 380, 444 and 450, and the new Desiro City Class 700.

The main electric locomotive designs are Class 91 built for East Coast high-speed services, designed for 140mph (225km/hr) running in semi-permanent 'InterCity225' (IC225) train formations; and Classes 86 and 90, used for both passenger and freight work.

The West Coast main line's Pendolino electric tilting trains are known as Class 390 and the Southeastern high-speed trains using High Speed 1 are Class 395. The new Hitachi trains for the InterCity Express Programme are Classes 800 (bi-mode) and 801 (electric).

The dominant freight diesel locomotive type is the Class 66 from General Motors / Electro-Motive Diesel, designed for 75mph freight work. The Class 67 is a mixed traffic express locomotive from the same stable, and Class 57 is a rebuilt ex-British Rail freight and passenger locomotive. Class 70 is the recent General Electric PowerHaul design operated by Freightliner and Colas. New Vossloh diesels for DRS are Class 68, and Vossloh dual-modes for DRS are Class 88.

Class 43 is the power car (locomotive) type used at both ends of diesel 'InterCity125' High Speed Trains: the ROSCOs also own substantial numbers of IC125 and IC225 passenger vehicles. ■

FINANCE AND LEASING

First Great Western workhorses await their next duty at Exeter depot. Porterbrook Leasing's Class 153 single-car No 153325 (centre) is still in London Midland livery. Angel Trains' Class 150/1 No 150104 is on the left and classmate No 150131, also owned by Angel, is in the shed on the right. **PAUL BIGLAND**

THE ROSCO FLEETS

MULTIPLE-UNIT VEHICLES, HST POWER CARS, AND LOCOMOTIVES - LISTED BY ROLLING STOCK LEASING COMPANY AND TRAIN OPERATING COMPANY

porterbrook

Class	No of vehicles
ARRIVA TRAINS WALES	
Class 143	22
Class 150/2	72
Class 153	3
C2C RAIL	
Class 357	184
CHILTERN	
Class 168/0	20
Class 168/1	17
Class 168/2	21
CROSSCOUNTRY	
Class 170 (2 Car)	26
Class 170 (3 Car)	48
Class 43 HST Power Car	5
EAST COAST	
Class 43 HST power car	9
EAST MIDLANDS TRAINS	
Class 43 HST power car	24
Class 153	11
Class 156	22
Class 158	18

FIRST GREAT WESTERN	
Class 43 HST Power Car	22
Class 57	4
Class 143	10
Class 150	34
Class 153	5
Class 158	43
FIRST SCOTRAIL	
Class 158	80
Class 170 (3-car)	150
FIRST TRANSPENNINE	
Class 170 (2-car)	18
GREATER ANGLIA	
Class 153	5
Class 156	18
Class 170 (2-car)	8
Class 170 (3-car)	24
Class 90	15
LONDON MIDLAND	
Class 139	2
Class 153	8
Class 170 (2-car)	34
Class 170 (3-car)	18
Class 172 (2-car)	24
Class 172 (3-car)	45

Class 323	78
Class 350	148
NORTHERN	
Class 144	56
Class 150	22
Class 153	8
Class 155	14
Class 156	36
Class 158	24
Class 319	4
Class 323	51
SOUTHERN	
Class 171 (2-car)	20
Class 171 (4-car)	24
Class 377	834
SOUTH WEST TRAINS	
Class 158	22
Class 159	90
Class 455	364
Class 456	48
Class 458	180
THAMESLINK	
Class 319/0	52
Class 319/2	28
Class 319/3	100

Class 319/4	160
Class 377	128
Class 387	116*

* - in service from 2015

FREIGHTLINER	
Class 66	35
Class 86	10
Class 90	10
NETWORK RAIL	
Class 43 HST Power Car	3
DIRECT RAIL SERVICES	
Class 57	14
GB RAILFREIGHT	
Class 66	9

EVERSHOLT RAIL GROUP

CHILTERN	
Class 168	9
EAST COAST	
Class 91	31

36

Ready for a new challenge?

A [2] B

Operations & train crew positions

jobs-in-rail.co.uk
your railway career

modern railways

Register now at Jobs-in-Rail.co.uk to start receiving weekly or daily job alerts **tailored** to your specialisms... Jobs-in-Rail.co.uk is an independent service which **combines the strengths of established market leading titles** and a dedicated team of recruitment specialists.

MANAGED SERVICE SOLUTIONS

RMF

RMF is a leading provider of railway reservation based international settlement and clearing services, providing sophisticated revenue and cost allocation, including business critical management information.

Client base
- Eurostar International Ltd
- Thalys International Sonl
- SNCF
- Department for Transport

Key partners
- Atos Origin
- Resarail 2000 GIE
- Kinagge and Company
- Davison & Shingleton

Times House, Bravingtons Walk, Regent Quarter, London N1 9AH
Telephone: + 44 (0) 20 7042 9961 | Fax: + 44 (0) 20 7833 0224
Email: david.hiscock@rmf.co.uk | www.rmf.co.uk

RSS
RAILWAY SUPPORT SERVICES

Re-railing, Recovery and Wheelskating Specialists

Montpellier House, Montpellier Drive, Cheltenham, GL50 1TY
www.railwaysupportservices.co.uk | info@railwaysupportservices.co.uk
Tel: 0870 803 4651 | Paul Fuller on 07787 256013

HITACHI
Inspire the Next

FINANCE AND LEASING

Bombardier built EMUs pass each other next to the new 'Access for All' footbridge and lifts at Denmark Hill station, on 25 January 2014. London Overground's 10.44 from Clapham Junction to Highbury & Islington is formed by Class 378 Capitalstar No 378135 (left), owned by QW Rail Leasing. On the rear of Southeastern's 09.30 from Ashford International to London Victoria is Class 375/6 Electrostar No 375608 'Bromley Travelwise', owned by Eversholt Rail Group. King's College Hospital is the building in the background. **BRIAN MORRISON**

EAST MIDLANDS TRAINS
Class 222	143

FIRST SCOTRAIL
Class 170	27
Class 318	63
Class 320	66
Class 334	120
Class 380	130

FIRST TRANSPENNINE EXPRESS
Class 185	153

GREATER ANGLIA
Class 315	244
Class 321	376

GREAT NORTHERN
Class 313	132
Class 321	52
Class 365	160

LONDON MIDLAND
Class 321	28

NORTHERN
Class 158	20

Class 321	12
Class 322	20

SOUTHEASTERN
Class 375	438
Class 376	180
Class 395	174
Class 465	388

SOUTHERN
Class 455	184

FREIGHTLINER
Class 66	56

GB RAILFREIGHT
Class 66	27

angel Trains — Rail People Real Expertise

ARRIVA TRAINS WALES
Class 142	30
Class 153	5
Class 158	48
Class 175 (2-car)	22
Class 175 (3-car)	48

C2C RAIL
Class 357/2	112

CHILTERN
165/0 (2-car)	56
165/0 (3-car)	33
172	8

CROSSCOUNTRY
Class 43 HST power car	5

EAST COAST
Class 43 HST power car	22

EAST MIDLANDS TRAINS
Class 153	6
Class 156	8
Class 158	32

FIRST GREAT WESTERN
Class 150	46
Class 153	9
Class 165/1 (2-car)	40
Class 165/1 (3-car)	48
Class 166	63

Class 180	25
Class 43 HST power car	86

FIRST SCOTRAIL
Class 156	96
Class 158	14
Class 314	48

FIRST TRANSPENNINE EXPRESS
Class 350/4	40

GRAND CENTRAL
Class 180	25
Class 43 HST power car	6

GREATER ANGLIA
Class 317/5	60
Class 317/6	96
Class 317/8	48
Class 360	84

GREAT NORTHERN
Class 317	48

HULL TRAINS
Class 180	20

LONDON MIDLAND
Class 150	6
Class 350/1	120
Class 350/4	40*

LONDON OVERGROUND
Class 172	16

MERSEYRAIL
Class 507	96
Class 508	81

NORTHERN
Class 142	158
Class 150	94
Class 153	11
Class 156	56
Class 158	52
Class 333	64

SOUTHERN
Class 442	120

SOUTH WEST TRAINS
Class 444	225
Class 450	508

SOUTHEASTERN
Class 465/2	64
Class 465/9	136
Class 466	86

VIRGIN TRAINS
Class 390	574

DB SCHENKER
Class 66	250
Class 67	30

TRAIN FLEET MAINTENANCE AND MANUFACTURE

IN ASSOCIATION WITH

TRAIN FLEET MAINTENANCE AND MANUFACTURE

KNORR-BREMSE
RailServices

THE CAPACITY AND CAPABILITY TO DELIVER SOLUTIONS TO THE RAIL INDUSTRY

With the largest total facilities of their kind in the UK, with a combined area of some 420,000 square metres, Knorr-Bremse RailServices has the capacity to deliver solutions to train operators who are based in the UK and Ireland.

The impressive RailServices facilities can undertake major 'whole train' and systems refurbishment projects which improves existing rail stock. Both Springburn and Wolverton facilities boast large and dedicated bogie shops, wheel overhaul shops and paint shops. The bogie shops include wash and strip facilities where all the bogie systems can be overhauled including the traction motors. The wheel shops have the capability to overhaul and carry out the heaviest of repairs on all wheel set types. The paint shops can handle the most challenging of refinish demands including repairs and they also include a complete vehicle re-livery service.

CAPABILITY

However, capacity and the sheer size of the RailServices facilities alone cannot deliver what customers need and RailServices possesses not only the capacity but also the capability to deliver support and solutions for customers. This capability is made possible by the four hundred plus highly skilled and experienced employees who work at the two RailServices sites; Springburn near Glasgow in the North and Wolverton near Milton Keynes in the South.

These employees are supported by the other five hundred plus Knorr-Bremse UK Rail Group employees who are based at Burton upon Trent in Staffordshire (the HVAC specialist facility) and at Melksham in Wiltshire (the UK headquarters and centre for original equipment brake control engineering, Knorr-Bremse Rail Group distribution and specialist platform screen system division, Westinghouse Platform Screen Doors).

EXPERIENCE AND EXPERTISE

Located at the Wolverton and Springburn facilities are highly experienced and qualified staff, including engineers, project managers and planners who, between them, can offer customers their expertise and support to provide a range of major service types to keep train running safely and reliably.

The types of service offered by RailServices include; vehicle overhaul, refurbishment, upgrade, re-livery and incident repair (on all EMUs/DMUs, coaching stock and locomotive types). In addition there are a wide range of flexible service types available to customers which include; component repair and overhaul, wheel set refurbishment, bogie overhaul, gear box and transmission repair and overhaul, peripheral equipment repair and overhaul, rail plant and equipment repair and overhaul and supply chain support and management using the latest in logistics techniques.

In addition to the services offered 'in-house' at either of the RailServices UK sites in Springburn and Wolverton, services can be provided at Customers' own locations and facilities. These include a 24 hour, 364 day incident and rectification service. Following a request for assistance with incident or rectification RailServices will visit the customer's site within 24 hours of the call and have the ability to transport and deliver the vehicle to a location as required. RailServices can offer customers RAIB investigation quarantine berths if they are required.

Components can also be supplied to customers whether the components are, overhauled, especially manufactured or re-manufactured or, from the original systems manufacturer. The extensive Knorr-Bremse Rail Group portfolio of systems and products is, of course, also available from RailServices.

Consumables and rotable product supply can also be managed on behalf of the customer by RailServices who can use the latest in logistics techniques to supply directly from their own extensive warehousing facilities. Parts supply can be from stock or against an agreed customer demand schedules and lead times through structured but flexible supply contracts. Customers' assets can be fully managed by RailServices to optimise in-service availability of trains.

FLEXIBILITY

In addition to offering capacity and capability, RailServices considers flexibility to be at the core of its proposition. Individual services can be demanded from the huge range available and provided to customers as and when needed or RailServices can manage the entire assets of the operator against pre-agreed targets with all of the variety of choices in-between through the entire life cycle of the train. RailServices sees its role as one of working together with and supporting the customer to keep their trains in safe, reliable, available and importantly, in revenue earning service. It certainly has the capability and capacity to do just that. ∎

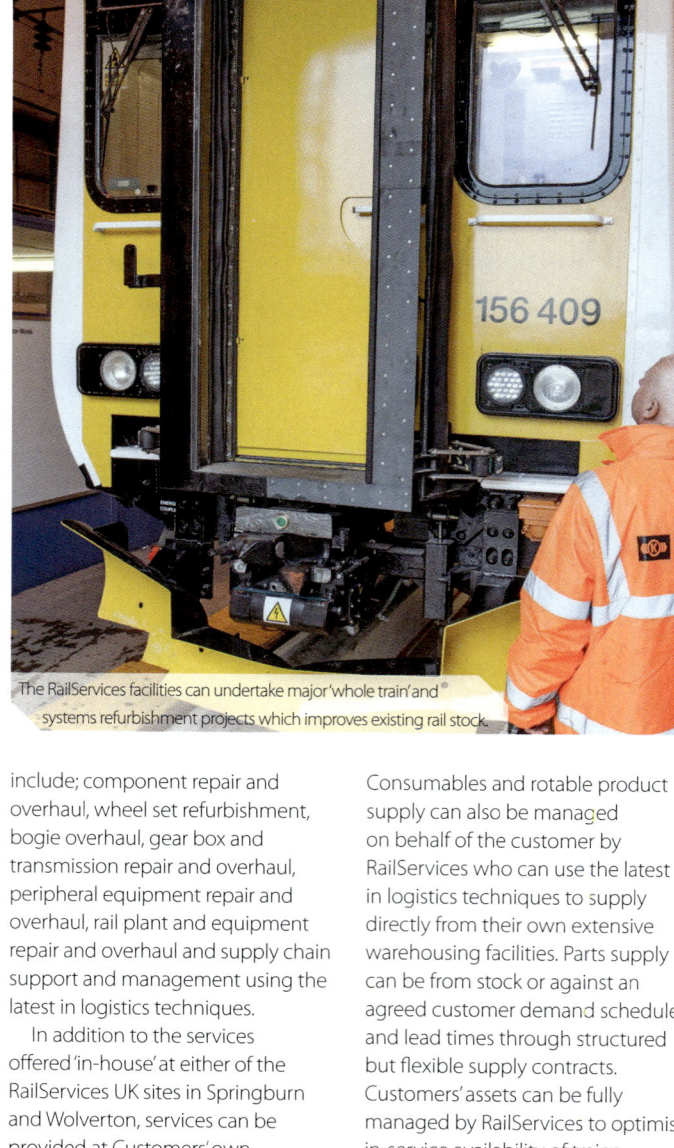

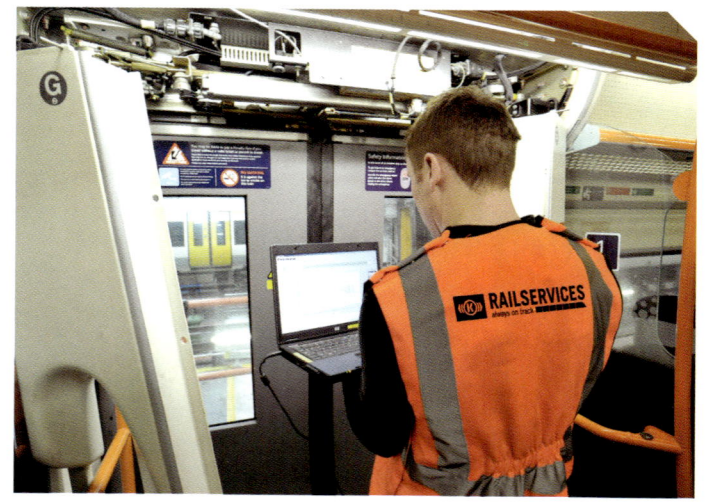

The RailServices facilities can undertake major 'whole train' and systems refurbishment projects which improves existing rail stock.

RailServices can manage the entire assets of the operator against pre-agreed targets.

DIRECT AWARDS REVIVE ROLLING STOCK MARKET

ROGER FORD, INDUSTRY & TECHNOLOGY EDITOR OF *MODERN RAILWAYS*, REPORTS ON HOW A QUALITY FACTOR IN RAIL FRANCHISE EVALUATION HAS INFLUENCED NEW PASSENGER TRAIN ORDERS

When the British Rail rolling stock fleet was sold off under privatisation, the aim was to create a leasing market. This meant setting the initial rentals which the new Rolling Stock Companies would charge for individual passenger train fleets ranging from nearly new to 20 years old.

A potential drawback was immediately apparent. If the lease rentals charged for the existing trains were too low, new rolling stock would be uneconomic at a time when ministers were promising that several of the new franchises would include replacement of life expired stock.

To overcome this obstacle, the new lease rentals were based on the concept of 'indifference pricing'. The aim was to make the total costs of existing trains broadly comparable with those of new rolling stock, so that operators would be 'indifferent' when it came to the choice between old or new.

Indifference pricing was a one-off exercise, and over the past two decades lease rentals for ex-British Rail rolling stock have become increasingly cheap, relative to new trains funded on the open market.

As a rule of thumb, if an existing train costs £x per month to lease, the refurbished and life extended version will cost £2x and the equivalent new train £4x.

GOVERNMENT ISSUE

When a franchise became due for replacement, competitive bids were evaluated solely on the basis of

PUTTING A VALUE ON QUALITY

Thameslink, Southern & Great Northern was the first franchise to be let using DfT's bid evaluation process which combines quality and cost. Under the new process, the Net Present Value of the bid, in terms of premium or subsidy, represents 70% of the score and Quality 30%.

To determine the winning bidder, DfT calculates what it terms the 'Combined Delivery & Funding Score' (CDFS). This requires a financial value to be put on the scores from the quality evaluation of each bid.

In consultation with the owning groups, a weighting factor has been determined which is applied to the quality scores. The CDFS for each bidder is then calculated using the formula:

$CDFS = P +/- (n \times Q)$, where P is the Net Present Value of the franchise premium/payments in £ million, Q is the quality score and n the quality weighting factor.

In the case of TSGN, P was the NPV of the franchise payments to cover operating costs plus a margin. As a result the quality score would offset these payments, making the formula:

$CDFS = P - (n \times Q)$.

In the example provided in the TSGN Invitation to Tender, 'n' was allocated a value of 33. This gave the following illustrative results:-

Bidder 1: P = 5,000; Q = 55
Bidder 2: P = 5,200, Q = 70

Under the previous bid evaluation process, Bidder 1 would have won with the lower cost NPV.

But when the CDFS formula is applied, the scoring becomes:-
Bidder 1: 5,000 - (33 x 55) = 3,185
Bidder 2: 5,200 - (33 x 70) = 2,890

This results in the higher quality bid winning with the lower CDFS.

Note that the value of 'n' is determined separately by DfT for each franchise competition to reflect the characteristics of that market and the quality DfT wants to buy.

Class 700 Desiro City train on Siemens' Wildenrath test track in Germany in June 2014. A large fleet of these trains has been procured by the DfT for the expanded Thameslink network. **SIEMENS**

TRAIN FLEET MAINTENANCE AND MANUFACTURE

TABLE 1: NEW SCOTRAIL FRANCHISE: ADDITIONAL ROLLING STOCK

FLEET	UNITS/SETS	FORMATION	VEHICLES	SERVICE DATE
New Hitachi AT200	24	4 car	96	From 2017
New Hitachi AT200	46	3 car	138	From 2017
New Hitachi AT200 (a)	10	3 car	30	By 2023
TOTAL NEW (MAX)	**80**		**264**	
Class 321	7	4 car	28	2015
IC125	13	2+5	65	December 2018
IC125	14	2+4	56	December 2018
TOTAL IC125	**27**		**121**	

(a) Option dependent on franchise running to full 10 year term.

lowest subsidy/highest premium. The relative cost of new trains made them unaffordable. An exception was where the introduction of new rolling stock was mandated in the Invitation to Tender.

Replacement of InterCity 125 fleets on the Great Western and East Coast main line, and the dedicated new train fleet for Thameslink, were two examples. In both cases the new fleets were procured directly by the Department for Transport (DfT). Similarly, Transport for London (TfL) and DfT, through Crossrail Ltd, have procured and funded the new trains for the new cross London route.

Other than these three mega-contracts, the prospects for new train orders in Control Period 5 were limited. And as the overview of the rolling stock market in last year's edition of The Modern Railway indicated, most of the prospective additional orders were linked to public sector operators, such as London Overground, or procured by a train operator on behalf of DfT.

BREAKTHROUGH

But a radical change in DfT's approach to franchise specification

TABLE 2: ROLLING STOCK ORDERS AND PROSPECTS

FLEET	CLASS NO	TYPE	QUANTITY (VEHICLES)	FORMATION	MANUFACTURER	FUNDER	STATUS (NOV 2014)
Intercity Express Programme (GWML)	800/801	EMU/bi-mode	369	various	Hitachi	Agility Trains West	Ordered
Intercity Express Programme (ECML)	800/801	EMU/bi-mode	497	various	Hitachi	Agility Trains East	Ordered
TOTAL IEP			**866**				
Thameslink	700	EMU	1140	8 & 12 car	Siemens	Cross London Trains	Ordered
Crossrail	345	EMU	585	9 car	Bombardier	DfT/TfL	Ordered
Southern [1]	387/1	EMU	116	4 car	Bombardier	Porterbrook Leasing	Delivering
Southern [2]	387	EMU	32	4 car	Bombardier		Option
London Overground [3]	378	EMU	57		Bombardier		Ordered
TSGN (Gatwick Express)	387/2	EMU	108	4 car	Bombardier [4]		Ordered
SWT (HLOS build)	707	EMU	150	5 car	Siemens	Angel Trains	Ordered
Caledonian Sleeper		Sleepers	74		CAF	SMBC [5]	Committed
ScotRail		EMU	234	3 & 4 car	Hitachi		Ordered
ScotRail		EMU	30	3 car	Hitachi		Option [6]
TOTAL (INCL IEP & OPTIONS)			**3392**				
PENDING							
London Overground [7]		EMU	270	4 car			Shortlisted
TSGN (Class 313 replacement)		EMU	150	6 car			Franchise commitment
Essex Thameside capacity enhancement		EMU	68	4 car			Franchise commitment
London Underground Northern Line [8]		Tube Stock	30	6 car		TfL	OJEU issued
London Underground Northern Line [9]		Tube Stock	270	6 car		TfL	OJEU issued
London Underground Jubilee Line [10, 11]		Tube Stock	126	7 car		TfL	OJEU issued
STATED REQUIREMENT							
Merseyrail [12, 13]		EMU	175	3 car			Pending OJEU
SPECULATIVE							
Trans Pennine Express electrification [14]		EMU	150	5 car			
Midland Main Line electrification [14]		EMU	175	5 car			
Alliance Rail open access	390	EMU	48	6 car			
Hull Trains open access [14, 15]		EMU	20	5 car			
CANCELLED							
Great Western [16]		EMU	120-160	4 car			

Notes
1. 110mph dual voltage. Additional Thameslink capacity pending new fleet.
2. Remaining option after Gatwick Express order.
3. Lengthening existing fleet to 5-car.
4. Drawn down from 140 vehicle option in Southern order for DfT.
5. Expected funder.
6. Subject to three year franchise extension option.
7. Greater Anglia Inner suburban, Gospel Oak-Barking, Euston-Watford.
8. Firm requirement.
9. Total of potential options.
10. Could include retractioning of exisiting fleet.
11. Option.
12. Max train length 60 metres.
13. Refurbishment option under consideration.
14. Likely quantities
15. Linked to private proposal for electrification to Hull.
16. Direct Award requirement dropped, could be reinstated under new Direct Award.

42

HITACHI
Inspire the Next

WE MOVE LONDON

London's transport network is one of the busiest and most complex in the world. As a global leader in rail technology, Bombardier plays a major role in keeping London moving. Our latest *BOMBARDIER MOVIA* metro trains on London Underground's Victoria and Sub-Surface lines and widely acclaimed *BOMBARDIER ELECTROSTAR* vehicles on London Overground are transporting thousands of passengers daily.

And the journey doesn't end there. For the new landmark London Crossrail project, we will deliver state-of-the-art trains based on the *BOMBARDIER AVENTRA* product platform. With Bombardier's latest trains and technology offering market-leading performance, we are driving The Evolution of Mobility.

www.bombardier.com

BOMBARDIER
the evolution of mobility

BOMBARDIER, AVENTRA, ELECTROSTAR & MOVIA are trademarks of Bombardier Inc. or its subsidiaries.

TRAIN FLEET MAINTENANCE AND MANUFACTURE

The most recent fleet of new trains to be completed is the Siemens-built Class 350/3 for London Midland, leased from Angel Trains. Some of the ten new 110mph trains entered service early with London Midland in October 2014. **DFT**

and evaluation has seen the number of main line vehicles ordered, in addition to the Intercity Express Programme, Thameslink and Crossrail, reach 800. Fleets currently out to tender or committed under franchise agreements (for London Overground, TSGN and Essex Thameside) add a further 488 main line vehicles.

Under its new franchise policy, DfT can include quality aspirations in the Invitations to Tender (ITT) for replacement franchises (see article on page 11). In effect, the Department can now quantify the value it puts on initiatives to improve quality of service – including new trains (see box). DfT's aim is to produce franchise agreements which are financially viable and affordable to government, while supporting investment and innovation for passengers.

Table 1 shows the result of the new approach, as adopted by Transport for Scotland (TfS). Reflecting national aspirations, the quality weighting was increased to 35% in the ScotRail ITT.

It was known that new four car EMUs would be needed for the Edinburgh-Glasgow Improvement Programme (EGIP) electrification, but the large number of three car units indicates the power of the 'quality factor'. According to TfS, the 46 three-car EMUs will be allocated to Dunblane, Alloa and Stirling services, plus a small quality for suburban services in South Glasgow. The seven Class 321 units will provide an immediate boost

TABLE 3: PASSENGER TRAIN ORDERS 2007-13

OPERATOR / FINANCIER	CLASS	VEHICLES	MANUFACTURER	DELIVERED
London Midland / Porterbrook	350/2	148	Siemens	2009
Southern / Porterbrook	377/5	92	Bombardier	2009
Southeastern (HS1) / Eversholt	395	174	Hitachi	2009
London Overground / QW	378	228	Bombardier	2011
London Overground / Angel	172/0 DMU	16	Bombardier	2010
ScotRail / Eversholt	380	130	Siemens	2010
London Midland / Porterbrook	139*	2	Parry People Movers	2008
Virgin West Coast / Angel	390	106	Alstom	2012
Greater Anglia / Lloyds	379	120	Bombardier	2011
London Midland / Porterbrook	172/2 and /3 DMU	69	Bombardier	2011
Chiltern / Angel	172/1 DMU	8	Bombardier	2011
Southern / Porterbrook	377/6	130	Bombardier	2013
Southern / Porterbrook	377/7	40	Bombardier	2014
London Midland / Angel	350/3	40	Siemens	2014
TransPennine / Angel	350/4	40	Siemens	2014

*LPG/flywheel hybrid drive railcars.
All are electric multiple-units except where shown (DMU - diesel multiple-unit)

44

HITACHI Inspire the Next

NEW TUBE FOR LONDON – FLEET SIZES

LINE	TRAIN SETS (APPROX)
Piccadilly	100
Central	100
Bakerloo	40
Waterloo & City	10

A contract between Transport for London and Bombardier covers the supply, delivery and maintenance of 65 new 9-car 'Aventra' trains and a depot at Old Oak Common for the new Crossrail route. There is an option to purchase 18 additional trains. **TFL**

to capacity on Glasgow commuter services this year.

Similarly the acquisition of re-engineered IC125 sets for the new services linking Scotland's seven cities was justified by a double quality benefit. Clearly the Mk3 coach, upgraded with power doors and Controlled Emission Toilet, will represent an improvement in quality of service compared with existing DMUs. However the extra performance of the shortened formations will cut journey times, attracting a separate quality bonus.

TUBE STOCK

Adding to demand are two London Underground requirements. In the near term the Jubilee and Northern Additional Train (JNAT) procurement programme has begun. The base requirement is for only five six-car Tube trains to cover the extension of the Northern Line to Battersea, but there are also options for up to a further 45 units.

Separate options under the new contract cover up to 18 7-car trains for the Jubilee Line. These are needed exploit the extra capacity provided by the ability of the new signalling to run 36 trains/hr.

However these requirements should be regarded as provisional because LU has told potential bidders that the allocation of trains between each line and between the base order and options will be further defined 'following completion of feasibility studies' and could be subject to change. One option would be to cascade trains between the Jubilee and Northern lines.

LU is looking for a 'modern equivalent train' which 'substantially replicates' the gauging and operational characteristics of the existing Alstom-supplied rolling stock in service on the two lines.

In the longer term LU has shortlisted Alstom, Bombardier, CAF, Hitachi and Siemens for a contract to supply up to 250 train sets for the Piccadilly, Bakerloo, Central and Waterloo & City lines under the 'New Tube for London' programme. The contract, valued at between £1.0bn and £2.5bn, is scheduled to be awarded in 2016 with the first trains entering service on the Piccadilly Line in 2022.

TABLE 4: PASSENGER TRAIN ORDERS FROM PRIVATISATION (1994) TO 2007

ORIGINAL CUSTOMER	MANUFACTURER	TYPE	NO OF VEHICLES	DELIVERY	FUNDER
Anglia Railways	Bombardier	Class 170 DMUs	32	2000	P
Arriva Tr Nthn	Siemens/CAF	16x4-car Class 333 EMUs	64	2000-04	A
c2c	Bombardier	74x4-car Electrostar EMUs	296	1999-2001	P,A
Central Trains[a]	Bombardier	23x2-car, 10x3-car Class 170 DMUs	76	2000-04	P
Central/Silverlink	Siemens	30x4-car Class 350/1 (West Coast route)	120	2004-05	A
Chiltern Railways	Bombardier	Class 168 DMUs	67	1998-2005	P, H
Connex (Southeastern)	Bombardier	Electrostar EMUs	618	2000-05	H
Connex / Southern	Bombardier	28x3-car, 154x4-car Electrostar EMUs	700	2002-05	P
First N Western	Alstom	16x3-car, 11x2-car Class 175 DMUs	70	2000	A
Gatwick Express	Alstom	8x8-car Juniper EMUs	64	1999	P
First Great Eastern	Siemens	21x4-car Desiro EMUs	84	2002	A
First Great Western	Alstom	14x5-car Class 180 DMUs	70	2000-01	A
Heathrow Connect	Siemens	5x5-car Class 360/2 EMUs	25	2005-06	T
Heathrow Express	CAF/Siemens	9x4-car, 5x5-car EMUs	61	1998-2002	T
Hull Trains	Bombardier	4x3-car Class 170 DMUs	12	2004	P
Hull Trains	Bombardier	4x4-car Class 222 DMUs	28	2005	H
Midland Mainline	Bombardier	17x2-car, 10x1-car Class 170 DMUs	44	2000-04	P
Midland Mainline	Bombardier	16x4-car, 7x9-car Class 222 DEMUs	127	2004-05	H
ScotRail	Alstom	40x3-car Class 334 Juniper EMUs	120	1999-2000	H
ScotRail	Bombardier	55x3-car Class 170 Turbostar DMUs	165	1999-2005	P, H
Southern	Bombardier	Class 170 DMUs	42	2003-04	P
South West Trains	Siemens	127 x 4-car Class 450 Desiro EMUs	508	2002-07	A
South West Trains	Bombardier	9x2-car Class 170 DMUs	18	2000-02	A
South West Trains	Siemens	45x5-car Class 444 Desiro EMUs	225	2002-05	A
TransPennine	Siemens	51x3-car Class 185 Desiro DMUs	153	2005-06	H
Virgin CrossCountry	Bombardier	40x5-car, 4x4-car tilting DEMUs	216	2001-03	V
Virgin CrossCountry	Bombardier	34x4-car non-tilting DEMUs	136	2000-02	V
Virgin West Coast	Alstom	53x9-car Pendolino trains	477	2001-05	A

[a] Plus 1x2-car and 2x3-car originally ordered by Porterbrook for spot hire
V Halifax Bank of Scotland and Royal Bank of Scotland.
T Owned by Heathrow Express.
A Angel Trains
P Porterbrook
H HSBC Rail (Eversholt)

TRAIN FLEET MAINTENANCE AND MANUFACTURE

HITACHI
BUILDING A BETTER RAILWAY

'Topping out' of the state-of-the-art Vehicle Manufacturing Facility in Newton Aycliffe was celebrated in October 2014.

Hitachi Rail Europe is now building on the success of the Class 395 Javelin train and Class 465 traction replacement project, and the company has set itself ambitious targets for growth in the UK and European markets. Not only is its service delivery solution for the Department for Transport's Intercity Express Programme (IEP) on schedule, but it is also progressing the design of its fleet of AT200 commuter trains for the Abellio ScotRail programme. In addition, following its successful bid to fit two Class 37 locomotives with on-board ETCS in-cab signalling, Hitachi Rail Europe is also emerging as a growing player in the signalling and on-board communications sector.

Progress is moving quickly on the IEP, for which Hitachi Rail Europe is designing and delivering, and maintaining, 122 Class 800/801 trains which will run on the Great Western Main Line and East Coast Main Line from 2017 and 2018 respectively.

The first three pre-series Class 800/801 trains have been under construction in Japan in 2014, with the first train due to arrive in the UK in March 2015. The first train was unveiled at Hitachi's Kasado-based factory in Japan in November, on programme, precipitating the advent of a flurry of interest surrounding the transportation of the train from Japan and its arrival in the UK.

On October 30, 2014, Hitachi Rail Europe and its key partners celebrated the topping out of its state-of-the-art Vehicle Manufacturing Facility in Newton Aycliffe, County Durham. This

46

HITACHI Inspire the Next

IN ASSOCIATION WITH **RAIL SERVICES** always on track

The first pre-series Intercity Express train is due to arrive in the UK in March 2015.

Hitachi is set to supply Abellio with 71 AT200 trains for operation in Scotland from 2017.

Hitachi successfully delivered one of the Traffic Management System prototype solutions for Network Rail.

marked a major milestone in bringing rail manufacturing back to the North-East: the completion of the external factory 'envelope'. The work on the interior of the factory is expected to be complete for mid-2015 when Hitachi will start commissioning equipment and training its new workforce. Developments at Newton Aycliffe are greeted with great interest in the North East, as the local economy and supply chain is already seeing the economic benefits of Hitachi Rail Europe's investment. Hitachi has committed to support education, training and apprenticeships in the area, investing in the future workforce.

Hitachi established a UK Design Office in Newton Aycliffe in October 2014 and is co-sponsoring the South Durham University Technical College, due to open in 2016. This UTC will have an intake of 120 pupils per year pursuing an academic and technical education, rising to between 550 and 600 pupils when in full operation. These pupils will add to the growing number of trainees and apprentices working for Hitachi at Newton Aycliffe.

As rolling stock, maintenance and service provider to the IEP, Hitachi Rail Europe actively promotes good practice in procurement. The organisation has worked hard to ensure that it sources parts, systems and operations from within the local supply chain wherever possible. Hitachi celebrated these partnerships with UK suppliers with a ceremony at leading rail trade fair InnoTrans 2014, attended by Clare Moriarty, Director General of the Rail Executive at the Department for Transport.

In addition, Hitachi Rail Europe is very proud to further promote investment in the UK, not only by investing in the first manufacturing plant to be built in the UK for over 100 years, but also in the construction of major new depots across the country. This adds considerably to the network's future assets.

In support of the maintenance of the IEP fleet, Hitachi Rail Europe's responsibility for 27.5 years, work is also underway to renovate a number of existing depots along both the East Coast and Great Western Main Lines, enhancing the capability of the existing infrastructure where possible.

This investment will build on Hitachi Rail Europe's track record of providing excellence in the maintenance of rolling stock, proven by the 100-strong team maintaining the iconic Class 395 Javelin trains which run on Southeastern's network. The Class 395 is Southeastern's most reliable fleet.

2014 has also seen the launch of the AT100/200 series product, Hitachi Rail Europe's offer to the commuter travel market. The AT200 mock-up was greeted with great acclaim at the 2014 InnoTrans in Berlin, and Hitachi is set to supply Abellio with 71 electric multiple units (EMUs). They will be route cleared to run throughout the wider network, which is currently being electrified. The AT200 trains will be operated by Abellio in Scotland from 2017.

The AT200 has been designed to transform the regional commuter travel experience. With a top speed of 100 miles per hour, each unit is 23 metres in length, and features cab-end and inter-vehicle gangways to facilitate the best use of passenger space. The train has a 35-year design life and places a heavy emphasis on energy efficiency and weight reduction to minimise the impact on the infrastructure. Passenger comfort is a priority, and this is reflected in the interior design with the ergonomic use of LED lighting, air conditioning, power sockets, WIFI, baggage storage and cantilever seats to provide additional room for luggage.

The AT200 trains will be built at the Newton Aycliffe factory and employ local and UK suppliers where possible.

Hitachi Rail Europe is also continuing to innovate in the field of ETCS. Following successful testing of the Class 97 locomotive in 2013, which was retro-fitted with Hitachi's ETCS system and operated successfully on the Cambrian line in Wales, there has been significant interest in other applications of this ground-breaking, interoperable technology. Hitachi expects this to be a significant growth area moving into 2015, with several opportunities under investigation, including throughout Europe.

After having successfully delivered one of the Traffic Management System (TMS) prototype solutions for Network Rail, the team is busy preparing for new challenges and opportunities to showcase its expertise in this field. As an enabler of the wider vision of a digital railway, Hitachi sees this as a major step forward towards a more reliable network.

Hitachi Rail Europe is proud to be bringing a fusion of Japanese engineering and UK manufacturing excellence to the European market and to be promoting growth in the UK manufacturing industry and supply chain. Hitachi looks forward to further opportunities to build a better railway through integrated infrastructure, train and technology solutions.

HITACHI Inspire the Next

TRAIN FLEET MAINTENANCE AND MANUFACTURE

BOMBARDIER
LEADER IN RAIL MANUFACTURING AND SERVICING

Bombardier Transportation is a global leader in the rail equipment manufacturing and servicing industry. It has a workforce of over 3,200 people and a presence at 31 locations throughout the UK. Bombardier has built, or has on order, around 60 per cent of the UK's rolling stock and is contracted to service over 5,200 vehicles (a third of the current fleet) across the UK. In 2014, Bombardier celebrated 175 years of continuous train manufacture in the city of Derby at its production site in Derby.

Bombardier offers the broadest product portfolio in the rail industry and delivers innovative products and services that set new standards in sustainable mobility – conserve energy, protect the environment and help to improve total train performance for passengers and operators. Bombardier's global expertise ensures that the UK continues to benefit from the latest technology that the rail industry has to offer. Bombardier's rail transportation products are in operation in all major British regions, in the full range of rail services - intercity, urban and suburban, metros and light rail systems.

The award winning Bombardier *ELECTROSTAR* is the most successful post-privatisation EMU in the UK, with more than 2,000 vehicles entering service in the past decade. The proven *ELECTROSTAR* consistently excels in performance league tables, achieving some of the highest reliability figures in the country. *ELECTROSTAR* trains are in operation on Southeastern, Southern, Thameslink, Greater Anglia, Essex Thameside and London Overground railways, where they help to bring thousands of commuters to, from and around London daily. In December 2011, Bombardier received a contract for the supply of 130 additional *ELECTROSTAR* vehicles for Southern to augment its existing fleet, with the new trains entering service in September 2013 - record time for a fleet of its size. In November 2012, an option for 40 additional new vehicles for Southern was exercised, and in July 2013 an order was placed for 116 *ELECTROSTAR* vehicles with a capability of 110mph operation. In May 2013, Bombardier also secured an order for the delivery of 57 new vehicles for London Overground.

The Gautrain Rapid Rail Link, a brand new complete rail system in South Africa also operates UK built *ELECTROSTAR* trains. In February 2014, Bombardier received the contract to deliver the new fleet of trains for the prestigious London Crossrail project. The contract is for the delivery and maintenance of 65 new trains - based on Bombardier's latest *AVENTRA* EMU product platform - and a new maintenance depot at Old Oak Common.

The *FLEXITY* 2 trams, in successful revenue service in Blackpool since 2012, incorporate the 'best of the best', bringing the outstanding, proven features of Bombardier trams into one vehicle.

191 *MOVIA* metro trains are being supplied for the London Underground Sub Surface Lines upgrade.

IN ASSOCIATION WITH **RAILSERVICES** always on track

Bombardier is to deliver the new fleet of trains for the prestigious London Crossrail project.

The CrossCountry and West Coast networks run Bombardier Voyager and Super Voyager diesel electric multiple-units (DEMUs). Bombardier Meridian DEMUs are also in daily passenger service with UK operator East Midlands Trains, and Bombardier's TURBOSTAR diesel multiple-units are in service with many operators, helping to connect towns and cities across Britain.

The 'greener' next generation TURBOSTARS are lighter and offer reduced CO2 emissions, improved fuel consumption and are over 90 per cent recyclable.

Traffic congestion in Croydon has been significantly reduced through the use of Bombardier FLEXITY Swift light rail vehicles on Transport for London's Tramlink system. And linking the centre of London with the eastern Docklands area, the Docklands Light Railway is served by the first fully automated, driverless public transport system, operating 94 Bombardier-built vehicles proving enormously popular and reliable during the London Olympics 2012. Manchester's Metrolink system also benefits from a new fleet of Bombardier FLEXITY Swift trams - a further 16 were ordered in 2014, bringing the fleet size to 120.

The FLEXITY 2 trams, which have been in successful revenue service in Blackpool since April 2012, incorporate the 'best of the best', bringing the outstanding, proven features of Bombardier trams into one vehicle.

Bombardier provides a complete portfolio of services from technical support and material solutions to total train care packages that are tailored to the needs of any operator. In the UK, Bombardier has total fleet management responsibility for, among other fleets, the diesel-electric trains operated by Arriva CrossCountry and Virgin West Coast, maintained at a purpose-built facility, Central Rivers, and a number of overnight out-station depots. Bombardier fleets throughout the UK are supported by highly skilled maintenance teams and also by ORBITA a leading edge predictive maintenance capability which helps operators to increase fleet utilisation, improve reliability and availability, reduce in-service failures and improve the passenger's overall journey experience.

During the London 2012 Olympics, Bombardier's maintenance teams supported 800 trains on 9 key routes into London, ensuring that fleets provided optimum reliability and availability to meet increased demand and attracting praise from visitors, train operators and the mayor of London. This, combined with Bombardier's contribution to the Victoria Line Upgrade, resulted in Bombardier receiving the award for 'Transport Supplier of the Year' at the 2013 National Transport Awards.

MAJOR LONDON UNDERGROUND CONTRACT

Bombardier is a participant in the renewal of the London Underground (LU) network, as the supplier of 191 MOVIA metro trains for the Sub Surface Lines (SSL) upgrade- the Metropolitan, District and Circle, Hammersmith and City lines -currently being built at Bombardier's production site at Derby and the first trains on the London Underground system to feature air-conditioning and walk through gangways. LU's Victoria Line service has been provided entirely by new Bombardier MOVIA trains since July 2011, which are providing exceptional levels of reliability and Bombardier's system upgrade project for the line, which also includes replacement of the signalling system, was completed, on schedule in 2012. ■

Bombardier is supplying 57 new vehicles for TfL's London Overground to lengthen all its EMUs to 5-car length.

After further orders in 2014, Manchester Metrolink's fleet of Bombardier FLEXITY Swift trams is set to reach a total of 120.

TRAIN FLEET MAINTENANCE AND MANUFACTURE

Class 700 train on the Siemens test track in Germany. **SIEMENS**

SIEMENS UNVEILS THAMESLINK TRAIN

Three fully-assembled cars for the new Desiro City train were unveiled for the first time by Siemens, funders Cross London Trains and operators Govia Thameslink Railway Limited, at Innotrans 2014 in Berlin in September. The Class 700 trains will form the main rolling stock fleet for the government sponsored £6.5bn Thameslink Programme, improving the north-south rail link across London.

The first trains will run on the Thameslink Bedford to Brighton service through central London in spring 2016, and on Peterborough and Cambridge Great Northern services a year later. By the end of 2018, when the Thameslink Programme is complete, the two services will join at St Pancras International, and run through central London every two to three minutes at the busiest times.

Many components for the Thameslink trains, approximately 25% lighter than previous generations and up to 50% more energy efficient, are manufactured in the UK, including at Siemens' site in Hebburn, near Newcastle, creating around 300 local jobs. The Thameslink Programme is expected to create around 8,000 jobs in total, including up to 2,000 in support of the new trains, across the UK supply chain.

The Desiro City train has also been chosen to provide additional capacity on the South West Trains franchise for passengers travelling into London Waterloo, the UK's busiest station, as part of a £210m deal. The 150 new vehicles will create capacity for more than 24,000 additional peak-time passengers every day, and will start running from 2017.

TRANSPENNINE

The 10th new Siemens-built Class 350/4 train was handed over to First TransPennine Express (FTPE) in March 2014, the final unit in a 10-strong fleet of Siemens electric trains. This is a key element of a project to create additional capacity and new services for passengers, and take advantage of newly electrified routes.

The new four-carriage Desiro trains, which have been designed with 110mph capability, increase capacity between Manchester in the northwest and Glasgow and Edinburgh in Scotland by 60%. They also improve space for luggage by 25% and reduce the carbon footprint of the service by over one third.

Siemens Rail Systems provides engineering and maintenance support for the new trains alongside its existing diesel Class 185 fleet at its newly electrified Ardwick depot in Manchester. Significant changes to the depot infrastructure saw it extended to accommodate both electric and diesel trains, with multi-skilled teams working on both technologies.

This investment in rolling stock has already led to the creation of 200 new jobs to date. It is expected improvements to rail connections as a result of the project will generate £10m per year in regional economic benefits.

The new trains took the number of Siemens vehicles in the UK to 1,558.

Siemens Rail Systems Division provides expertise and technology in the full range of rail vehicles – from heavy rail to metros to trams and light-rail vehicles. In the UK, the Division employs around 750 people and maintains over 360 Siemens passenger trains for First TransPennine Express, South West Trains, Heathrow Express, Greater Anglia, Northern Rail, London Midland and ScotRail. In addition to manufacturing the new trains for Thameslink, the company is also supplying Eurostar with its new high speed fleet of trains.

NATIONAL TRAINING ACADEMY

Opening in autumn 2015, the National Training Academy for Rail (NTAR) will grow the UK talent pool in rail engineering, plugging the skills gap that could otherwise become a barrier to growth.

NTAR is a joint project between the National Skills Academy for Railway Engineering (NSARE), the Department for Business, Innovation & Skills (BIS) and the Department for Transport (DfT), who have provided half the funds required, with industry partner Siemens contributing the other half.

Located at Northampton, NTAR will also collaborate with other organisations nationwide to help build up a network of complementary 'spokes' to maximise the reach of next generation training, including the National College for High Speed Rail.

Currently, some 13,500 people work in specialist traction and rolling stock roles across the UK, but a future skills shortage of around 4,000 people over the next five years is forecast – caused by factors including an ageing workforce, the technological advancement of rolling stock, and investment and growth in the industry.

NTAR will enable all organisations across the sector to access excellent training and development facilities, including passenger and freight train operating companies, train manufacturers and maintainers, equipment manufacturers and the wider supply chain including SMEs.

WHEN YOU'RE PULLING OUT ALL THE STOPS, YOU CAN RELY ON OUR FIRST CLASS SUPPORT

Our fluid analysis laboratory is one of the largest in the UK, providing 24-hour response and real-time reporting to the rail industry, preventing downtime and minimising maintenance costs.

POWER FOR A NEW GENERATION. SUPPORT THAT LASTS.

Finning is partnering with Direct Rail Services to support the new Class 68 locomotive. Powered by our proven Cat® C175 engine and supported by our bespoke parts and fluid analysis package, we're always on hand to keep things moving.

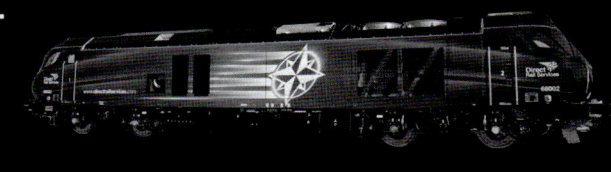

For more information contact us
Phone: 0113 201 2065
Email: oillab@finning.co.uk
Web: www.fluid-analysis.com

FINNING®

TRUSTED BY EXPERTS

TRAIN FLEET MAINTENANCE AND MANUFACTURE

Colas Rail Freight's Class 70 No 70805 at Dawlish with a Westbury-Newton Abbot engineering train on 4 June 2014. **STEWART ARMSTRONG**

NEW DIESELS FROM GE AND EMD

CLASS 70S FOR COLAS

Ten GE Transportation UK PowerHaul Series locomotives joined the Colas Rail Freight fleet in 2014, bringing the total of these Class 70 locomotives in operation in the UK to 29.

Freightliner Group placed the original order for these locomotives in 2007, partnering with GE on the new design configured to take into account current and future requirements for efficiency, emissions control and safety.

The 129-ton PowerHaul Series locomotive is designed to generate more horsepower and tractive effort while lowering fuel consumption and greenhouse gas emissions. The locomotive features several leading technologies to achieve this performance including a V16-cylinder, twin-turbo PowerHaul series engine – a product of Ecomagination, a GE-wide initiative to help meet customer demand for more energy-efficient products.

GE's unique AC individual-axle traction-control technology enables the PowerHaul Series to haul heavier loads by significantly reducing slippage on start-ups, inclines and sub-optimal track conditions. The PowerHaul Series also features dynamic braking in addition to air brakes to provide smoother handling when hauling heavier loads.

GE Transportation's PowerHaul Series PH37ACai locomotive, unveiled at InnoTrans 2012 in Berlin, meets interoperability requirements and has a full-width continental-gauge body, in contrast to the UK-gauge version.

German open-access freight-hauler Heavy Haul Power International (HHPI) was the customer for the pilot batch of PowerHauls.

GE Transportation has partnered with Turkish company Tülomsas to manufacture state-of-the-art PowerHaul locomotives for the Turkish State Railways (TCDD) as well as customers in Europe, Middle East and North Africa.

ELECTRO-MOTIVE DIESEL

GB Railfreight announced in February 2014 a deal with Electro-Motive Diesel Inc to purchase a further 13 Class-66 locomotives.

On top of the purchase of eight Class 66 locomotives from EMD announced in September 2013, this brought the total number of additional locomotives on order for the GB Railfreight fleet to 37.

The purchase of 21 Class-66s will take GB Railfreight's Class-66 fleet to 71 locomotives. They were being delivered by Chicago-based Electro-Motive from July 2014. The locomotives were secured ahead of the change in EU emissions legislation which, from January 2015, sees new regulations coming into force that could impact the ability to obtain compliant and affordable locomotives.

Electro-Motive Diesel was acquired by Progress Rail Services, a wholly-owned subsidiary of Caterpillar Inc, in 2010 from previous owners Greenbriar Equity Group and Berkshire Partners. EMD became a wholly-owned subsidiary of Progress Rail, creating a global locomotive manufacturing and rail services company.

Progress Rail Services is one of the largest providers of rail and transit products and services in North America, including: locomotive upgrade and repair; railcar remanufacturing; trackwork; rail welding; rail repair and replacement; signal design and installation; maintenance of way equipment; parts reclamation and recycling.

EMD's Class 66 locomotive has become the UK standard, and gained acceptance more widely in Europe, with DB Schenker company Euro Cargo Rail using its Class 66 locomotives for cross-border operations between France, Belgium and Germany. They are equipped with safety systems and radios for all three countries, with automatic switching when crossing borders.

UK company EMDL - a subsidiary of Electro-Motive Diesel - signed a 10-year contract with GBRf in 2012 to maintain its fleet of Class 66 locomotives – the company's first full-maintenance contract.

The company provides all post delivery services, including commissioning, locomotive modification and maintenance of EMD locomotives in Europe, Scandinavia and parts of the Middle East.

EMDL has invested in a new maintenance and warehouse facility, with new cranes and wheel lathe, at its Doncaster base. ■

RAILWAY SYSTEMS ENGINEERING & INTEGRATION (RSEI) AT THE UNIVERSITY OF BIRMINGHAM

POSTGRADUATE PROGRAMMES IN RAILWAY SYSTEMS ENGINEERING AND RISK MANAGEMENT

400 years after their invention, railways are transporting ever more people and goods at higher speeds and over greater distances. Railway systems engineers ensure the reliability and safety of 5 km long iron ore trains, of a 574.8 km/h world record train and of peak flows of 40,000 passengers per hour and direction. In Britain, they have started the design of a high speed railway for 400 km/h between London, Manchester and Leeds.

The postgraduate programmes in Railway Systems Engineering and in Railway Risk and Safety Management allow participants to acquire the skills and know-how to become recognised experts in the railway domain, ready to tackle the challenges of climate change and rapidly growing demand. The modular programmes are suitable for experienced railway staff as well as new entrants to the industry, available in both part-time and full-time modes of study. They lead to the degree of MSc, the Postgraduate Diploma or a Postgraduate Certificate of the University.

Our Master of Research (MRes) programme in RSI (Railway Systems Integration) has been offered since 2011/12. This one year period of postgraduate study involves the equivalent of 2 months of taught courses 2 months of research training and 8 months of research under the guidance of one of our experts. Some MRes projects are supported by major international sponsors and research bodies.

Alumni of the taught postgraduate programmes at Birmingham can be found in senior positions in railways and railway consultancies around the world. MRes graduates join this select group on successful completion of their studies.

The University of Birmingham encourages equality of opportunity for all and offers railway systems engineering studies as part of its provision of higher education in a research-led environment.

UNIVERSITY OF BIRMINGHAM

Further information and registration:
contact Joy Grey (0121 414 4342, j.grey@bham.ac.uk)

or in writing to
Administrator RSEI, BCRRE,
Gisbert Kapp,
University of Birmingham,
B15 2TT.

MSc RSEI

Research and technical consultancy enquiries to f.schmid@bham.ac.uk

CONTINUOUS PROFESSIONAL DEVELOPMENT

---

creating desire

Confidence,
gobsmacking style,
excellent design,
attention to detail and
raw, heartfelt passion are
the hallmarks of our approach.

Head-turning liveries are just one of the areas of brand communication for which we are legendary.

We've created many commanding transport brands, and designed powerful advertising and marketing that turns heads, changes opinions, inspires loyalty, wins awards and ultimately makes money

... as the country's more progressive transport companies keep discovering.

best impr

Best Impressions
15 Starfield Road
London W12 9SN

t 020 8740 6443
e talk2us@best-impressions.co.uk

TRAIN FLEET MAINTENANCE AND MANUFACTURE

CONTRACT WINS FOR ALSTOM

Alstom Transport employs some 2,000 people in the UK at over 20 locations. Alstom has full service provision and technical support contracts with a number of train and metro operating companies, notably for the Alstom-designed and built Pendolino fleet for Virgin.

Alstom built several current fleets of trains running on the London Underground and today provides maintenance for the Northern Line fleet. From its Preston site, Alstom provides dual expertise as the company's UK supplier of spare parts and logistics and global centre of excellence for lifetime traction support. The site is the only traction systems engineering knowledge centre in the UK.

Around a third of all rail journeys in the UK are made on Alstom rolling stock.

NOTTINGHAM

The first Alstom trams to be delivered to the UK are the 22 Citadis trams ordered by Nottingham Express Transit (NET) for the tramway extension project.

The Citadis for Nottingham is 32 metres long and can carry up to 200 people. The trams have been built in Alstom's facility in Barcelona.

As part of the Tramlink consortium, Alstom was also awarded the contract to maintain the trams, including the 15 Bombardier trams already in service. Refurbishment worth over £300,000 has been carried out for the existing fleet.

Alstom is also building the two new lines, with associated overhead wires, track and signalling, with its consortium partner Taylor Woodrow.

Alstom's unique Appitrack machine was used for the first time in the UK on NET. Appitrack can lay the platform and insert the shoes for the rails with total accuracy, at rates averaging 150m a day. It holds the world record of 403m of single track laid in one day, in Orleans.

PENDOLINO

Alstom was awarded a contract worth over Euro 12 million by Virgin Trains in October 2013 to modernise its entire Pendolino fleet. The contract included refurbishment of the interiors, bar, kitchen facilities and toilets, over a period of eight months.

To help solve problems on the Pendolino fleet more quickly, Alstom has created a dedicated Customer Care Centre that will allow Virgin train crew to report technical issues in real time, between 06.00 and 22.00, seven-days-a-week.

The third heavy overhaul ('H3') of the Pendolino fleet was completed by Alstom in July 2013 - the end of a £60m process that saw 1.3 million parts changed on the trains, and 936 bogies overhauled. The Longsight team also extended 31 of the nine-car trains to 11 cars.

Eversholt Rail in 2014 awarded Alstom a two year contract worth £36.1 million to improve the passenger environment and reliability of the 40 ScotRail Class 334 trains, and has also extended a DC motor contract by two years. As part of the £4m extension, Alstom will upgrade the motors, used on Class 318, 320, 321 and 322 trains.

UNDERGROUND

The London Underground Northern Line mid-life project is a refurbishment of the Alstom-built fleet comprising upgrades to the interior and exterior of the 106 trains, and Alstom is due to complete this in 2015.

Alstom was awarded a contract by UK Power Networks Services in 2013 to supply its innovative Harmonic and Energy Saving Optimiser (HESOP) energy recovery system for the Victoria Line. The contract, worth about Euro 1 million, was for a trial of inverting substation technology. HESOP works by converting and transferring any unused power, generated by the trains during braking, to accelerating trains elsewhere on the line or to the grid.

ELECTRIFICATION PROGRAMME

ABC Electrification (Alstom, Babcock and Costain) won its first contract in 2013, a £48m project for the third phase of the West Coast power supply upgrade – then ABC was appointed in 2014 as one of four suppliers to deliver Network Rail's £2 billion electrification programme. The total contract for ABC is estimated at around £900 million over an initial seven year term. ABC was awarded two out of the six areas.

Terence Watson, President of Alstom UK said, 'Being selected as one of the framework suppliers working with Network Rail is a really important win for ABC and for Alstom. The project is an opportunity to invest in training and development and attract new comers to the sector.'

The ATC joint venture (Alstom, TSO and Costain) has been awarded the contract to fit out and commission track and power equipment in the Crossrail tunnels under London. The contract is worth over Euro 350 million.

Crossrail's contract for high voltage traction power supply, valued at about £15m, was awarded to the AC Joint Venture (Alstom and Costain) – as was the non-traction high-voltage power supply contract (value about £25m).

New Citadis trams for Nottingham. **ALSTOM**

We design and manufacture equipment for your trains, so who better to service it

- Engineering support
- Repairs & Overhauls
- Upgrades & Retrofits
- Reliability & LCC improvements

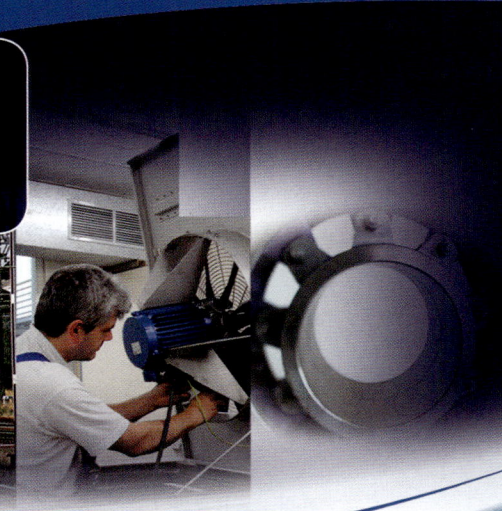

RANGE OF RAIL PRODUCTS
Brake Systems including WSP
Couplers
Doors
Pantographs
Platform Screen doors
HVAC
CCTV including DOO
Train Data Recorders
Wireless Systems

Faiveley Transport
Morpeth Wharf, Twelve Quays,
Birkenhead CH41 1LF
Tel: +44 (0) 151 649 5000
Fax: +44 (0) 151 649 5002
sales@faiveleytransport.com
www.faiveleytransport.com

Faiveley Transport
Unit 21/22 Darwell Park,
Mica Close, Amington
Tamworth
Staffordshire B77 4DR
Tel: +44 (0) 182 726 2830
Fax: +44 (0) 182 726 2831

For New Build Projects contact:
Kevin Smith
Sales & Marketing Manager
New Equipment & Maintenance
Tel: +44 (0)7808 364417
kevin.smith@faiveleytransport.com

For After Market Products & Services contact:
John Summers
Customer Services Manager
Tel: +44 (0)7778 590799
john.summers@faiveleytransport.com

Faiveley TRANSPORT

MECHAN
Strength with Technology

RAILCAR LIFTING JACKS

RAIL DEPOT LIFTING AND HANDLING EQUIPMENT

› Railcar Lifting Jacks
› Bogie/Equipment Drops
› Traversers
› Turntables
› Bogie Test Machines
› Under Car Equipment Handling
› Rail Depot Workshop Equipment

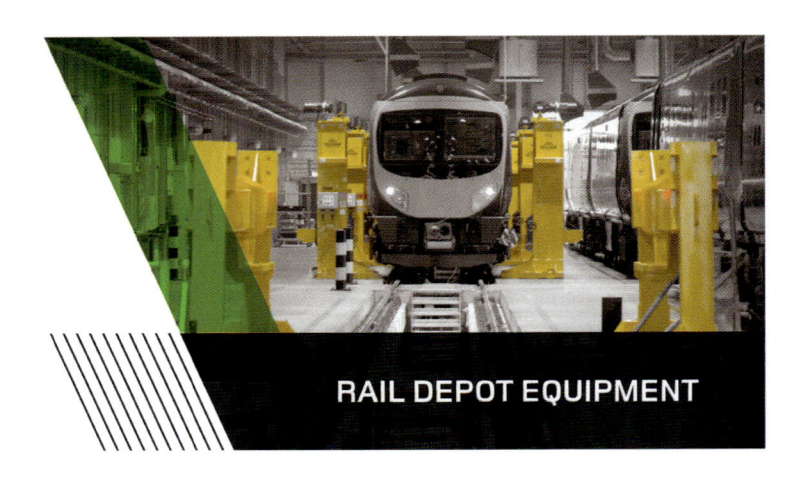

RAIL DEPOT EQUIPMENT

✉ info@mechan.co.uk 📱 +44 (0)114 257 0563 💻 www.mechan.co.uk

HITACHI
Inspire the Next

TRAIN FLEET MAINTENANCE AND MANUFACTURE

CAF DELIVERS NEW FLEETS

New CAF trams for Midland Metro. **CENTRO**

CAF - Construcciones y Auxiliar de Ferrocarriles, SA - has constructed several fleets of electric multiple-units and diesel multiple-units for railway operators in the UK and Ireland and provided the fleet for Edinburgh Tram, its first light-rail project in the UK.

CAF followed this by being selected as the supplier of up to 25 five-car Urbos 3 trams for the Midland Metro in the West Midlands, in a deal worth in the region of £40 million. The first of an initial order of 20 was unveiled at Wednesbury depot in October 2013.

The first new tram came into service on the existing line in September 2014. The five-section air-conditioned trams have a passenger capacity of approximately 200, with two dedicated spaces for wheelchair users, and their features are fully compliant with the Disability Discrimination Act. Each section has passenger information systems and CCTV, and passenger assistance units at each door. The trams are 30 metres long and 2.65 metres wide, with an aluminium body, 100% low floor access, and 70 km/h maximum speed.

The company has also demonstrated its intentions for the UK main line market by adapting its Civity electric multiple-unit platform design specifically to the UK.

CAF completed the delivery of 20 x 3 car diesel multiple-units to Northern Ireland Railways in 2012, under a contract which includes maintenance by CAF Rail Services UK Ltd for a 15 year period. The 100mph trains are arranged as 3 car units, with provision to increase the number of cars per unit in the future.

The Class 4000 is a development of the Class 3000 design, following a comprehensive review to produce a more environmentally-friendly train - adapting the traction system to meet new European emission regulations, cutting fuel consumption and maintenance costs.

Representing an investment of £105 million, the 20 Class-4000 trains operate alongside the fleet of 23 Class 3000 trains delivered by CAF in 2005.

CAF has also supplied diesel multiple-units and 125mph intercity vehicles for Iarnród Éireann (IE - Irish Rail). CAF provided the 14 electric multiple-unit trains for Heathrow Express, in conjunction with Siemens, and 16 similar trains for West Yorkshire.

The company's products range from complete transportation systems for urban, suburban and long-distance routes and turnkey solutions, to custom-made parts and components. With several manufacturing plants in Spain, and others in North and South America, CAF has the capability and experience to manufacture using steel, aluminium or stainless steel. CAF also offers maintenance, upgrading and overhaul of vehicles and components.

CAF, through its subsidiary company Eliop Seinalia is now also a developer and supplier of both onboard and trackside railway signalling equipment. ■

DRS ORDERS 35 VOSSLOH LOCOS

Vossloh España was awarded a follow-up order for ten UKLight (Class 68) locomotives by Direct Rail Services (DRS) in April 2014. This brought the total number of Class 68s ordered by DRS to 25.

The Bo-Bo mixed traffic diesel-electric locomotives, developed in conjunction with Beacon Rail Leasing, have an axle load of 21.4 tonnes, and a 2,800 kW Caterpillar engine. The locomotives are built at Vossloh's plant in Valencia, Spain.

The locomotives are fitted with AC traction equipment from ABB, have a top speed of 100mph, and are designed for use on both intermodal and passenger trains.

The locomotives meet Stage IIIA emission standards.

Vossloh España is also supplying ten Dual Mode locomotives to DRS, with delivery to start in 2015. Key features of this Class 88 locomotive include 4MW ABB equipment delivering a continuous electric power rating on the 25kV electrified network, a 700kW diesel engine for work away from the electrified network (delivering 317KN of tractive effort in both modes), plus superior adhesion capacity. The Class 88 has a nominal 100mph top speed, 500KW train-heating rating and regenerative braking.

These dual-powered locomotives are designed for heavy-haul freight and high-speed passenger services (with a self-rescue capability and flexibility to adapt to various passenger applications), while complying with Euro IIIB environmental targets.

Vossloh España is also supplying seven tram-trains, with modern traction systems from Vossloh Kiepe, to South Yorkshire Passenger Transport Executive, to operate between the centre of Sheffield and Rotherham Parkgate. They will be delivered from 2015 and will be compatible with operation on the existing Sheffield Supertram network as well the heavy rail route from Meadowhall to Rotherham Parkgate.

MOVERIGHT INTERNATIONAL

UK European Worldwide

Heavy Haulage and Abnormal Load Specialists

www.moverightinternational.com | andrew@moverightinternational.com
Telephone: 01675 475590 | Mobile: 07974 755105

Dura Grating
Fibreglass Anti-Slip Bridge Decking

+44 (0)1255 423601
enquiries@duracomposites.com
www.duracomposites.com

- **High load capacity**
- **Gritted surface prevents slips, trips & falls**
- **Quick & easy to lift and install**
- **Corrosion resistant and maintenance free**

Cookspond Bridge with grey Dura Grating 50mm fibreglass decking

RISQS QUALIFIED

Dura Composites is the leading UK supplier of precision engineered FRP composite open grid or solid cover structural walkway products. Dura Grating open mesh structural walkway products are Form 3 approved and allow contractors to take advantage of their light weight handle ability, their workability using standard hand tools both on and off site, their short lead times, and their rapid installation speeds. Dura are renowned for providing innovative fixing solutions in real-time thus ensuring that site works on projects such as bridge decks operate smoothly and to time-scales required.

dura composites™

...designed for the future

■ Industrial ■ Rail ■ Marine ■ Landscaping ■ Architectural

HITACHI Inspire the Next

57

TRAIN FLEET MAINTENANCE AND MANUFACTURE

The Class 321 EMU rebuilt by Wabtec at Doncaster, for Eversholt Rail Group, as a demonstrator for Abellio Greater Anglia passengers to evaluate. **TONY MILES**

Wabtec RAIL LIMITED

The Wabtec Group has the combined resources to provide an all-encompassing range of services to the UK rail industry. It is part of Wabtec Corporation, a worldwide leading supplier of value-added, technology-based products and services for rail, transit and other industries.

The group includes Wabtec Rail Limited, Wabtec Rail Scotland and Brush Traction, and now also LH Group, including the Hunslet Engine Company.

Based at Barton under Needwood in Staffordshire, LH is a leading supplier of multiple unit passenger rail products and services. A key part of the company's activities is the overhaul of rail vehicles, engines and transmission systems. Resources include a gear cutting and machining facility specialising in the manufacture of components, all types of gears, spiral bevels, castings, machining and reverse engineering. There is also a general fabrication facility offering a broad range of engineering capabilities. The Hunslet Engine Company is renowned throughout the world as a designer and manufacturer of quality industrial shunting, tunnelling and specialised locomotives.

The acquisition of LH was complementary to Wabtec Group's activities as one of the UK's leading rail vehicle engineering companies. Through Wabtec Rail Limited's works at Doncaster and Wabtec Rail Scotland's works at Kilmarnock in Scotland, the Group undertakes the refurbishment and maintenance of railway rolling stock, locomotives, passenger trains and freight wagons. Brush Traction's facilities at Loughborough provide locomotive overhauls, services and aftermarket components, including traction motors, electrical control systems and wheelsets.

In 2014 Wabtec Corporation acquired Fandstan Electric Group, the leading rail and industrial equipment manufacturer. The company's highly engineered products include pantographs, third rail shoe gears, electrical contacts and brush holders, and its brand names include Brecknell Willis, Stemmann Technik and Transtech. Fandstan Electric has about 1,000 employees and operations in the UK, Europe, China, Australia, and the US.

Wabtec said Fandstan Electric would expand its high-technology content on rail vehicles and provided another entry into the infrastructure segment of the market.

Major refurbishment and overhaul contracts presently under way at Wabtec's works include creation of six additional Class 458 EMUs for Porterbrook, South West Trains and Alstom - reconfiguring the Class 458 fleet into 5-car units and incorporating equipment from the Class 460 fleet previously used on Gatwick Express.

One of the Greater Anglia fleet of Class 321 EMUs has been rebuilt by Wabtec at Doncaster, for Eversholt Rail Group, as a demonstrator for passengers to evaluate. The interiors have been revamped in two formats, suburban and metro.

Two cars have the new suburban-style interior, with air conditioning, double-glazed windows, energy-efficient LED lighting, redesigned seats, two wheelchair spaces and an accessible toilet. Two metro-style cars have air conditioning, new lights and windows, with slimline 2+2 seating, clear access and increased standing space.

Modernisation and conversion work on Class 73 electro-diesel locomotives for GB Railfreight, including fitting them with more powerful 1,600hp MTU engines, is currently under way at Brush - giving them up to 25 more years in service, according to GBRf. The '73/9s' are initially expected to work on infrastructure monitoring and railhead treatment duties for Network Rail.

Major coupler and brake interface modifications were completed on Class 57/3 locomotives at Wabtec's Brush Traction facility, to enable the haulage of virtually every electric multiple-unit class with full compliance to the Rule Book.

Further conversions and modernisation of Mk3 coaches for First Great Western got under way at Wabtec Rail Scotland in Kilmarnock in autumn 2014, with 18 Trailer Firsts to be converted to First/Standard composite vehicles and 24 to full Standard class. Wabtec also refurbished Mk3 vehicles for Chiltern Mainline services, fitting them with external sliding plug doors, with driving-van trailer vehicles also undergoing overhaul and modification.

Refurbishment and C6X overhaul of the 21 Class 318 electric multiple-unit fleet by Wabtec for Eversholt is also under way, as is a C6 repair for Northern Rail's Class 322s and 321/9s.

Other major recent contracts include the 'as new' refurbishment of Tyne & Wear Metrocars for DB Regio Tyne & Wear Ltd.

PASSENGER TRAIN OPERATORS

IN ASSOCIATION WITH

ESG
Designed to deliver

PASSENGER TRAIN OPERATORS

One of ESG's experts offering consultancy advice during a visit to Wimbledon depot.

ESG UNRIVALLED TECHNICAL EXPERTISE AND SERVICES

LEADING UK RAIL ENGINEERING CONSULTANCY GOES FROM STRENGTH TO STRENGTH

Derby based ESG offers highly creative and value-led railway rolling stock engineering consultancy. With a rapidly expanding UK team, the company prides itself on combining innovation and responsiveness with a broad base of experience.

Additionally, as part of the Deutsche Bahn Technology Division, ESG and its parent company DB Systemtechnik can access the full range of DB test facilities as well as the collective 950+ high calibre engineers from across mainland Europe. This contributes to ESG's unique, considerable and deep understanding of the UK's rail network.

Martin Horsman, Managing Director of ESG Rail explained why the company is achieving great growth and success in the market: 'Our organisation has a relentless focus on our customers' needs - with an obsession to deliver right-first-time, on time, every time. We recognise that changes occur as projects mature. This is reflected in our adaptability, speed of response and the transparency of our communication. All of this means we deliver at the least cost whilst helping our customers to avoid commercial or operational barriers that can slow progress'.

ESG's business encompasses the following services:

CONSULTANCY

ESG's highly experienced rolling stock engineers encompass all specialisms of railway technology, with the skills to support train operators, rolling stock companies and original equipment manufacturers and maintainers. Project experience ranges from the development of documentation through to complex design projects and from rolling stock upgrades to whole life-cycle cost modelling. The company's team of dedicated system specialists provide expert advice on unique industry challenges, such as wheel-rail interface issues, passenger information, energy metering and the industry's unique WSPER facility that provides the capability to evaluate and optimise brake performance.

DESIGN

ESG's team of expert designers and engineers offer a comprehensive rolling stock design service, enabling the development of solutions for both new build vehicles and fleet modernisation. These include the creation of concept design, 3D CAD modelling, 2D drawings, wiring diagrams and schematics for modernization, upgrade, refurbishment and supporting compliance with legislative requirements, such as facilitating access for Persons with Reduced Mobility (PRM).

INTEGRATION

ESG's experienced project management team enable the company to provide a turnkey service of design, procurement and installation of complex system projects, including for example the installation of on-board systems such as ETCS, Driver Advisory System (DAS) and Remote Condition Monitoring.

Additionally, its comprehensive service encompasses all aspects of managing a project – including a design approvals service – provided by sister company - Railway Approvals Limited.

RE-FRANCHISING

The specialist re-franchising team provide Train Operating Companies (TOCs) with bidding, negotiating, mobilizing or franchise deployment support – with particular focus on rolling stock strategy and maintenance, together with the activities associated with franchise end and hand back.

These activities include:
- Bespoke fleet maintenance and depot strategies
- Innovative leasing and risk sharing techniques
- Asset management
- Resource investment and governance
- Sustainability
- Equality of access
- Bid writing contribution
- Business case preparation
- Contractualisation of franchise committed obligations

RAILWAY APPROVALS

ESG's sister company Railway Approvals Limited is dedicated to providing impartial certification services to the railway industry. Certification work carried out by Railway Approvals Ltd is governed by UK/European Legislation, standards and Industry Regulations covering railway vehicle and product certification.

In addition Railway Approvals are a leading Rail Industry Supplier Assessment Body (RISAB) for the supply of safety critical products to the UK rail industry.

Clients include train operating companies (TOCs), Rolling Stock Leasing Companies (RoSCo), Freight Operating Companies (ECR, DB Schenker, Freightliner, GBRf, and DRS), Private Vehicle Owners (PO), rolling stock manufacturers and Network Rail.

An ESG specialist engineer surveys a sandbox as part of a unique modification.

TRAIN OPERATING COMPANIES - INDEX

The eastern approaches to Manchester Piccadilly with a First TransPennine Express Class 170 diesel multiple-unit (left) and Northern Rail Class 323 electric multiple-unit arriving. **PAUL BIGLAND**

COMPANY	OWNING GROUP	NEW FRANCHISE START [E]	PAGE NO
First Great Western	First	Mar 2019	p69
First TransPennine Express	First/Keolis	Feb 2016	p70
*First Hull Trains	First/Renaissance	-	p71
*ScotRail	First	Apr 2015	p72
Northern Rail	Serco/Abellio	Feb 2016	P74
*Merseyrail (a)	Serco/Abellio		P76
GreaterAnglia	Abellio	Oct 2016	P77
Govia Thameslink Railway (GTR)	Govia	Sept 2014	p79
Southern	Govia	[d]	p80
Southeastern	Govia	June 2018	p82
London Midland	Govia	June 2017	p85
Chiltern Railways	Arriva	Dec 2021	p87
Wales & Borders (c)	Arriva	Oct 2018	p88
Cross Country	Arriva	Oct 2019	p89
*Grand Central	Arriva	-	p91
South West Trains	Stagecoach	Apr 2019	p92
East Midlands Trains	Stagecoach	Oct 2017	p93
InterCity West Coast	Virgin/Stagecoach	April 2017	p95
c2c	National Express	Nov 2014	p96
East Coast	Directly Operated Railways (DfT)	March 2015	p97
*Heathrow Express	Heathrow airport	-	p100
*Eurostar	London & Continental (DfT)	-	p98
*Eurotunnel	-	-	p99
*London Overground Concession (b)	LOROL (MTR and Arriva)		p162

Notes:

* Not franchised by Department for Transport.
(a) concession agreement with Merseytravel.
(b) concession agreement with Transport for London.
(c) Management of franchise devolved to the Welsh Government, but DfT is the procuring authority.
(d) To join GTR at end of present Southern franchise in July 2015.
(e) As planned in Department for Transport programme, October 2014.

PASSENGER TRAIN OPERATORS

The ScotRail franchise changes hands, to Abellio, in April 2015. FirstGroup saw its profits fall by over a third during its penultimate year in charge. **ABELLIO**

PASSENGER OPERATOR FINANCES

CHRIS CHEEK OF PASSENGER TRANSPORT SPECIALISTS TAS ANALYSES TRAIN OPERATING COMPANIES' FINANCIAL PERFORMANCE, AND FINDS THAT REVENUE GROWTH IS NOT GENERALLY REFLECTED IN TRAIN OPERATOR PROFITS

2013-14 was the year in which the long bull market in rail demand resumed with a vengeance, driven by a pace of economic recovery which took even the economic pundits by surprise. Four straight quarters of growth throughout 2013/14 – even despite the catastrophic storms during the winter which severed parts of the network completely: it is perhaps a measure of the underlying strength of the rail market that growth could be maintained and even accelerated during a period of such high profile disruption.

As well as reflecting the difficulties with storms and flooding, the sluggish performance of both the InterCity and regional markets could also offer support to those who claim that – as yet – the economic recovery is very much driven by what is happening in the capital, and the home counties which surround it.

The national patronage totals for the twelve months ended 31 March 2014 show the number of passenger journeys rising by 5.7% to 1,588 million. Passenger kilometres travelled rose by 2.9% to 59.6 billion.

Looking at the individual sectors, passenger journeys on the London and South East routes grew at the fastest rate, winning another 74 million journeys – a rise of 7.2%, taking the total to 1,108 million. It is a measure of the growth we have seen that this is higher than the total carried by the whole network as recently as 2005/06.

The longer distance operators experienced much lower growth, winning an extra 1.4 million passenger journeys, a rise of just 1.1%. This took the total to 129.1 million. Growth resumed on the regional networks after the previous year's virtual standstill: an extra ten million journeys were made, taking the total to 351 million, growth of 2.8%.

On the revenue front, all three sectors saw growth during 2013/14, as total railway revenue hit £8.2 billion – 6.4% up on the previous year. Commuter services gained 7.5%, regional routes 6.7% and InterCity services 4.8%. After taking inflation into account, revenue was ahead in real terms by around 4.8%.

This growth is not, however, generally reflected in train operator profits: the benefits have mainly gone straight into the Whitehall pot: DfT Rail earned enough in premium payments to cover the subsidies paid to the regional franchises and still have £420m over.

OPERATOR PROFITS

According to the latest analysis from passenger transport specialists TAS, profits at Britain's privatised train operating companies (TOCs) deteriorated again in 2012/13. Overall, the figures show that operating profits fell by 7% during the year, marking the fifth fall in six years: a partial recovery in margins achieved in 2010/11 is now but a distant memory.

The analysis covers all the TOCs lodging accounts with financial year ends between 31 December 2012 and 30 June 2013. Across the franchised train operating companies as a whole, turnover was up by 8.1% at £10,280m, whilst operating profits totalled £196.8m (previous year: £238m on £9,509m), to give an operating margin of 1.9% (previous year: 2.5%).

62

HITACHI Inspire the Next

Operating costs reached a total of £10,083m, 8.8% higher the 2011/12 total of £9,271.4m. The bulk of the increases were driven by increases in premium payments to Government – which extracted a net £419m in premium payments from the train operators in fiscal year 2012/13.

The companies continued to be net earners of interest during the year – a figure that now includes pension scheme income. Proceeds earned rose sharply as investment returns improved. The total was just £61.9m, up from £60.8m a year earlier. Pre-tax profits were therefore 13.5% lower at £258.6m (2012: £299.0m). Pre-tax profit margins were 2.5% (last year: 3.1%).

Total capital expenditure by the TOCs during the year fell by 10.7%, from the previous year's £155.9 to £139.2m. The value of net assets employed by the operators fell once again, by over 51% to £53.7m.

As is often the case, however, there were sharp variations between different rail industry sectors and between train operators. Overall, three of the 19 TOCs made an operating loss, down from five last year. First Greater Western was the biggest loser with an operating margin of minus 0.9%, whilst Chiltern and London Midland each recorded a loss of 0.3%. Two other big loss-makers from the previous year - Stagecoach Group's East Midlands Trains and Arriva's XC Trains - moved into profit as revenue support from the Department for Transport kicked in.

InterCity operators returned to profit after recording big losses in 2011/12, driven by the descent into the red at Cross Country, Greater Western and East Midlands. Total turnover amongst the companies rose by 8.9% to £3,760m, whilst operating costs rose by 6.7% to £3,716m. The resulting operating profit of £44.0m compared with the loss of £31.3m recorded in 2011/12, and was achieved at a margin of just 1.2% (2010/11: -0.9%). Biggest gainer in all this was the Department for Transport, which extracted £457m in premium payments from these operators during the year – though this was down from £497m in 2011/12.

Operators in London and the South East remain in the black, but saw profits fall by 48%. Again, the government was a big winner, extracting premium payments worth £747m (last year: £420m) from the sector as a whole: only Southeastern, Chiltern (just) and London Midland were in receipt of subsidy from DfT, with London Overground getting its £50.1m subvention from Transport for London.

Turnover at these mostly commuter companies rose by 7.2%, taking the total to £4,485m, whilst operating costs rose by 8.8% to £4,424m. The resulting operating profit of £60.8m compared with £117.3m in the previous year, at a margin of 1.4% (previous year: 2.8%). Margins are well below the peak they hit before the recession – this was the 4.8% achieved in 2006/07.

The regional franchises also saw falls in profit levels – though interestingly those TOCs most heavily reliant on public funding also deliver the highest returns. Turnover rose by 8.6% to £2,035m, whilst operating costs were 12.9% higher, totalling £1,943m. Operating profits were 39.5% down at £92.2m (previous year £152.9m), at a margin of 4.5% (8.1%). As usual, this sector consumed the bulk of the subsidy paid to the train operators, soaking up £863m worth of taxpayer funding, £10m less than in 2011/12.

Individually, the most profitable TOC was the Merseyrail Electrics operation, which returned an operating margin of 10.2%. Next came National Express Group's surviving franchise, c2c Rail, on 7.0%, followed by TransPennine Express on 6.9%.

In the summaries below, figures are extracted from accounts lodged at Companies House. Practice concerning the declaration and calculation of different cost and revenue items varies between train operators. This occasionally makes interpretation and reconciliation difficult: major issues are noted in the brief commentaries.

LONG DISTANCE OPERATORS

CROSS COUNTRY

The company returned to profit during the year as revenue support from the Department for Transport was payable for the full year, offsetting the first premium payable by the company.

Department for Transport support was worth a total of £80.3m during the year, up from £3.6m in 2011. Offsetting this was a premium payable to DfT under the franchise agreement of £53.0m (previous year: Nil). Passenger revenue grew by £35.6m.

PERIOD TO:	31/12/2012	31/12/2011
	£000	£000
Turnover	501,577	387,163
Operating Costs:	485,527	417,145
Operating Profit:	16,050	(29,982)
Operating Margin:	3.2%	-7.7%
Turnover per Employee	£306,026	£237,669
Track Access	98,345	94,325
Rolling stock lease	50,574	48,507
Revenue Grant	80,287	3,641

FIRST GREAT WESTERN

The company's performance deteriorated during the year, as operating losses rose by 22% ahead of exceptional items. Though revenue grew at well above inflation, operating costs increased at a faster rate to produce the deterioration, though the size of the losses relative to the turnover meant that there was a tiny effect on overall margins.

PERIOD TO:	31/03/2013	31/03/2012
	£000	£000
Turnover	1,130,274	1,018,928
Operating Costs:	1,140,976	1,027,696
Operating Profit:	(10,702)	(8,768)
Operating Margin:	-0.9%	-0.9%
Turnover per Employee	£222,451	£210,175
Track Access	138,655	135,893
Rolling stock lease	69,553	65,130
Revenue Grant	269,905	205,399

Northern Rail saw operating profits dip slightly in 2012 though passenger revenue was 8.7% higher. A Class 142 Pacer passes through Gateshead. **NORTHERN**

PASSENGER TRAIN OPERATORS

The cramped Southeastern terminus at London Charing Cross is packed in the evening rush hour on 24 April 2014. Despite the success of the company's operation during the Olympic Games, it experienced a difficult year financially in 2012-13. **PAUL BIGLAND**

EAST COAST

The company's performance deteriorated slightly during the year, as the rise in operating costs just exceeded revenue growth. Key to the operating costs, though, was another substantial £190m premium payment to government.

PERIOD TO:	31/03/2013	31/03/2012
	£000	£000
Turnover	692,498	665,864
Operating Costs:	688,085	660,721
Operating Profit:	4,413	5,143
Operating Margin:	0.6%	0.8%
Turnover per Employee	£241,541	£238,832
Track Access	48,839	45,258
Rolling stock lease	83,026	82,777

VIRGIN WEST COAST

The company saw profits dip sharply during the year, partly as a result of the change in franchise agreement, on the expiry of the previous deal in December 2012. From that point onwards, the franchise changed to a management contract with a 1% margin.

PERIOD TO:	31/03/2013	31/03/2012
	£000	£000
Turnover	966,651	1,001,470
Operating Costs:	946,281	965,141
Operating Profit:	20,370	36,329
Operating Margin:	2.1%	3.6%
Turnover per Employee	£331,613	£347,010
Rolling stock lease	302,333	236,283
Track Access	156,215	161,175
Revenue Grant	27,611	46,336

EAST MIDLANDS TRAINS

The company improved its results substantially during the year, returning to profit after several years of substantial losses. Revenue support from the DfT became available during the year, resulting in a change in net payments from a £40m premium to a net subsidy of £2.3m.

PERIOD TO:	30/04/2013	30/04/2012
	£000	£000
Turnover	469,127	378,523
Operating Costs:	455,294	412,566
Operating Profit:	13,833	(34,043)
Operating Margin:	2.9%	-9.0%
Turnover per Employee	£228,175	£186,373
Track Access	76,485	71,225
Rolling stock lease	27,856	27,760
Revenue Grant	121,927	36,340

LONDON AND SOUTH EAST OPERATORS

C2C RAIL

The company saw profits dip by over a third during the year, as an impressive double digit increase in passenger revenue was more than swallowed up by increases in operating costs – including track access charges, train leasing, maintenance and rising premium payments to government.

PERIOD TO:	31/12/2012	31/12/2011
	£000	£000
Turnover	137,360	127,827
Operating Costs:	127,801	113,135
Operating Profit:	9,559	14,692
Operating Margin:	7.0%	11.5%
Turnover per Employee	£239,721	£231,571
Track Access	12,144	11,224
Rolling stock lease	23,344	22,696

CHILTERN

The company improved its results during the year, sharply reducing operating and pre-tax losses after achieving strong revenue growth following completion of infrastructure upgrades in 2011. Meanwhile, the company moved back into net premium payments after a year of receiving net subsidy in 2010/11. The project to extend services to Oxford is now under construction, and the continuing effects of the Evergreen 3 projects make the accounts for this business very complex.

TAS - THE PASSENGER TRANSPORT SPECIALISTS

For 25 years, TAS has been providing research, analysis and advisory services to a huge range of organisations involved in passenger transport - including government at national, regional and local level, together with operators of rail, light rail and bus and community transport services.

TAS's market-leading market intelligence reports have achieved a worldwide reputation for being the definitive analysis of the financial and market performance of the UK's rail, light rail and bus industries, being widely quoted by government, the media and academics. These are now available online via the popular and successful TAS Business Monitor subscription service.

Passenger transport in all its forms is about delivery providing services and networks that get customers to where they want to be quickly, comfortably and above all safely, whilst at the same time delivering value for money to customers and stakeholders.

TAS is an employee-owned company that exists to help transport providers to deliver these services and to deliver continuous improvement in today's demanding and ever-changing world.

For further details, visit www.tas.uk.net

PERIOD TO:	31/12/2012	31/12/2011
	£000	£000
Turnover	155,575	130,964
Operating Costs:	156,000	141,109
Operating Profit:	(425)	(10,145)
Operating Margin:	-0.3%	-7.7%
Turnover per Employee	£203,101	£170,526
Rolling stock lease	19,161	17,970
Track Access	36,663	27,194

FIRST CAPITAL CONNECT

The company, which ceased to operate in September 2014, improved its performance during its penultimate year, recording strong revenue growth. However, the business remained only marginally profitable, being barely above break-even.

PERIOD TO:	31/03/2013	31/03/2012
	£000	£000
Turnover	604,332	547,755
Operating Costs:	599,269	544,165
Operating Profit:	5,063	3,590
Operating Margin:	0.8%	0.7%
Turnover per Employee	£249,827	£234,585
Rolling stock lease	57,522	41,530
Track Access	56,102	65,380
Revenue Grant	45,900	33,300

GREATER ANGLIA

This was the company's first year of trading, which commenced with the takeover of the Greater Anglia franchise from National Express on 5 February 2012.

PERIOD TO:	31/12/2012
	£000
Turnover	569,635
Operating Costs:	564,945
Operating Profit:	4,690
Operating Margin:	0.8%
Turnover per Employee	£198,756
Rolling stock lease	121,348
Track Access	70,941
Revenue Grant	12,225

LONDON MIDLAND

The company continued to make a loss as first staffing problems and then weather difficulties hindered its revenue growth during the year. However, at least losses were reduced substantially compared with the previous year. This resulted from strong above-inflation revenue growth, accompanied by lower – albeit still substantial – rises in costs.

PERIOD TO:	29/06/2013	30/06/2012
	£000	£000
Turnover	356,756	333,327
Operating Costs:	357,834	335,742
Operating Profit:	(1,078)	(2,415)
Operating Margin:	-0.3%	-0.7%
Turnover per Employee	£153,774	£143,799
Track Access	85,293	75,299
Rolling stock lease	52,463	52,470
Revenue Grant	57,319	65,268

LONDON OVERGROUND

The company's profits dipped during the year as operating cost growth outstripped the increase in revenue. Services expanded with the opening of the line from Surrey Quays to Clapham Junction during the year, requiring the recruitment and training of an additional 51 drivers. Meanwhile, the concession agreement was extended by two years to 12 November 2016.

PERIOD TO:	31/03/2013	31/03/2012
	£000	£000
Turnover	126,829	110,481
Operating Costs:	120,388	102,941
Operating Profit:	6,441	7,540
Operating Margin:	5.1%	6.8%
Turnover per Employee	£104,991	£95,489
Track Access	12,486	10,488
Rolling stock lease	2,088	2,091
Revenue Grant	98,507	86,473

SOUTHERN

The company improved its profits by almost a third during the year, as strong 6% passenger revenue growth outstripped the rises in costs, despite a huge £46m increase in the premium paid to government.

PERIOD TO:	29/06/2013	30/06/2012
	£000	£000
Turnover	725,591	677,880
Operating Costs:	707,395	664,067
Operating Profit:	18,196	13,813
Operating Margin:	2.5%	2.0%
Turnover per Employee	£180,675	£166,678
Track Access	138,978	122,769
Rolling stock lease	110,898	109,481

SOUTHEASTERN

Despite the success of the company's operation during the Olympic Games, it experienced a difficult year financially, as profits fell to just above break-even level. Despite the Games, passenger revenue growth was limited to 2.4%, whilst operating costs rose by 4%.

PERIOD TO:	29/06/2013	30/06/2012
	£000	£000
Turnover	764,151	750,802
Operating Costs:	763,168	733,799
Operating Profit:	983	17,003
Operating Margin:	0.1%	2.3%
Turnover per Employee	£200,934	£199,469
Rail contracts	425,097	404,279

SOUTH WEST TRAINS

The company saw a sharp reduction in operating and pre-tax profits during the year, as rises in operating costs – particularly increases in track access and electricity costs - outstripped otherwise strong revenue growth. The £133.5m revenue grant partially offset a premium of £415m paid to DfT.

PERIOD TO:	27/04/2013	28/04/2012
	£000	£000
Turnover	1,044,910	945,130
Operating Costs:	1,027,563	901,507
Operating Profit:	17,347	43,623
Operating Margin:	1.7%	4.6%
Turnover per Employee	£229,046	£213,637
Track Access	89,099	80,780
Rolling stock lease	109,481	105,309
Revenue Grant	133,457	87,133

REGIONAL, SCOTLAND AND WALES

ARRIVA TRAINS WALES

The company saw profits dip as operating cost increases – particularly track access and other property rental charges - outstripped otherwise strong revenue growth – with passenger income up by 9.7% and subsidy by 4.6%.

PERIOD TO:	31/12/2012	31/12/2011
	£000	£000
Turnover	287,210	272,402
Operating Costs:	270,069	251,874
Operating Profit:	17,141	20,528
Operating Margin:	6.0%	7.5%
Turnover per Employee	£143,462	£136,337
Rolling stock lease	40,176	38,654
Track Access	52,863	48,740
Revenue Grant	147,522	141,022

FIRST SCOTRAIL

Another franchise which is in the process of changing hands, this time for the second time. FirstGroup saw its profits fall by over a third during its penultimate year in charge, as increases in operating costs – particularly hefty rises in rolling stock and track access charges - outstripped rises in revenue. These included a 6% rise in passenger income and a sharp 50% increase in revenue grant to offset track access changes.

PERIOD TO:	31/03/2013	31/03/2012
	£000	£000
Turnover	778,672	613,686
Operating Costs:	767,752	596,259
Operating Profit:	10,920	17,427
Operating Margin:	1.4%	2.8%
Turnover per Employee	£166,954	£137,321
Rail contracts	375,458	231,514
Revenue Grant	447,196	297,536

FIRST TRANSPENNINE

The company saw turnover and profits fall sharply, as expected, following a new franchise extension deal with DfT. This saw a halving of the previous levels of subsidy paid and reductions in track

The new £5.2m Energlyn and Churchill Park station near Caerphilly opened in December 2013, funded by the European Regional Development Fund through the Welsh Government. Arriva Trains Wales saw profits dip in 2012 despite strong revenue growth. **NETWORK RAIL**

PASSENGER TRAIN OPERATORS

East Midlands Trains combines Midland main line inter-city services with regional and rural operations. The company improved its results substantially during 2012-13, with revenue support from the DfT becoming available. Passengers board a Class 156 DMU at Lincoln. **EAST MIDLANDS TRAINS**

access charges. Rolling stock lease costs increased following the delivery of the new electric stock for the Manchester Airport-Scotland services.

PERIOD TO:	31/03/2013	31/03/2012
	£000	£000
Turnover	241,472	284,941
Operating Costs:	224,866	218,943
Operating Profit:	16,606	65,998
Operating Margin:	6.9%	23.2%
Turnover per Employee	£226,947	£279,903
Track Access	48,438	75,630
Rolling stock lease	62,758	49,969
Revenue Grant	52,354	107,724

MERSEYRAIL ELECTRICS

The company improved its performance during the year, as revenue rose roughly in line with inflation whilst cost increases were held below this level.

PERIOD TO:	05/01/2013	07/01/2012
	£000	£000
Turnover	135,224	131,649
Operating Costs:	121,400	119,403
Operating Profit:	13,824	12,246
Operating Margin:	10.2%	9.3%
Turnover per Employee	£109,582	£108,175
Track Access	11,281	10,847
Rolling stock lease	12,218	12,126
Revenue Grant (ORR figures)	75,520	74,700

NORTHERN RAIL

The company saw operating profits dip slightly as the increase in operating costs – mainly pensions, depreciation and materials costs - outstripped revenue growth. Subsidy payments moved in line with inflation but passenger revenue was 8.7% higher.

PERIOD TO:	05/01/2013	07/01/2012
	£000	£000
Turnover	592,458	570,567
Operating Costs:	558,928	534,580
Operating Profit:	33,530	35,987
Operating Margin:	5.7%	6.3%
Turnover per Employee	£121,405	£117,473
Track Access	100,319	92,945
Rolling stock lease	37,168	35,546
Revenue Grant	324,111	317,432

NON-FRANCHISED OPERATORS

EUROSTAR INTERNATIONAL

The company saw a significant growth in profitability during the year, the second year of its existence as a fully integrated business co-owned by SNCF, the UK Department for Transport and SNCB. However, revenue growth was sluggish and the improvement in profits came about primarily as a result of cost reductions – notably £8.3m worth of cuts in track access charges.

PERIOD TO:	31/12/2012	31/12/2011
	£000	£000
Turnover	829,400	824,700
Operating Costs:	776,100	793,300
Operating Profit:	53,300	31,400
Operating Margin:	6.4%	3.8%
Turnover per Employee	£499,940	£487,700
Track Access - Europe	82,200	87,300
Track Access – Eurotunnel	206,500	208,700
Track Access – HS1	71,800	72,800

HULL TRAINS

The company improved its performance during the year, returning to a small operating profit after the previous losses, assisted by reduced rolling stock leasing costs.

PERIOD TO:	31/03/2013	31/03/2012
	£000	£000
Turnover	22,762	21,629
Operating Costs:	22,383	21,971
Operating Profit:	379	(342)
Operating Margin:	1.7%	-1.6%
Turnover per Employee	£212,729	£212,049
Rolling stock lease	2,462	2,621

GRAND CENTRAL

The company improved its performance sharply during the period, the first full year following Arriva's acquisition in November 2011. After several years of heavy losses during the set up phase, the business virtually achieved break even in operating profit terms. The company commenced the operation of a fifth daily departure on the Sunderland service in December 2012. On an estimated annualised basis, revenue was up by over 22% whilst operating costs were reduced by 18%, resulting in the dramatic improvement in the bottom line.

PERIOD TO:	31/12/2012	31/12/2011
	£000	£000
Turnover	27,071	16,656
Operating Costs:	27,346	25,096
Operating Profit:	(275)	(8,440)
Operating Margin:	-1.0%	-50.7%
Turnover per Employee	£237,465	£137,653
Rolling stock lease	7,209	6,995

PASSENGER OPERATOR ARTICLES

In the following pages, statistics for train operating companies (TOCs) are drawn from data published by the Office of Rail Regulation and Department for Transport (DfT).

Punctuality figures are the Public Performance Measure annual average - for long distance operators, the percentage of trains arriving within ten minutes of planned arrival time at final destination; and for London & South East operators and regional, Scotland and Wales operators, the percentage arriving within 5min of planned arrival time.

The subsidy figures include franchise payments and revenue support: negative values mean the DfT was receiving payments. Network grant figures are DfT estimates based on each TOC's share of track access charges. The grant is paid directly to Network Rail but is acknowledged by the DfT as an indirect subsidy to TOCs, reducing the track access charges they pay.

IM POSSIBLE

Difficult brief?

Why not let us take a closer look.

It's the way we like it.

- Engineering Consultancy
- Project Management
- Vehicle Systems Expertise
- Rolling Stock Enhancement
- PRM-TSI Specialists
- Fleet and Maintenance Strategy
- Documentation and Data
- Asset Value Maximisation
- Franchising Support
- Approvals and Certification

ESG
Designed to deliver

www.esg-rail.com   01332 483800   sales@esg-rail.com

PASSENGER TRAIN OPERATORS

- **HULL TRAINS**
- **FIRST GREAT WESTERN**
- **FIRST TRANSPENNINE EXPRESS**
- **SCOTRAIL** (franchise handover April 2015)

IN ASSOCIATION WITH ESG Designed to deliver

FIRSTGROUP

FirstGroup's rail operations carried more than 330m passengers in the year to 31 March 2014, an increase of 70m since 2006-07 when the group began operating the same franchise mix.

FirstGroup operates three UK rail franchises - First Great Western, First TransPennine Express, and (until March 2015) ScotRail – plus an open access passenger rail service, First Hull Trains. The group also operates London Tramlink on behalf of Transport for London, and the Heathrow Connect service jointly with Heathrow Express. The Thameslink & Great Northern (First Capital Connect) franchise ended in September 2014 and was merged into the new Thameslink, Southern and Great Northern franchise operated by Govia. First's other major operations are in UK Bus and North America. In October 2014 Transport Scotland announced the award of the next ScotRail franchise to Abellio, with the transfer from FirstGroup on 1 April 2015. The Caledonian Sleeper service will transfer to Serco on the same date.

Revenue in FirstGroup's UK Rail division was £2,870.1m in 2013/14 (2012/13: £2,795.1m) and operating profit was £55.2m (2012/13: £19.3m). The group says that in part this reflects First Great Western moving from a loss-making position to more normal terms under the direct award agreed in October 2013, and the successful delivery of a number of fleet and infrastructure projects in conjunction with industry partners. Like-for-like passenger revenue increased by 5.9%, reflecting strong volume growth across all First's train operating companies.

The group has proposed and delivered over £650m capital investment into its franchises since 2006. Since FirstGroup began rail operations, it has introduced a total of 740 additional vehicles in its various franchises, which has also led to the creation of new depot facilities and jobs.

UK Rail Managing Director is Vernon Barker, appointed in September 2011.

First Great Western

DIRECT AWARD TO 2019 EXPECTED

The Greater Western franchise, branded as First Great Western (FGW), began operation on 1 April 2006, combining the previous Great Western inter-city, London and Thames Valley, and West Country regional franchises. Services run from London Paddington across the South and West of England and South Wales.

In 2011 a contractual three-year franchise extension was not taken up by FirstGroup, and the Department for Transport (DfT) planned a longer term franchise to help deliver route electrification, Crossrail and introduction of Intercity Express Programme trains. After the DfT paused its franchising programme in October 2012, a 28-week extension for FGW was been followed by a 23-month direct award agreement from 14 October 2013. The DfT indicated in October 2014 that it intended to negotiate a further direct award until March 2019, with an extension of up to a year at DfT's discretion.

FGW has developed initiatives to improve performance and customer service since the start of the franchise, as well as delivering additional capacity, with plans for a significant number of additional and improved trains formulated with the DfT.

In March 2014 an increase in Standard class capacity on High Speed Trains was announced, through converting some First class carriages. The programme will create almost 3,000 more Standard seats a day, with nearly 16% more Standard accommodation on morning peak high-speed services into London. In addition work will be undertaken to refresh First class accommodation, including newly-designed leather reclining seats. 4,500 more peak-time seats were previously provided by FGW in summer 2012, by rebuilding disused buffet cars.

KEY STATISTICS
FIRST GREAT WESTERN

	2012-13	2013-14
Punctuality	89.1%	87.9%
Passenger journeys (millions)	97.3	99.7
Passenger km (millions)	5,867.8	5,785.0
Timetabled train km (millions)	42.8	43.0
Route km operated	1,997.2	1,997.2
Number of stations operated	209	206
Number of employees	5,156	5.353
Subsidy per passenger km (pence)	-2.9	-1.3
Network grant / pass km (p)	5.7	5.3

Free wi-fi is available on Night Riviera sleeper trains as well as FGW's Class 180 fleet, with completion on the HST fleet due in early 2015.

FGW is expanding the number of Pullman restaurant services, and changing its Travelling Chef offer. It is

First Great Western's No 158951 at Bristol Temple Meads. **TONY MILES**

PASSENGER TRAIN OPERATORS

SENIOR PERSONNEL
FIRST GREAT WESTERN

MANAGING DIRECTOR Mark Hopwood (in photo)
ENGINEERING DIRECTOR Andrew Mellors
OPERATIONS DIRECTOR Ben Rule
PROJECTS AND PLANNING DIRECTOR Mike Hogg
BID DIRECTOR Matthew Golton
DIRECTOR OF COMMUNICATIONS Sue Evans
FINANCE DIRECTOR Ben Caswell
HEAD OF SALES & MARKETING Diane Burke
HEAD OF HR Sharon Johnston
HEAD OF SAFETY Paul Williams

also considering re-introduction of a retail trolley in Standard, and an at-seat service at weekends in First class. The South Wales Pullman was reintroduced in September 2014 along with an additional Devon and Cornwall service.

A £146.6m package of rail improvements for Cornwall will see a major upgrade to the Night Riviera London-Penzance sleeper trains, improved signalling on the main line, and enhancements to the traincare centre in Penzance. In 2014 FGW and the Cornwall and Isles of Scilly Local Enterprise Partnership secured two additional carriages for the sleeper.

The December 2014 timetable provides an earlier morning direct train from London to Plymouth and Cornwall, arriving at many destinations 40min earlier.

The government has also announced investment from its Local Growth Fund (LGF), which will, among many projects, see £16m of work at Chippenham station.

Half-hourly cross Bristol rail services will be introduced with the MetroWest programme, which has received £3.2 million from the LGF, and a provisional further £8.5 million. This will mean reopening the Portishead and Henbury lines and will see the West of England Local Enterprise Partnership investing an additional £23.2m in the scheme.

FGW has seven train maintenance and servicing depots; Old Oak Common, London; Laira, Plymouth; St Philips Marsh, Bristol; Long Rock, Penzance; Landore, Swansea; Exeter; and Reading. A new depot at Reading, to replace the existing facility as a result of the infrastructure remodelling, opened in 2013.

The FGW diesel multiple-unit fleet consists has these 2-car units: Class 143 (8 units), Class 150/1 (15), Class 150/2 (19), Class 158 (2), Class 165/1 (20); and 3-car units: Class 150/0 (2), Class 158 (13), Class 165/1 (16), Class 166 (21); plus 14 Class-153 single-car units. There are five Class 180 trains (25 vehicles).

The HST fleet has 119 Class 43 power cars and 447 Mk3 coaches (12 of the power cars and 42 Mk3 vehicles are owned by FirstGroup).

There are 18 Mk3 Sleeper vehicles and four Class 57/6 locomotives mainly used on sleeper trains.

First TransPennine Express

DIRECT AWARD TO FEBRUARY 2016 PLANNED

Half way through 2013/14, First TransPennine Express (FTPE) celebrated carrying its 200 millionth passenger since the start of the franchise on 1 February 2004.

FTPE is a joint operation by First Group (55% share) and Keolis. French Railways (SNCF) is a major shareholder in Keolis, which operates trains, buses and metros across Europe and in other countries. Initially the franchise was awarded for eight years with an optional five-year extension: in August 2011 the Department for Transport (DfT) announced an extension, to April 2015 at the latest. Following the franchising review, in March 2013 the DfT scheduled a new direct award, running to February 2016. This would see the next TPE and Northern Rail franchises starting at the same time, allowing the DfT the flexibility to remap the franchises if it opts to do so.

Shortlisted bidders for the new franchise are: First Trans Pennine Express Ltd; Keolis Go-Ahead Ltd; and Stagecoach Trans Pennine Express Trains Ltd.

SENIOR PERSONNEL
FIRST TRANSPENNINE EXPRESS

MANAGING DIRECTOR Nick Donovan (in photo)
COMMERCIAL DIRECTOR Darren Higgins
ENGINEERING DIRECTOR Paul Staples
PROGRAMME DIRECTOR Chris Nutton
OPERATIONS DIRECTOR Paul Watson
FINANCE DIRECTOR Liz Collins
HUMAN RESOURCES DIRECTOR Sue Whaley
CUSTOMER SERVICE DIRECTOR Kathryn O'Brien

FTPE runs inter-city train services linking Liverpool and Manchester with Leeds, York and the Northeast, with Sheffield and Doncaster, and the Lake District. In 2006/07 it took over the Manchester Airport-Blackpool North and Manchester-Glasgow/Edinburgh routes.

The new £60m fleet of ten 4-car Desiro electric multiple-units, which

New Class 350/4 No 350404 runs between Manchester Oxford Rd and Manchester Piccadilly on 4 August 2014, working the 07.10 Glasgow Central to Manchester Airport. **TONY MILES**

were fully deployed by May 2014, is providing 90,000 extra seats a week and a 25% increase in luggage space across the FTPE fleet.

The new EMUs have taken over the majority of Manchester Airport-Glasgow/Edinburgh services and have released Class 185 DMUs to provide additional capacity on other routes, and work a new service between between Liverpool, Manchester, Leeds and Newcastle from May 2014 giving significant journey time reductions.

The Scottish service became hourly, through the daytime, with 15 services a day each way, a 36% increase in frequency and an extra 18,000 seats a week between Manchester and Scotland.

Since the franchise began, passenger journeys have increased from 13.5m to almost 26m in 2013/14, a 0.6% year-on-year increase. This has resulted in an underlying income growth significantly ahead of the industry average.

FTPE has been particularly successful in developing advance purchase ticket sales with a 100% increase in sales between 2009/10 and 2012/13. Advance purchase sales made up 11.5% of revenue in 2009/10 and 17.6% in 2012/13. In 2013/14 FTPE had the second highest seat occupancy of any UK operator and has, to date, reduced taxpayer subsidy as a proportion of farebox revenue by 80% during the life of the franchise.

When FTPE took over Anglo-Scottish services annual passenger journeys were just over 0.5m, but this total has risen to almost 1.4million. Much of this growth has been achieved through significant improvements to the timetable, faster journey times and more attractive departure times better suited to meet the needs of the leisure and business markets.

The weekend Manchester-Scotland timetable in particular has seen major improvements. From May 2014 the number of Sunday services increased to ten each way, with a number of trains strengthened to handle weekend demand. Initiatives such as strengthening of Glasgow services during the 2014 Commonwealth Games and Edinburgh services in summer including for the Edinburgh Festival were popular.

KEY STATISTICS
FIRST TRANSPENNINE EXPRESS

	2012-13	2013-14
Punctuality (0-10min)	91.7%	90.4%
Passenger journeys (millions)	24.9	26.1
Passenger km (millions)	1,603.9	1,663.3
Timetabled train km (millions)	17.4	17.4
Route km operated	1,250.5	1,250.5
Number of stations operated	30	30
Number of employees	1,126	1,175
Subsidy per passenger km (pence)	2.6	3.7
Network grant / pass km (p)	7.6	6.8

The ten 110mph Siemens Class 350/4 four-car Desiro EMUs and 51 three-car 100mph Siemens Desiro DMUs are supplemented by nine 2-car Class 170 Turbostar DMUs which are to transfer to Chiltern Railways from May 2015. While this may be deferred for a short time, FTPE is working to secure alternative rolling stock to maintain capacity. ■

First Hull Trains
NON-FRANCHISED INTERCITY TRAIN COMPANY

First Hull Trains is a non-franchised ('open access') intercity train company operating between Hull and London King's Cross, calling at Brough, Howden, Selby, Doncaster, Retford and Grantham.

Now approaching its 15th anniversary (on 25 September 2015), in its first year the company carried just 80,000 passengers between Hull and London on its three daily services. Now it runs 90 trains to London per week, with over 860,000 passenger journeys a year as at late 2014.

The company is 80% owned by FirstGroup, following the buyout of its previous parent company, GB Railways. The original promoter of Hull Trains, Renaissance Trains, set up by two former British Rail managers, John Nelson and Michael Jones, own the remaining 20%.

In 2002 the Rail Regulator awarded the company 10-year rights, providing security of access at least until May 2010. A £36m investment in a new fleet of 4-car Class 222 'Pioneer' trains in 2005 was followed by a new leasing deal with Angel Trains for four 5-Car Class 180s in their place; delivering an extra 500,000 seats a year.

Following regulatory decisions on East Coast main line capacity, First

KEY STATISTICS
FIRST HULL TRAINS

	2012-13	2013-14
Punctuality (0-10min)	81.8%	82.0%
Passenger journeys	735,358	774,159
Timetabled train km (millions)	1.48	1.48
Route km operated	329.0	329.0
Staff employed	106	106

A First Hull Trains Class 180 train on the East Coast main line. **FIRST HULL TRAINS**

PASSENGER TRAIN OPERATORS

SENIOR PERSONNEL
FIRST HULL TRAINS

MANAGING DIRECTOR Will Dunnett (in photo)
SERVICE DELIVERY DIRECTOR Keith Doughty
FINANCE MANAGER Glenn McLeish-Longthorn
HEAD OF ENGINEERING Jonathan Plowright
PERFORMANCE MANAGER Louise Mendham
ON BOARD STANDARDS MANAGER John Dooley
HEAD OF HR Victoria Evans

Hull Trains was granted firm rights for seven weekday and five weekend return services until December 2014. Further negotiations with the Office of Rail Regulation (ORR) brought an extension, alongside firm rights for all trains to operate during the week and weekdays until the end of 2016, in exchange for a commitment to undertake a train refurbishment programme and other improvements.

The business is pursuing plans to electrify the Hull-Selby line, to create electrified routes from Hull to London, and to Leeds and Manchester, potentially linking Hull to High Speed 2. A £7.5 million grant was allocated in the 2014 Growth Deal funding by the Department for Transport, following nine months of intensive negotiations with the Local Enterprise Partnership, Hull City Council and the DfT. This followed a £2.5m DfT grant to fund a feasibility study into the project.

In late 2014, First Hull Trains was in discussions with the ORR to agree a long-term track access arrangement, as well as negotiations with manufacturers of electric trains.

2012 and 2013 saw significant investment in engineering overhauls on the Class 180 diesel train fleet, with modifications to design implemented in conjunction with Angel Trains.

Strong growth in online sales has been achieved, with more passengers buying print at home and mobile phone tickets. On board, travelling cleaners have been introduced, and all toilet facilities upgraded.

In 2014, First Hull Trains became the first rail operator to trial the use of 4G-enabled, single-sign-up free wi-fi on all its trains. ■

ScotRail
FRANCHISE HANDOVER IN APRIL 2015

The Scottish Government announced In October 2015 that Abellio had been awarded the new ScotRail franchise, transferring from First Group on 1 April 2015.

A new, separate Caledonian Sleeper franchise was awarded to Serco in May 2014 and will also begin on 1 April 2015.

ScotRail includes 95% of passenger services in Scotland, and until March 2015 the cross-border Caledonian Sleeper services to London. In 2004, the Scottish Government took on full funding responsibility and FirstGroup's present franchise began. In 2006 Transport Scotland assumed responsibility for most rail powers in Scotland and also for infrastructure projects, working in conjunction with regional transport partnerships. In 2008 the franchise was extended by three years to November 2014, and in December 2012 by an additional 28 weeks, to allow time to assess Westminster's franchising review.

The ScotRail livery and colour scheme which incorporates Scotland's national flag, the Saltire, will not change as the franchise transfers to new operators.

In 2013 Scotland's Transport Minister, Keith Brown, announced that peak fares would be capped in January 2014 and 2015 to RPI. In 2014 he said regulated ScotRail fare increases can be no higher than RPI and off-peak regulated fare increases will be capped at 1% below RPI.

Completion of the £80m programme to electrify the Cumbernauld line enabled electric services to be introduced on the route in May 2014, with many trains

KEY STATISTICS
SCOTRAIL

	2012-13	2013-14
Punctuality (0-5min)	93.0%	91.4%
Passenger journeys (millions)	83.3	86.3
Passenger km (millions)	2,712.8	2,827.5
Timetabled train km (millions)	44.4	45.3
Route km operated	3,065.8	3,065.8
Number of stations operated	347	347
Number of employees	4,741	4,845
Subsidy per passenger km (pence)	10.7	17.5

operating via Glasgow Queen Street low level as an extension of existing Springburn-Dalmuir services.

In 2014 ScotRail introduced more frequent services between Glasgow and Ayr, improved services to Oban, additional Sunday services between Aberdeen and the central belt, as well as improved commuter services serving Aberdeen.

ScotRail drew praise for its work during the 2014 Commonwealth Games: trains carried more than 1.1m people to 13 venues in Scotland's biggest-ever public transport operation. Over 150,000 journeys were made through Glasgow event stations each day: Exhibition Centre station, gateway to a number of venues, saw a total of over 350,000 passengers.

The Ryder Cup at Gleneagles in September 2014 saw ScotRail carry 7,500 people each way daily. Preparation included major investment to improve access and the appearance of the station buildings and platforms.

Whilst First ScotRail's franchise commitment included £40m worth of investment, it has delivered £56million of investment in station improvements and also £26million of improvements to rolling stock. The 2,300 daily services represent an increase of 300 from the start of the franchise in 2004. First ScotRail worked closely with Transport Scotland to deliver a 38-strong new fleet of Class 380 electric trains with 130 carriages. More than 130 trains have been fitted with mobile Wi-Fi, which collates the best available signal from all mobile providers. Since 2004 ScotRail has delivered punctuality to an all time high, up from 84% to 95.3%, while customer satisfaction at 90% in 2014 was eight percentage points higher than UK average and six points higher than at the franchise start.

The company has introduced new channels to communicate with customers using Facebook, Twitter, YouTube and a smartphone app. Smartcard technology is being rolled out on key commuter routes.

Caledonian Sleeper services are hauled by locomotives hired from DBS (Class 90 electrics between London and Glasgow/Edinburgh, and Class 67 on to Aberdeen, Fort William and Inverness).

The ScotRail fleet has 2-car diesel multiple-units of Class 156 (48 trains) and Class 158 (48 trains). 3-car DMUs are of Class 170/3 (4 trains), and Class 170/4 (55). 3-car electric multiple-units are of Class 314 (16 trains), Class 318 (21), Class 320 (22), Class 334 (40). There are 22 three-car and 16 four-car Class 380 EMUs, delivered by Siemens from 2010. A Class 67-hauled train from DBS is hired for peak runs on the Fife Circle.

NEW FRANCHISES

The new ScotRail franchise from April 2015, which will be worth up to £6billion, will run for a minimum of seven years, with an option to extend to 10 years by mutual consent after five years.

Abellio has committed to introduce 70 new Hitachi electric multiple-units, rising to 80 if the franchise runs for its full term, with 24 four-car trains for Edinburgh-Glasgow and 46 three-car for other routes being electrified. Seven 4-car Class 321 EMUs will transfer for duties in the Glasgow area, and by December 2018, 27 HSTs from First Great Western will take over services between Scotland's major cities. These will be formed into 2+4 or 2+5 sets with vehicles fully refurbished to meet accessibility regulations, with power doors, a new interior layout, buffet and at-seat catering. A new Great Scenic Railway scheme for the north, southwest and Borders will use trains refurbished to align seats with windows, with some carrying a 'tourist ambassador' and offering catering showcasing local produce.

Station improvements include and Aberdeen concourse and retail development with improved links to Union Street, and also schemes at Inverness, Perth and Stirling. 'Stations2Stations' business centres will be developed.

Abellio will offer more bus, sea and air through ticketing, reduced fares for jobseekers, and advance fares between cities starting at £5. More luggage, cycle and ski storage will be provided on trains, an additional train will run to Oban in peak season, and special events in low season will be staged to attract customers. Abellio will also put in place a 'deep alliance' with Network Rail aiming to drive improved performance. It promises no compulsory redundancies for the life of the contract, an employee gain share scheme, and at least 100 apprenticeships.

The 15-year Caledonian Sleeper franchise is to bring a new fleet of vehicles, built by CAF, by the summer of 2018 - a £100m contract part-funded by a £60m capital grant from the Scottish Government. Significant improvements include en-suite berths, Pod Flatbeds for the first time on a train, and a brasserie-style Club Car.

Serco promises a hospitality service 'emblematic of the best of Scotland' among changes aimed at increasing passenger numbers in business, leisure and tourist sectors. Traction is to be provided by GBRf, using Class 92 electric locomotives between London and Glasgow/Edinburgh and newly rebuilt Class 73s onwards to Aberdeen, Inverness and Fort William. ■

A ScotRail Class 156 train at Morar on the West Highland line. **SCOTRAIL**

SENIOR PERSONNEL
FIRST SCOTRAIL

MANAGING DIRECTOR Steve Montgomery (in photo)
COMMERCIAL DIRECTOR Sean Duffy
OPERATIONS DIRECTOR Jacqueline Dey
ENGINEERING DIRECTOR Ken Docherty
CUSTOMER SERVICES DIRECTOR Jacqueline Taggart.
DIRECTOR OF BUSINESS PLANNING Jerry Farquharson
DIRECTOR OF FACILITIES & BUSINESS Services Pat Callaghan
ACTING FINANCE DIRECTOR Billy Connelly
HUMAN RESOURCES DIRECTOR Julie McComasky

PASSENGER TRAIN OPERATORS

SERCO AND ABELLIO

A 50-50 partnership of Serco and Abellio (formerly NedRailways) holds the Northern Rail and Merseyrail franchises. Abellio alone has the Greater Anglia franchise. The companies decided to 'pursue separate paths' in respect of the new Northern franchise, for which Abellio was shortlisted in August 2014. Serco was selected by Transport Scotland in May 2014 to manage the new 15-year franchise for the Caledonian Sleeper service, and in October 2014 Abellio was awarded the new ScotRail franchise (see preceding pages).

Serco, an international service company, operated, maintained and supported the Docklands Light Railway in London from 2006, securing an 18-month extension, valued at about £100m, until September 2014. After a further short extension a new franchise, won by Keolis Amey Docklands, began in December 2014. Serco began operating and maintaining the new Dubai Metro in 2009, and in 2013 won a contract to operate the Dubai Tram for five years. Serco Rail Technical Services offers services including vehicle testing and condition monitoring. Operations in transport and local authority direct services account for about 40% of UK and Europe revenues. The Northern franchise represented about 6% of group revenue and 13% of the UK & Europe division in 2013.

Abellio is the international passenger transport subsidiary of the Dutch national railway company, Nederlandse Spoorwegen. Its 13,000 employees provides rail, bus and tram services to over one million customers across the UK, Germany and in the Netherlands each day.

Combined with an ambition to grow a sustainable portfolio of public transport businesses in Europe by further expanding within existing markets and exploring new markets, Abellio says it promotes a broader vision to deliver public transport services that serve its clients and improve the quality of life in the communities it serves.

northern

DIRECT AWARD AGREEMENT TO FEBRUARY 2016

The Department for Transport (DfT) in 2012 granted a continuation of Serco and Abellio's Northern Rail's franchise (originally awarded in December 2004) from 15 September 2013 until 1 April 2014. Then in March 2014 the DfT announced a further Direct Award agreement with Serco and Abellio, until a planned new franchise begins in February 2016.

Off-peak tickets were no longer valid in the evening peak on many services, from September 2014, intended to help reduce subsidy as part of the new agreement.

Northern runs inter-urban, commuter and local train services for northwest and northeast England, Yorkshire, and Humberside, and Serco and Abellio previously secured a two-year extension in 2010, triggered by improved punctuality and reliability.

In August 2014, the DfT shortlisted three companies for the new franchise: Abellio Northern Ltd, Arriva Rail North Limited, and Govia Northern Ltd.

The DfT has been working together with Rail North, a consortium of 30 local transport authorities covering the north

A Northern Class-158 train at Brough. **NORTHERN**

KEY STATISTICS
NORTHERN

	2012-13	2013-14
Punctuality (0-5min)	90.7%	91.0%
Passenger journeys (millions)	89.8	94.0
Passenger km (millions)	2,122.1	2,210.5
Timetabled train km (millions)	44.6	44.8
Route km operated	2,716.6	2,734.3
Number of stations operated	463	463
Number of employees	4,900	4,980
Subsidy per passenger km (p)*	7.1	7.8
Network grant / pass km (p)	18.0	15.9

*- not including PTE grants

of England. In January 2014 the Secretary of State announced an intention to work in partnership on collaborative development of the Northern and TransPennine Express franchises, with the DfT in the lead. The Secretary of State retained ultimate responsibility for all design and procurement decisions – and also on development of an integrated partnership structure with a more formally constituted Rail North, which would be capable of managing the franchises after they had been let.

The DfT was considering transfer of some services from TPE to Northern: Manchester Airport-Blackpool North, Oxenholme-Windermere, Lancaster to Barrow-in-Furness, York-Scarborough, and Doncaster-Cleethorpes. A potential transfer from Northern to East Midlands Trains was Cleethorpes to Barton-on-Humber. Bidders were asked to draw up plans for withdrawal of all Pacer trains, for the DfT to consider.

Since its franchise began in 2004, Northern has provided a more punctual and reliable railway, increasing the number of trains arriving on time from 83.7%, to over 90%; and it has attracted over 47% growth in passenger numbers. Around 75% of the fleet has been refurbished, with reliability improved by 60%.

Against a 'no growth, no investment' franchise specification, it attracted over £100m of external investment. Serco and Abellio invested £30m.

Northern secured 60 additional carriages up to 2011, as part of an agreement to meet the government's High Level Output Specification, adding 2.2m additional peak seats per year.

Northern Rail and Network Rail signed a framework agreement for an alliance in 2012, seeking ways to improve industry efficiency and reduce costs to deliver improved facilities and services.

Franchise bidders were made aware of the possibility of transferring Station Facility Owner responsibility for a small number of stations to a third party, either Network Rail (as a managed station) or to a Passenger Transport Executive (PTE) or successor body. Northern includes 14 of the 36 designated Community Rail routes, and members of the Association of Community Rail Partnerships are also active on five other routes, with most stations adopted by volunteers and community groups. A Community Ambassadors Scheme has been created to promote the use of local rail services with Black and Minority Ethnic (BME) and socially excluded groups.

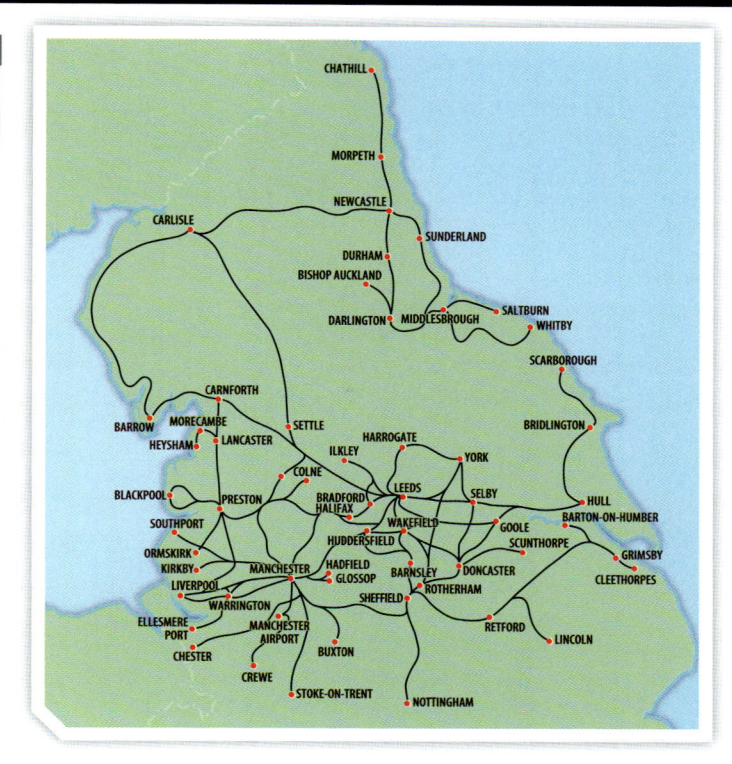

Northern operates a diverse fleet of diesel multiple-units: 79 Class-142, and 13 two-car and 10 three-car Class 144 'Pacers'; 58 Class-150s; 7 Class-155s; 42 Class-156s; 37 two-car and 8 three-car Class-158s; and 18 single car Class-153s. There are eight Class-321/322 electric multiple-units and 16 Class-333s operated in West Yorkshire, with 17 Class-323s used mainly in Greater Manchester.

In April 2014 Northern Rail reached agreement with the DfT on trains for newly electrified routes. With electrification from Manchester to Liverpool via Newton-le-Willows due for 2015, three Class 319 EMUs, transferred from Thameslink, are to be available - due to rise to 14 by the time the new franchise starts, with services progressively converted to electric operation.

Driver-only operated on Thameslink, the '319s' will be modified for driver and conductor operation. Diesel trains released by them will provide extra capacity, including to Bolton and via the new Todmorden curve to Burnley.

The main maintenance depots are at Newcastle (Heaton), Manchester (Newton Heath), Leeds (Neville Hill) and a new depot opened in 2011 at Liverpool (Allerton). Concentrating maintenance of each type of train at particular depots has helped to improve reliability. Alstom's West Coast Traincare maintains the Class 323s at Manchester.

Northern operates 2,550 services each weekday, more than any other franchise operator, and covers around 20% of the national network.

SENIOR PERSONNEL
NORTHERN

MANAGING DIRECTOR Alex Hynes (in photo)
SERVICE DELIVERY DIRECTOR Alan Chaplin
CUSTOMER SERVICE DIRECTOR Natalie Loughborough
DIRECTOR OF OPERATIONS Paul Barnfield
ENGINEERING DIRECTOR Stuart Draper
PLANNING AND PROGRAMMES DIRECTOR Rob Warnes
SAFETY AND ASSURANCE DIRECTOR Gary Stewart
COMMERCIAL DIRECTOR Richard Allan
TRANSITION DIRECTOR Lee Wasnidge

PASSENGER TRAIN OPERATORS

Merseyrail
25-YEAR CONCESSION FROM JULY 2003

The Merseyrail electric network is one of the most heavily used outside London, with almost 800 trains carrying 110,000 passengers per weekday, on 15min train frequencies, increasing to 5min on city centre sections. Nearly half of Merseyrail passengers are daily users.

Merseytravel, the Merseyside Public Transport Executive, manages the unique operating concession for this 75-mile, self-contained network of 750V DC, third-rail electrified railway, for the Liverpool City Region Combined Authority.

The 25-year contract, with a total value of £3.6bn, was awarded in 2003 to the Serco and Abellio joint venture 'Merseyrail Electrics 2002', subject to five-yearly reviews. Merseytravel livery is carried on trains and stations. Average fares are among the cheapest in the country, with rises capped at the Retail Price Index level.

The Northern Line links Southport, Ormskirk and Kirkby to Hunts Cross, and the Wirral Line serves West Kirby, New Brighton, Chester, Ellesmere Port and a central Liverpool loop line - 6.5 miles in tunnel with four underground stations in Liverpool and one in Birkenhead.

A £40m-plus overhaul for all five underground stations began with £20m of improvements completed in 2012 at Liverpool Central, the network's busiest station, and the underground station with the highest footfall outside London.

The funding package was shared between Network Rail, Merseytravel and the European Rail Development Fund. Work was completed in 2013 at James Street and Lime Street, and began at Hamilton Square station in Birkenhead in September 2014.

KEY STATISTICS
MERSEYRAIL

	2012-13	2013-14
Punctuality (0-5min)	95.4%	95.8%
Passenger journeys (millions)	41.7	42.7
Passenger km (millions)	611.7	661.2
Timetabled train km (millions)	6.4	6.4
Route km operated	120.7	120.7
Number of stations operated	66	66
Number of employees	1,267	1,242
Subsidy per passenger km (p)	12.3	12.7

At Central, transformation of the concourse was carried out by Merseyrail and contractor Strategic Team Group, while Network Rail and contractor Morgan Sindall improved the platforms, escalators and passageways. The station has gained an additional lift, replacement escalators to the Northern Line; additional platform space; and improved toilets and waiting areas. A clear glazed roof and glass external walls allow natural lighting.

Merseytravel has been considering a major project to modernise or replace the train fleet by 2019, the end of the lease on the current fleet of 59 Class 507 and Class 508 trains (built in 1978-79). 50 are required in service each day. A further £8.5m refurbishment of the existing trains is due to be completed by mid 2015. Angel Trains is contributing £5.5m as part of its lease agreement and a further £3m is being provided by Merseyrail. Trains are maintained at Kirkdale and Birkenhead North depots.

A wide range of service improvement and expansion plans in the Liverpool City region have been put forward in a 30-year strategy, including improved links to cities and towns further afield for both Merseyrail and other rail routes in the region. Electrification of the Ormskirk-Preston, and Kirkby-Wigan lines, and a new rail service for Skelmersdale, are outlined, and the Wrexham-Bidston line could also be improved and incorporated into the Merseyrail Wirral line. Some options could require dual-voltage Merseyrail trains.

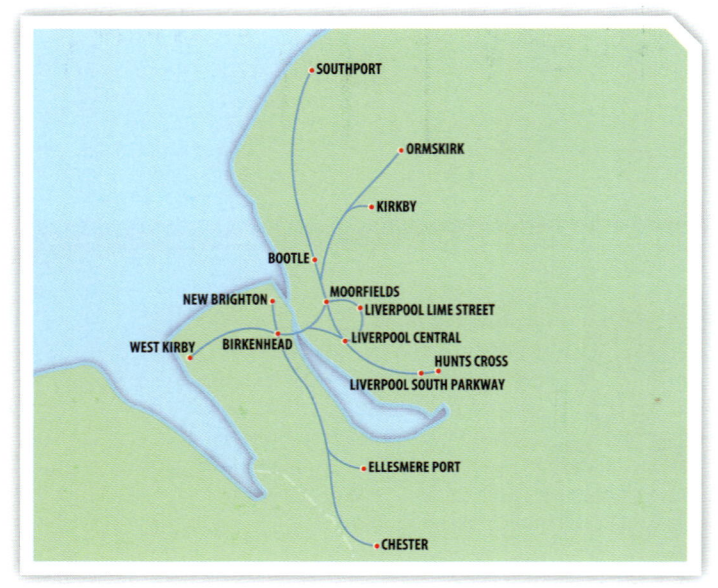

In previous years, Merseytravel has invested more than £100m in Merseyrail, refurbished eight stations and built six new ones, with £32m invested in refurbishing rolling stock. A further £3.7m programme of station improvements was confirmed in 2014, with work over three years funded by the National Stations Improvement Programme at seven stations.

Commissioning of the GSM-R leaky feeder radio system within Merseyrail's tunnels was completed in 2014, the final part of Network Rail's nationwide GSM-R train radio roll out.

In the Spring 2014 National Passenger Survey, Merseyrail secured the highest score among train operating companies for overall satisfaction. The operator has excellent results for public performance measure punctuality, typically averaging over 95% and in mid 2014 reaching the highest score in almost four years.

Merseyrail in 2010 became the first 'fully secure' rail network in the UK with all 66 stations and 36 car parks accredited under the Secure Station and Safer Parking schemes by the British Transport Police. Merseyrail staff, police and partners such as byelaw enforcement officers work together to create a consistent high visibility presence to counter anti-social behaviour and ticketless travel. A penalty fare scheme covers all stations.

Liverpool South Parkway, a £32m new station, was opened in 2006 at the intersection of the Merseyrail electric and Liverpool-Crewe routes. It has a bus shuttle to Liverpool John Lennon Airport, acts as a hub for local bus routes, and offers park-and-ride.

Merseyrail has nine 'Mtogo' stores, combined retail outlet and ticket offices tailored to suit both large and smaller stations. Mtogo is aimed at enhancing the customer experience and making passengers feel more secure.

Merseyrail celebrated the first anniversary of its Bike&Go scheme in Sepember 2014 by adding facilities at three more stations to the 11 already equipped with cycle hire. The scheme has 1,000 subscribers and 600 bicycles.

Merseyrail Class 507 No 507017 in new livery at Formby on 11 February 2014. Six different designs relate to the journey purposes of workers, students and leisure passengers. TONY MILES

SENIOR PERSONNEL
MERSEYRAIL

INTERIM MANAGING DIRECTOR Alan Chaplin (in photo)
DEPUTY MANAGING DIRECTOR Andy Heath
ENGINEERING DIRECTOR Mike Roe
FINANCE AND COMMERCIAL DIRECTOR Paul Bowen
SAFETY AND ASSURANCE DIRECTOR David Foster
CUSTOMER SERVICES DIRECTOR Kaj Mook

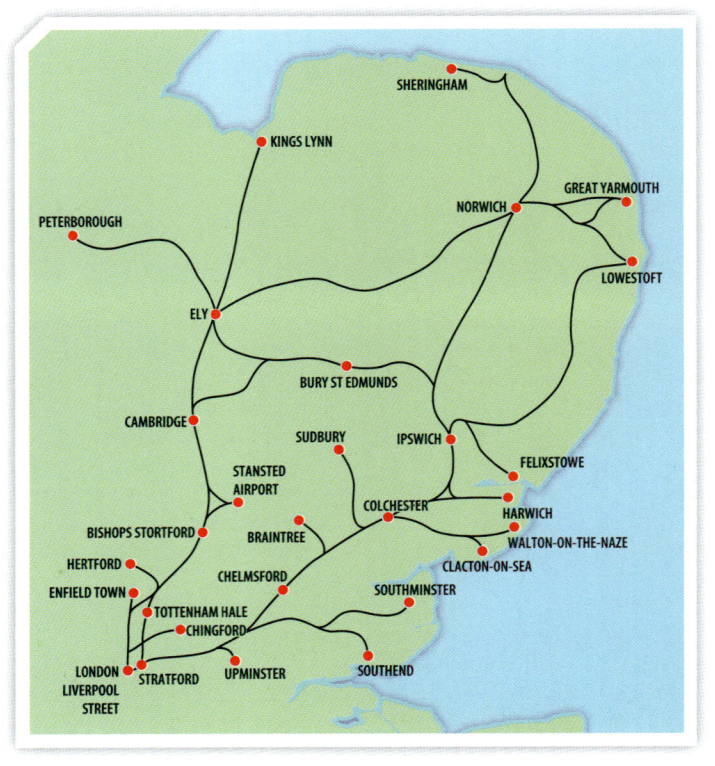

abellio greateranglia

NEW FRANCHISE UNTIL OCTOBER 2016

The Greater Anglia franchise was awarded to Abellio from 5 February 2012 for 29 months, a relatively short term, as the DfT prepared for revisions in franchising policy. In April 2014 a new short franchise was agreed, in place from July 2014 until 15 October 2016. The previous franchise, National Express East Anglia, ran from April 2004.

The agreement with the DfT includes a package of over £20m in service enhancements by Abellio Greater Anglia (AGA), including: additional train services between Cambridge and Stansted Airport; and between Norwich and Sheringham with a year-round hourly Sunday service introduced from 5 October 2014. On summer Sundays two additional services will run on the Norwich-London route and Norwich-Lowestoft will have an hourly service. Plans are being developed to introduce on-line 'delay repay' arrangements for season-ticket holders.

A major refresh will be undertaken on the Mk3 carriages on the Norwich-London intercity services, to include controlled emission toilet (CET) tanks. Seven catering vehicles will be converted to offer 44 Standard instead

KEY STATISTICS
ABELLIO GREATER ANGLIA

	2012-13	2013-14
Punctuality	90.9%	92.3%
Passenger journeys (millions)	126.4	135.2
Passenger km (millions)	4,146.9	4,350.3
Timetabled train km (millions)	34.0	33.8
Route km operated	1,611.0	1,611.0
Number of stations operated	167	167
Number of employees	2,973	3,008
Subsidy per passenger km (pence)	-3.4	-3.7
Network grant / pass km (p)	5.3	4.7

PASSENGER TRAIN OPERATORS

A Driving Van Trailer heads an Abellio Greater Anglia London-Norwich intercity train at Colchester. **NETWORK RAIL**

of 24 First Class seats, while continuing to offer the existing catering service.

A programme to also fit CET to Class 321 trains, with a £2m investment at train maintenance depots, will also be rolled out. Passenger accessibility improvements will be made to 12 of the Class 321 train fleet and AGA will evaluate options with its train leasing partner to begin a wider refurbishment on a small number of these trains before the end of the franchise term. More frequent heavy cleaning of trains is also to take place, with new systems introduced on trains to manage fuel and power consumption more efficiently.

Services between Liverpool Street and Enfield Town, Cheshunt (via Seven Sisters) and Chingford, as well as the Romford-Upminster line, are to transfer to the London Overground concession from 31 May 2015.

AGA has made consistent improvements in punctuality since taking the franchise over, working more closely with Network Rail through an alliance to deliver improved performance. A new agreement with Network Rail has ensured a revised approach to engineering work, significantly reducing disruption at weekends. In March 2014 a new joint investment of £1m was announced to raise performance standards. AGA continues to work with the DfT, Network Rail and other stakeholders as part of the Great Eastern rail campaign, to develop plans to improve journey times and service. Overall customer satisfaction in the spring 2014 NPS was 81%, up from 77% in spring 2013.

In December 2012, an hourly Ipswich-Lowestoft service was introduced, following installation of a new passing loop at Beccles. Work on a £1.8m refurbishment of Bishop's Stortford station has been completed and work is also underway on major enhancement schemes at Chelmsford and Cambridge. A new transport interchange has opened at Lowestoft, in partnership with Suffolk County Council. Car park and cycle facilities at a number of locations including Cambridge and Chelmsford are to be improved. 15 stations on the AGA network are now part of Bike & Go, the UK's first major station cycle hire programme.

A bus link at Saffron Walden was launched in September 2013 and an integrated bus link from Halesworth station to Southwold has also been implemented.

Another key element of the franchise is a renewed focus on marketing to encourage more passenger journeys, including an innovative partnership with Visit East Anglia. AGA is strengthening its commitment to the Community Rail Partnerships in the region by increasing their funding contribution by 20%.

In conjunction with Eversholt Rail, a fully refurbished high specification Class 321 demonstrator EMU has entered service, showcasing how these trains could be upgraded, to help shape plans for future enhancements. A similar initiative is underway with Angel Trains to operate a pilot Class 317 train on the West Anglia network.

AGA became the first operator in the country to fit a Driving Van Trailer with new equipment that helps to help tackle low adhesion in autumn by applying gel to tracks. Following positive results the programme is now being extended to some EMUs.

Greater Anglia's main train depots are at Ilford, Norwich and Clacton, with cleaning and stabling at other locations. The fleet of four-car electric multiple-units, based at Ilford, is made up of: 61 Class 315s, 51 Class 317s, 94 Class 321s, 21 Class 360s, and 30 Class 379s.

The diesel fleet is made up of five single-car Class 153s, nine Class 156s, four two-car Class 170s and eight three-car Class 170s. The locomotive-hauled fleet is comprised of 15 Class 90 locomotives and 15 Mk3 Driving Van Trailers along with 119 Mk3 coaches. Two Class 08 shunters are hired; and also Class 47 diesel locomotives for 'Thunderbird' rescue duties and to power the Norwich-Great Yarmouth legs of high season London-Great Yarmouth services, as well as additional trains for special events.

SENIOR PERSONNEL
ABELLIO GREATER ANGLIA

MANAGING DIRECTOR Jamie Burles (in photo)
OPERATIONS DIRECTOR Peter Lensik
CUSTOMER SERVICE DIRECTOR Andrew Goodrum
FINANCE DIRECTOR Adam Golton
ENGINEERING DIRECTOR Kate Marjoribanks
ASSET MANAGEMENT DIRECTOR Simone Bailey
HR AND SAFETY DIRECTOR Michelle Smart
COMMERCIAL DIRECTOR Andy Camp

GOVIA

Govia is a joint venture partnership between British company The Go-Ahead Group and Keolis. Go-Ahead, the 65% majority partner, employs 26,000 people in UK rail and bus. More than one billion passenger journeys were undertaken on Go-Ahead's bus and rail companies in 2013-14.

Keolis - in which French Railways (SNCF) is a major shareholder - operates trains, buses and metros across the world.

Rail has been a key element of Go-Ahead's transport strategy since privatisation. By autumn 2014 it was responsible for about 35% of national rail journeys.

Go-Ahead operated the Thames Trains franchise from 1996 to 2004 and Govia the Thameslink franchise from 1997 to 2006. Govia took over the South Central franchise in 2001, later rebranding it as Southern, and retained it from September 2009. In 2008, Gatwick Express became part of the franchise.

Govia was awarded the Integrated Kent franchise, operated as Southeastern, in 2006 and launched the UK's first domestic high speed service in 2009. In November 2007 it began operating the new West Midlands franchise, as London Midland.

Following the recent franchising review, a Southeastern direct award contract was agreed, running until 24 June 2018, and it was planned for Govia to continue operating London Midland until June 2017.

Govia began running the new Thameslink, Southern and Great Northern (TSGN) rail franchise on 14 September 2014.

Govia was shortlisted in 2014 to bid for the Northern franchise, and in another joint venture with Keolis (Keolis is the 65% majority shareholder) was shortlisted to bid for TransPennine Express franchise.

GTR

SEVEN YEAR MANAGEMENT CONTRACT

The Thameslink, Southern, Great Northern (TSGN) franchise, operated by Govia from 14 September 2014, replaced the previous Thameslink and Great Northern franchise held by First Capital Connect (FCC). TSGN will also include the present South Central franchise (Southern plus Gatwick Express, also operated by Govia) when it expires on 26 July 2015. A small number of services and stations were scheduled to transfer from the South Eastern franchise to TSGN by 21 December 2014.

Branded as Govia Thameslink Railway (GTR), the basis of the new TSGN franchise is a seven year management contract: this means that Govia passes ticket revenue directly to the government. This arrangement was chosen because of the extensive work being carried out on the Thameslink route through the centre of London, including resignalling of the central part of the route, and the extensive rebuilding of London Bridge station.

The Thameslink and Great Northern routes connect important regional centres north and south of London such as Peterborough, Cambridge, Bedford, Luton and Brighton. They provide rail links to Gatwick and Luton airports, and to Eurostar at St Pancras International. From 2018, Farringdon station will provide interchange between Thameslink and Crossrail, bringing connections to Heathrow, Canary Wharf and central London.

GTR is the largest rail franchise in the UK in terms of passenger numbers, trains, revenue and staff. It is forecast to carry 273m passenger journeys per year, employ around 6,500 people and generate annual passenger revenues of £1.3bn.

From the start of the franchise in September 2014 until June 2015, Govia's revenue from franchise payments is estimated to be about £350m. In the first full year to June 2016, which includes the Southern franchise from July 2015, Govia's revenue from franchise payments is estimated to be about £1.1bn. Target operating profit margins average about 3% over the life of the franchise.

There are performance regimes in place to incentivise or penalise Govia to meet a range of service quality targets (including for punctuality, customer experience at stations and on trains, and revenue protection). In addition to performance regimes, Govia can also achieve up to £25m for delivery of key performance milestones in the

KEY STATISTICS
THAMESLINK & GREAT NORTHERN (FIRST CAPITAL CONNECT)

	2012-13	2013-14
Punctuality (0-5min)	88.3%	86.1%
Passenger journeys (millions)	106.3	117.8
Passenger km (millions)	3,637.6	3,848.2
Timetabled train km (millions)	24.8	25.1
Route km operated	500.9	494.1
Number of stations operated	78	75
Number of employees	2,459	2,541
Subsidy per passenger km (pence)	-5.1	-5.3
Network grant / pass km (p)	3.3	2.9

Class 319 No 319009 in GTR Thameslink livery at Blackfriars on 15 September 2014. **TONY MILES**

PASSENGER TRAIN OPERATORS

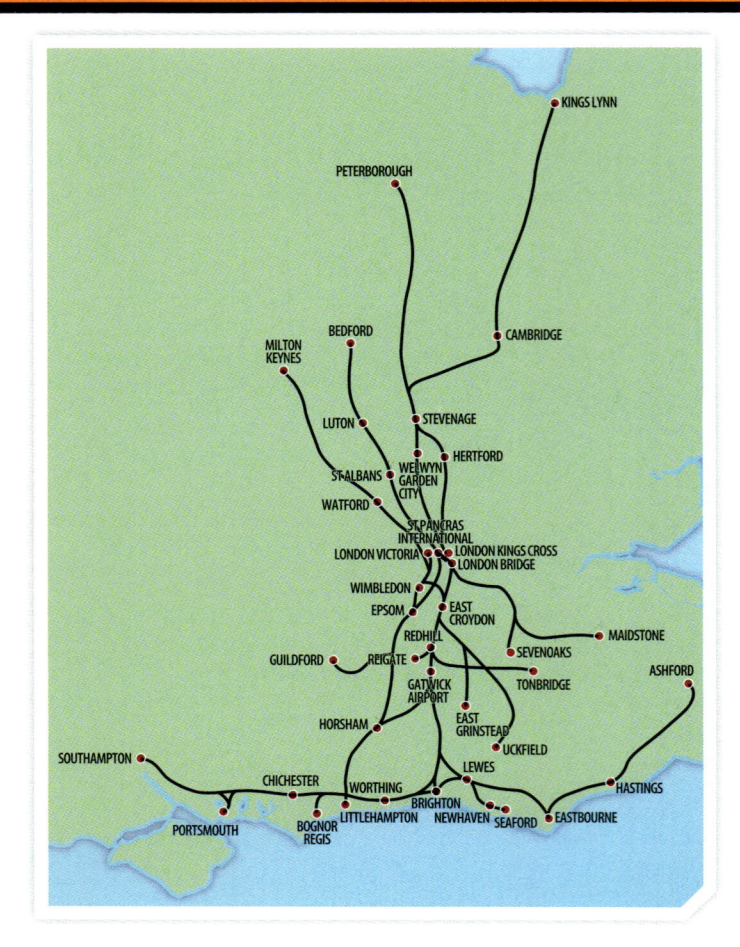

Thameslink Programme, which would largely be payable in the mid-term of the franchise.

Govia will work with the DfT to generate passenger revenue of an estimated £12.4bn over the life of the franchise. Franchise payments from the DfT to Govia will amount to an estimated £8.9bn, to reflect operating costs and a small margin allowance. Based on DfT methodology, the net present value (NPV) of the franchise payments is estimated to be around £6.8bn.

Govia has committed to the procurement of around £430m of investment over the life of the franchise, including significant investment in rolling stock and franchise improvements. Approximately £40m of capital expenditure will be made by Govia directly, with most of this investment in the first two years.

Major projects include the introduction of three new train fleets for Thameslink, Great Northern and Gatwick Express, providing 26% more carriages and 10,000 additional seats on trains to London in the morning peak, and additional services.

The franchise will play a crucial role in delivering the government's £6.5bn Thameslink programme - the major infrastructure project that will allow 24 trains per hour to travel in each direction from Blackfriars to St Pancras. New tunnels will link the Great Northern route to the existing Thameslink route, providing easy access across London via St Pancras.

The franchise will introduce 1,140 new Class 700 'Desiro City' carriages - being constructed by Siemens - on the Thameslink network.

The first of 29 four-car Class 387/1 EMUs for use on the Thameslink route were entering service in late 2014. Built by Bombardier with Porterbrook providing capital funding, these 110mph EMUs will allow the release of existing Thameslink rolling stock to newly electrified routes in other parts of the country. When Class 700 trains enter service, the Class 387s will also be redeployed elsewhere.

Govia was also planning to lease a new fleet of 27 four-car Class 387/2 EMUs for the Gatwick Express service, replacing the current Class 442 with a fleet better suited to the needs of airport passengers.

The Gatwick Express timetable will be changed to see a half-hourly through service between Brighton, Gatwick Airport and London Victoria (a key part of the business case for the new trains) alternating every 15min with services between Gatwick and Victoria only.

Govia is also working to acquire a fleet of 25 six-car EMUs to replace the 40-year-old Class 313s currently operating on the route between Moorgate, north London and Hertfordshire. With the introduction also of the Siemens Class 700s, the majority of the Class 365 fleet is planned to be withdrawn, and Great Northern services to Cambridge and King's Lynn will be handed over to Class 377 EMUs.

There is also a commitment to bring in longer trains on the non-electrified Uckfield branch, and additional diesel multiple-units to supplement the Class 171s currently working on this route and the Ashford-Hastings line are planned to be transferred from ScotRail.

From September 2014 the franchise introduced separate branding for Thameslink and Great Northern with each service group having its own

SOUTHERN

5 YEAR 10 MONTH FRANCHISE FROM SEPTEMBER 2009

The South Central franchise, operated by Govia as 'Southern', is due to become part of the new Thameslink, Southern and Great Northern franchise in 2015.

The current franchise runs from 20 September 2009 to 25 July 2015: Govia also held the previous franchise, from 2003. Southern provides train services in South London and connects central London to the South Coast, East and West Sussex, Surrey and parts of Kent and Hampshire.

The franchise met a commitment to deliver an additional 10% capacity by December 2013, including extending eight-car trains to ten cars on key inner-suburban 'Metro' routes. To meet this commitment Southern ordered 26 five-car Class 377/6 Electrostar EMUs, worth £200m, from Bombardier.

An option for eight 5-car dual-voltage trains was also exercised, and these Class 377/7s entered service in 2014, mainly on Croydon-Milton Keynes services, increasing capacity and enabling the release of six 4-car dual-voltage Class 377/2s to Thameslink.

As part of the Thameslink Programme, Southern transferred the last eight of its Class 319 trains to First Capital Connect in early 2009, and sub-leased 23 four-car dual-voltage Class-377/5 trains to Thameslink (First Capital Connect). This gave FCC sufficient rolling stock to deliver key stages of the programme. Southern sub-leased a further 3 Class-377/2s to FCC/Thameslink in December 2011 to enable it to run 12-car trains (six more '377/2s' transferred to Thameslink in 2014). Additional capacity at Southern was created through reinstatement of five stored Class 442 trains, and transfer of 19 Class-313 units released by London Overground. The '313s'

KEY STATISTICS
SOUTHERN

	2012-13	2013-14
Punctuality (0-5min)	88.0%	85.8%
Passenger journeys (millions)	171.4	181.8
Passenger km (millions)	4,386.0	4,548.5
Timetabled train km (millions)	37.8	37.8
Route km operated	666.3	666.3
Number of stations operated	156	156
Number of employees	3,979	4,045
Subsidy per passenger km (p)	-4.9	-3.6
Network grant / pass km (p)	4.5	4.0

were refreshed, gaining passenger information systems and CCTV, and operate on Coastway services out of Brighton. This enabled 3-car Class 377/3s to be transferred to strengthen services in London.

The flagship route of the franchise is the Brighton main line and Southern operates Gatwick Express services using five and ten-car Class 442 sets. Two services an hour are extended to Brighton in morning and evening peaks.

During 2014 Southern has been equipping its fleet with GSM-R cab radios and a new Driver Advisory System has been fitted to its Class 171 diesel fleet.

website. The Southern and Gatwick Express brands will be retained when the Southern franchise joins GTR in July 2015. The GTR name is not used on trains or stations.

The franchise will see several key timetable changes, beginning with the full incorporation of services currently operated jointly by FCC and Southeastern from December 2014, along with transfer of seven stations.

In December 2015 a recast of the Brighton main line timetable will set in place many service changes planned for the full 2018 Thameslink timetable. Thameslink services will all run via Elephant & Castle from January 2015 until 2018 as the London Bridge route will not be available during work to rebuild the station and the tracks serving it.

December 2015 will also see opening hours of the Moorgate branch extended on weekdays and trains will also serve it at weekends. The completion of track work north of Ely by May 2017 will enable off-peak King's Lynn–London King's Cross services to go half-hourly.

In 2018, with the ending of the London Bridge blockade, the high frequency service through the Thameslink core will be launched. Initially at 21 trains per hour, it is planned to grow to 24 by the end of the year.

New Thameslink services will include fast trains between Cambridge and Brighton, which will link Cambridge and Gatwick in about 1hr 40min and the full journey taking just 2hr. Other services include Cambridge-Tattenham Corner and Peterborough-Horsham via Gatwick Airport.

Service frequency for Hertford North and Welwyn Garden City will be increased with trains to Moorgate increasing from 12 to 14 an hour in the high peak.

The new franchise has committed to deliver smartcard ticketing across the franchise area, using the Key smartcard, and to extend Oyster pay-as-you-go to Epsom, Gatwick Airport, Luton Airport Parkway, Welwyn Garden City and Hertford North.

Evening restrictions on off-peak fares that FCC introduced will remain through the first part of the franchise. There is an obligation to retain some FCC fare discounts while the London Bridge rebuilding is going on, and there is a desire to harmonise fares and structures by 2018 which may see some restrictions disappear. Single-leg pricing is to be introduced, benefiting passengers making journeys that are 'peak' in one direction and 'off-peak' in the other, and 'super off-peak' fares are to become available during the week in the north part of franchise.

GTR will also deliver £50m of station improvements, with every station seeing a level of upgrade based on its assets. St Albans, Luton and possibly Stevenage will get high levels of refurbishment and an additional fund for improvements to small stations is pledged, with community involvement also encouraged. The DfT is requiring 'first to last train' staffing at the 101 busiest stations which have more than a one million passenger footfall per year at the start of the franchise. Free wi-fi will be rolled out at 104 stations. Gatelines will be installed at 21 stations.

GTR says its Passenger Service Directors (PSDs) are empowered to lead all aspects of service delivery within their directorates, responsible for drivers, conductors and station staff within their areas. The full team will be: (Great Northern) Keith Jipps, (Thameslink) Stuart Cheshire, (Southern Mainline) David Scorey, (Southern Metro) Alex Foulds.

In 2014 the Thameslink and Great Northern train fleet comprised: Class 313 (44 trains); 317/1 (12), 319/0 (13); 319/2 (7); 319/3 (26); 319/4 (40); Class 321 (13 trains); 365 (40); Class 377/5 (23); 377/2 (3). All are 4-car units apart from Class 313 (3-car). Class 319 trains began to be released in mid 2014 for newly electrified routes in the Northern franchise – a total of 14 transferred by 2016 was initially planned.

FirstGroup operated the First Capital Connect franchise from 1 April 2006 to 13 September 2014. Along with active involvement in the development of the Thameslink Programme and the delivery of additional capacity across its routes, highlights included the introduction of 144 new vehicles onto the Thameslink route which provided an extra 14,500 seats at the busiest times of the day, a 29% increase. FCC also doubled the number of cross-London rush hour trains from 7/8 per hour to 15 between St Pancras International and Blackfriars. 12,500 extra seats were introduced at the busiest times of the day on Great Northern services, to increase peak capacity by more than 22%.

FCC also improved the way it communicated with customers with the introduction of a 24/7 Twitter service, free SMS and email feed alerts and a new website with mobile capability and real time feeds. ■

SENIOR PERSONNEL
GOVIA THAMESLINK RAILWAY

CHIEF EXECUTIVE OFFICER Charles Horton (in photo)
CHIEF OPERATING OFFICER Dyan Crowther
CHIEF FINANCIAL OFFICER Wilma Allan
ENGINEERING DIRECTOR Gerry McFadden
PROGRAMME DIRECTOR Keith Wallace
COMMERCIAL DIRECTOR David Innis
HEAD OF SAFETY AND SUSTAINABILITY Colin Clifton
INTEGRATION DIRECTOR Jonathan Kennedy
HR DIRECTOR Andy Bindon

A new Class 377/6 train in a newly opened platform in the Southern part of London Bridge, early on 1 September 2014. **NETWORK RAIL**

PASSENGER TRAIN OPERATORS

Southern's entire fleet of Class 377 Electrostars now operate with third-rail regenerative braking. All of the '377s' are being refreshed inside and out, with work due to be completed in spring 2015. The company's Class 455 trains are also currently being refreshed while the Class 171 Turbostar diesels have all been refurbished. The company's driving simulators have been upgraded to enable energy efficient, eco-driving training.

Govia's Smartcard system, 'the Key', is in use at most Southern stations. Passengers can use the Key to buy a comprehensive suite of tickets, and trials of flexi-seasons and 'keyGo' (similar to pay-as-you-go) began in 2014. Southern's work with smartcards is laying the foundation for other train operators as part of the government's South East Flexible Ticketing scheme (SEFT).

The initiatives promised by Southern have been supported by capital investment of £76m, of which approximately £50m is being funded by Govia. Revenue share has applied from the start of the franchise, sharing with the DfT 50% of incremental revenue above 102% of the bid revenue, and 80% above 106% of bid. Revenue support has applied from 21 September 2013, with the DfT to provide 50% of any incremental shortfall in revenue below 98% of bid revenue and 80% support for any shortfall below 94% of bid.

At the busy East Croydon station, a new footbridge at the London end provides a new entrance, along with new retail units and lifts: also under way was an upgrade of the station concourse and platform facilities. At Brighton station, £5m has recently been invested transforming the concourse, opening the whole area up to expose the magnificent train shed. Additional car parking spaces have been created at a number of Southern's busiest stations.

All Southern routes are electrified at 750V DC, except for Oxted-Uckfield and Ashford-Hastings, which are worked by Class 171 diesel units (six 4-car and ten 2-car).

Electric multiple-units are of: Class 313 (19 x 3-car); Class 377/1 (64 x 4-car), 377/3 (28 x 3-car), 377/4 (75 x 4-car), 377/6 (26 x 5-car); dual-voltage 377/2 (6 x 4-car) and 377/7 (8 x 5-car); Class 442 (24 x 5-car); Class 455 (46 x 4-car).

The main train depots are at Selhurst (also responsible for overhaul), Brighton, and Stewarts Lane, Battersea.

SENIOR PERSONNEL
SOUTHERN

MANAGING DIRECTOR Charles Horton
INTERIM FINANCE & CONTRACTS DIRECTOR Nigel Ball
FLEET DIRECTOR Gerry McFadden
COMMERCIAL DIRECTOR Alex Foulds
OPERATIONS DIRECTOR David Scorey
HR DIRECTOR Andy Binden
HEAD OF SAFETY & OPERATIONAL STANDARDS Colin Morris

southeastern.

DIRECT AWARD UNTIL JUNE 2018

The Southeastern franchise serves Kent, south east London and part of East Sussex and includes high-speed domestic services on the High Speed 1 (HS1).

After being awarded an initial six-year franchise from 1 April 2006, Southeastern was granted a 2 year extension to 12 October 2014 after performance targets had been met. Following the DfT review of franchising a new direct award contract until June 2018 was agreed. It covers the duration of the Thameslink Programme infrastructure upgrade and London Bridge rebuild.

The new agreement includes commitments to more high-speed services with extra peak capacity, and new journey opportunities designed to help passengers during the three year rebuild of London Bridge.

New faster peak trains for Hastings, direct services between Maidstone East and Canterbury West, more services between Dartford and London Victoria and a new Blackfriars-Maidstone East service are also to be introduced.

Up to 75 extra staff will be deployed at gatelines at key stations and the opening hours of Cannon Street station will be extended to accommodate services running into the station later in the day. Train crew and station staff will have tablet devices to ensure better access to service information and 20 new information screens will be installed at key stations.

Southeastern will also offer more off-peak discount fares and will work with TfL to seek to have Dartford and Swanley stations included in the Oyster fare area, and to make Oyster available through stored-ticket value on HS1 between St Pancras and Stratford International.

The company will invest a further £4.8m in station improvements, carry out a deep clean of all stations, and install more self-service ticket machines.

In December 2014 a small number of services (on the Catford Loop) were incorporated into the GTR franchise and become part of the Thameslink service group.

The introduction of the high-speed service to St Pancras, worked exclusively by the fleet of 29 six-car Class 395 trains, brought a dramatic reduction in journey times for many passengers.

The 11.26 from London Charing Cross to Gravesend, via Sidcup, arrives at New Eltham on 22 September 2014, passing under the new 'Access for All' footbridge and lifts. The eight-car Class 465/1 Networker set is led by No 465185. **BRIAN MORRISON**

SENIOR PERSONNEL
SOUTHEASTERN

MANAGING DIRECTOR David Statham (in photo)
FINANCE DIRECTOR Elodie Brian
ENGINEERING DIRECTOR Mark Johnson
ACTING HR DIRECTOR John Morey
PASSENGER SERVICES DIRECTOR Barbara Thomas
TRAIN SERVICES DIRECTOR Richard Dean

Trains reach Ebbsfleet from St Pancras in just 17min and reduce peak times from across Kent, including London to Ashford in 37min. The high-speed 'Javelin' trains have been named after Olympians, and Southeastern has retained the connection with the Kent-born Olympic Gold medallist Dame Kelly Holmes, teaming up with her charity to help Kent youngsters gain skills to improve job prospects.

Over the past couple of years Southeastern's alliance with Network Rail has delivered benefits as the companies worked together to upgrade stations, such as at the award-winning rebuild of Gravesend station, as well as working to 'weather-proof' the rail infrastructure and deliver the largest resignalling scheme in over 60 years. Underlying punctuality performance has improved and emergency response times have shortened.

Some 50% of all employees hold a National Vocational Qualification with the majority of these in customer services. Senior managers across the company have also taken Institute of Learning Management qualifications with an aim to improve the way the company manages and develops staff. The internal professional social networking site, 'Workmate', allows all 3,800 Southeastern employees to connect, communicate and share information in real time about work-related on social matters.

Southeastern's engineering department has won several awards for its engineering 'wiki'; an internal online resource to help engineers remedy and repair faults. An innovative partnership between the engineering team and start-up technology company Perpetuum was rewarded with a national accolade at the *Modern Railways* Railway Industry Innovation Awards, for application of technology that monitors vibration levels on train wheel axles, and helps prevent damage that can cause cancellations.

Southeastern's commitment to reducing traction energy has seen the increased use of regenerative breaking, the re-training of drivers and the promotion of eco-driving techniques supported by the creation of an award for good driving. A 'driving energy further' initiative has reduced carbon emissions by 42,000 tonnes of CO2, saving around £6.2m. Southeastern was also the first stand-alone train company to commit to the '10:10' carbon reduction commitment. 70% of all waste is now recycled.

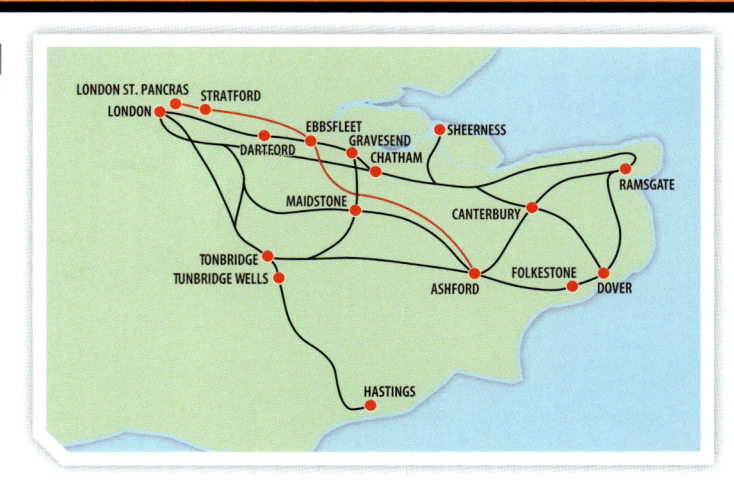

Southeastern runs a completely electric train fleet. Maintenance is carried out at Slade Green near Dartford (suburban) and Ramsgate (main line), with smaller depots for maintenance and cleaning at Ashford, Grove Park and Gillingham. Hitachi's depot at Ashford maintains the 29 Class-395 six-car high-speed trains. The remainder of the fleet is made up of 10 three-car and 102 four-car Class 375s; 36 five-car Class 376s; 147 four-car Class 465s; and 43 two-car Class 466s.

KEY STATISTICS
SOUTHEASTERN

	2012-13	2013-14
Punctuality (0-5min)	91.7%	89.0%
Passenger journeys (millions)	169.3	178.6
Passenger km (millions)	4,218.1	4,347.2
Timetabled train km (millions)	38.1	38.2
Route km operated	748.3	748.3
Number of stations operated	173	173
Number of employees	3,820	3,866
Subsidy per passenger km (p)	2.0	2.2
Network grant / pass km (p)	6.1	5.5

london midland
EXTENSION TO JUNE 2017 PLANNED

The London Midland (LM) franchise began on 11 November 2007, combining the Silverlink franchise's County routes and most of Central Trains.

The company has two brands, London Midland City (West Midlands conurbation and the wider region, with Centro's Network West Midlands brand prominent) and London Midland Express (longer distance routes connecting London Euston, the Midlands and Northwest).

Following its review of franchising, the DfT extended LM's franchise by 28 weeks until March 2016, prior to a new direct award contract planned to extend its tenure to June 2017.

Early in its franchise, LM introduced a new timetable structure in 2008, with through services between Birmingham and London, and a new service between London Euston and Crewe via the Trent Valley and Stoke-on-Trent. 37 new Siemens Class 350/2 Desiro electric trains were introduced, and Class 172 Bombardier Turbostars replaced most Class 150 Sprinters from 2011. Seven Class 321 EMUs were retained to increase capacity between Watford Junction and London Euston.

A joint initiative with Siemens has upgraded the Class 350/1 EMUs to run at 110mph, to cut journey times on the West Coast main line (WCML) and introduce additional services. Phase two of the project, which allows longer trains of 8 or 12-vehicles to run at 110mph, was completed in 2014. 110mph running allows some services to avoid Northampton and cut journey times to London by up to 30min, and capacity was created for an additional train per hour, off-peak, between Milton Keynes and London.

Ten new 4-car 110mph Class 350/3 Desiros were delivered in 2014. Seven are allocated to the WCML, providing around 4,000 more peak seats per day in and out of Euston, and the other three release Class 323s to provide extra services on the Cross-City line through Birmingham.

London Midland began using some '350/3s' more than two months early to lengthen some of the busiest peak services. From December 2014 an improved timetable for WCML services sees more strengthening, changes to calling patterns, further 110mph operation, and additional services.

KEY STATISTICS
LONDON MIDLAND

	2012-13	2013-14
Punctuality (0-5min)	86.0%	85.9%
Passenger journeys (millions)	60.5	64.0
Passenger km (millions)	2,241.2	2,363.7
Timetabled train km (millions)	25.4	25.7
Route km operated	898.8	898.8
Number of stations operated	147	148
Number of employees	2,327	2,401
Subsidy per passenger km (p)	2.6	2.8
Network grant / pass km (p)	6.5	6.1

modern railways

Established for 50 years, **Modern Railways** has earned its reputation in the industry as a highly respected monthly railway journal. Providing in-depth coverage of all aspects of the industry, from traction and rolling stock to signalling and infrastructure management, **Modern Railways** carries the latest news alongside detailed analysis, making it essential reading for industry professionals and railway enthusiasts alike.

FREE APP with sample issue
IN APP ISSUES £3.99

Available monthly from **WHSmith** and other leading newsagents

ALSO AVAILABLE FOR DOWNLOAD

SEARCH RAILWAYS ILLUSTRATED
FREE APP with sample issue
IN APP ISSUES £3.99

SEARCH STEAM DAYS
FREE APP with sample issue
IN APP ISSUES £3.99

NEW FREE Specials App **NEW**

IN APP ISSUES £3.99

Simply download to purchase digital versions of your favourite aviation specials in one handy place! Once you have the app, you will be able to download new, out of print or archive specials for less than the cover price!

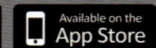

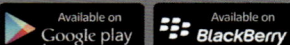

SEARCH: Aviation Specials

How it Works.

Simply download the Modern Railways app and receive your sample issue completely free. Once you have the app, you will be able to download new or back issues (from January 2011 onwards) for less than newsstand price or, alternatively, subscribe to save even more!

Don't forget to register for your Pocketmags account. This will protect your purchase in the event of a damaged or lost device. It will also allow you to view your purchases on multiple platforms.

Available on iTunes • Available on the App Store • Available on Google play • Available on BlackBerry • Available on kindle fire • Available on PC, Mac & Windows 8

Available on PC, Mac, Blackberry and Windows 8 from **pocketmags.com**

Requirements for app: registered iTunes account on Apple iPhone 3G, 3GS, 4S, 5, iPod Touch or iPad 1, 2, 3 or 4. Internet connection required for initial download. Published by Key Publishing Ltd. The entire contents of these titles are © copyright 2014. All rights reserved. App prices subject to change. 973/14

A pair of Class 172 diesel multiple-units, led by No 172213, calls at Acocks Green with the 14.55 Kidderminster-Dorridge on 24 April 2014. **TONY MILES**

These are possible with the additional capacity created by the faster trains.

LM has now installed meters on all of its Class 323 and Class 350 EMUs which monitor and record how much electricity is used and the amount regenerated in braking. The data can be downloaded and analysed to help the company work with its drivers to drive in a more energy efficient way.

A commitment to addressing passenger needs, raising punctuality, reducing cancellations and providing 'quality journeys for everyone' was the basis of a 'Strong Foundations' improvement programme implemented in March 2013. Work has included building a greater level of resilience into timetables so LM is better prepared to address challenges such as major public events, where additional services are scheduled.

LM's Public Performance Measure figures have shown progress, with the October 2014 score reaching 89.2% and a Moving Annual Average of 86.7% - seen as an important improvement on the 2013 figure, given continuing high levels of disruption on the highly congested West Coast main line.

London Midland has four 'heads of route' who have overall responsibility for the West Coast main line, Birmingham Snow Hill services, Regional, and Cross City services. They focus on train performance, customer service and passenger information, as well as working closely with Network Rail and other partners.

London Midland has taken full advantage of the DfT's National Station Improvement Programme (NSIP) to provide passenger benefits at 21 stations. This was achieved through a mixture of £12m of NSIP funds and an additional £2.5m of outside funding.

In a £100m investment package in north Worcestershire, Network Rail installed a new 3km section of double track in summer 2014, allowing LM to run three services an hour between Barnt Green and Redditch. Work is also under way on a £17.4m replacement station at Bromsgrove, with four platforms, supported by electrification between Bromsgrove and Barnt Green, which will enable Cross-City services to be extended to the new station.

The opening of the new Stratford-upon-Avon Parkway station in 2013 took London Midland's managed station total to 148, and work to create new stations at Ricoh Arena and Bermuda Park, on the on the Coventry-Nuneaton line, is underway. Work to improve the station at Northampton has also begun, and a new station for Kenilworth is also being developed, with construction due to begin in late 2015.

London Midland's diesel train fleet consists of: Class 172 Turbostars (12 two-car and 15 three-car), Class 170 Turbostars (17 two-car and six three-car), Class 150 Sprinters (3 two-car); Class 153 (8 single-car), Class 139 (2 single-car, LPG/flywheel-powered Parry People Movers).

The electric train fleet mainly has four-car trains: 30 Class-350/1, 37 Class-350/2, and 10 Class 350/3 Desiros; 7 Class-321; plus 26 three-car Class-323s.

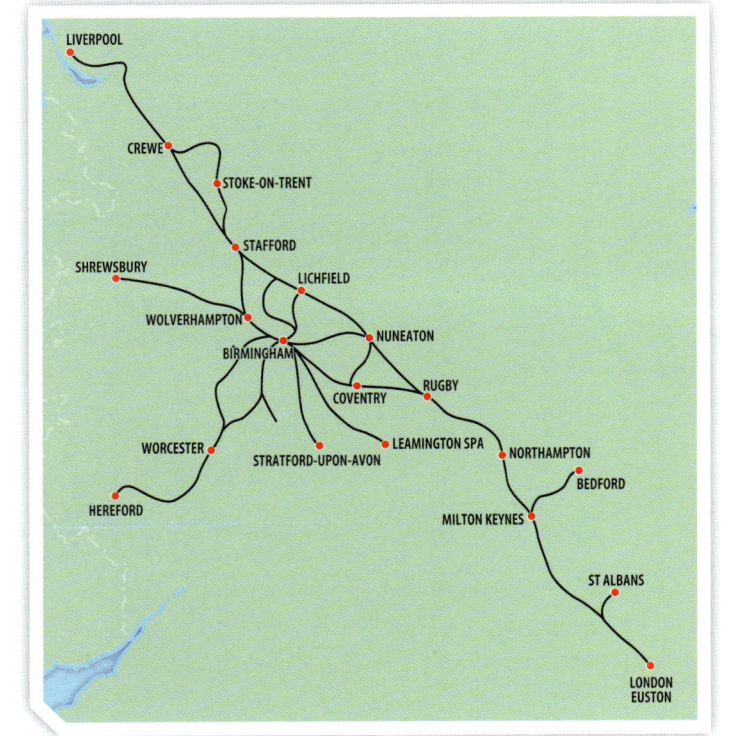

SENIOR PERSONNEL
LONDON MIDLAND

MANAGING DIRECTOR Patrick Verwer (in photo)
FINANCE & CONTRACTS DIRECTOR Ian McLaren
PASSENGER SERVICES DIRECTOR Tom Joyner
COMMERCIAL DIRECTOR Richard Brooks
ASSET MAINTENANCE DIRECTOR Neil Bamford
HEAD OF DRIVERS Terry Brissenden
HEAD OF CONDUCTORS Sean McBroome
HEAD OF CURRENT OPERATIONS Olly Glover
HEAD OF HR Lynsey Rice

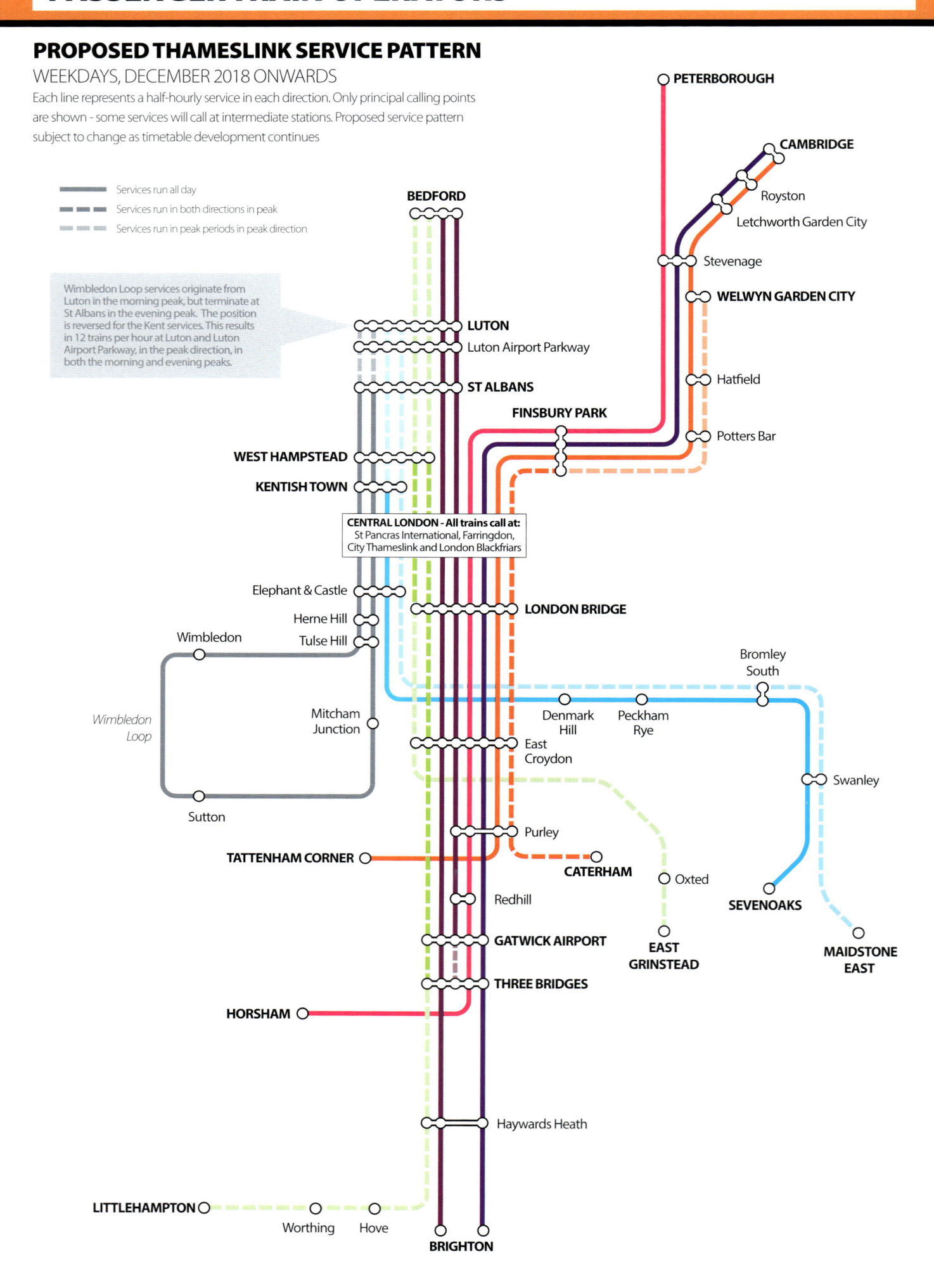

PASSENGER TRAIN OPERATORS

PROPOSED THAMESLINK SERVICE PATTERN

WEEKDAYS, DECEMBER 2018 ONWARDS

Each line represents a half-hourly service in each direction. Only principal calling points are shown - some services will call at intermediate stations. Proposed service pattern subject to change as timetable development continues

- Services run all day
- Services run in both directions in peak
- Services run in peak periods in peak direction

Wimbledon Loop services originate from Luton in the morning peak, but terminate at St Albans in the evening peak. The position is reversed for the Kent services. This results in 12 trains per hour at Luton and Luton Airport Parkway, in the peak direction, in both the morning and evening peaks.

CENTRAL LONDON - All trains call at: St Pancras International, Farringdon, City Thameslink and London Blackfriars

Stations shown:
- PETERBOROUGH
- CAMBRIDGE
- Royston
- Letchworth Garden City
- Stevenage
- WELWYN GARDEN CITY
- Hatfield
- Potters Bar
- BEDFORD
- LUTON
- Luton Airport Parkway
- ST ALBANS
- FINSBURY PARK
- WEST HAMPSTEAD
- KENTISH TOWN
- Elephant & Castle
- Herne Hill
- Tulse Hill
- Wimbledon
- Mitcham Junction
- Sutton
- LONDON BRIDGE
- Denmark Hill
- Peckham Rye
- Bromley South
- East Croydon
- Swanley
- Purley
- TATTENHAM CORNER
- CATERHAM
- Oxted
- SEVENOAKS
- Redhill
- EAST GRINSTEAD
- MAIDSTONE EAST
- GATWICK AIRPORT
- THREE BRIDGES
- HORSHAM
- Haywards Heath
- LITTLEHAMPTON
- Worthing
- Hove
- BRIGHTON

Wimbledon Loop

86

HITACHI Inspire the Next

ARRIVA

Part of the German state rail group Deutsche Bahn (DB) since it acquired Arriva plc in August 2010, Arriva is responsible for regional passenger transport outside Germany. In 2013 it had 46,700 (full time equivalent) employees operating in 14 countries, with revenue of Euro 4.18billion.

Arriva UK Trains estimates that it operates about 14% of the UK passenger network. It has three rail franchises: CrossCountry and Arriva Trains Wales (Arriva held these two prior to the DB acquisition), and Chiltern Railways, which DB had run since acquiring its parent Laing Rail in 2008. Open-access train company Grand Central was acquired in November 2011.

Also involved in the Laing acquisition was the London Rail concession for London Overground, awarded in 2007 to London Overground Rail Operations Ltd (LOROL), a joint venture of Laing with Hong Kong's MTR. A two-year extension to November 2016 was confirmed in 2013.

Arriva operates a seven-year Tyne & Wear Metro contract for Nexus, the Passenger Transport Executive. It covers the train service, fleet maintenance and modernisation, and day-to-day station management.

Arriva also owns rail maintenance business LNWR, based in Crewe and founded in 1996. Depots in Gateshead, Bristol, Cambridge and Eastleigh service CrossCountry trains on behalf of Bombardier.

Alliance Rail Holdings, acquired by DB in 2010, undertakes strategic development work for Grand Central as well as for other proposed open-access services.

Network Rail in 2014 agreed access rights for two-hourly services from London Euston to Huddersfield and Leeds via Manchester Victoria, and to Blackpool. Network Rail and GNWR then submitted an agreed application to the Office of Rail Regulation: services are proposed to commence by December 2017, using 6-car Alstom Pendolino trains.

A two-hourly service from London King's Cross to Bradford and Ilkley, calling at a new 'parkway' station east of Leeds as well as Leeds itself, is proposed, as well as services to Scunthorpe, Grimsby and Cleethorpes, using new Hitachi Super Express Trains or equivalent. Alliance also plans an express service between King's Cross and Edinburgh, calling only at Newcastle. With end to end journey times of 3hr 43min, this is aimed at competing with air using 9 car tilting Alstom Pendolino trains to bring the significant time advantage.

Chiltern Railways

20 YEAR FRANCHISE FROM FEBRUARY 2002

Awarded in 2002 by the former Strategic Rail Authority, Chiltern Railways' unique 20-year franchise is linked to delivery of investment.

The first part of a current development package, 'Evergreen 3', was launched in 2011, with new London-Birmingham 'Mainline' services offering fast journeys to London Marylebone (currently from 94min from Birmingham Moor Street). Over 50 miles of track were upgraded for 100mph, with key junctions improved. In the first year, Chiltern recorded a 33% increase in West Midlands-London journeys. A revised timetable from December 2012 gave 600 extra seats in the peaks.

In early 2014, Chiltern Railways announced an agreement with Direct Rail Services (DRS) for six new Class 68 locomotives for 'Mainline' trains, replacing six Class 67s hired from DB Schenker.

Free Wi-Fi and a new Business Zone, designed as a cost efficient alternative to First class, are offered on Mainline trains. The company also restructured ticketing, and improved station facilities and parking capacity.

After Transport & Works Act approval in 2013, Phase 2 of Evergreen 3 will provide a new Oxford-Marylebone service, with upgrading and partial doubling of the Oxford-Bicester line, a new link to the Chiltern line at Bicester, and a new multi-modal interchange, Oxford

KEY STATISTICS
CHILTERN RAILWAYS

	2012-13	2013-14
Punctuality (0-5min)	94.9%	94.9%
Passenger journeys (millions)	21.4	22.8
Passenger km (millions)	1,132.5	1,198.0
Timetabled train km (millions)	10.7	10.9
Route km operated	341.2	341.2
Number of stations operated	32	32
Number of employees	778	780
Subsidy per passenger km (p)	0.6	-0.4
Network grant / pass km (p)	6.9	5.3

Headed by a Driving Van Trailer, a Chiltern Railways 'Mainline' train arrives at Birmingham Moor Street. **CHILTERN RAILWAYS**

PASSENGER TRAIN OPERATORS

Parkway, north of the city.

A collaboration with Network Rail is overseeing this and the first phase of work on East West Rail (Oxford-Bicester-Bletchley-Bedford/Milton Keynes, with Chiltern services extended from Aylesbury to Bletchley and Milton Keynes). An £87m design-and-build contract was awarded to Carillion and Buckingham Group in March 2014.

Marylebone services are due to begin in September 2015 from Oxford Parkway (fastest journey 58min to London), serving Oxford from spring 2016.

Funding of about £259m for Evergreen 3, from Network Rail, is to be repaid by the train operator over 30 years. With this project, Chiltern says a total of £600m will have been invested since the start of its original franchise in 1996.

The £80m 'Evergreen 2', completed in 2006, was a Design, Build, Finance & Transfer project, improving capacity for 20 trains per peak hour to use Marylebone. 'Evergreen 1' doubled single track between Aynho Junction and Princes Risborough.

Aylesbury Vale Parkway, 3km north of Aylesbury, designed to serve housing development and park-and-ride, opened in 2008. Warwick Parkway, the first non-Railtrack station delivered on the rail network, opened in 2000.

Chiltern Railways in July 2013 became the first operator to roll out 'App and Go' tickets, with mobile ticketing company Masabi. On-phone tickets can be scanned at barriers.

In the four weeks to 24 May 2014, Chiltern achieved its best public performance measure score since 1996, at 97.8%.

Nine 2-car Class 170 diesel multiple-units currently with First TransPennine Express, are to transfer to Chiltern to enlarge the fleet with introduction of the Oxford services. The four Mainline trains of Mk3 coaches have undergone major refurbishment by Wabtec, including new power-operated bodyside doors, and controlled-emission toilets. The Class 168 'Clubman' diesel multiple-units are being refurbished by Wabtec with the same silver livery, in a £5.3m programme. There are ten 4-car and nine 3-car Class 168s, used for longer-distance services. A fifth loco-hauled train is used for commuter services.

Four new two-car Class 172 DMUs went into service in 2011. There are 28 two-car and 11 three-car Class 165 'Turbo' trains. Two refurbished Class-121 single-car diesels are used on Aylesbury-Princes Risborough shuttles. The main maintenance depot is at Aylesbury, with another at Wembley, and a new one is proposed at Banbury.

In May 2013, Chiltern Railways was awarded 5-star European Foundation for Quality Management accreditation. ■

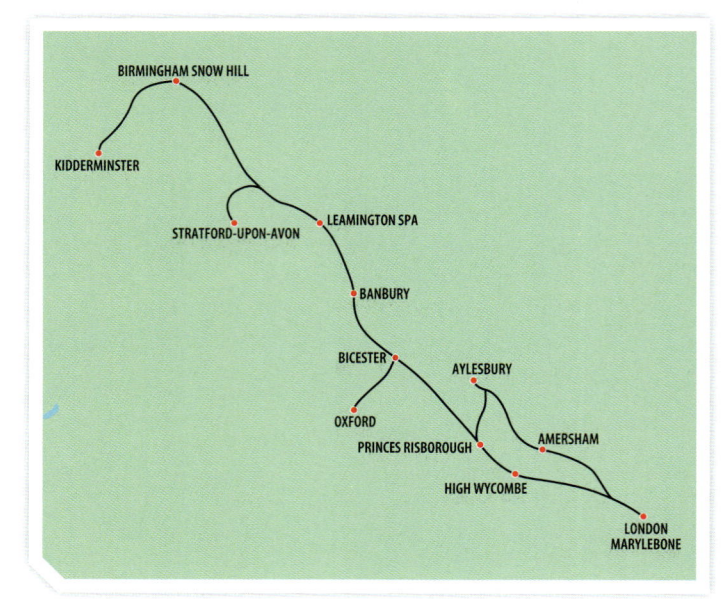

SENIOR PERSONNEL
CHILTERN RAILWAYS

MANAGING DIRECTOR Rob Brighouse (in photo)
BUSINESS DEVELOPMENT DIRECTOR Graham Cross
CUSTOMER SERVICES DIRECTOR Jennifer Payne
ENGINEERING DIRECTOR Dave Penney
FINANCE DIRECTOR Duncan Rimmer
OPERATIONS AND SAFETY DIRECTOR Andrew Munden
COMMERCIAL DIRECTOR Thomas Ableman

ARRIVA Trains Wales / Trenau Arriva Cymru

15 YEAR FRANCHISE FROM DECEMBER 2003

Arriva Trains Wales/Trenau Arriva Cymru (ATW) includes national, regional and local routes within Wales; through services to Birmingham, Chester, Manchester and Cheltenham; and the 'Borders' route via Shrewsbury.

The 15-year Wales & Borders franchise commenced on 7 December 2003, and in April 2006 the Welsh Government took responsibility for it, gaining powers to fund improvements: National Assembly and devolution commission reports have both recommended full devolution of the next franchise.

Contrary to assumptions of little growth, there has been a 60% increase in journeys since 2003, and PPM performance has improved from around 80% to over 93%. ATW has invested more than £30m in train maintenance and improvements, station upgrades, ticketing, information and security, and government has funded additional trains and stations.

Electrification of the Valley Lines network around Cardiff is planned by about 2019. Current enhancements include a £220m modernisation, bringing an extra four trains per hour through the Cardiff area, other capacity measures, and a new station opened in 2013 at Energlyn near Caerphilly.

The doubling of five miles of Swansea-Llanelli single track, aimed at improving reliability and capacity, was completed in 2013. In June 2014, work started on a £44m project to double part of the Wrexham-Chester line.

Four more Aberystwyth-Shrewsbury trains will run from May 2015, as a three-year Welsh Government-funded trial, with extra commuter trains for the Heart of Wales. The Welsh Government funded five extra daily trains for Fishguard, from 2011, now extended until 2018.

Train capacity of 330,000 extra seats a year was added in May 2012, benefiting places including Aberystwyth, North and West Wales. Another 125,000 seats a year were added from September 2012 on several commuter flows, with a revised loco-hauled express linking Holyhead with Cardiff via Wrexham.

Another loco-hauled train,

An Arriva Trains Wales Class 175 train at Fishguard Harbour. **ATW**

boosting services between North Wales and Manchester from December 2014, was enabled by a £1.2m deal with the Department for Transport, involving a change of control fee paid by Deutsche Bahn after acquiring Arriva plc.

A new Ebbw Vale town station is expected to open in 2015, with 1.3 miles of new track from Ebbw Vale Parkway. The Welsh Government in 2013 announced £11.5m funding.

A new Pye Corner station, on the Ebbw Vale line was funded by £2.5m from the Department for Transport's New Station Fund and £1m from the Welsh Government. The Wales Stations Improvement Programme has seen major enhancements at Swansea and Chester, with Port Talbot and Aberystwyth to benefit in the next round.

Severe winter storm damage on the Cambrian Coast line had been repaired by May 2014. The Harlech-Pwllheli section reopened in September 2014, using the new Pont Briwet viaduct over the Afon Dwyryd.

A complete upgrade of ATW's Class 158 fleet (carried out by LNWR) was completed in 2012, with the Welsh Government providing £7.5m. Class 175s have also recently been refurbished.

Apart from the Class-67-loco-hauled trains, long-distance services use 24 Class-158 diesel multiple-units and 27 Class-175s. A fleet of 30 Class-142/143 Pacer railbuses is mainly used in the Cardiff area. There are also 36 Class-150s and 8 single-car Class-153s.

Most of the fleet is based at Cardiff Canton, with a £3million facility at Machynlleth servicing Class 158s, while Class 175s are maintained at manufacturer Alstom's Chester depot.

KEY STATISTICS
ARRIVA TRAINS WALES

	2012-13	2013-14
Punctuality (0-5min)	93.3%	93.1%
Passenger journeys (millions)	29.0	29.9
Passenger km (millions)	1,154	1,167
Timetabled train km (millions)	24.2	24.3
Route km operated	1,670.5	1,670.5
Number of stations operated	244	245
Number of employees	2,010	2,072
Subsidy per passenger km (p)	12.2	13.2

SENIOR PERSONNEL
ARRIVA TRAINS WALES

MANAGING DIRECTOR Ian Bullock (in photo)
OPERATIONS AND SAFETY DIRECTOR Claire Mann
CUSTOMER SERVICES DIRECTOR Lynne Milligan
COMMERCIAL DIRECTOR Mike Bagshaw
ENGINEERING DIRECTOR Matt Prosser
HUMAN RESOURCES DIRECTOR Gareth Thomas
FINANCE DIRECTOR Rob Phillips

crosscountry

FRANCHISE EXTENSION TO NOVEMBER 2019 PLANNED

The CrossCountry (XC) network is the most extensive GB rail franchise, stretching from Aberdeen to Penzance, and from Stansted to Cardiff. Arriva's franchise, starting on 11 November 2007, was due to run until 31 March 2016. The Department for Transport in 2013 announced a proposed 43-month extended contract, running until November 2019.

There are regular half-hourly services on key route sections, including Birmingham to Bristol, Reading, Manchester, Sheffield and Leicester; hourly direct services between Bristol and Manchester; hourly through services for all destinations between Plymouth and Edinburgh (via Leeds), Southampton, Reading and Newcastle (via Doncaster), Bournemouth and Manchester, Cardiff and Nottingham, Birmingham and Stansted Airport. CrossCountry trains via Motherwell and Edinburgh connect Glasgow with Northeast England, Yorkshire, the Midlands and Southwest. Britain's longest direct train service is CrossCountry's 08.20 Aberdeen to Penzance (774 miles).

CrossCountry has introduced a series of commercial innovations, including pioneering print-at-home tickets in the UK. Its train tickets app, developed by Masabi, offers train times and real-time running information, and ticket purchase by smartphone. XC Advance tickets can be delivered to the app and displayed for inspection, while other tickets can be collected from a machine at the station.

Travellers can register for alerts when advance tickets become available, and students can

PASSENGER TRAIN OPERATORS

KEY STATISTICS
CROSSCOUNTRY

	2012-13	2013-14
Punctuality (0-10min)	86.8%	86.7%
Passenger journeys (millions)	33.4	34.2
Passenger km (millions)	3,254.1	3,247.2
Timetabled train km (millions)	32.6	32.7
Route km operated	2,661.9	2,710.1
Number of stations operated	0	0
Number of employees	1,694	1,705
Subsidy per passenger km (p)	0.6	1.0
Network grant / pass km (p)	9.5	8.7

receive an extra 10% discount on XC Advance tickets. The 'Advance Purchase On the Day' initiative enables purchase of discounted advance purchase fares (and seat reservations on many services) on the day of travel, up to 10min before boarding a train – via website, mobile app, or a call centre. It won the Passenger Experience award at the 2014 Rail Industry Innovation Awards, organised by *Modern Railways*.

CrossCountry operates 34 Class-220 (4-car) and 23 Class-221 Voyager trains (most 5-car); 29 Class-170 Turbostar diesel multiple-units (16 x 3-car, 13 x 2-car) and 5 High-Speed Trains.

Since the beginning of the franchise CrossCountry has carried out £40m worth of improvements to its fleet, with reconfiguration to provide additional seating and luggage space producing a 35% increase in capacity on principal routes in the evening peaks. The Voyager fleet has won the *Modern Railways* 'Golden Spanner' for the most reliable InterCity train for five consecutive years.

The HSTs were fully refurbished by Wabtec at Doncaster, with a number of additional trailers converted from loco-hauled vehicles. MTU engines were fitted to the power cars.

The Class 170 Turbostars operate on Cardiff/Birmingham-Nottingham/Stansted Airport/Leicester routes. Various sub-classes were configured to a standard layout (120 seats in the two-car and 200 in three-car units) during a refurbishment by Transys Projects (now Vossloh Kiepe UK) with exterior repainting by Axiom Rail.

Work in conjunction with Nomad Digital to equip all HSTs and Voyagers with wi-fi was completed in 2012. At-seat catering is provided on most services, providing hot and cold refreshments appropriate to the time of day.

CrossCountry has achieved EFQM 'Recognised for Excellence' status - the first Arriva train company to gain the maximum '5 star' rating - and was also awarded the 2013 British Quality Foundation prize for 'Excellence in Employee Engagement'.

Installation of the Energymiser driver advisory system by Arriva began with CrossCountry in 2014. It is designed to maximise train performance and reduce fuel consumption and emissions. A forward-facing CCTV system has also been installed on all trains to monitor the rail infrastructure. ∎

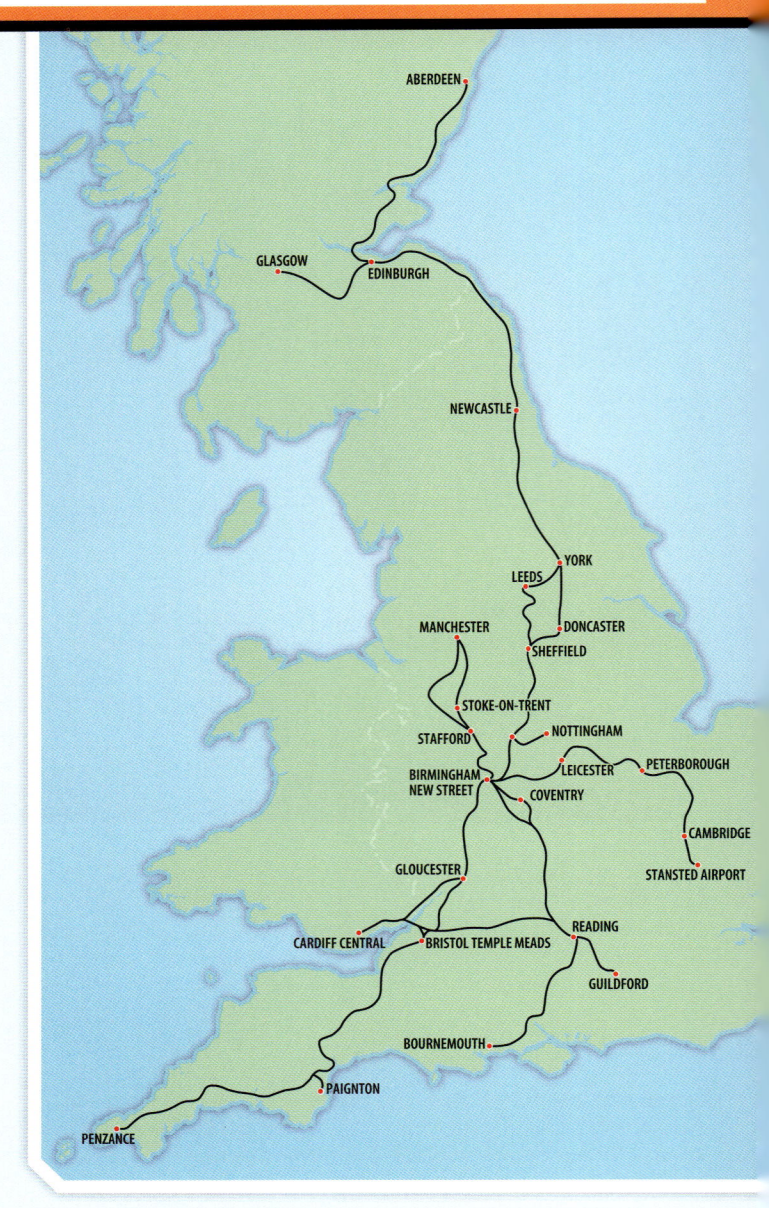

SENIOR PERSONNEL
CROSSCOUNTRY

MANAGING DIRECTOR Andy Cooper (in photo)
COMMERCIAL DIRECTOR David Watkin
CUSTOMER SERVICE DIRECTOR Jeremy Higgins
PRODUCTION DIRECTOR Will Rogers
HEAD OF SAFETY Des Lowe
HR DIRECTOR Maria Zywica
FINANCE DIRECTOR Jonathan Roberts

Power car No 43304 heads an HST descending Dainton Bank, near Stoneycombe, with the 12.25 Plymouth-Glasgow on 23 September 2014. **STEWART ARMSTRONG**

IN ASSOCIATION WITH **ESG** Designed to deliver

Grand Central's Class 180 No 180114 races through Peterborough en route from King's Cross to Bradford. **TONY MILES**

GRAND CENTRAL

OPEN ACCESS OPERATOR ON TRACK TO 2026

Grand Central Rail (GC) has been awarded an extended access contract, by 10 years, until 2026, and is beginning £7.8m of investment in its fleet and at stations.

GC is to take over the five Class 180s currently working with First Great Western from December 2016. They may be sub-leased back to FGW for a period, before GC begins operating a uniform fleet of Class 180s after 2017, when its three Class 43 High Speed Trains will be retired. A Class 180 refurbishment programme will commence in 2015. GC currently leases five Class 180 and three HSTs from Angel Trains.

GC's open access service from Sunderland to London King's Cross was launched in December 2007: a three trains a day service began in July 2008. By 2012, GC was running five return journeys. The West Riding service started in May 2010, offering three trains a day between Bradford Interchange and King's Cross (calling at Halifax, Brighouse, Wakefield Kirkgate, Pontefract Monkhill and Doncaster – and from December 2011, Mirfield). GC was permitted a fourth Bradford service from December 2013.

A series of changes in ownership culminated in GC becoming part of Arriva in November 2011. GC has invested over £40m of private capital in trains and people, as well as covering its start-up costs, with a £400,000 programme of investment in stations completing in late 2014.

Notable among improvements to stations through partnerships has been the transformation of Wakefield Kirkgate - once dubbed by former transport minister Lord Adonis as the worst medium sized station on the network.

GC is the UK's most trusted long-distance rail company, according to research by Passenger Focus. The spring 2014 National Rail Passenger Survey found 94% of its passengers were satisfied, or very satisfied.

In mid-2014, GC introduced a Twitter feed, and also manages a Facebook page, responding to passenger feedback, helping with queries and sharing information.

GC's award-winning Station Ambassador scheme was extended during 2014: voluntary representatives help passengers on Sundays when booking offices are closed and most disruption due to engineering work occurs.

All West Riding services are presently worked by Class 180s, and the North Eastern route is shared between '180s' and HST sets. In 2010 the 21 HST vehicles (6 Class 43 power cars and 15 Mk3 coaches) were sold by GC sister company Sovereign Trains to Angel Trains, which agreed to invest in a substantial engineering programme, to improve performance and reliability. This included installation of new MTU engines in power cars. GC agreed to lease the sets until at least December 2016.

Working with Angel, First Hull Trains and First Great Western, Grand Central entered into a unique technical support contract with Alstom which covers all Class 180s. This is delivering significant improvements in arrangements for maintenance, including fitment of remote conditioning monitoring equipment on key systems. Northern Rail maintains Grand Central's trains at Heaton depot, Newcastle and provides riding inspectors to check on trains en route. Two '180s' are serviced overnight at Crofton, Wakefield, by Bombardier.

2014 saw a continuation of rapid growth, especially on the West Riding route, driven by additional services, generation of awareness, and increased availability of advance fares. Growth in First Class custom is based on more competitively priced tickets. 2014 also saw the launch of additional student discounts on advance tickets. Carnet tickets for frequent travellers were revised and made available via stations and business travel agents as well as by phone.

With a total staff of 130, Grand Central Rail has created more than 65 jobs in Sunderland, 44 in Bradford and 22 in York. It says these are skilled, permanent positions which make a real contribution to economic development.

The punctuality statistic for 2013/14 was 80.7%. ∎

SENIOR PERSONNEL
GRAND CENTRAL RAIL

MANAGING DIRECTOR Richard McClean (in photo)
CHIEF OPERATING OFFICER Sean English
FLEET DIRECTOR Dave Hatfield
COMMERCIAL DIRECTOR Louise Blyth
CUSTOMER EXPERIENCE MANAGER Celia Knott
HEAD OF OPERATIONS David Neil
HEAD OF FINANCE Mark Robinson

HITACHI Inspire the Next

PASSENGER TRAIN OPERATORS

STAGECOACH GROUP

Stagecoach Group has extensive bus, rail and light rail operations in the UK and North America, employing around 35,000 people, over 7,000 of them in UK Rail. Holder of the South West Trains franchise since it was first awarded in 1996, it was awarded the East Midlands rail franchise in 2007, and has a 49% shareholding in Virgin Rail Group which will continue to operate the West Coast intercity rail franchise until at least March 2017. Stagecoach is currently involved in running around 20% of the UK's passenger rail network. Stagecoach Supertram holds a 27-year concession until 2024 for Sheffield's 28km light rail network.

UK rail subsidiaries' revenue for the year to 30 April 2014 was up 4.2% at £1,252m (2013: £1,201.3m). Operating profit was £34.3m (2013: £41.2m). The operating margin fell slightly from 3.4 to 2.7%. South West Trains and East Midlands Trains continued to receive revenue support, partly offsetting shortfall in revenue forecast in the franchise bids. Stagecoach spent £9m in 2013-14 pursuing new rail franchise opportunities.

SOUTH WEST TRAINS

EXTENSION PLANNED UNTIL APRIL 2019

The 10-year South West Trains (SWT) franchise, held by Stagecoach, began on 4 February 2007 combining the previous SWT and Island Line (Isle of Wight) franchises. The DfT plans an extended award, of 26 months, to April 2019.

SWT is carrying more than 100 million more passengers on its services every year than at privatisation in 1995 and demand continues to grow.

An alliance between SWT and Network Rail, established in April 2012 (the 'South Western Railway' or SWR), sees a single management team is responsible for one of the busiest, most intensely used and complex railways in Europe. Service performance has improved through the work of the alliance to create better working relationships between the two companies. The teams are co-located and aim for an increased focus on even the smallest delays, and recovery from incidents is significantly improved.

SWT says that the proposed extended franchise award could co-ordinate beneficially with Network Rail's Control Period 5 plans. A capacity programme for SWR is based on two phases of improvement which could deliver up to 35% extra capacity by the end of 2024, including procurement of extra trains, opening the remaining Waterloo International platforms, and infrastructure schemes including resignalling, power supply improvements and further platform extensions.

Moving towards providing a 10-car railway on some of the busiest routes, Class 460 (former Gatwick Express) vehicles are being used to extend the 30 Class 458 sets to 5-cars and create six new 5-car EMUs, all designated Class 458/5. This will provide space for around 16,400 additional peak time passengers a day. 60 stations on the Windsor suburban and main suburban routes are having

KEY STATISTICS
SOUTH WEST TRAINS

	2012-13	2013-14
Punctuality (0-5min)	91.4%	89.7%
Passenger journeys (millions)	210.8	222.8
Passenger km (millions)	5,777.5	6,045.8
Timetabled train km (millions)	39.5	39.5
Route km operated	944.7	944.7
Number of stations operated	186	186
Number of employees	4,720	4,827
Subsidy per passenger km (p)	-5.4	-5.2

A Siemens built Class 450 heads west through Weybridge en route to Portsmouth, with a classmate waiting to depart for the Chertsey line from the bay platform (left), and a Class 455 bound for Woking (right). SIEMENS/SWT

their platforms extended. After the contractors experienced delays, it is hoped that all of the remaining '458/5s' will be introduced before summer 2015.

In September 2014, SWT announced its intention to award a contract for a £210m fleet of 30 new 5-car Desiro City trains to Siemens and Angel Trains. Due in service by early 2018, they will provide for more than 18,000 extra peak passengers a day, contributing to a total peak-time capacity increase of around 30% by 2018.

The former Waterloo International Terminal will be fully reopened for domestic services by March 2017 and this will allow 20 trains an hour on the Waterloo-Reading line. Platforms 1-4 at Waterloo will be lengthened in 2017, to allow 10 car trains to operate on suburban lines.

Passengers served by the SWT-Network Rail Alliance have seen over £18 million worth of improvements at stations over the last year. Investment in new and improved facilities at 30 different stations has delivered a wide range of benefits. In July 2014 a new heated and air conditioned waiting room and retail outlet was opened on platforms 13 and 14 at Clapham Junction, as part of a £950,000 National Stations Improvement Programme (NSIP) scheme.

SWT achieves some of the highest train performance standards for both electric and diesel fleets. The electric multiple-unit fleet has 45 Class-444 five-car Siemens Desiro trains (designed for longer distance services), 127 Class-450 four-car Desiros. 24 two-car Class-456s were transferred from Southern in 2014, and the 91-strong Class 455 fleet is being upgraded through the fitment of new traction equipment to help improve reliability. Work started in 2012 on the £23m overhaul of the '455' fleet at Bournemouth, home to a new £3.2 million state-of-the-art paint shop. 30 three-car Class 159 and 11 two-car Class 158 diesel multiple-units are used on the non-electrified routes from Southampton and Basingstoke to Salisbury and beyond.

Main train depots are at Wimbledon, Salisbury and, for the Siemens-built Desiro units, Northam near Southampton. Work is being carried out to upgrade facilities at Wimbledon and Farnham for the additional trains being introduced. At Wimbledon, around £6m has been invested, with a new bogie drop system to detach bogies and other mechanical equipment at track level, while work on other parts of the train can continue, delivering greater efficiency during maintenance.

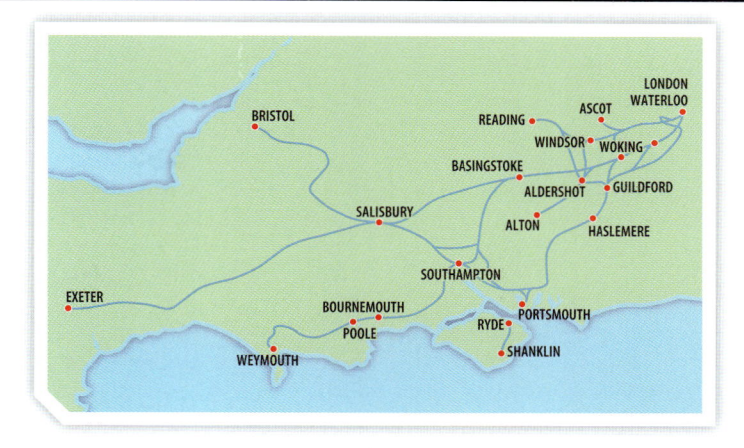

SENIOR PERSONNEL
SOUTH WEST TRAINS

CHIEF EXECUTIVE Tim Shoveller (in photo)
DEVELOPMENT DIRECTOR Jake Kelly
CUSTOMER SERVICE DIRECTOR Arthur Pretorius
INFRASTRUCTURE DIRECTOR John Halsall
COMMERCIAL DIRECTOR Sam McCarthy
OPERATIONS DIRECTOR Mark Steward
SAFETY & ENVIRONMENT DIRECTOR Sharon Vye-Parminter
FINANCE DIRECTOR Andy West
HR DIRECTOR Kelly Barlow

EAST MIDLANDS TRAINS
EXTENSION PLANNED UNTIL 2017

The East Midlands franchise - combining the previous Midland main line intercity franchise with the eastern section of Central Trains - began operation on 11 November 2007 and was due to continue until 1 April 2015, subject to performance. The DfT in 2013 announced plans for a new Direct Award, taking the franchise to October 2017.

For every 200 passengers who travelled on the InterCity Midland main line services in 1995, EMT is now carrying 500. The route to London now carries over 13 million passengers a year and is a vital artery for South Yorkshire, the East Midlands and Northamptonshire.

Passenger numbers have held up despite the challenging economic circumstances, but revenue growth did not met expected targets and EMT became eligible for revenue support from the DfT from November 2011. EMT has now marked its fifth year as the UK's most punctual long distance train operator.

A range of station improvements are being delivered, with the most significant being the Nottingham Hub redevelopment, with extensive remodelling and resignalling in a £100m project. £50m of improvement to the station itself was completed in May 2014, creating a new, glass-fronted southern concourse, with fully accessible connections with the car park and tram network.

Derby station's forecourt was transformed in a £2.7 million scheme, with a new transport interchange for buses and taxis. Other schemes include the £100,000 project to improve Chesterfield station, and a £250,000 project at Lincoln.

In 2013/14 EMT invested over £350,000 in accessibility improvements at stations, and now has 69 with step-free access. 36 have Secure Station accreditation, and 30 car parks have Park Mark status.

A new initiative launched in 2013/14 is 'magic moments', which have included free chips at major stations during National Chip Week, fortune cookies and free noodles at Chinese New Year, free bacon butties to launch the new First Class offer, free wine on Valentine's Day, and free Guinness flavoured crisps for St Patrick's Day.

KEY STATISTICS
EAST MIDLANDS TRAINS

	2012-13	2013-14
Punctuality	92.5%	91.3%
Passenger journeys (millions)	24.1	24.1
Passenger km (millions)	2,252.4	2,231.8
Timetabled train km (millions)	22.2	22.0
Route km operated	1,549.8	1,549.8
Number of stations operated	89	89
Number of employees	2,025	2,052
Subsidy per passenger km (p)	0.1	0.2
Network grant / pass km (p)	8.6	8.0

PASSENGER TRAIN OPERATORS

EMT has continued to develop the on-board service on London trains, now offering complimentary breakfast in First Class on many peak trains, with a new all-day menu. All long-distance trains have a market-leading wi-fi router which aggregates signals from multiple networks to provide an enhanced service.

A £30m programme to refurbish all 93 trains was completed in 2012. It included the £10m refurbishment of the 25 two-car Class 158 sets, a £5m project to refurbish the 17 Class-153 and 15 Class-156 sets, while a £9m programme for the InterCity 125 High Speed Train fleet brought updated interiors, and technical modifications to increase reliability. Class 222 Meridian trains was refurbished in a £6 million project. CCTV has been installed on all trains. The Energy Saving Mode on Meridian trains allows some engines to be turned off when trains are sitting in stations, resulting in reduced noise and emissions.

Fleet delay minutes have reduced by nearly 20% year on year. For the Class 222 fleet, miles covered between each technical incident increased by almost 90%.

In partnership with Network Rail, EMT worked on a £70m line speed improvement scheme on the Midland main line to enable trains to run at up to 125mph on some sections, with almost 160 miles of track upgraded. From December 2013 the average journey between Sheffield and London was reduced by 7 minutes and between Nottingham and London by 5 minutes. Electrification and further improvements are planned.

The busy Liverpool-Norwich route saw a significant increase in capacity from December 2011 with the transfer of four additional diesel multiple-units from Northern Rail, funded by the DfT under its HLOS programme.

EMT's 11 HSTs are formed from a pool of 26 power cars with eight coaches per train. The Class 222 Meridian fleet was reorganised in 2008 to form six 7-car and seventeen 5-car sets, and four additional 4-car Class 222s were transferred from Hull Trains.

EMT was named Passenger Operator of the Year at the 2014 National Rail Awards and topped the rail league table in a national customer survey carried out by the Institute of Customer Service.

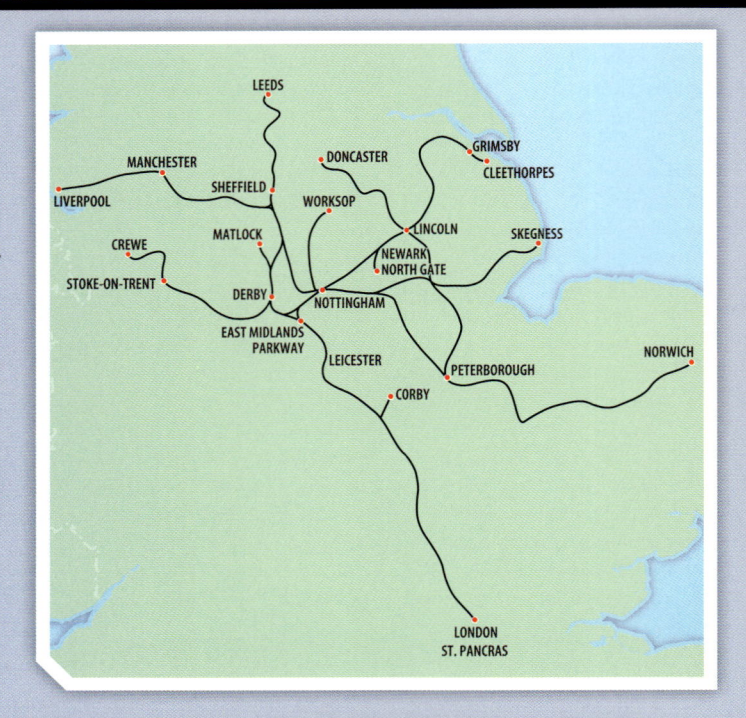

SENIOR PERSONNEL
EAST MIDLANDS TRAINS

MANAGING DIRECTOR David Horne (in photo)
CUSTOMER SERVICE & COMMERCIAL DIRECTOR Neil Micklethwaite
SAFETY & OPERATIONS DIRECTOR Ian Smith
FLEET DIRECTOR Tim Sayer
FINANCE DIRECTOR Tim Gledhill
HR DIRECTOR Clare Burles

East Midlands Trains' No 158865 heads a Norwich-Liverpool service at Humphrey Park, west of Manchester. **TONY MILES**

IN ASSOCIATION WITH **ESG** Designed to deliver

Virgin Trains
NEW DIRECT AWARD UNTIL MARCH 2017

The Virgin Trains West Coast intercity franchise is run by Virgin Rail Group a joint venture between Virgin Group (51%) and Stagecoach Group (49%). Main routes are from London Euston to Glasgow, Liverpool, Manchester and Birmingham. After a difficult period following the collapse of Railtrack, with a reduced scope for the West Coast Route Modernisation project, the original franchise terms were replaced by an interim agreement in 2002 and then by a new deal, agreed with the Department for Transport (DfT) in December 2006.

This arrangement was extended from March 2012 to December 2012 as the DfT revisited terms for a new franchising competition. Then a 'pause' was announced in October 2012 after the West Coast franchising process was challenged and cancelled. Virgin was awarded an interim extension, initially earning a fee equivalent to 1% of revenue, with DfT taking revenue and cost risk, but a new Direct Award franchise took effect from 22 June 2014. It will run until 31 March 2017: then the next competed franchise is expected to start.

Virgin Trains will pay a guaranteed premium of £430m (about £155.3m a year) under the new contract, if the economy performs as expected. If returns exceed expectations, government will take an increasing share. Virgin has committed to convert Coach G on all 21 nine-car Pendolinos from First to Standard Class by September 2015. All trains are to be equipped with superfast wi-fi, which Network Rail intends to support with trackside infrastructure the first major UK intercity rail deployment of 4G technology, enabling Virgin to provide free wi-fi.

The deal also includes more than £20m on modernising stations; an upgraded website; more staff on stations; increased emphasis on apprenticeships and traineeships; a pledge to have 10% more small and medium enterprises in the supply base; a commitment to make station and training centre facilities available for community use; plus a range of environmental commitments.

The 'VHF' (Virgin High Frequency) timetable, introduced in 2008 after the West Coast Route Modernisation, sees nine Virgin trains departing from London every hour in the off-peak periods, and 11 in the peak. Virgin also runs the hourly Birmingham-Scotland service and London-Holyhead and Wrexham trains.

After a lengthy submissions process, the company was given clearance to start direct trains between London and Shrewsbury and Blackpool from December 2014, using existing train paths south of Preston or the West Midlands.

Demand projections led the DfT to sanction capacity increases in 2008, when train lessor Angel Trains signed contracts with Alstom for four new 11-car Pendolinos and two extra cars for 31 existing trains (106 additional vehicles in all), along with a 10-year maintenance regime, worth a total of £1.5bn. The project was completed in December 2012.

Virgin's train fleet now comprises 35 eleven-car and 21 nine-car Pendolino electric tilting trains, and 20 five-car Class-221 diesel Super Voyager units. A supplementary loco-hauled train was withdrawn in October 2014, requiring a further increase in fleet availability.

The Pendolino fleet clocked up 150m miles in May 2014, and a month later No 390122 became the first train to pass 3m miles.

A refurbishment of the entire fleet started in 2013, including improved catering equipment in the Pendolinos.

Virgin Trains achieved an overall satisfaction rating of 90% in the Spring 2014 National Passenger Survey the average for the long distance sector was 86%.

Class 221 Super Voyager No 221107 'Sir Martin Frobisher' hurries north between South Kenton and Kenton on a wet 9 May 2014, forming the 11.10 Virgin Trains service from Euston to Chester. **BRIAN MORRISON**

SENIOR PERSONNEL
VIRGIN TRAINS

LEAD EXECUTIVE Phil Whittingham (in photo)
EXECUTIVE DIRECTOR, OPERATIONS AND PROJECTS Phil Bearpark
PROJECT DIRECTOR Samantha Wadsworth
EXECUTIVE DIRECTOR, CUSTOMER EXPERIENCE Steve Tennant
EXECUTIVE DIRECTOR, COMMERCIAL Graham Leech
CUSTOMER STRATEGY DIRECTOR Bob Powell

KEY STATISTICS
VIRGIN TRAINS

	2012-13	2013-14
Punctuality (0-10min)	83.6%	85.8%
Passenger journeys (millions)	30.4	31.9
Passenger km (millions)	5,958.4	6,215.4
Timetabled train km (millions)	35.8	35.8
Route km operated	1,190.9	1,190.9
Number of stations operated	17	17
Number of employees	2,914	2,999
Subsidy per passenger km (p)	-1.6	-1.6
Network grant / pass km (p)	5.2	4.5

HITACHI Inspire the Next

95

PASSENGER TRAIN OPERATORS

c2c
15-YEAR FRANCHISE UNTIL NOVEMBER 2029

National Express Group has retained the 'c2c' Essex Thameside franchise, with a new 15-year term starting on 9 November 2014. c2c is to have new trains, extra services, and a Passenger Charter 'Personal Performance Promise'.

From December 2015, a new timetable is to add 20% more trains each weekday and 38% more morning-peak capacity into London Fenchurch Street. In the high peaks, all London-bound trains (morning) and trains from London (evening) will call at the key interchanges of Barking, West Ham and Limehouse, and a 'metro' service between Upminster and Fenchurch Street will run at 3min intervals.

The train fleet will be refurbished and upgraded, and 68 new carriages (17 trains) are to be introduced from 2019, increasing capacity by over 4,500 seats a day.

A quarter of weekend trains will call at Stratford, for access to Westfield shopping centre, and will run to Liverpool Street, offering new connections. By the end of the franchise, there are to be 25,000 additional seats serving London in the morning peak every week.

There will be automatic compensation for registered smartcard customers for delays over 2min. Registered customers will also receive personalised performance reports, and passengers will have the right to be sold the cheapest ticket for any c2c journey, or be compensated.

Every station will be staffed from first until last train, and CCTV will be renewed and expanded. Smart ticketing, flexible season tickets and carnets of 10 return tickets will be provided, and improvements to wi-fi, information, and stations are promised.

National Express will pay around £1.5bn to the Department for Transport (DfT) over the 15 years. Based on DfT methodology, the net present value of payments was estimated at £1.1bn. National Express is providing parent company guarantees for capital expenditure and liquidity funding. External bonds will cover 50% of liquidity funding and a £6m performance bond, together with season ticket bonding.

The c2c franchise is the only one currently held by National Express, which became responsible for it in 2000, when it took over Prism Rail after financial problems at other Prism franchises. The franchise had been awarded in May 1996 in a 15-year deal. The company adopted its name in 2002, and suggested 'c2c' could indicate 'coast to capital' or 'commitment to customers'.

Following the Department for Transport (DfT) review of rail franchising, a new short term contract was announced in May 2013. The franchise was previously extended for two years during previous reconsideration of franchising policy.

Passenger demand broke records for c2c during the London 2012 Games, with 1.96m journeys during the 17 days of the games.

c2c holds the UK record for any four-week performance period, at 98.8% by the Public Performance Measure, and also holds the record for punctuality on a moving annual average (97.5%). c2c held top position in the national table for over two and a half years to August 2014.

All maintenance and servicing on the 74-strong fleet of four-car Class 357 Electrostar electric multiple-units are performed, in partnership with manufacturer Bombardier, at East Ham depot, along with some heavy maintenance: other heavy repairs including tyre turning, bogie overhauls, corrosion repairs, and painting are carried out at Bombardier's Ilford heavy maintenance depot. Stabling also takes place at Shoeburyness. The company switched its entire fleet to regenerative braking in 2007.

c2c works in an alliance with Network Rail, building since 2012 on an established partnership, which included joint signalling and operating control based at Upminster.

Driver-only operation (DOO) is used for trains of up to 8 cars: the invitation to tender for the new franchise envisaged DOO of 12-car trains by 2024.

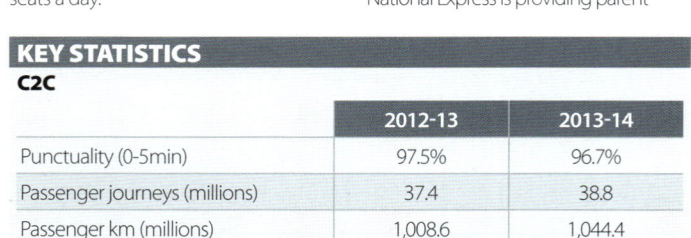

SENIOR PERSONNEL
C2C

MANAGING DIRECTOR Julian Drury (in photo)
OPERATIONS DIRECTOR Kevin Frazer
FINANCE DIRECTOR Richard Bowley
ENGINEERING DIRECTOR Ben Ackroyd

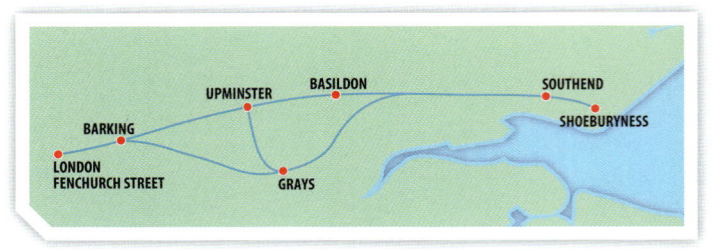

KEY STATISTICS
C2C

	2012-13	2013-14
Punctuality (0-5min)	97.5%	96.7%
Passenger journeys (millions)	37.4	38.8
Passenger km (millions)	1,008.6	1,044.4
Timetabled train km (millions)	6.5	6.5
Route km operated	115.5	115.5
Number of stations operated	25	25
Number of employees	702	762
Subsidy per passenger km (p)	-1.7	-0.4
Network grant / pass km (p)	4.4	3.9

A pair of c2c's Class 357 electric multiple-units, heading east at Barking on 28 January 2014. TONY MILES

EAST COAST

NEW FRANCHISE PLANNED FROM MARCH 2015

East Coast's trains link London with Scotland, serving York, Newcastle, Edinburgh, Aberdeen, and also link London and Leeds, with less frequent services to Inverness, Hull, Lincoln, Harrogate, Skipton, Bradford and Glasgow.

A subsidiary of government-owned holding company Directly Operated Railways, East Coast Main Line Company Limited has operated intercity services since November 2009 when National Express's East Coast franchise was terminated: this was due to pay total premium payments of £1.4bn from December 2007 to March 2015, but revenue was undermined by the economic downturn.

Turnover for the year 2013-14 amounted to £720.0m (2012/13: £693.8m). Operating expenditure was £715.3m (2012/13: £690.0m). This generated an operating profit for DOR before DfT service payments and taxation, of £225.3m (2012/13: £208.7m), and an operating profit after DfT service payments before taxation, of £8.4m (2012/13: £5.9m).

At 91%, East Coast achieved the top customer satisfaction result for a long-distance franchised rail operator, in the 2014 National Rail Passenger Survey, matching the autumn 2013 result.

In 2014, a new station at Wakefield Westgate was opened, and new design cafe-bar and new staff uniforms introduced.

The Secretary of State confirmed in March 2014 that East Coast was planned to be returned to private sector ownership in March 2015, under a new 8 year 4 week franchise with a possible one year extension. Unlike previous franchise changes, the East Coast company will be the subject of a business sale to a new private sector owner. First Group, Keolis/Eurostar and Stagecoach/Virgin were shortlisted to bid, and could consider five new routes: to Huddersfield, Middlesbrough, Scarborough, Sunderland (via Newcastle), and Harrogate (via York). York and Newcastle stations are to transfer to Network Rail management during the franchise term, while the entire train fleet is to be replaced under the InterCity Express Programme.

The current East Coast timetable provides 55 services each weekday, 19 more than prior to May 2011. Highlights are the early morning 4hr 'Flying Scotsman' from Edinburgh to London, calling only at Newcastle, and a 2hr non-stop train from Leeds to London. One new daily Lincoln-London return train was introduced, instead of the two-hourly service previously proposed - a change estimated to save £9m a year, avoiding acquisition of additional trains. Most East Coast services on the Edinburgh-Glasgow section were replaced by CrossCountry trains.

A new First-class complimentary food and drinks offer saw some £10.2m invested in depots, trains and equipment. The company went from serving typically 100,000 meals a year to over a million. The new catering offer was projected to reduce losses by the previous operator of some £20m per year.

Given the nature of the current rail infrastructure the company has said delays to customers during disruption remains its single biggest challenge, and it continued to work closely with Network Rail to facilitate integrated working where possible, to mitigate delays and to understand the root causes. High winds and overhead line incidents were the most detrimental during 2013-14.

After significant investment in depot facilities and the capabilities of the engineering team, availability and reliability of the fleet improved, with the number of cancellations reduced in 2013-14 and delays attributable to fleet performance starting to improve.

The fleet consists of 31 Class-91 electric locomotives, powering 30 rakes of Mk4 coaches to make up InterCity225 trains; and 14 diesel HST sets. It operates from three depots: Bounds Green, London; Craigentinny, Edinburgh; and Clayhills, Aberdeen.

KEY STATISTICS
EAST COAST

	2012-13	2013-14
Punctuality (0-10min)	83.9%	84.2%
Passenger journeys (millions)	19.0	19.9
Passenger km (millions)	4,934.3	5,107.8
Timetabled train km (millions)	22.0	22.0
Route km operated	1,480.6	1,480.6
Number of stations operated	12	12
Number of employees	2,988	3,031
Subsidy per passenger km (p)	-3.9	-4.0
Network grant / pass km (p)	4.1	3.7

SENIOR PERSONNEL
EAST COAST

MANAGING DIRECTOR Karen Boswell (in photo)
OPERATIONS DIRECTOR Danny Williams
FINANCE DIRECTOR Tim Kavanagh
COMMERCIAL AND CUSTOMER SERVICE DIRECTOR Peter Williams
ENGINEERING DIRECTOR Jack Commandeur
BUSINESS PLANNING DIRECTOR Phil Cameron
PROPERTY AND PROJECTS DIRECTOR Tim Hedley-Jones

PASSENGER TRAIN OPERATORS

Eurostar train at the London terminus, St Pancras International. **EUROSTAR**

EUROSTAR
INTERNATIONAL INTER-CITY TRAINS

Eurostar marked its 20th year of operation in 2014: its trains have carried more than 145m passengers on the high-speed service linking Britain with France and Belgium via the Channel Tunnel.

Eurostar was launched by the three countries' state railways, with the British interest sold to London & Continental Railways (LCR) when chosen as Channel Tunnel Rail Link developer by the government in 1996. As it prepared to sell the Channel Tunnel Rail Link (High Speed 1 HS1), the government took control of LCR in 2009, and in 2010, a new standalone joint venture company, Eurostar International (EI), replaced the unincorporated joint venture of the three national companies. The UK has a 40% shareholding, SNCF (French Railways) 55%, and SNCB (Belgian Railways) 5%. European Commission approval for EI was subject to conditions including access to stations, information systems and maintenance services for competitors.

Sale of the UK government stake was being pursued in 2014, with expressions of interest invited in October: the stake was transferred from the Department for Transport to HM Treasury in June 2014, 'to address any perceived or actual conflict of interests' in the Inter-City East Coast passenger rail franchise competition (a joint venture of Keolis and Eurostar International was shortlisted for this in early 2014).

Eurostar is to introduce a new fleet of 10 Siemens-Velaro-based 320km/hr trains (named 'e320') in 2015. A £700m rolling stock programme also includes overhaul and refurbishment of the existing 300km/hr trains, and rebranding. Nomad Digital is to supply onboard wi-fi on new and existing fleets. The same length as existing trains, the e320 will have about 150 more seats.

Eurostar links St Pancras International, Ebbsfleet International, and Ashford International in the UK with Paris, Brussels, Lille, Calais, Disneyland Resort Paris, Avignon and the French Alps. Trial direct services ran to Lyon and Provence in 2013, and Eurostar is to run a fuller South of France service from 2015. In partnership with international operator TGV Lyria, a connection is available via Lille to Geneva (from December 2014), as well to Swiss ski resorts in winter.

Eurostar in 2013 announced an agreement with Netherlands Railways to launch direct, 4hr London-Amsterdam services from December 2016, using e320 trains, which will be interoperable and compatible with the Netherlands' high-speed infrastructure. Eurostar plans two services a day, calling at Antwerp, Rotterdam, and Schiphol Airport.

A programme of station improvements saw the London St Pancras ticket office relocated and improvements to the business lounge in Brussels-Midi station in 2014, with Lille Europe and Gare du Nord, Paris also due to benefit. A new design of uniform for Eurostar staff was introduced in January 2014.

Eurostar carried more than 10m travellers in one year for the first time in 2013, with passenger volumes up 2% year-on-year. Sales revenues were up 7% to £857m, and operating profit up 4% to £54m.

In the first six months of 2014, sales revenues were up 0.5% year-on-year to £456m, and passenger numbers up 2% to 5.0m. The number of international customers rose by 7%.

Following major disruption to services during adverse winter weather in December 2009, new investment of £28m was committed, to improve resilience of trains, as well as passenger care, and communication systems inside and outside the Channel Tunnel.

The opening in 2007 of HS1, the new line from London to the Channel Tunnel, with its new London St Pancras terminal, saw journey times cut by about 20min. The London-Paris non-stop timing is now 2hr 16min. Record journey times were achieved on special runs before normal services began on HS1 in 2007: Paris-London, 2hr 3min, and Brussels-London, 1hr 43min.

New menus for Business Premier passengers have been introduced in partnership with Eurostar's new Culinary Director, Raymond Blanc. Since 2013, supermarket Waitrose has supplied refreshments to Eurostar's bar buffets, for passengers travelling in Standard class.

The flagship Business Premier class features a guaranteed boarding service; express check-in; on-board taxi bookings; and exclusive business traveller facilities at main stations. Standard Premier is a 'mid-class' designed for cost-conscious business travellers, and others who want extra space and service.

Under its Tread Lightly environmental plan, Eurostar has set targets of reducing carbon dioxide emissions per traveller journey by 35%, with a 25% cut in wider Eurostar business emissions by 2015, alongside studies of Eurostar's direct and indirect carbon footprint, and new Sustainable Travel Awards to promote local initiatives in the UK, France and Belgium.

Eurostar operates a fleet of 27 of its original 'Trans Manche Super Trains' each 400 metres long, weighing 750 tonnes and carrying 750 passengers in 18 carriages. Three more trains are used only on French domestic services (as are most of a further seven, 14-car, trains built for aborted UK regional services). ■

SENIOR PERSONNEL
EUROSTAR

CHIEF EXECUTIVE OFFICER Nicolas Petrovic (in photo)
CHAIRMAN Clare Hollingsworth
OPERATIONS DELIVERY DIRECTOR Frank Renault
COMMERCIAL DIRECTOR Nicholas Mercer
SERVICE AND PEOPLE DIRECTOR Marc Noaro
DIRECTOR OF STATIONS Mikaël Lemarchand
DIRECTOR OF REGULATORY AFFAIRS & COMPANY SECRETARY Gareth Williams
CHIEF FINANCIAL OFFICER James Cheesewright

EUROTUNNEL

CROSS-CHANNEL AND RAIL FREIGHT GROUP

To celebrate the 20th anniversary of the opening of the Channel Tunnel and the launch of international high-speed trains, HM The Queen unveiled a plaque at London St Pancras International station on 5 June 2014. Since 1994, 65 million vehicles and 330m people had travelled through the Tunnel.

The Channel Tunnel with twin railway tunnels and a service tunnel is operated by Eurotunnel under a 100-year concession signed in 1986 with the French and British governments. Terminals at Folkestone and Coquelles provide car, coach and lorry access to shuttle trains. International passenger and freight trains also run through the Tunnel.

Eurotunnel's international rail freight subsidiary, Europorte, includes operations in France and the British operator GB Railfreight.

Tests with new-generation Siemens Vectron and Alstom Prima II locomotives were conducted in 2012 and 2013 to check compatibility with Tunnel systems. Eurotunnel is pursuing application of European Interoperability Specifications, one aim being that rail freight trains can run in the Tunnel without the specialised Class 92 locos.

16 Class-92 electric locomotives were bought from Europorte by GB Railfreight in February 2014. They are equipped for North of London, Tunnel and North of France 25kV 50Hz pantograph supply; and for the UK 750V-DC third-rail network. Europorte has also encouraged the idea of a piggyback rail network to carry lorry trailers across Europe and into Britain.

Eurotunnel owns three ferries previously used by Sea France, purchased in 2012 for Euro 65m, with financial support from French local authorities, and leased to independent operator MyFerryLink. The UK Competition Commission in September 2014 confirmed its decision to prohibit their operation: an appeal was scheduled for late 2014.

The basis of Channel Tunnel track access charges was challenged by the European Commission in 2013: in April 2014, this was dropped after the extension of the ETICA programme (Eurotunnel Incentive for Capacity Additions) to support new rail freight services, plus reduction of some off-peak tariffs for rail freight.

The Eurotunnel group's consolidated revenues in 2013 exceeded one billion Euros for the first time, increasing by 12% compared to 2012, to Euro 1,092m. Excluding the impact of insurance indemnities in 2012, the operating profit increased by Euro 31m to Euro 285m.

The number of through rail freight trains increased by 10% in 2013, mainly attributed to an increase in steel transport, upturn in certain intermodal traffic and, at the end of the year, the new services generated by ETICA.

For the first half of 2014, revenue from Eurostar high-speed trains and rail freight trains increased by 3% to Euro 149m. The number of rail freight trains increased by 15%.

A 2011 European Railway Agency report found passenger trains with distributed traction (rather than power cars at train ends) could be permitted in the Tunnel, as required by Eurostar and Deutsche Bahn plans for new international passenger services. In June 2013, the UK/France Intergovernmental Commission (the supervisory authority for safety and regulation) granted Deutsche Bahn a certificate to operate passenger services through the Tunnel, though (in late 2014) there was no target date.

Four SAFE fire-fighting points, installed in the tunnels in 2011, are designed to suppress fires on lorry shuttles, and hot-spot detectors are used on lorries.

Eurotunnel has nine passenger shuttles for cars and coaches (one was restored in 2012 after being out of use), and 15 lorry shuttles. Each 800-metre long shuttle has two locomotives.

Shuttle locos have three bogies, each with two motorised axles for good wheel/rail adhesion. There are 45 locos of 7MW rating, many uprated from 5.7MW, with 13 remaining at 5.7MW. There are also seven Krupp/MaK diesel auxiliary locos. Eurotunnel increased the top speed of its shuttles from 140km/h to 160km/h in 2012.

Work began in 2014 on increasing the capacity of terminals to offer up to eight departures an hour for truck shuttles, rather than six. Eurotunnel also plans to acquire three new truck shuttles, for which aerodynamic studies have been carried out.

A 1,000MW electrical interconnector between Great Britain and France is under development by ElecLink, a Eurotunnel joint venture with STAR Capital.

Mobile phone services were provided inside the North running tunnel (usual direction UK to France) in 2014 with the help of three UK telecom operators and equipment supplier Alcatel-Lucent. The South tunnel was equipped in 2012 by French operators.

SENIOR PERSONNEL
EUROTUNNEL

CHAIRMAN AND CHIEF EXECUTIVE Jacques Gounon (in photo)
DEPUTY CHIEF EXECUTIVE Emmanuel Moulin
CHIEF OPERATING OFFICER, CHANNEL TUNNEL Michel Boudoussier
COMMERCIAL DIRECTOR Jo Willacy
BUSINESS SERVICES DIRECTOR Patrick Etienne
CHIEF OPERATING OFFICER, EUROPORTE Pascal Sainson

Eurotunnel 7kW Shuttle locomotive No 9802 at Folkestone. **EUROTUNNEL**

PASSENGER TRAIN OPERATORS

Heathrow Express's No 332002 awaits departure from London Paddington on 19 February 2014. **PAUL BIGLAND**

Heathrow Express

FAST AIR-RAIL LINK

A fast and frequent service between Heathrow and London Paddington, Heathrow Express trains depart every 15min each way, for most of the day, taking just 15min to/from Terminals 1-3.

Heathrow Express is a private train operating company and subsidiary of the airport owner: its infrastructure within the airport was built as part of a long-term strategy to increase public transport use for airport access.

During 2013 the Heathrow Express service carried a total of 5.84 million passengers, and the stopping service Heathrow Connect carried 0.5m passengers, with a market share of 11.1%. Combined passenger numbers increased by 5.0%, from 6.04m in 2012 to 6.35m in 2013.

Trains reach the airport on a dedicated line, tunnelling from near Hayes & Harlington on the Great Western main line, for about 3.5km to Heathrow Terminals 1-3 and about 6.5km to Terminal 4 (both opened in 1998). A 1.8km extension to Terminal 5 opened in 2008.

Terminal 5 station has two platform spaces for western rail links: a proposed link via Staines was shelved in 2011, but a new study of southern rail access was begun by the Department for Transport in 2014. Plans for a link towards Reading via the Great Western main line are being taken forward for possible completion in 2021.

Terminals 1-3 and 5 are served direct by Heathrow Express. A regular shuttle runs between Terminal 4 and Terminals 1-3. The Class 332 electric trains are owned (under a leaseback arrangement) by Heathrow, and were built by Siemens in partnership with CAF of Spain.

Heathrow Express launched new branding and a train refurbishment programme in 2012, a £16m project. The major refurbishment, with input from Siemens and Interfleet Technology, was completed in 2013. Designs by the Tangerine agency aim to create an airliner ambience. Internet access is available throughout the journey. Heathrow Express was the first UK train company to launch an app which allows users to buy a ticket and receive it on a phone.

Pre-purchased fares (late 2014) for Express Class are £21 single, £34 return (£29/£52 First Class). Tickets can be purchased on-board trains, with an extra charge in Express Class. Promotional fares for two or more passengers travelling together, or adults with children, were introduced in 2012, and new Advance purchase fares were announced in late 2014.

Since April 2013, an online partnership with Aer Lingus has allowed customers to book train travel with flights receiving both Heathrow Express and airline e-tickets. From January 2014, travellers from some First Great Western stations could arrange flights and rail fares in one booking, in a partnership with Singapore Airlines and Heathrow Express.

Heathrow Connect was introduced in 2005, representing a £35m investment by Heathrow, in partnership with FirstGroup, aimed at providing access to the airport for London and Thames Valley residents and airport workers. Trains run generally half-hourly between Paddington and Terminals 1-3 (32min journey), calling at five stations. Fares are aligned with price-sensitive and local markets: a London-Heathrow single (late 2014) is £9.90. Trains and on-board staff are supplied by Heathrow Express, and between Paddington and Hayes & Harlington, operation is by First Great Western. Between Hayes & Harlington and Airport Junction, open-access rights apply. Heathrow Connect uses five 5-car Class 360/2 trains built by Siemens.

The 14 Class-332 Heathrow Express trains generally run in pairs, making up eight or nine-car trains. (Five additional carriages, valued at £6m, increased five trains to five-car length.) Siemens carries out train maintenance, with reliability standards specified in the contract. The purpose-built depot is at Old Oak Common, near Paddington.

In March 2014, Heathrow Express proposed efficiencies to help cut operating costs by nearly £6m by 2019, with a new a 'customer host' role.

A separate Heathrow rail infrastructure management is to be set up when Crossrail replaces Heathrow Connect services, with access charges, set by the Office of Rail Regulation, paid to it by Heathrow Express, and by TfL for Crossrail which will run four trains an hour to Terminal 4.

In July 2014, Heathrow Express created a platform office, manned by senior managers at Heathrow Terminal 5 from 9am to 5pm Monday to Friday, aiming to listen and talk to customers and frontline employees.

In 2013, according to the airport company's accounts, rail income increased by 6.9% compared with 2012 to £116m. The 2012 income figure increased by 4.4% compared with 2011.

Heathrow Express Public Performance Measure punctuality (moving annual average) for 2013/14 was 93.8%. Heathrow Express has 435 employees. It achieved an overall satisfaction rating of 94% in the spring 2014 National Rail Passenger Survey.

SENIOR PERSONNEL
HEATHROW EXPRESS

MANAGING DIRECTOR Keith Greenfield (in photo)
OPERATIONS DIRECTOR Keith Harding
COMMERCIAL DIRECTOR Fraser Brown
ENGINEERING MANAGER Mark Chestney

HITACHI Inspire the Next

FREIGHT AND HAULAGE

IN ASSOCIATION WITH

FINNING

FREIGHT AND HAULAGE

RAILFREIGHT LOOKS TO THE FUTURE

THE MODERN RAILWAY'S RAILFREIGHT REVIEW FINDS GROUNDS FOR OPTIMISM IN MOST SECTORS

In summer 2014 DB Schenker started using a set of coal wagons on aggregates traffic from the Mendips to London. An interesting development for wagon buffs perhaps, but, from a strategic business perspective - so what? The answer is that this switch of assets is an interesting metaphor for the changing face of railfreight in the UK.

Coal traffic was sharply down (30%) in Quarter 1 of 2014-15, not only on the previous quarter – which could have been seasonal variation – but on the comparable quarter in 2013-14. Aggregates traffic, by contrast, produced its best ever result, and was booming to the point of wagon shortage, hence the use of otherwise idle coal wagons, complications with different discharge equipment and wagon/train length notwithstanding.

Nor is this just a 'coal versus construction' issue – all non-coal commodities other than petroleum (which was marginally down) grew: non-coal business was up 4.5% on the previous quarter and 7% up on the same period a year earlier, well above the level of growth in the economy at large. Yet, because of the big fall in coal, railfreight overall was down 2-3%, and therein lies the changing nature of the railfreight business – will other traffics grow fast enough to offset the decline in coal?

Before we look at these other traffics, the future of coal requires analysis - even at the reduced levels seen in Q1 2014-15, coal remains the biggest single business sector at just under 30% of the total (although domestic intermodal is now only just behind at 29%). The coal business is, of course, almost entirely dependent on electricity generation – tonnages to the steel and cement industries are small by comparison. So why has the coal burn dropped so sharply?

COAL REBOUND?

2014 has seen power station closures (at Didcot and Cockenzie) as government policy seeks to reduce the amount of coal used. There have also been problems at some of the remaining coal stations, with Ferrybridge suffering a serious fire which took out a significant slice of capacity. More positively, Drax is burning an increasing proportion of biomass in favour of coal, but this is recorded as 'Other' freight rather than coal. Finally, and perhaps most significantly, the weather was unusually mild in winter 2013-14, depressing demand for electricity and leaving stocks at a relatively high level going into spring and summer.

The key question is will demand for coal rebound? A number of factors suggest that it will. Firstly, and most importantly, coal prices on the world market have been low – the surge in shale gas and oil production in the USA has driven energy prices down, and created a surplus of coal for export at competitive prices. In Europe, conversely, gas seemed likely to be scarcer, due to the situation in Ukraine and Russia's use of gas exports as a negotiating tool. Closer to home, the ageing nuclear stations (notably Heysham and Hartlepool) continued to suffer from technical problems, and the gas stations, as well as burning an expensive fuel, also encountered problems – Didcot B lost half its capacity due to a fire in autumn 2014. Despite substantial subsidy and much construction activity, renewable sources such as wind

Colas Rail Freight's Class 56 No 56302 emerges from Kennaway Tunnel, Dawlish with the 09.55 Teigngrace (near Newton Abbot) to Chirk loaded timber on 24 April 2014. **STEWART ARMSTRONG**

and solar, at around 6%, remain minor contributors to total electricity production.

Much as government policy – and perhaps public sentiment – has remained in favour of decarbonising electricity generation, the UK's capacity reserve to meet peak winter demand is becoming perilously thin (barely 4% in winter 2014/5), in spite of attempts to secure standby gas capacity and additional volumes through the interconnector from the continent (at ruinously high prices). The crunch point may be getting very close and reconsideration of the optimum energy mix could well be a consequence.

It may only take a few instances of the lights going off, or industry suffering power rationing, to produce a very vocal challenge to current energy policy – an acid test, if ever there was one, of how 'brave' ministers would be, especially in the crucial months leading up to a general election. What are the odds on carbon reduction targets being pushed back and, in the interim, conversion of some large stations (such as Eggborough) to burn biomass, on which the government have blown hot and cold over the past year. A rational investor (or freight operator) would, no doubt, prefer rather more certainty when committing resources for the months and years ahead.

COAL PORT

So much for the macro level. Down at the coal face (a pun that, sadly, will soon lose its original meaning), the UK mining industry is having a torrid time, with reduced world prices putting unsustainable pressures on the profitability of producers. Scottish Coal went into administration and, in the face of big losses, UK Coal has announced the closure of its remaining pits (Thoresby and Kellingley), leaving Hatfield near Doncaster as the country's only deep mine, and even this has a large question mark over it. Open cast operations continue in Scotland (Hargreaves having taken over some of Scottish Coal's assets), Wales and North East England, but the proportion of imports grows ever higher.

Immingham remains the pre-eminent coal port, followed by Hunterston, the North East ports of Tyne Dock, Redcar and Blyth, plus Liverpool, Hull and Portbury. Overall, DB Schenker (DBS), Freightliner Heavy Haul (FHH) and GB Railfreight (GBRf) share most of the coal business, with Colas keeping a loco and one set of wagons occupied on coal. Inevitably, the big two – DBS and FHH – had significant numbers of wagons under-occupied in mid 2014 due to the reduced volumes moving.

Biomass movements continue to increase, with Immingham's import facility being commissioned in mid 2014. Drax, with three generating units now converted, receives biomass from Tyne Dock using GBRf resources and from Immingham and Hull in its own wagons hauled by DBS. Ironbridge (which is set for closure in 2015) also burns biomass, mostly imported via Liverpool and hauled by GBRf in a combination of its covered hoppers and 20ft containers on flat wagons.

STEEL

Britain's other traditional industry – steel – whilst recovering well in the short term, has been facing strategic uncertainty on the East Coast. Tata Steel sold the Lackenby plant to SSI, a Thai steelmaker, in 2011 and the company had produced over 5m tonnes of slab by early 2014. However, although it returned a monthly profit for the first time in June, an audit report in autumn 2014 cast serious doubt on the plant's viability and there were concerns about its future. GBRf provides internal shunting within the plant and to Tees Dock, from where virtually all the slab is exported, and there are inbound flows of limestone from Rylstone and Shap (DBS) and dolomite from Thrislington (FHH).

Even more worryingly, Tata announced in October 2014 that it planned to sell the whole of its Long Products business to Klesch Group, a Swiss steel trading company. This involves the integrated works at Scunthorpe, sections mills at Redcar and Skinningrove on Teesside, plate mills at Dalzell and Clydebridge in Scotland, plus other plants in the UK and Continental Europe, notably the rail mill at Hayange in north eastern France. It also includes Immingham Bulk Terminal, which imports iron and coal for Scunthorpe and the power generators. Tata said 'We have decided to concentrate our resources mainly on our strip products activities, where we have greater cross-European production and technical synergies'.

It followed that the other integrated works at Port Talbot together with its associated rolling mills and processing plants at Llanwern, Corby, Hartlepool, Trostre, Shotton and Mauberge in northern France would remain within Tata. It also appears that the Engineering Steels works in the Sheffield area and the narrow strip mill at Brinsworth near Rotherham are similarly unaffected. Nevertheless, the move created major uncertainty over the East Coast and Scottish plants, not least because in the UK little was known about Klesch. It describes itself as a 'global commodities business' and has two steel production sites and a finishing plant in Northern Italy. The Chairman stated the company has 'deep experience in the long products sector... we believe there is a growing market for the first class products made by this business and we intend to capitalise on this demand'.

Encouraging words, but any rationalisation that Klesch might think necessary could have a significant impact on railfreight and especially on DBS. The last remaining iron ore flow – 4m tonnes a year from Immingham to Scunthorpe – and a parallel 1m tonnes movement of coking coal are core business, as are the flows of semi-finished bloom and billet from Scunthorpe to Teesside, Scotland and France, the latter being the largest flow through the Channel Tunnel.

Away from the heady world of Mergers and Acquisitions, the railfreight metals business is doing reasonably well as the economy recovers. With more cars being sold and buildings constructed, carryings have risen for each of the last four quarters and have been 5-10% higher than the comparative period a year earlier. The flow of automotive coil from South Wales to Nissan in Sunderland is increasing, and Dawsons are investing in additional high quality warehousing at Middlesbrough to handle the business. A similar investment by Maritime Transport at Tilbury has seen a new route to the Continent emerging, for both tinplate from Trostre and coil from Port Talbot/Llanwern. DBS operate the former and share the latter with Colas, the combined flow amounting to an almost daily train.

Aluminium is not a commodity that has featured large in UK railfreight in recent years, but an encouraging development in 2014 saw the introduction of a two-way flow for Novelis from Neuss in Germany, via the Channel Tunnel, to Runcorn. DBS moves three trains a week of high capacity ferry vans conveying coil from Germany to the UK and returning with slab produced from recycled cans at a facility in Warrington.

CONSTRUCTION

The railfreight metals and construction businesses were neck and neck through the 1990s but, with long term trends of contraction in the UK

Freightliner's Class 66 No 66541 approaches Eastleigh with the 12.54 Southampton to Manchester Trafford Park container train on 28 July 2014, with work in progress on a new loop. **STEWART ARMSTRONG**

FREIGHT AND HAULAGE

A substantial part of the freight operating companies' business is haulage of infrastructure materials and equipment for Network Rail. DB Schenker Rail UK is one of Network Rail's Top 20 suppliers by value (£100m in 2013/14): its Class 66 locomotive No 66015 heads a ballast train at Watford Junction on 3 May 2014. **NETWORK RAIL**

steel industry and growth in the rail movement of aggregates, the latter is now twice as large as the former. Construction had its highest ever quarter in Q1 2014/15 (9% up on the comparable quarter a year earlier), taking it to over 17% of total railfreight. While the movement of Crossrail spoil from Paddington to Northfleet would have contributed to this result, much of it was due to intensification of baseload business from quarries and wharves to established terminals – excellent news for asset utilisation in both the aggregates industry and the freight operating companies (FOCs). One notable trend is the growing tonnage of sand and gravel moving within the Southeast from sources such as Marks Tey, Dagenham, Cliffe and Angerstein to a wide range of terminals around London, most of which also receive trains of limestone from the Mendips. DBS has been successful in retaining the lion's share of the aggregates business, although FHH and GBRf have a presence and FHH are strong in cement.

One new flow of interest is gypsum from West Burton to Portbury for the Siniat (formerly Lafarge) plasterboard factory, replacing imported material. In contrast to the movements for British Gypsum, which are containerised, the Siniat flow employs open box wagons. Worth noting, en passant, that sand for glass manufacture from Middleton Towers (King's Lynn) to Ince similarly uses open box wagons in contrast to the covered hoppers required on the established flows to Yorkshire. Clearly, in both cases, keeping the product dry in transit is not the imperative it once was.

Whereas construction is seeing additional volume to established terminals, petroleum is gradually diminishing. Consumption of petroleum products is declining and most UK refineries are old. Grangemouth only just survived a long running labour dispute and Robeston (Milford Haven) is set to become only a distribution/storage facility. Only the flows from Immingham seem assured in the long term. Robeston's flows to Westerleigh (Bristol) and Theale could potentially be sourced from the Humber instead.

BETTER OFFER

Whilst not one of the larger commodity sectors, the 'Other' category is showing spectacular growth and in Q1 was 21% up on the previous year. Three products dominate this grouping, all of which are seeing increased use of rail – biomass, automotive, timber. The substitution of biomass for coal, as described earlier, certainly accounts for a lot of the growth, but automotive is growing too. The UK car industry is resurgent and production is close to 2m cars a year, last seen in the 1980s, when Ford and British Leyland were churning out vehicles of varying quality, and most rail movements were British built cars for the domestic market. Now, most rail hauls are for export, through Southampton and Purfleet, although there are growing movements of imported vehicles from Dagenham, Portbury and Southampton to the Northwest of England, Yorkshire and Scotland.

Channel Tunnel railfreight is similarly small but shows even more impressive growth. Up 15% on the previous quarter and fully 36% on the same quarter a year earlier, it is now back to levels last seen in the early 2000s. Steel and aluminium are the major growth commodities, but there are encouraging signs that non-bulk freight is starting to return to the route. Various factors lie behind this: Eurotunnel, in the face of increasing EU interest in its charges, has reduced its prices significantly for freight trains moving in off-peak periods and, given the proportion of total costs accounted for by the Tunnel toll, this has made through rail more competitive. In addition, both DBS and Eurotunnel Group's GBRf can now provide rail haulage on both sides of the Channel and thereby assemble a better offer to the client – flows are no longer at the mercy of SNCF operating performance and labour relations.

With a more robust product, albeit not yet where it needs to be in terms of punctuality, services such DBS's Wroclaw to Barking train are of interest to manufacturers and retailers who are seeking an alternative to long distance road haulage. In November 2014, a flow of products for Procter & Gamble began between Dourges (near Lille) and Barking, with John G Russell (for customers 2XL and Novatrans) contracting Europorte to run five Cross-Channel intermodal trains/week. That such a blue-chip client is using rail via the Channel Tunnel for a key supply chain movement can only be regarded as immensely encouraging, particularly since the journey is relatively short and not a long haul from Italy, Spain or Poland.

INTERMODAL

All of which brings us neatly to domestic intermodal. After spectacular growth (close to doubling) in the 10 years to 2012, as Deep Sea imports roared ahead and the supermarkets, notably Tesco, started to use rail on a regular and sustained basis, the last two years have seen volumes stagnate. It was with some relief, therefore, that Q1 2014/15 witnessed a resumption of growth – up 6% on the previous quarter and 3.5% on Q1 2013/14. With no major advances in domestic distribution, growth seems to have come from Deep Sea. Additional services are running from Felixstowe (now up to 30 trains a day) and from London Gateway, although build up of volumes at the new port has been slower than the promoters had hoped and most major lines had remained at Felixstowe or Southampton.

Investment in new wagons, locos and infrastructure is paying off and much longer trains are now commonplace from all three ports, providing extra capacity, reducing the unit cost of movement and thus making rail more competitive. The timing is excellent since, with the introduction in September 2014 of the HGV Driver's Certificate of Professional Competence, a shortage of road haulage in the container market emerged, which can only be good news for railfreight. With consolidation amongst road container hauliers (Maritime Transport acquired Roadways in mid 2014), it may not be too long before we see some of the bigger road operators chartering trains in their own right, particularly where they own and operate rail container terminals themselves.

STRIKING BACK

Further cause for optimism exists with domestic UK distribution. One of the reasons frequently mentioned by logisticians over the last few years for not getting into rail was the introduction of double deck trailers for road trunking, which significantly increased payload and productivity. Now, railfreight is striking back – WH Malcolm have developed a 50ft swap body which gives a 10% or more payload increase compared to the standard 45ft unit. The new equipment is going into service on Malcolm's Anglo Scottish trains to/from Daventry, the haulage of which switched from Direct Rail Services (DRS) to DBS in 2014. As a result, Class 92 electrics are now used in lieu of Class 66 diesels – giving a further improvement in productivity (extra haulage capability), performance (much faster hill climbing on Shap and Beattock) and emissions. The HGV driver issue mentioned above will also impact on long distance domestic haulage, further strengthening rail's position. Intermodal volumes in forthcoming quarters will be awaited with much interest.

With the introduction of Freightliner's Class 70 and DRS's Class 68, together with DBS and GBRf making better use of the Class 92, the traction capabilities of the FOCs are improving markedly, and this will take a further step with DRS's Class 88s entering service in 2015. Their 'last mile' capability, via the diesel power unit, will give useful flexibility, albeit this comes at a price – the cost is rumoured to be approaching £4m per loco. Others may well find that the 'last mile' is better covered by a low-cost rail subcontractor – these have existed on the continent for some years and the first UK example emerged in 2014 when Victa Railfreight applied for a licence to provide a 'last mile' service, initially in the Barking/Dagenham area, but with the potential to go nationwide. The scope to use expensive main line locos and drivers more productively and leave local shunting and tripping to a lower cost operator will probably not be lost FOC MDs.

INFRASTRUCTURE BOOST

Finally, to infrastructure, where we see visible progress almost everywhere we look. Reading is moving ahead in leaps and bounds and will considerably ease the path of Southampton intermodal and Mendip stone trains. The Bacon Factory curve at Ipswich is already demonstrating its value and the remodelling of Ipswich yard was completed in summer 2014, albeit with some commissioning problems. Further north, Doncaster North Chord is in use and work is about to start on grade separation at Norton Bridge. Less dramatic, but equally important, are new loops at Eastleigh (commissioned in October 2014), Oxford North and Sundon (north of Luton), the latter adding capacity for stone trains from Leicestershire to London.

Yet there remain some issues – grade separation at Werrington (north of Peterborough) will be essential if the considerable expenditure on improving the GN/GE Joint Line is to be exploited, Basingstoke is a bottleneck for Southampton traffic and Oxford will need sorting out prior to the East-West route opening towards the end of the decade.

At least there is some clarity on Felixstowe. The branch is to be partially redoubled in the next few years, but it would surely be better to do the job properly now rather than go for a scheme which caters for the next 5-10 years of growth, but will have to be unpicked in the 2020s to provide for long term needs. Further inland, having achieved W10 (9ft 6in high container) gauge clearance and some additional capacity on Felixstowe-Nuneaton, the next step must be to tackle the Syston-Leicester-Wigston corridor (in conjunction with Midland main line electrification), very likely with additional freight lines and grade separation at Wigston – hopefully with Midland main line fast passenger trains flying over long and heavy freights routed to/from the West Coast main line at Nuneaton.

Notwithstanding improvements through Leicester, a new W10 route from Felixstowe is set to open in 2016/17, heading north from Syston through Loughborough, then west through Castle Donnington and Uttoxeter to reach the West Coast main line at Stoke on Trent and thence on already gauge-cleared and electrified lines to Manchester and Crewe.

Ah, electrification – at least one FOC MD believes, with some justification, that much the best freight electrification scheme would be Felixstowe-Nuneaton. Given the growth predicted from Felixstowe and the need to avoid cross-London lines, with their ever more frequent 'Boris Johnson Metro' services, there is much to be said for the notion. How many devotees outside the civil service does the current Department of Transport favourite – an Electric Spine from Southampton – have? It is worth remembering that, from a historic position of dominance in deep-sea container movements by rail and, more recently, equivalence with Felixstowe, Southampton now generates only around half the number of trains that emanate each day from its East Anglian competitor.

Whatever - the fact we are debating not 'if' but 'where' shows just how far freight infrastructure investment has come in recent years. Long may it continue!

FREIGHT OPERATOR FINANCES

The freight industry's recovery from the impact of the recession came to

Steel flow - one of DB Schenker's upgraded 'Super 60s', No 60044, passes Severn Tunnel Junction with the 10.01 Round Oak to Margam working on 24 July 2014. **STEWART ARMSTRONG**

FREIGHT AND HAULAGE

Electric freight - the 11.16 Manchester Trafford Park to Felixstowe North Freightliner intermodal working (routed via London), headed by Class 90 No 90043, heads away from Trafford Park and Oxford Road station towards Manchester Piccadilly on 4 August 2014. **TONY MILES**

a halt in 2012/13, with falls of over 17% in operating and of over 21% in pre-tax profits, according to analysis undertaken by consultants TAS in Rail Industry Monitor.

Cash operating profits fell from the previous year's £63.8m to £52.7m, with margins falling from 7.2% back to 5.8%.

The combined turnover of the companies analysed was 2.3% higher at £911m, whilst the rise in operating costs was 3.9%, taking the total to £858.3m. Improved returns on pension scheme assets met that the industry recorded £0.4m worth of interest earnings, down from the previous year's £3.6m inflow. As a result, pre-tax profits were down by more than a fifth, reaching £53.1m at a margin of 5.8% (last year: £67.5m at 7.6%).

TAS also reports on market share, as measured by turnover. DB Schenker retained its majority share of the business – just: market share was 50.8% compared with 54.0% the previous year: it is interesting to reflect that this figure stood at over 80% in the late 1990s. Freightliner was next with 32.8%, up by 0.7%. The two post privatisation new entrants, Eurotunnel's GB Railfreight subsidiary and Direct Rail Services, have steadily built up their market shares over the last decade, reaching 9.9% and 6.6% respectively. Both saw further increases in their share for the second year in a row.

GB RAILFREIGHT

The former FirstGroup subsidiary, sold to Eurotunnel in 2010, improved its profits in cash terms during the year, as business expanded, but it traded at slightly lower margins. The company reported that additional contracts were won in the power generation, petroleum and steel industries, whilst activity in the infrastructure sector remained strong.

PERIOD TO:	31/12/2012	31/12/2011
	£000	£000
Turnover	90,047	73,056
Operating Costs:	84,783	68,685
Operating Profit:	5,264	4,371
Operating Margin:	5.8%	6.0%
Turnover per Employee	£211,378	£211,757
Rolling stock lease	11,433	6,702

DIRECT RAIL SERVICES

The company improved its results during the year, achieving strong revenue growth across its market sectors, and improving margins at the same time.

PERIOD TO:	31/03/2013	31/03/2012
	£000	£000
Turnover	60,014	50,243
Operating Costs:	56,271	47,560
Operating Profit:	3,743	2,683
Operating Margin:	6.2%	5.3%
Turnover per Employee	£197,414	£173,252
Rolling stock lease	5,477	5,502
Revenue Grant	805	702

DB SCHENKER

The company saw a fall in profitability during the year, as turnover fell by over 5% but the reduction was not matched by savings in operating costs. As a result the company's market share slipped once more and was in danger of falling below 50% for the first time.

PERIOD TO:	31/12/2012	31/12/2011
	£000	£000
Turnover	429,000	452,000
Operating Costs:	404,000	413,000
Operating Profit:	25,000	39,000
Operating Margin:	5.8%	8.6%
Turnover per Employee	£160,734	£164,723

FREIGHTLINER

The intermodal company's performance deteriorated slightly during the year, as income grew roughly in line with inflation whilst operating costs rose at a faster rate. The directors report some increase in volumes of containers in 2013, which should enable improvements in performance in 2013/14.

PERIOD TO:	30/03/2013	31/03/2012
	£000	£000
Turnover	181,091	177,503
Operating Costs:	173,264	168,521
Operating Profit:	7,827	8,982
Operating Margin:	4.3%	5.1%
Turnover per Employee	£159,692	£158,626

DB SCHENKER INTERNATIONAL

International freight revenue grew strongly during the year, enabling a significant improvement in its results. Though the business remained in the red, losses were halved and are reducing steadily.

PERIOD TO:	31/12/2012	31/12/2011
	£000	£000
Turnover	33,475	29,077
Operating Costs:	35,871	33,463
Operating Profit:	(2,396)	(4,386)
Operating Margin:	-7.2%	-15.1%
Turnover per Employee	£190,199	£143,946
Revenue Grant	73	64

FREIGHTLINER HEAVY HAUL

The company formed to specialise in and compete for bulk trainload movements achieved above-inflation revenue growth during the year. However, the growth was outstripped by rising operating costs. As a result, although operating profits rose in cash terms very slightly, the business traded at lower margins.

PERIOD TO:	30/03/2013	31/03/2012
	£000	£000
Turnover	117,350	108,241
Operating Costs:	104,068	95,050
Operating Profit:	13,282	13,191
Operating Margin:	11.3%	12.2%
Turnover per Employee	£185,680	£178,321

IN ASSOCIATION WITH **FINNING**

The Finning fluid and condition monitoring laboratory.

FLUID ANALYSIS

THE KEY TO SAFETY, RELIABILITY AND COST REDUCTION

Train operating companies (TOCs) are facing increasing scrutiny regarding the performance of both passenger and freight operations, with delays or cancellations incurring significant penalties.

For TOCs, this creates a number of challenges, not least, to ensure that all rolling stock remains fully operational in order to meet key performance obligations and reduce the impact of delays or missed services. As there is little 'redundancy' in the system, with the majority of stock required to be available at all times, TOCs must be confident in their fleet's reliability on a daily basis.

Finning UK, an expert in fluid testing and analysis, discusses the benefits of fluid and condition monitoring for the rail industry – a form of preventative maintenance that can protect availability, performance and ultimately profitability.

FROM REACTIVE TO PREDICTIVE MAINTENANCE

Fluid analysis is not a new concept. Since the introduction of diesel trains in the mid-fifties, operators have benefitted from regular oil sample checks and cooling system monitoring. However, in those early days of diesel engine technology, such analysis was typically secondary to the maintenance schedule. This reactionary approach to condition-based monitoring has now given way to proactive, predictive maintenance.

Today, train maintenance teams are demanding far more from their condition monitoring service provider. There is now a greater emphasis on trend analysis to provide understanding across fleets to highlight performance and reduce maintenance concerns. This, coupled with live data streams, is improving reliability and safety and helping to extend component life.

FLUID SAMPLING BENEFITS

An effective fluid and conditioning monitoring service will deliver the performance insight that operators need and, crucially, will provide recommendations for action that can help maintain train availability and reduce fleet running costs.

For example, there is a strong argument for changing from scheduled maintenance to condition monitoring, which can reduce operating costs by extending oil drain intervals and the associated cost of supply, disposal and labour.

In the case of the older DMU fleets, where much of the stock was originally built in the 1980s and is still in operation today, it is paramount that maintenance teams have all the information at hand to ensure their fleets are in good working order. Likewise with the new EMU and hybrid fleets, fluid analysis data provides a critical insight into performance alongside live data streams.

When operators consider fluid analysis they may think only of the lubricating oil. There are however a high proportion of engine issues that result from problems with the cooling system which, if left unchecked can cause expensive failures. This is critical to efficient performance and equipment longevity and by analysing the coolant condition, engine damage and resulting repair costs can be avoided through proactive action.

The benefits to the rail sector are clear. Today, fluid analysis is far more than a method to resolve disparate engineering issues but a powerful tool to improve reliability and availability, reduce risk and enhance operator image.

FLUID ANALYSIS EXPLAINED

Fluids are removed from the working parts of the traction system be it engine, gearbox or final drive or in the case of electric traction, the transformer and final drives. These could include oil, fuel and coolant. The extraction of the fluid is a simple process and can be carried out at the depot during routine examination.

Samples are then sent back to the laboratory where a team of specialist rail sector diagnosticians will carry out a series of tests and interpret the results.

At the Finning fluid and condition monitoring laboratory, fluid samples can be analysed and reports published within 24 hours, with the results emailed directly to the customer and posted on an online reporting system (Infotrak). The Finning diagnostician team is supported by a dedicated rail reliability engineer, to provide technical and engineering advice to the depot.

The Infotrak system provides up-to-the-minute information and historical data, allowing the customer to see at-a-glance which samples require attention. The system provides full history and can highlight trends by vehicle, component or across an entire fleet.

HITACHI Inspire the Next

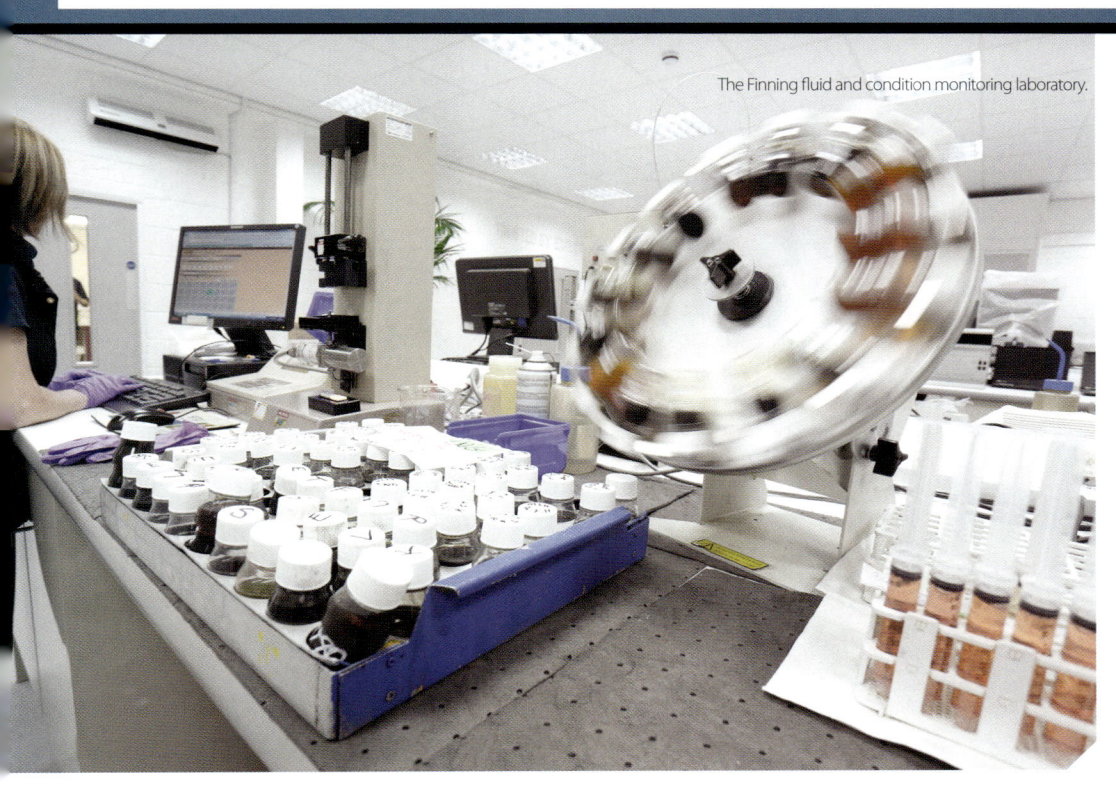

FREIGHT AND HAULAGE

One of the overhauled Class 60s – No 60019 heads north through Doncaster on 5 September 2014. **TONY MILES**

DB SCHENKER
BRITAIN'S BIGGEST

DB Schenker Rail UK Ltd is Britain's largest rail freight operator, running around 3,200 trains per week and employing some 3,400 people. It delivers services through four divisions:
- Energy, serving the electricity supply industry.
- Industrial, moving materials such as metals and petroleum products.
- Construction, conveying construction products and domestic waste.
- Network, providing rail industry, intermodal and logistics services.

The company focuses strongly on developing international logistics. A twice-weekly service between Barking and Wroclaw, Poland running over the HS1 high-speed line between London and the Channel Tunnel was launched in 2012, enabling continental gauge wagons to reach the capital. In January 2014 a service also using HS1 was introduced from Spain carrying foodstuffs in refrigerated containers and automotive components.

International traffic using classic routes includes a Padua (Italy)-Hams Hall intermodal service, with some traffic forwarded to Mossend. Steel slabs for rail manufacture are conveyed from Scunthorpe to Ebange in France, and in December 2013 a flow of outbound aluminium ingots and inbound coil was started between Ditton and Neuss in Germany. Bottled water from France is brought in to Daventry and a train of china clay slurry for paper-making runs from Antwerp to Irvine in Scotland.

August 2014 saw the commencement of a new daily Anglo-Scottish service for Malcolm Logistics between Daventry and Grangemouth. This carries 50 ft containers by rail for the first time in the UK. Four months earlier DBSR UK had recaptured the established Daventry-Mossend flow for Malcolm under a three-year contract.

DBSR UK runs trains of maritime containers from Southampton and Felixstowe to Birch Coppice in the Midlands, Doncaster, Trafford Park and Wakefield. In September 2013 it operated the first train out of the new DP World London Gateway port on the Thames Estuary. Since then some 4,000 containers have been moved by the company from and to this port, with services now connecting Daventry, Manchester, Wakefield and South Wales.

More than 700 trains per week are operated for the power generation industry. In April 2014 ScottishPower awarded DBSR UK a two and three-quarter year contract to convey up to 4 million tonnes of coal per year from Hunterston to Longannet Power Station. A recent development in the wagon fleet for this market is a high-capacity biomass vehicle converted from an HTA coal hopper by subsidiary Axion Rail.

In the Industrial sector there are flows of petroleum products from Humberside, Fawley and Grangemouth. Services are operated to support steel manufacturing, serving sites at Scunthorpe, in South Wales and on Teesside. Imported iron ore trains run between Immingham and Scunthorpe, and there is an extensive network of inter-plant services plus trains delivering finished steel products. Scrap metal is also handled. A shuttle service for Tata Steel connects IJmuiden in the Netherlands with Trostre in South Wales to convey steel coils.

Nearly 400 trains a week are run for the construction and waste industries. A contract with Mendip Rail covers operation of trains from the Mendips quarries of Aggregates Industries (Merehead) and HeidelbergCement subsidiary Hanson (Whatley), some using the shippers' own locomotives and wagons. DBSR UK has a contract with Cemex UK covering aggregates haulage, including flows from the Peak District. The Lafarge Tarmac quarry at Mountsorrel is served and sea-dredged aggregates are moved from Thames-side terminals for Brett Aggregates and Marcon. China clay, cement and domestic waste are also carried.

The automotive market generates movements of Jaguar Land Rover cars for export from Halewood and Castle Bromwich to Southampton and BMW Minis from Cowley to Southampton and Purfleet. Imported vehicles are conveyed from Dagenham and Portbury to Mossend.

The company fulfils a Ministry of Defence rail freight haulage contract, with some movements incorporating other traffic to form a wagonload network. It operates London-Warrington-Glasgow and London-Tyneside Royal Mail postal trains using Class 325 mail EMUs, and also holds the Network Rail Infrastructure Monitoring contract, operating test trains across the system.

DBSR UK is one of five rail freight companies awarded a Network Rail contract in 2014 covering National Supply Chain services and haulage of engineering trains to support works undertaken during CP5 (2014-19).

The diesel fleet includes 250 EMD-built Class 66 locomotives, although more than 70 of these are in use by Euro Cargo Rail in France and other group companies in continental Europe. DBSR UK has overhauled and refurbished 21 of its 26 active Class 60 locomotives. There are also six Class 59/2s used on Mendips aggregates traffic. The 30 Class 67 locomotives are mainly used on charter passenger services or hired to franchised TOCs. Electric traction comprises operational examples of 30 Class 92 dual-voltage machines plus 25 Class 90s. Six Class 92s have been modified to operate on HS1. ■

SENIOR PERSONNEL

CHIEF EXECUTIVE Geoff Spencer
CHIEF FINANCIAL OFFICER Andrea Rossi
HEAD OF SALES Neil McDonald
HEAD OF PRODUCTION Graham Young
HEAD OF MAINTENANCE AND INFRASTRUCTURE Andrew Byrne
HEAD OF PLANNING Nigel Jones
HEAD OF SERVICE DESIGN AND RESOURCE Chris Tingle

GB Railfreight
1,000 TRAINS PER WEEK

Part of the Eurotunnel subsidiary Europorte, GB Railfreight continues to see its business grow and by late 2014 was running up to 1,000 trains per week. Starting in 2000 with contracts for infrastructure support work for Railtrack, the company has since expanded to become a major force in both intermodal and bulk traffic markets.

GBRf is a now major operator of intermodal services for maritime containers, especially from Felixstowe, where it handles some 20% of rail traffic. Services run from the port to Doncaster, Hams Hall, Selby and Trafford Park. A key client is Mediterranean Shipping Company (UK), for which a three-year extension contract took effect in February 2014. This sees continuation of three daily container services from Felixstowe – two to Hams Hall and one to Selby, including an agreement to provide additional capacity on each train. Growing business in this sector led to GBRf signing a lease with VTG Rail UK in May 2014 for 18 Ecofret triple-platform wagons.

International traffic has been developing too. Collaboration with sister company Europorte Channel saw the introduction in 2011 of a Daventry to Novarra, Italy, intermodal service via the Channel Tunnel for container shipper DFDS. And in November 2014 GBRf ran its first train through the Channel Tunnel and over HS1 for Europorte France (EPF) on behalf of John G Russell, transporting containers five times per week from Dourges in France to Barking. Acting as a supplier to EPF, GBRf provides a hook-and-haul service using Class 92 locomotives on the Frethun to Barking HS1 exchange leg.

GBRf handles up to 30% of the coal moved by rail for power generation in Britain, operating imported flows out of the ports of Tyne, Immingham, Hull and Redcar, as well as carrying domestically mined coal from UK Coal's Thoresby and Potland Burn railheads. Cottam, Drax and West Burton are among power stations served. The company has recently invested in rolling stock for conveying biomass, moving 1.5 million tonnes annually between Liverpool and Ironbridge for E.ON and a similar volume between Tyne and Drax.

Bulk traffic flows also include petroleum products from Humberside to Cardiff, gas condensate from North Walsham to Harwich and alumina from North Blyth to Fort William. For the automotive industry GBRf runs a daily Dagenham-Garston train carrying Ford vehicles and 2014 saw trial services moving Renault cars from Southampton to Mossend.

A growing portfolio in the construction materials sector lists Aggregate Industries, British Gypsum, Lafarge Tarmac and Yeoman among the firm's clients. A contract which started in 2012 has seen more than 1 million tonnes of excavated tunnelling spoil from the Crossrail project taken from West London to Northfleet.

The company continues to run infrastructure materials trains for Network Rail and London Underground. For the latter it has an £80 million 10-year contract awarded by Metronet in 2006, including operation of a materials depot at Wellingborough. It provides haulage for deliveries of LUL's new Bombardier-built 'S' Stock trains and in 2013 signed a contract with Hitachi to facilitate commissioning and testing of Class 800/801 IEP high-speed trainsets. Other services for the rail industry include provision of traction or traincrew for rolling stock moves for TOCs and Roscos and supplying locomotives for infrastructure monitoring trains on the third rail network.

On Tees-side GBRf operates the internal rail system at Sahaviriya Steel Industries (SSI UK) Redcar plant, including the lease and maintenance of 10 Vossloh-built Class Di8 locomotives obtained from Norway.

The traction fleet has seen major recent developments. In July 2014 the company took delivery of the first tranche of an order for 21 additional EMD Class 66s, bringing the pool of these locomotives to 71. This latest batch was secured ahead of a change in EU emissions legislation taking effect in January 2015 expected to preclude further orders for this type. The company also purchased locomotive 59003, one of the five Class 59s acquired by Foster Yeoman in the 1980s, from Heavy Haul Power International in Germany. And three Class 47s have been hired from Riviera Trains for haulage of gypsum and sand traffic in Yorkshire.

In February 2014 16 Class 92 electric locomotives owned by parent company Europorte were purchased by GBRf. Five of these were operational, some others are to be returned to traffic. A programme to refurbish and upgrade 10 of the versatile Class 73 electro-diesels is being undertaken by Wabtec subsidiary Brush Traction. Work includes replacement of the original 600 hp English Electric engine with an MTU 1,500 hp unit.

SENIOR PERSONNEL
MANAGING DIRECTOR John Smith (in photo)
FINANCE DIRECTOR Karl Goulding-Davis
PRODUCTION DIRECTOR David Knowles
COMMERCIAL DIRECTOR Phil Webster
ENGINEERING AND STRATEGY DIRECTOR Jim Macfadyen

To mark the 150th anniversary of the London Underground, and a new partnership with the London Transport Museum, two GBRf locomotives with new liveries were named after Transport for London Commissioner, Sir Peter Hendy CBE (No 66718), and Harry Beck, the designer of the original Tube map (No 66721). Displaying various TfL themes, No 66718 arrives at London Victoria for the ceremony on 5 November 2013. **BRIAN MORRISON**

FREIGHT AND HAULAGE

Freightliner

Freightliner Group is owned by Bahrain-based investment firm Arcapita. It has two rail operating subsidiaries in Britain: Freightliner Ltd, serving the UK deep-sea rail-borne container market; and Freightliner Heavy Haul (FHH), specialising in bulk commodities. Freightliner Maintenance Ltd is the Group's third UK subsidiary, dedicated to traction and rolling stock maintenance and repair. Subdivisions include Logico, a division of Freightliner Ltd offering bespoke rail space to new markets.

International subsidiaries are Freightliner Australia, Freightliner Poland Ltd and European intermodal rail operator ERS Railways BV, acquired in 2013 from Maersk Line. ERS also owns 47% of German-based intermodal rail operator boxXpress. de GmbH.

FREIGHTLINER LTD

Freightliner Ltd is the UK's largest rail carrier of maritime containers, operating from the deep-sea ports of Felixstowe, London Gateway, Seaforth, Southampton and Tilbury. Services run to 14 interchanges, nine of which are owned and operated by Freightliner. It moves around 3,000 containers per day on more than 100 services, with 34 direct route offerings.

Main locations are:
- Ports: Felixstowe, Seaforth (Garston, Liverpool), Southampton, London Gateway and Tilbury.
- Inland terminals: Birmingham, Bristol, Wentloog (Cardiff), Wilton (Cleveland), Coatbridge (Glasgow), Doncaster, Leeds, Liverpool and Manchester.
- Independent terminals served include Birch Coppice (Birmingham International Freight Terminal), Daventry (DIRFT), Hams Hall (Birmingham) and Ditton (Widnes).

In late 2013 Freightliner Ltd ran its first service from DP World's new London Gateway port in the Thames Estuary.

Following recent W10 gauge enhancements from Southampton to the West Midlands and on the Felixstowe to Nuneaton (F2N) route, a further significant development to benefit container movements was commissioning in 2014 of a 1 km chord linking the East Suffolk line and the Great Eastern main line in Ipswich to avoid trains to using the F2N route having to reverse there.

Class 70s No 70017/18 approach Basingstoke with the 09.58 Wentloog to Southampton container train on 10 July 2013. **STEWART ARMSTRONG**

Freightliner has the largest intermodal contract in the UK with Maersk Line, the container arm of the Danish conglomerate A P Moller-Maersk, signing a new multi-year contract in 2011 to provide committed space for the transport of containers from Felixstowe. In the same year a second 10-year contract with OOCL was concluded.

FREIGHTLINER HEAVY HAUL

Freightliner Heavy Haul (FHH) operates around 1,200 trains per week, moving more than 20 million tonnes annually. The company's largest bulk market is coal. It serves all UK rail-connected coal-fired power stations from opencast sites and surviving collieries in Britain, and from import terminals at Ellesmere Port, Hull, Hunterston, Immingham, Liverpool and Portbury.

Aggregates sector clients include Lafarge Tarmac, Aggregate Industries and Hanson, with quarried stone and sand among products carried. Limestone is conveyed from Tunstead to several coal-fired power stations for emissions cleaning processes.

Cement from Lafarge Tarmac's Hope plant is carried to Dewsbury and Theale, and from Oxwellmains to Aberdeen, Inverness and Uddingston in Scotland, and south to Leeds and Seaham. From Tunstead FHH handles cement flows to West Thurrock and Westbury.

FHH works with Greater Manchester Waste Disposal Authority (GMWDA) and Viridor moving municipal waste from several locations to a Combined Heat and Power plant at Runcorn, following a move away from the use of landfill, though in 2014 some trains feeding this method of disposal were being operated to Oxwellmains. FHH also runs a containerised household waste service from Cricklewood in north London to Calvert.

Potash and rock salt are moved between Boulby on the Cleveland coast and Tees-side, and for steelmaker Celsa FHH transports scrap metal from Dagenham to Cardiff.

Infrastructure actvities for Network Rail include haulage of high-output ballast cleaning and track renewal systems, ballast movements and operation of the major distribution centre at Basford Hall, Crewe.

Freightliner Maintenance Ltd (FML) undertakes repair and maintenance of traction and rolling stock both for group companies and third parties. Its main site is Leeds Midland Road depot, with supplementary facilities at Crewe, Dunbar, Hope and York. There is a dedicated maintenance facility for Freightliner Ltd at Southampton.

Freightliner's UK fleet comprises 137 Class 66 and 19 Class 70 diesels, Class 86 (16) and Class 90 (10) electrics, plus shunters. The Class 70 GE PowerHaul diesel locomotives are divided between intermodal (7) and FHH (12) businesses.

The wagon fleet totals more than 3,000, of which some 1,700 are container flats. In 2014 Freightliner placed an order with VTG for 21 additional 43 twin-platform Ecofret 'Shortliner' wagons to supplement the 43 already in use. Manufactured by Greenbrier in Poland, each comprises a twin set of two 40ft deck length sections. ■

SENIOR PERSONNEL
FREIGHTLINER GROUP

CHIEF EXECUTIVE OFFICER Russell Mears (in photo)
CHIEF FINANCIAL OFFICER Darren Leigh
MD, FREIGHTLINER LTD Adam Cunliffe
MD, HEAVY HAUL Paul Smart
ENGINEERING DIRECTOR Tim Shakerley
CORPORATE DEVELOPMENT DIRECTOR Dom McKenna

Colas Rail is the first UK freight operator to adopt HaCon's train planning system, TPS. It will help Colas to respond to customer demands and plan train services using up to date infrastructure and timetable data, and benefit from automated orchestration of access requests (bids and offers) with Network Rail. A Colas Rail Class 70 locomotive is seen hauling a Network Rail infrastructure train. **HACON**

COLAS RAIL FREIGHT

Active since 2007, Colas Rail Freight is part of the Colas Group, a subsidiary of the French-based multinational Bouygues construction and services conglomerate.

Haulage activities to support Network Rail's renewals and enhancements programmes now form a key part of the company's portfolio. In 2014 Colas was awarded a £90 million contract to provide haulage for engineering trains during CP5 (2014-19), mainly for the Western and Southern regions. Since 2013 Colas had already been operating engineering materials trains for Network Rail as part of the National Supply Chain network, including the Hoo Junction-Whitemoor, Hoo Junction-Eastleigh, Eastleigh-Westbury and Westbury-Hinksey-Bescot circuits.

Other commodities carried include steel for the automotive industry. Originating at Dunkerque, France, this is shipped to Boston docks for transfer to Washwood Heath in Birmingham. There is also a flow of export steel from Llanwern to Tilbury.

Imported coal is conveyed from Avonmouth to Ratcliffe Power Station for E.ON and Colas has a contract with Air BP to move aviation fuel from the Ineos refinery at Grangemouth to Prestwick Airport and the Rolls Royce factory in Derby. Trains of timber for building materials manufacturer Kronospan are operated to Chirk from Baglan Bay in South Wales and Carlisle, supplemented by loads from Newton Abbot and Ribblehead.

The traction fleet has seen a significant recent expansion. In 2014, 10 Class-70 2,750 kW Type PH37ACmi locomotives were received from GE Transportation. The company also concluded a deal to acquire 10 surplus Class 60s from DB Schenker Rail UK including overhaul at the latter's Toton depot. By late 2014 three had entered service. These acquisitions complement five Class 66s, three Class 47s and operational members of pools of 10 Class 56s and four Class 37s.

DIRECT RAIL SERVICES

A wholly owned subsidiary of the Nuclear Decommissioning Authority (NDA), Direct Rail Services Limited (DRS) was established to provide British Nuclear Fuels Limited with a strategic rail transport service. It has since expanded into the general railfreight market. In its original role, it operates trains between 10 UK power station sites and Sellafield, Cumbria. Additional flows link Sellafield with Drigg and Barrow Dock.

Intermodal movements include trains operated for Tesco in conjunction with Stobart Rail from Daventry to Purfleet and Wentloog, plus Daventry-Coatbridge services in collaboration with logistics firm John G Russell. In Scotland DRS operates an intermodal service between Grangemouth and Aberdeen carrying mainly Asda supermarket traffic. There is also a daily train of Tesco swap-bodies between Mossend and Inverness.

Services for Network Rail include operation of autumn railhead treatment trains, winter snow clearance movements, provision of traction for infrastructure monitoring trains and haulage of National Supply Chain traffic in northern and central England.

In the passenger sector DRS supplies Belmond Ltd with locomotives for the Northern Belle luxury train, provides support for TOCs and traction for charter operators. It has a fleet of refurbished Mark 2 coaches, some of which are used for a two-year contract from June 2014 with Greater Anglia to supply locomotives and stock for Norwich area services. DRS also deploys strategically sited Class 57/3 'Thunderbird' locomotives for West Coast main line rescue services.

Operations with Vossloh-built Class 68 diesel locomotives began in 2014, initially on intermodal services in Scotland and National Supply Chain trains. Six of the initial 15 machines ordered have been sub-leased to Chiltern Railways to replace Class 67s hired from DB Schenker Rail UK. In 2014 DRS ordered 10 more Class 68s. Also on order from Vossloh are ten bi-mode Class 88 locomotives for delivery in 2015. These will be rated at 5,360 hp under a 25 kV AC supply and at 900 hp in diesel mode from a Caterpillar 12-cylinder engine.

The fleet also includes 19 Class 66s, 12 Class 57/3s and nine Class 57s. There are eight Class 47s, 35 Class 37s and eight Class 20s. Examples of some of the older types are stored or awaiting refurbishment.

SENIOR PERSONNEL
COLAS RAIL

CEO, COLAS RAIL UK
Richard Fostier
MD, COLAS RAIL SERVICES
Stephen Haynes

New Class 68 built by Vossloh for DRS. **DIRECT RAIL SERVICES**

SENIOR PERSONNEL
DIRECT RAIL SERVICES (DRS)

MANAGING DIRECTOR Neil McNicholas
DIRECTOR OF COMMERCIAL & BUSINESS DEVELOPMENT Chris Connelly
OPERATIONS AND COMPLIANCE DIRECTOR Jeffery Marshall
ENGINEERING AND PERFORMANCE DIRECTOR Tony Bush

FREIGHT AND HAULAGE

WEST COAST RAILWAY COMPANY

With its main base at Carnforth, WCR specialises in operating charter trains both on its own account and for other tour operators, using diesel and steam traction. In 1998 it was the first privately owned company to obtain an operating licence to coordinate and run its own trains.

In addition to an extensive programme of tours throughout the year, WCR runs two regular seasonal steam-hauled trains – the Fort William-Mallaig 'Jacobite' and the York-Scarborough 'Scarborough Spa Express'. Beyond the passenger sector, traction is occasionally provided for stock and plant moves.

The active diesel fleet includes three Class 33s, five Class 37s, 11 Class 47s and seven Class 57s, including four ex-Virgin Trains Class 57/3s. WCR also manages the operation of steam locomotives belonging to various owners. Its pool of coaching stock numbers more than 80 vehicles including a rake of Metro-Cammell 1960s-built Pullman carriages. A subsidiary depot and maintenance facility is located at Southall in west London.

RIVIERA TRAINS LIMITED

Active since 1996, Riviera Trains claims to be the UK's largest and only independent coaching stock provider, supplying both the charter train market and TOCs when extra short-term capacity is needed, such as during major sporting events. The fleet of around 120 coaches includes later Mk2 air-conditioned stock as well as Mk1 vehicles, meeting requirements ranging from VIP charters to enthusiast railtours.

In addition to providing coaching stock for a number of railtour clients, the company works in association with three principal charter train operators – DB Schenker Rail (UK), Direct Rail Services and GBRf.

Riviera Trains also owns five Class 47 diesel locomotives. In late 2014 three of these were on hire to GB Railfreight. Its main base is at Crewe, with some coaching stock based at Eastleigh.

DEVON AND CORNWALL RAILWAYS LIMITED

DCR is a freight operating subsidiary of British American Railway Services Limited, which was formed by US shortline railroad holding company Iowa Pacific Holdings.

Other BARS group companies include RMS Locotec Locomotive Hire, RMS Locotec Track Maintenance and RMS Locotec Rail Projects. The group also owns the Dartmoor Railway between Yeoford and Meldon Quarry in Devon and the Weardale Railway linking Bishop Auckland with Wolsingham and Eastgate. Both lines are connected to the Network Rail system.

A recent ongoing contract for DCR has been provision of traction for RailVac air-vacuum excavators used in cooperation with Bridgeway Railcare for wetbed removal during overnight possessions. The company has handled short-term flows of scrap metal to the Celsa plant in Cardiff, blending coal from opencast sites in northeast England, aggregates from the Peak District and spoil from Willesden to Calvert. It also undertakes stock moves for train operating companies and supplies locomotives on hire, as well as collaborating with other rail freight operators.

The company's traction fleet comprises six Class 56s and four Class 31s.

West Coast Railway Company runs the regular seasonal steam-hauled 'Jacobite' train between Fort William and Mallaig, seen here at Glenfinnan. **ABELLIO**

INNOVATION AND ENVIRONMENT

IN ASSOCIATION WITH

KNORR-BREMSE

INNOVATION AND ENVIRONMENT

Knorr-Bremse offers a complete braking system solution, including the unique, mechatronic EP2002 Distributed Brake Control system.

CREATIVE SOLUTIONS FROM KNORR-BREMSE

Global experience and continuous innovation combined with locally based expertise and capacity, means that Knorr-Bremse can offer customers an outstanding range of both system and service solutions.

These systems and services are delivered by over 900 employees based at four, major Knorr-Bremse Rail sites, conveniently located around the UK. From Melksham in Wiltshire OE systems and support, from Burton upon Trent in Staffordshire, HVAC systems and support, from Springburn in Glasgow and Wolverton in Milton Keynes specialist maintenance, service and modernisation is available under the RailServices banner.

Knorr-Bremse Rail UK facilities are the local source for the extensive range of products, systems and services that are available from the entire global Knorr-Bremse Rail Group.

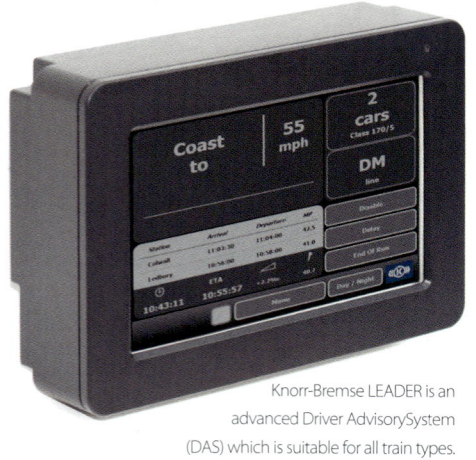

EXPERTLY INTEGRATED

Renowned throughout the rail world for its rail braking systems expertise, Knorr-Bremse offers a complete braking system solution. Covering brake control, including the unique, mechatronic EP2002 Distributed Brake Control system, air supply systems, bogie equipment, brake resistors and controllers, sanding systems and wheel slide protection systems, Knorr-Bremse engineers expertly integrate these components to provide the optimum solution for any rail vehicle.

The Knorr-Bremse Group also offers an extensive and globally proven rail portfolio for both on and off board applications. This range includes derailment detectors, driver simulators, platform screen systems, power converters, power supply, train doors (internal and external), wiper systems and level crossing and signalling systems.

However, Knorr-Bremse has always been a forward looking Group and a leader in innovation. Recently the Group has been using its technological expertise from around the world to develop systems which can support customers in keeping trains in safe, reliable and cost effective service through the entire life-cycle.

Knorr-Bremse LEADER is an advanced Driver AdvisorySystem (DAS) which is suitable for all train types.

ENERGY SAVING

Rail energy costs will continue to rise and the impact on the environment of rail operations is becoming more important. Knorr-Bremse offers a range of energy saving systems which are designed to optimise energy use and support a reduction in environmental impact.

Knorr-Bremse LEADER is such a system. LEADER is an advanced Driver Advisory System (DAS) which is suitable for all train types. Developed especially for rail routes in the UK and Ireland LEADER improves train handling and timetable adherence and delivers significant energy savings.

Further supporting a reduction in energy use is Knorr-Bremse EUROMETER. This Energy Monitoring System (EMS) empowers train operators to fully understand how energy is being used and wasted. By fully understanding this, operators are empowered to save energy, reduce operational costs and minimise environmental impact. EUROMETER is the ideal partner for LEADER. Used together they can provide an integrated system with which operators can manage their energy usage.

Knorr-Bremse COMORAN is another innovative system which delivers monitoring and diagnostic for powered and unpowered bogies and their components. Integrated into the braking system, COMORAN identifies critical and safety-relevant conditions such as damage to wheel set bearings, hot axle boxes, unstable running or derailment and allows for conditioned based maintenance work to be carried out more economically.

INCREASING TRAIN AVAILABILITY

In addition to addressing energy saving in rail Knorr-Bremse engineers and designers have also recognised that understanding the true status of a train's systems, in real time, can be invaluable for rail operators in increasing train availability. By identifying and addressing any issues before they become major problems, trains can be kept on track, operating safely and in revenue earning service.

Developed by Knorr-Bremse in the UK especially for the UK and Ireland markets, Knorr-Bremse Z300 facilitates both monitoring and control, both in real time, for example the HVAC system. Its modular design uses advanced, web-based smart technology with apps providing advanced condition based maintenance to improve the train's reliability and availability.

The latest development in this area from Knorr-Bremse is iCOM. iCOM identifies the true status of the vital systems on a train, minimising disruption and costs through *predicting* equipment failures. Detecting, diagnosing and *prioritising* equipment failures in advance, iCOM can improve both maintenance planning and scheduling. This maximises system and component life whilst increasing train availability.

HITACHI
Inspire the Next

IN ASSOCIATION WITH **KNORR-BREMSE**

NEW BOOST FOR COMMUNITY RAIL?

THE DEPARTMENT FOR TRANSPORT IS FIRMLY IN SUPPORT OF COMMUNITY RAIL WITH A PROMISE OF MORE SECURE FUNDING. BUT A WIDE RANGING NEW REPORT HAS IDENTIFIED BOTH OPPORTUNITIES AND CHALLENGES AHEAD. *MODERN RAILWAYS* COLUMNIST AND COMMUNITY RAIL PARTNERSHIP CHAIRMAN **ALAN WILLIAMS** REPORTS.

Change is afoot. Following several years of frustration and concerns about the future, especially around reduced funding, the Department for Transport has set itself firmly in support of community rail. Peter Wilkinson, Director of Rail Franchising at the Department for Transport (DfT) and now Managing Director of the Office of Rail Passenger Services, has declared that 'Community Rail Partnerships are not of marginal importance. They are providing real service and deserve to be supported.'

In the run-up to the competition for the next Northern franchise, which alone encompasses 18 separate Community Rail Partnerships (CRPs), including the latest to be designated, the Tyne Valley line from Carlisle to Newcastle, the Department has required the three short-listed bidders to engage with CRPs much more than in the past.

And speaking at the 2014 Community Rail Awards in Scarborough, Minister of State for Transport Baroness Kramer squarely addressed shortfalls in funding, one of the main issues confronting most CRPs at present. 'I don't want to see Community Rail simply surviving, I want to see it thriving. I want to ensure that there is long term funding available for partnerships so they can plan effectively for the future. So we are making sure that Community Rail is fully recognised in all future rail franchises.'

But in what seemed like a shot across the bows of some local authorities who have reduced or even withdrawn funding, while recognising that there are pressures on local authority budgets, she insisted that 'supporting Community Rail makes sound business sense, providing economic social and environmental value to their lines and communities'.

VALUE

This new enthusiasm for Community Rail is supported by a weighty new piece of research prepared for the National Rail Steering Group, a partnership of central and local government, Network Rail, the Association of Train Operating Companies and the Association of Community Rail Partnerships (ACoRP). With the perhaps more descriptive than snappy title 'The Value of Community Rail Partnerships and the Value of Community Rail Volunteers', the report finds that percentage growth in ridership on CRP-supported lines continues to march well ahead of both the national rail network overall and non-supported regional lines, with CRP lines growing by 45% over the six years 2006/07 to 2012/13 against only 23% for the regional sector overall.

Using the regional sector as a whole as a comparator for what would have happened without CRPs, the report concludes that CRPs create substantially more income than they cost to run. And it estimates that the 3,200 volunteers who give 250,000

A First TransPennine Express Class 185 diesel multiple-unit heads towards Carnforth at Arnside, on the route of the Furness line Community Rail Partnership. **PAUL BIGLAND**

INNOVATION AND ENVIRONMENT

Passengers board a train bound for Derby at Stoke-on-Trent, a line covered by the North Staffordshire Community Rail Partnership. **EAST MIDLANDS TRAINS**

The famous 'Harrington hump' in Cumbria – the station just south of Workington has the prototype raised section of platform to enable easier boarding of trains. **NETWORK RAIL**

hours per year to support community rail across the country have an annual financial value, using the national average wage rate, of £3.4 million.

The report identifies continuity of funding as a key challenge for most CRPs, a distraction now seemingly acknowledged by DfT. But there are other major concerns. More than half of the CRPs consulted reported that train capacity is limiting their efforts, with severe overcrowding on some lines which, whilst a measure of their success, is now becoming a disincentive to users. With no additional rolling stock likely to be available to most CRP supported lines in the near future, this is a problem which is likely to get worse. On some lines, the so-called 'PIXC percentage', based on the number of passengers carried in excess of capacity, is huge, often approaching and sometimes even exceeding 100% - much, much more than the oft-reported overcrowding on commuter lines leading into London. An additional 150 people standing for 90 minutes on a two-car 150-seat Northern Class 156, as for example happens routinely on the Middlesbrough-Whitby Esk Valley line in high summer, is every bit as unacceptable – and possibly dangerous – as 900 standing on a peak-hour 12-car train into Waterloo. But how often does SWT see that level of overcrowding, and for that length of time? And when the next train is more than two hours away rather than 20 minutes, being left behind waiting for the next train is not much of an option. The report identifies the East Suffolk and Heart of Wessex lines as suffering similar problems.

FARES

Another concern seemingly affecting almost all CRPs, and now exacerbated by the growing overcrowding problem, is non-payment of fares, either because of deliberate evasion or because the conductor simply cannot pass through the train. By their very nature, most CRP-supported lines serve unstaffed stations, so the majority of fares are paid to the conductor. But he or she also has to return to the end of the train at each station to open and then close the doors. Using the Esk Valley line again as an example, there are 16 intermediate unstaffed stations on the 90 minute Middlesbrough-Whitby journey, bringing an interruption to revenue collection every five minutes. Based on information supplied by CRPs, including individual passenger counts at stations, the report concludes that actual ridership on CRP lines is up to 1.36 greater than the official LENNON figures, which only record actual fares sold, would imply. The report notes that CRPs find this doubly frustrating, because it both understates usage of their line and undermines their efforts to increase revenue.

Almost all CRPs call for better revenue protection, suggesting that Driver Only Operation be introduced to allow conductors to concentrate on revenue protection. Unfortunately, this widely held view has brought confrontation with the trade unions, who are opposed to DOO on the grounds that it will mean loss of jobs. Historically, the unions have always been somewhat ambivalent towards Community Rail, with some union spokespeople complaining that community rail volunteers are being used to do jobs that would otherwise be carried out by their members. They need to be persuaded that, while CRPs support DOO, they absolutely do not want to see conductors removed from trains. And likewise that, far from replacing paid staff, the tasks that CRP volunteers undertake would almost always otherwise simply go undone.

And while we are talking ambivalence, several at the Community Rail Awards questioned just how much Network Rail really supports the Community Rail concept. In its early years, CR protagonists found NR difficult to engage with. Then it set up a small Community Rail Unit and suddenly NR had a human face, a contact through which you could navigate the shadowy structure of NR. The unit won plaudits, including an award for its part in developing the 'Harrington hump', the raised section of platform at wayside stations with otherwise low platforms that allows easier boarding of trains. But in 2014, just as both Peter Wilkinson and Ministers were extolling the virtues of community rail and telling us all how it deserved more support, Network Rail announced it was closing the unit as part of a 15% reduction in staff. Despite widespread protestations that the savings on such an important role would be peanuts compared to NR's overall spend, and an intervention

The new Northern franchise will have 18 Community Rail Partnerships on its patch. A Class 158 train on the Settle & Carlisle line. **NORTHERN**

116

HITACHI Inspire the Next

from Baroness Kramer who feared that the move might jeopardise delivery of the DfT's Community Rail Strategy, NR insisted that the closure went ahead. Contact with CRPs has been devolved to staff in the Route Directorships – some of whom say that the task has simply been added to their already heavy workload and that their involvement is therefore likely to be limited. Inevitably, veteran community rail supporters fear a return to the lack of focus or consistency of yesteryear.

OUTSIDE THE BOX

The report observes that, although Community Rail designation is intended to open up opportunities for innovation and managing costs down, and to encourage CRPs to 'think outside the box', in practice implementation has been limited. CRPs complain that their suggestions and proposals are too often simply ignored, with TOCs content to maintain the status quo of their franchise contracts, while Network Rail insists on its 'one size fits all', risk-averse structure. At a recent meeting of CRPs in the north of England, there was general agreement that, while relationships with the relevant TOCs was probably improving, that with Network Rail was getting worse. DfT ministers and Officials are clearly encouraging new franchises to give more credence to community rail. If they really believe what they are saying, now that NR is effectively a nationalised industry, they should surely be insisting that community rail has a markedly higher priority there, too.

Micro franchising was one of the initial objectives of the Strategic Rail Authority when it set up the six pilot Community Rail schemes a decade ago, but was quickly dropped when the SRA was abolished and DfT took ownership of the Community Rail agenda. Now it has come to the fore again because the DfT is encouraging those bidding for new franchises to consider new business models. The report suggests that involvement of a CRP in micro franchising would involve significant issues around management, finance, insurance and public liability. I suspect most would not wish to go that far. But there is certainly recognition that, if CRPs are to become more involved in decisions about the management of their lines, some form of grouping may be necessary, perhaps along the lines of the successful Devon and Cornwall Rail Partnership which represents the six individual CRPs in the two counties. Will the new Northern franchise, for example, be able to adequately liaise with those now 18 separate CRPs on its patch?

VOLUNTEERS

As you might expect, the Report found that most community rail volunteers are practically-orientated, and that some 80% are retired or semi-retired. More surprisingly, given that the rail industry in general remains male-dominated, the male-female split of volunteers was almost exactly 50/50. The report finds that most 'come from a similar social background with an above average level of education, including degrees and relevant technical or specialist qualifications'.

So a good pool of talent. But there are warnings, too, about risks to volunteering in the future, including increasing alternative demands on volunteer's time, both personal and from the growing number of alternative volunteering options; from the staged increases in the national retirement age; and concern about the lack of public awareness and appreciation of the work that CRPs do, making it difficult to recruit new volunteers in competition with better known organisations such as the National Trust, or even heritage railways. That said, it is clear that, while they would like more recognition, volunteers have no desire for payment of any kind. There is though concern among volunteers that many of the travelling public wrongly perceive them as paid employees of a railway company, and react to them as such. What they want is wider recognition of their work, both at national level and, particularly, on stations and trains on their lines, coupled with practical assistance from TOCs for the work they do in terms of material and equipment.

Awareness of what Community Rail Partnerships do certainly needs to be improved, both among the public and within the industry; despite a National policy, in practice some train operating companies are far less supportive of community rail than others. And Network Rail in particular needs to be more responsive. After all, as Chris Austin, ACoRP Board Member, and former Director of Community Rail Development at the SRA, rightly asks, what other industry has such a willing band of volunteers to clear up years of neglect on its property?

So despite the challenges, with 37 lines now formally designated, many more stations enjoying the support of 'Friends' groups, and ridership handsomely outstripping the national average, it seems clear that community rail is here to stay. ■

INNOVATION AND ENVIRONMENT

Roger Ford, Industry & Technology Editor of *Modern Railways*, was the compere for the 2014 Rail Industry Innovation Awards. **TONY MILES**

MODERN RAILWAYS AWARDS
HIGHLIGHT INNOVATION

The 2014 Rail Industry Innovation Awards were presented in London at a meeting of the *Modern Railways* Fourth Friday Club in June, with Baroness Kramer, Minister of State for Transport, as guest of honour, and Roger Ford, Industry & Technology Editor of *Modern Railways*, as compere.

Originating in 1998, this is the longest standing award scheme in the industry.

MAJOR PROJECT
The Innovation Award for a Major Project, sponsored by Arriva, was awarded to the remodelling of Gravesend station - part of the Kent train lengthening programme. Spencer Rail was the principal contractor, commissioned to manage the £19 million multi-disciplinary project, providing an extra 12-car length platform and extension of the existing two platforms, using advanced construction methods and new technologies.

The project centred around a crucial 15-day blockade, so the team put in a large amount of preparatory work to ensure disruption to services was kept to an absolute minimum. This featured trials of different pre-cast concrete platform units, and redesign of the footbridge so that it didn't have to be lifted in during the blockade. Oakwood Engineering was commissioned to produce a 4D virtual construction model of all aspects of the blockade, which won the Global Award for Visual Planning 2014.

Highly Commended was an entry from Signalling Solutions, the transformation at Nottingham, where commissioning of the station area resignalling completed two years' work to deliver significant improvements.

ENGINEERING AND SAFETY
A remote condition monitoring system for wheel bearings won this year's Innovation Award for Engineering and Safety, sponsored by the Railway Industry Association. Developed, implemented and improved through partnership working by Southeastern and Perpetuum, the system uses bogie-mounted vibration and temperature sensors, and has achieved significant savings in cost and man hours.

Vortok's Modular Automatic Warning System and First Capital Connect's Customer Safety Campaign were Highly Commended.

PASSENGER EXPERIENCE
Ticketing and revenue initiatives took all three places on the shortlist for the Innovation Award for Passenger Experience. It was presented to CrossCountry for 'Advance Purchase On the Day', its industry-leading initiative that is revolutionising the way customers buy tickets and reserve seats. You can buy discounted advance purchase fares, and make seat reservations on the day of travel, up to 10min before boarding a train – and you can do it via website, a mobile app, or a call centre.

'RailFly' - a collaboration between First Great Western, Singapore Airlines and Heathrow Express – was Highly Commended, as were Southern Railway and Cubic Transportation Systems, for their work to revolutionise the way passengers buy tickets.

OPERATIONS AND PERFORMANCE
The Multi Purpose Vehicle (MPV) fleet of the South Western Railway was the winner of the Innovation Award for Operations and Performance, sponsored by Unipart Rail. As of last autumn, Multi Purpose Vehicles used for track treatment and similar work have been driven by South West Trains drivers, as part of the South Western Railway alliance with Network Rail. Availability of staff and vehicles has improved, as have operational command and responsiveness,

118

IN ASSOCIATION WITH **KNORR-BREMSE**

Celebrating the Major Project award for the Gravesend station remodelling are (left to right) Julian Allan, Spencer Rail Project Surveyor; Stephen Spencer-Jones, Gravesend Station Manager for Southeastern; prize presenter, Roger Cobbe of Arriva; Tom Kerins, Spencer Rail Operations Director; Kieran Spence, NR Scheme Project Manager; and Paul Devoy, NR Project Manager. **TONY MILES**

The first train calls at Gravesend on 6 January 2014 after major remodelling work over Christmas and New Year. This project won the 2014 Innovation Award for a Major Project. **NETWORK RAIL**

and alongside other initiatives, this innovation has resulted in significant improvement in autumn and winter track treatment.

Highly Commended were Altitude, the instant train tracking system developed by Southern and Data Alchemist, and Interfleet's Metered Billing for electric trains, Energyx.

CROSS-INDUSTRY

The award for Innovation in a Cross-Industry Project was a unique software tool, known as AEGIS, developed by Northern Rail, with Network Rail, Nomad Rail and Incremental Computing, to provide economical monitoring of train movements across the network using GPS data. A fully measurable performance map is now available, showing stations, junctions, passing points and signals, with journey times classed by time of day and season – unlocking a host of information on what customers experience.

Highly Commended were the high pressure solution used by Network Rail and a large team of specialist companies to deal with the cliff failure near Teignmouth, and ScotRail and First Glasgow for a partnership to help ticket holders during times of railway disruption.

SMALL SCALE

The Innovation Award for a Small Scale project went to a remote monitoring system from Park Signalling, for the older but still vital signalling equipment that is dispersed around the rail network. Park's Remote Indicator Status System gives technicians the ability to see indications on equipment that is not equipped with full Remote Condition Monitoring.

Highly Commended were a modification to the windscreen wiper system on CrossCountry's Class 170 fleet, and a fresh approach to rail replacement buses, by Chiltern Railways.

ENVIRONMENT

The Innovation Award for the Environment was awarded to a new door design for lightweight trains, using state-of-the-art composite materials and manufacturing processes from the aerospace industry. It has been developed by a consortium led by London Underground and including Atkins Aerospace, the National Composites Centre, Wabtec Rail, and University College London, as part of the Technology Strategy Board's competition on 'Accelerating Innovation in Rail'.

Highly Commended were a 'Smart' approach to energy monitoring from Arriva Trains Wales, and the bike hire scheme provided by Merseyrail, Northern Rail, and Abellio Greater Anglia.

'GOLDEN SPANNERS' FOR ROLLING STOCK EXCELLENCE

The 12th annual review of traction and rolling stock fleet reliability is published in the January 2015 issue of *Modern Railways* magazine. An awards luncheon the previous November - one of the *Modern Railways* Fourth Friday Club events - sees 'Golden Spanners' awarded to the best performers, with gold (best in class), silver (most improved) and bronze (fastest incident recovery) categories.

The brainchild of Roger Ford, Industry & Technology Editor of *Modern Railways*, the awards divide the national rolling stock fleet into categories: Pacers; Ex BR electric multiple-units; Ex BR diesel multiple-units; InterCity, New-generation DMUs and New-generation EMUs. Spanners for each category are awarded based on actual performance data, Miles Per Technical Incident (MTIN). The awards are widely credited within the industry as contributing to improvements in train reliability.

GOLDEN WHISTLES AWARDS

Skilful operators can make the trains run safely and on time – and the best operators deserve recognition.

For this reason the Institution of Railway Operators and *Modern Railways* magazine joined forces to launch the Golden Whistles Awards. These awards acknowledge best practice and congratulate railway operators that have done a good job by rewarding them with that ultimate symbol of smart operating – a whistle!

The Golden Whistles, based on objective data, emulate the successful Golden Spanners Awards already run by *Modern Railways*. There are categories for: Operational Safety, Operational Performance, and Managing Disruption, with awards for best performance and most improved performance in several categories.

Based on nominations from their peers, Golden Whistles are also awarded to the Outstanding Individual Operator of the Year, and Best Operating Team of the Year.

A panel of senior railway executives interpret the data and ensure fair play.

The 2015 Golden Whistles Awards will be presented at the January meeting of the *Modern Railways* Fourth Friday Club.

THE FOURTH FRIDAY CLUB

The *Modern Railways* Fourth Friday Club provides a unique networking forum for executives from all sectors in the railway industry. There are club meetings on five Fridays in each year, the season running from September to June. The club was the idea of *Modern Railways* Editor, James Abbott who is also Club Secretary.

Since the first meeting in 2003, the growing reputation of the Club for attracting senior policy makers and top railway managers as guest speakers has seen membership expand rapidly.

For more information, see - www.4thfriday.co.uk

A new door design for lightweight trains, developed by a consortium led by London Underground, won the Innovation Award for the Environment. Baroness Kramer, Minister of State for Transport, presented the award to London Underground's Francesco Cavallo (left), Simon Chung (second left) and Kuldeep Gharatya (right). **TONY MILES**

HITACHI Inspire the Next

INNOVATION AND ENVIRONMENT

12th RAILTEX TO SHOWCASE INDUSTRY INNOVATIONS

Halls 3 and 3a at the National Exhibition Centre in Birmingham will be the setting for Railtex 2015, which takes place from 12 to 14 May. This will be the 12th of these popular events, bringing together leading companies from all areas of the rail supply industry to present their capabilities and latest innovations.

Organisers Mack Brooks Exhibitions aim to build on the success of the last exhibition in 2013. That was the biggest Railtex since 2007, with 434 companies from 17 countries taking part. It was visited by more than 8,200 industry professionals, an increase of 19% on the previous show.

Complementing stands hosting many of the most prominent suppliers to the UK rail market, the show will again include familiar features such as dedicated display areas for specialised equipment and plant, and the Recruitment Wall, highlighting job opportunities from participating companies.

And as well showcasing the very latest in railway systems, products and services, Railtex will also offer valuable insights into trends in rail policy and technology through an extensive programme of supporting activities.

The Knowledge Hub will be one of two areas at the show where seminars and keynote speeches will take place, including high-profile presentations providing insights into prospects and opportunities for the UK rail sector. The Knowledge Hub will also be the venue for a programme of Project Updates detailing progress on current UK rail schemes, and for The Platform, a series of open discussion forums on topical industry themes. Both have drawn appreciative audiences at previous Railtex and Infrarail shows. These sessions will be open to all, free of charge.

In addition, the event provides a great opportunity for friends and colleagues to meet and for new business relationships to be developed. The opening day's Networking Reception will welcome exhibitors and show visitors and further networking opportunities will be provided by the second Railtex Awards dinner, taking place on 13 May to mark significant achievements by exhibiting companies.

As usual, entry to Railtex will be free for pre-registered visitors. Registration via the show website *www.railtex.co.uk* will open at the end of January 2015 and remain open until 11 May 2015. For non-registered visitors an entrance fee will be payable on the door.

The website is frequently updated, providing the latest list of exhibiting companies, plus details of all associated activities including keynote addresses, technical seminars and project updates as they are finalised.

Infrarail will return in 2016 – visit *www.infrarail.com* for the dates and venue.

Railtex 2015 will host many of the most prominent suppliers to the UK rail market.

RAIL VEHICLE ENHANCEMENTS EXPO

The Rail Vehicle Enhancements Expo and Forum in October 2014 at the Derby IPRO Football Stadium saw footfall increase significantly, the technical forum was oversubscribed and the number of exhibitors doubled.

The show, organised by Onyxrail and sponsored by *Modern Railways*, brought together many technical achievements as visitors were able to see live Darwin feeds to Televic Rail's Passenger Information Systems, Volo TV and Media demonstrated their content streaming to personal devices, Infodev detailed their real time highly accurate passenger counting systems, and DC Airco presented their developments in saloon air conditioning.

The unique profile of the show focuses on improving the passenger travelling experience through the provision of technical uplifts and the refurbishment of rail vehicles.

The organisation of RVE 2015 is already in progress. The event will be twice as large as RVE 2014 and will be in a new venue in Derby, offering a much larger single hall with a number of side halls that enable the running of forums in parallel.

RVE 2014 brought together many technical innovations.

KEY PROJECTS
AND CONSULTANTS

IN ASSOCIATION WITH

DeltaRail
Imagine the journey

KEY PROJECTS AND CONSULTANTS

THE DIGITAL RAILWAY

'There are 10 kinds of people in the Rail Industry. Those that understand digital, and those that don't.'
(With apologies to Professor Ian Stewart, FRS.)

In the 19th century, the railway was the engine of social change. The engine driving the 20th century was internal combustion, but the 21st will be digital. Will Rail embrace the digital age and once again be seen as a vehicle for change and innovation?

The management consultancy Accenture has declared that 'every business is a digital business' whether it recognises it or not, and that for businesses 'the next three years will be about determining their organisations' pace in this digital race – and their place in the new world of digital'. In a service industry like Rail, digital is no longer an option, but a necessity.

Network Rail's CEO, Mark Carne, brings a much needed new perspective to the railway. He has been unambiguous that the digital railway is one of his core strategic objectives. However, his cultural task is immense; requiring change to the fundamental dialogue within his business and to the businesses and organisations it works with.

So what does it mean to be digital? What is it that has driven the phenomenal transformation in industries that have already embraced digital? Three crucial features are open standards, the importance of data, and the consumer-led pull economy.

Open standards provide freely available interfaces, without restrictions on use, developed by communities where mutual benefit is greater than individual. They encourage the creation of ecosystems for development and platforms for exploitation, stimulating innovation, rapid growth, and blending of best in-class components to produce optimum solutions for the consumer. They displace closed standards that have used proprietary protocols to lock out competition and have delivered lowest common denominator solutions for the benefit of the large suppliers.

The emergence of the digital economy has relied on recognition of the importance of data. Valuable information that has previously been trapped within individual systems is released, and combined with other data, to drive a vortex of value creation. This digitisation of the world has transformed banking, insurance, retail, communications, logistics, media, entertainment, and even healthcare.

The government command paper 'Reforming our Railways: Putting the Customer First', published in 2012 to set the Agenda ahead of Control Period 5, put making life better for customers at the heart of necessary reform. But the Rail Industry still mostly sees itself as 'running a railway', focused on moving metal boxes around as close as possible to a timetable, and challenging the consumer to adapt to it using the cryptic clues.

The key feature in the success of a digital transformation is the move from push to pull. A pull economy places the consumer at the centre, pulling services to meet individual need rather than at the edge trying to make the best of services being pushed. This is most visible from digital television where (in much less time than the duration of a Rail Technical Strategy) we have moved from three channels pushing fixed schedules, through hundreds of channels to choose from, to on-demand delivery of what you want, when you want, on any device you want. When complete, such a transformation sees the consumer as a crucial collaborator in the design of the service – participating in its timing, location, and provision.

At DeltaRail we have embraced the digital future and introduced a step change into railway signalling control through our IECC Scalable product. IECC Scalable has delivered a world-leading digital architecture and platform based on best-in-class components used by other industries, even though key rail 'experts' said they would never work in rail.

Importantly, this move into digital has been delivered without compromising on the performance of our 'world-class' Enhanced Automatic Route Setting (EARS) and a Timetable Processor (TTP); enabling larger areas of control per workstation and user configuration of the ARS decision data.

Industries across the globe have used the digital revolution to deliver a transformation in business performance and cost. 'Rail is different' has often been defended by use of the safety card, but IECC Scalable has used architecture to both ensure a robust safety environment and provide a platform for transformation. The flexibility and agility of open standards and COTS components combined with a design driven by data has already led to significant improvements in performance and reduced costs for the railway. Our platform and ecosystem are ready. Who else wants to get on board?

The UK government has recognised the need to drive innovation through its Digital by Default programme and is building on the accepted wisdom that innovation comes from small players, not giants. Innovation is then distributed across many parties able to move with agility and seize opportunity. The government has shown strong leadership through this digital strategy and is delivering a transformation in government services, increasing usage, improving satisfaction and dramatically reducing costs.

So will the Rail Industry respond in time? Recognition of the need for innovation is clear from the proliferation of innovation initiatives. But in an industry where progress has traditionally only been made when a large number of complex stakeholders are aligned, there is still a Sir Humphrey-like tendency to set up a new committee to consider rather than take the responsibility that comes with action.

The digital age doesn't wait. With disruptors from blablacar to autonomous vehicles challenging Rail's traditional customer base, it's no longer a given that consumers will continue to use Rail. The digital race is on, ask London cabbies!

And what happens to those too slow to catch the digital express? Look at Kodak who denied the benefits of digital photography, even though it invented it. Or Blackberry who persisted with the view that smartphones would never catch on. As consumers of rail services look out enviously at those being served elsewhere, will Rail also be in denial?

What is needed now is strong leadership. As tomorrow's business leaders look up from their digital world, how will they judge what the Rail Industry did?

Graham Scott,
Group Development Director,
Delta Rail

IN ASSOCIATION WITH **Delta**Rail
Imagine the journey

The Carillion and SPL Powerlines partnership has invested in training facilities to help meet the need for skilled lines staff for the electrification programme. **TONY MILES**

ELECTRIFICATION AT THE CROSSROADS

ROGER FORD, INDUSTRY & TECHNOLOGY EDITOR OF *MODERN RAILWAYS*, REPORTS THAT 2015 WILL BE A CRUCIAL YEAR IN THE DELIVERY OF A ROLLING PROGRAMME OF ELECTRIFICATION

As recently as 2007, the Department for Transport's policy was that uncertainty over future traction power technology meant that proposals for further electrification of the network should pay off over 15 years instead of the usual 30-35 years for capital investment. Civil servants believed that by 2022 technologies such as hydrogen fuel cells could make electrification obsolete.

This policy was enshrined in the 2007 White Paper which included the High Level Output Specification (HLOS) for Control Period 4 (2009-2014). However, in October that year, Network Rail Chief Executive, Ian Coucher, and the Chairman of the Association of Train Operating Companies, Adrian Shooter, wrote to Director General Rail & National Networks, Mike Mitchell, challenging DfT's decision to defer consideration of 'a wider electrification programme' to Control Period 5 (2014-2019).

Their message was blunt. 'We believe that this is wrong', because 'there are real benefits to be gained from doing this now and deferral simply delays the realisation of these benefits'.

NEW PROGRAMME

This robust challenge from a united railway industry stunned the Department and initiated the reversal of the policy. By July 2009, Transport Secretary Lord Andrew Adonis was able to authorise an 'immediate start' of detailed planning for electrification of the Great Western main line (GWML) and the Manchester Victoria-Liverpool Lime Street route – later expanded to form the 'Northern triangle' with the addition of Manchester-Bolton-Euxton Junction (near Preston), Huyton-Wigan, and Preston-Blackpool.

Under the Adonis plan, included in the Control Period 5 HLOS, electrification from London to Bristol, Cardiff and Swansea was due to be completed by 2017, together with the lines to Oxford and Newbury, at a cost of £1 billion. Manchester-Liverpool electrification was scheduled for completion in 2013 at a cost of £100 million.

It should be noted that Scotland had escaped the misguided policy which blighted the railway in England and Wales. After devolution in 2005, the Scottish Ministers' 2007 HLOS for CP4 (later subject to some reconsideration) featured electrification of the core route between Edinburgh and Glasgow, plus a programme of infill electrification covering Paisley Canal, Whifflet, Cumbernauld, Maryhill and Stirling/Dunblane and Alloa services. Follow-on schemes (not yet in a detailed programme) would add East Kilbride and Barrhead/Kilmarnock.

CRUCIAL

South of the border, following the 2010 General Election, the Coalition Government made railway investment one of its spending priorities. This has created a long term programme of electrification, building on the original Adonis schemes, as shown in the table.

As a result, 2015 will be a crucial year in the delivery of what has become a rolling programme of electrification on a scale matching that implemented by British Rail during the 1980s. A telling statistic is that between 1980 and 1993, electrification schemes totalling 912 route miles were commissioned. In the following 15 years, the total was 22 route miles.

123

KEY PROJECTS AND CONSULTANTS

This 15 year hiatus inevitably meant the loss of experienced designers and estimators while the practiced installation teams melted away. The decision by Railtrack to outsource Overhead Line Equipment (OHLE) maintenance only compounded the loss of skill and experience.

As the accident report into the dewirement at Littleport, north of Ely, in January 2012 and Chris Gibb's earlier report on the condition of the West Coast OHLE confirmed, much of the unreliability attributed to British Rail electrifying 'on the cheap' was, in fact, the result of inadequate maintenance, which is still recovering from the Railtrack era.

NEW EQUIPMENT

Faced with a major long term rolling programme, NR has commissioned its own OHLE designs to replace the British Rail Mk3b used on the East Coast main line and other 1980s schemes. A major change is the return to portals over three and four track sections in place of the head-span construction of the Mk3b.

Portal gantries were used on the first major electrification scheme in the UK, the London and Manchester/Liverpool scheme completed in 1966. As the name implies, with a gantry, the registration arms supporting the individual catenaries are mounted on a rigid beam between a pair of support masts.

Developed by British Rail for the subsequent extension from Crewe to Glasgow, head-span construction has wire cables (the head-span) between each pair of masts, from which the registration arms are suspended. While this form of support requires lighter structures and is easier to install, it has the disadvantage that in the case of a dewirement all the wires can be brought down if the head-span is damaged.

With an increasingly busy railway, minimising disruption in the event of OHLE failure is a key consideration, hence the return to gantries. At the same time Network Rail has developed an entirely new range of OHLE equipment known as Series 1 and 2. These draw heavily on European experience. Series 1 is for 125mph operation and uses a Fuller+Frey design: it is already being installed under the Great Eastern main line OHLE upgrade programme. Series 2 is rated for 100 mph.

Network Rail's second technical 'innovation' is the £40 million Windhoff factory train, more correctly known as the High Output Plant System (HOPS). This train is made up of 23 specialised vehicles grouped into 'consists', each with a specific task, from sinking up to 30 of the piles which support the masts per night shift, to installing the catenary and contact wire. The consists have their own power units and can be driven independently.

With several consists in the train, the HOPS leaves the purpose-built depot in Swindon and runs to the section being electrified, where the consists separate and head to their work sites running at 60 mph. Each consist carries all the supplies and

ELECTRIFICATION SCHEMES IN CP 5 (2014-19)

ELECTRIFICATION SCHEME	COMPLETION DATE
North West [see note 6]	
Liverpool to Wigan	May 2015
Liverpool to Manchester (Victoria and Piccadilly)	May 2015
Preston to Blackpool [note 5]	December 2016
Manchester Victoria to Stalybridge	December 2016
Preston to Manchester	December 2016
North Transpennine (West)	
Manchester Victoria to Stalybridge Jct	December 2016*
Guide Bridge to Stalybridge grid feed	December 2018*
Northern	
Leeds to York	December 2018*
Leeds to Selby	December 2018*
Stalybridge to Leeds	December 2018*
West Midlands	
Walsall to Rugeley	December 2017*
Barnt Green to Bromsgrove	July 2016
Electric Spine	
Oxford to Bletchley	March 2019*
Sheffield to East Coast main line	June 2021*
Leamington Spa to Coventry	under development
Midland main line	
Bedford to Kettering and Corby	December 2017
Kettering to Nottingham	December 2019
Trent Junction to Derby	December 2019
Derby to Sheffield	December 2020
London	
Gospel Oak-Barking	June 2017*
Carlton Road Jct to Junction Road Jct [note 3]	December 2018*
Acton (GWML) to Willesden (WCML)	Under development
Great Western main line	
Maidenhead to Newbury, Oxford, Chippenham (incl) and Bristol Parkway	December 2016*
Reading (Southcote Jct) to Basingstoke [note 1]	under development
Chippenham (excl) to Bristol Temple Meads	May 2017*
Bristol Temple Meads / Parkway to Cardiff	December 2017*
Cardiff (excl) to Swansea	May 2018*
Thames Valley branch lines [note 2]	December 2017*
Welsh Valley lines	December 2019*
Tram train	
Rotherham to Meadowhall (DC)	May 2016*
Scotland	
Glasgow Queen St to Newbridge Junction (via Falkirk High)	March 2017
Cumbernauld to Greenhill Lower Junction	March 2017
Rolling Programme [note 4]	March 2019

Notes
* Indicative. Otherwise dates are an ORR regulated output
1. Previously part of Electric Spine.
2. Twyford-Henley on Thames; Maidenhead-Bourne End and Marlow; and Slough-Windsor & Eton Central.
3. Add on to Gospel Oak-Barking: plus links to Thameshaven and Tilbury container ports.
4. Greenhill Lower-Carmuirs West Junction-Falkirk Grahamston and Polmont; Carmuirs West-Stirling-Dunblane-Alloa (including Larbert Junction-Carmuirs East); Holytown Junction-Shotts-Midcalder Junction. (Springburn-Cumbernauld and Rutherglen-Whifflet brought forward to 2014.)
5. Later rescheduled for March 2017, with additional resignalling and remodelling.
6. Bolton-Wigan North Western electrification also announced in December 2013, due by 2017; Oxenholme-Windermere electrification favoured by DfT and being assessed.
Completion dates as shown in Network Rail CP5 Enhancements Delivery Plan, June 2014.

MC Electronics
Railway Safety Solutions

New Lightweight, more compact and portable possession equipment

MCE Worksite Marker Board

Only 2Kg in weight

MCE Possession Limit Board

Visit our website for all your

Depot

Trackside

Platform

Emergency

Requirements

www.mcelectronics.co.uk
For more information call 020 8428 2027
E-mail us on info@mcelectronics.co.uk

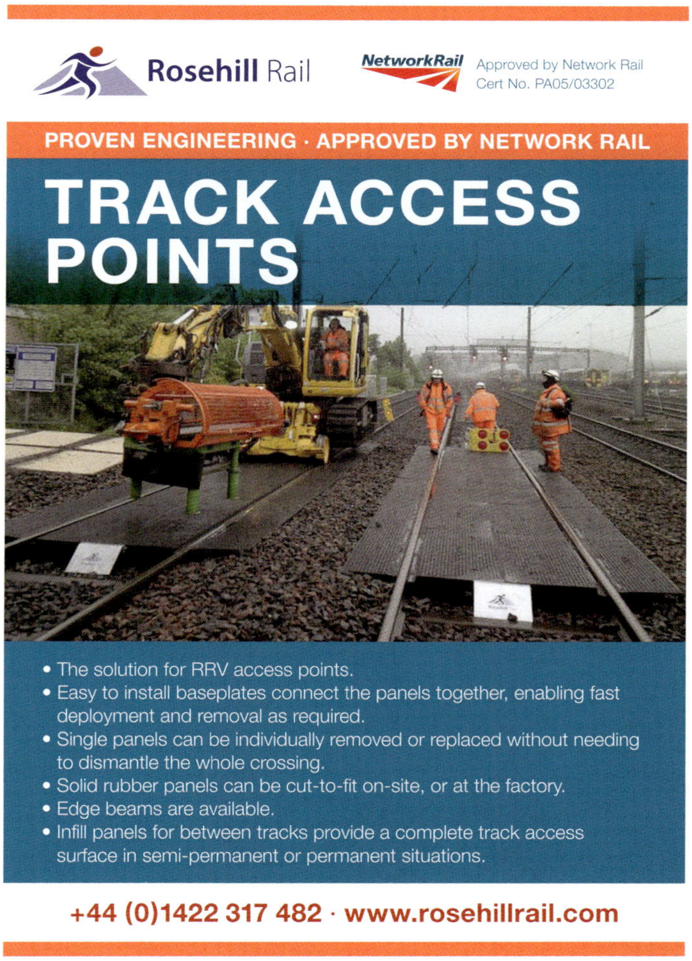

Rosehill Rail

NetworkRail Approved by Network Rail
Cert No. PA05/03302

PROVEN ENGINEERING · APPROVED BY NETWORK RAIL

TRACK ACCESS POINTS

- The solution for RRV access points.
- Easy to install baseplates connect the panels together, enabling fast deployment and removal as required.
- Single panels can be individually removed or replaced without needing to dismantle the whole crossing.
- Solid rubber panels can be cut-to-fit on-site, or at the factory.
- Edge beams are available.
- Infill panels for between tracks provide a complete track access surface in semi-permanent or permanent situations.

+44 (0)1422 317 482 · www.rosehillrail.com

Furrer+Frey AG
Overhead contact line engineering
Design, manufacturing, installation
Thunstrasse 35, P.O. Box 182
CH-3000 Berne 6, Switzerland

Telephone   + 41 31 357 61 11
Fax   + 41 31 357 61 00

www.furrerfrey.ch

Furrer+Frey®
Overhead contact lines

HITACHI
Inspire the Next

KEY PROJECTS AND CONSULTANTS

Electrification work under way at Alvechurch on the Redditch branch, where a new stretch of double track (with a new, second platform here) has increased capacity. In the second part of the current £100m north Worcestershire improvements, work continues on a new station at Bromsgrove and electrification from Barnt Green to Bromsgrove. **NETWORK RAIL**

RAIL HLOS ELECTRIFICATION BY 2019

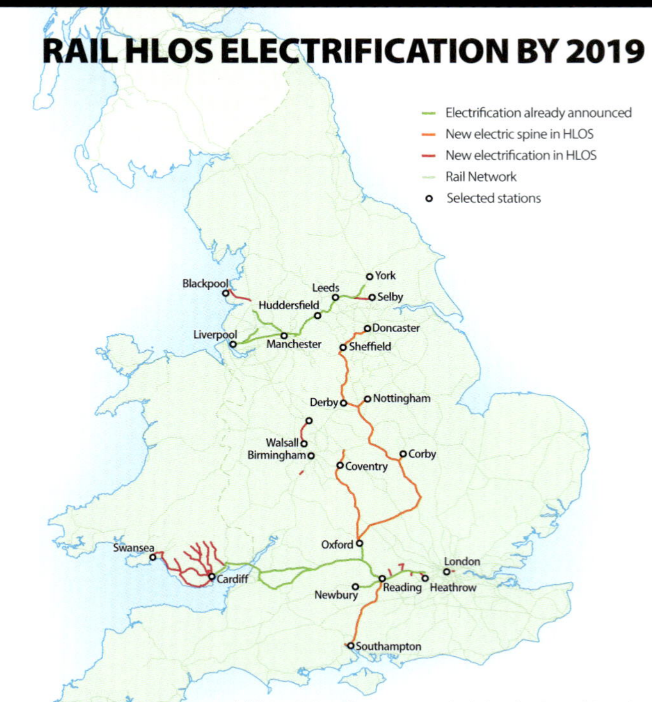

- Electrification already announced
- New electric spine in HLOS
- New electrification in HLOS
- Rail Network
- Selected stations

Additional electrification was included in the Control Period 5 High Level Output Specification (HLOS), published in 2012.

equipment needed for one night's work.

Consist functions include a piling rig, an excavation and concrete batching unit (with its own supplies of aggregate, cement and water), and a structures consist, which will erect the Series One masts, portal booms and cantilevers for twin track sections. It can carry 30 masts for erection, per night.

An ancillary conductor consist installs the earthing wires, return wires and small parts such as registration arms and other equipment. The process is completed by the contact and catenary consist, which will string up the remaining wires.

CAUTION

However, the electrification programme is making a slow start. While there have been successes, such as the avoidance of costly clearance works on the Paisley Canal scheme in Scotland, the Northern Triangle has suffered delays, in part due to inexperience after the long hiatus.

As we went to press, work was behind schedule on Phase 2 of the programme including Edge Hill-Earlestown, and Huyton-Wigan. A full review was underway with the aim of completion early in 2015. Full service introduction of the HOPS has also been slowed during discussions over aspects of the specification.

However the main concern was the fact that the cost of much of the Great Western route modernisation and other electrification schemes was still passing through the Office of Rail Regulation's Enhancements Cost Adjustment Mechanism (ECAM) process which will determine whether the cost is efficient. In addition, Network Rail's latest Control Period 5 Enhancements Delivery Plan, on which the table is based, added this caveat to many of the electrification schemes: 'It should be noted that an efficient profiling workstream is considering all electrification projects and the outcome of this workstream may result in reprofiling the delivery dates of some electrification projects'.

There were already suggestions that electrification of the Trans-Pennine route could slip back by up to two years. With electrification one of the government's flagship projects, the industry needs to show it can deliver. For electrification, 2015 could be a make or break year.

A stretch of the Springburn-Cumbernauld electrification, which was brought forward to 2014, to improve capacity in advance of the Commonwealth Games in Glasgow, and to free up diesel trains for the Borders Railway. **NETWORK RAIL**

CP5 ELECTRIFICATION IN SCOTLAND

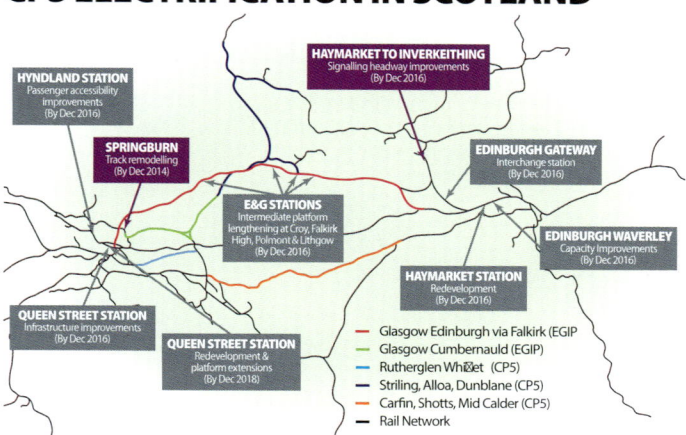

HYNDLAND STATION
Passenger accessibility improvements
(By Dec 2016)

SPRINGBURN
Track remodelling
(By Dec 2014)

HAYMARKET TO INVERKEITHING
Signalling headway improvements
(By Dec 2016)

E&G STATIONS
Intermediate platform lengthening at Croy, Falkirk High, Polmont & Lithgow
(By Dec 2016)

EDINBURGH GATEWAY
Interchange station
(By Dec 2016)

EDINBURGH WAVERLEY
Capacity improvements
(By Dec 2016)

HAYMARKET STATION
Redevelopment
(By Dec 2016)

QUEEN STREET STATION
Infrastructure improvements
(By Dec 2016)

QUEEN STREET STATION
Redevelopment & platform extensions
(By Dec 2018)

- Glasgow Edinburgh via Falkirk (EGIP)
- Glasgow Cumbernauld (EGIP)
- Rutherglen Whifflet (CP5)
- Stirling, Alloa, Dunblane (CP5)
- Carfin, Shotts, Mid Calder (CP5)
- Rail Network

MORE WIRES?

In December 2013, the Department for Transport announced a joint taskforce to explore 'where next' for electrification in the North of England, made up of experts from Network Rail and the DfT, and involving train operators, local authorities, supply companies, and local MPs. Routes to be examined included: Leeds-Harrogate-York; Selby-Hull; Sheffield-Leeds; Sheffield-Doncaster; East Coast main line-Middlesbrough; Sheffield-Manchester; Warrington-Chester; Crewe-Chester.

£7.5m of support for plans to electrify Selby-Hull was included in the Local Growth Deal announcements in July 2014 (subject to agreement on feasibility, value for money, and funding mechanism).

Principally for freight services, electrification to Grangemouth, and of the Edinburgh 'suburban' line bypassing Edinburgh Waverley was also under consideration, with whole or part funding from a Control Period 5 allocation for Scottish railfreight investment.

IN ASSOCIATION WITH **DeltaRail**

THALES GETS METROLINK
TO MANCHESTER AIRPORT A YEAR EARLY

Thales, in consortium with M-Pact (Laing O'Rourke and VolkerRail) and in partnership with Transport for Greater Manchester, has delivered the new 14.5 km Metrolink line to Wythenshawe and Manchester airport more than 12 months ahead of schedule.

On opening day, 3 November 2014, Chancellor George Osborne joined a driver in the cab and travelled on the airport line to see the work for himself. He said: 'I am delighted to be able to mark the opening of the new Metrolink line to Manchester Airport over 12 months ahead of schedule. The network now covers over 92km and is a vital economic asset for Manchester.'

Thales supplies a fully-integrated tramway management, control and communication solution that enables all aspects of the tramway to be operated safely, efficient and quickly. In addition, Thales as a consortium member of the principal contractor MPT (M-Pact Thales) also deliver overhead line, power, communications, passenger information and CCTV with the associated systems integration and maintenance of the expanded Metrolink network.

Thales has done over 2 million hours on this project and M-Pact Thales 13.3 million to September 2014. Martin Murphy, Programme Director MML, Thales said: 'We work against an aggressive schedule. What we do is complex; we do it at night and on construction sites, we're working with high voltage power at times, we're conducting dynamic tests, working near trams, and some of our work sites are close to live environments. The most important thing we do is manage the safety of the team and throughout the programme we embedded a very strong safety culture.'

The Metrolink expansion is the largest single public transport investment outside London and the early opening of the new line brings the network to nearly 100km of tramway in Greater Manchester.

Alistair McPhee, Vice President, Ground Transportation Systems (GTS) at Thales UK said, 'The opportunity to open the 14.5km Metrolink line to Wythenshawe and Manchester Airport a year early demonstrates Thales's capability in the delivery of complex systems in collaboration with our client, consortium partners and suppliers.'

Councillor Andrew Fender, Chair of the Transport for Greater Manchester Committee, said: 'Seeing our trams reach Manchester Airport more than a year ahead of schedule is a truly amazing achievement – and a game-changer for the communities set to benefit from its 15 new stops and frequent, fully accessible services.'

The airport line opening was the latest in a series of successful commissionings for the Manchester Metrolink Programme. When Oldham's new Town Centre line opened in January 2014 it was the third line commissioning in a row to be completed several months ahead of schedule. Then Rochdale's new town centre Metrolink line opened to passengers in March 2014, with the opening of the new line going hand-in-hand with a multi-million pound regeneration of the town centre.

Victor Chavez, CEO, Thales UK said, 'Yet again we have demonstrated our ability to exceed customer expectations on major infrastructure projects. This vital network will be a tremendous boost for Manchester and we are delighted to have been a major part of the project.'

Metrolink's airport line took off on 3 November 2014. **TFGM**

Thales provides a fully-integrated tramway management, control and communication system for Manchester Metrolink.

KEY PROJECTS AND CONSULTANTS

COLLABORATION:
LET'S MAKE IT OFFICIAL

Collaboration, in its simplest form is 'working with someone to produce something'. While working in this way isn't a new concept to the UK rail industry, we are starting to see more partnerships formalised under the standard for collaborative working, BS 11000.

BS 11000 is helping companies to work more effectively with their clients and business partners by reducing duplication of effort, creating additional value and managing joint risks which saves time and money. Having achieved BS 11000 certification in 2012 for its Rail Engineering Projects (REP) business, Atkins is seeing the benefits of formal partnerships.

As Atkins was one of the first businesses in the UK rail industry to achieve BS 11000 certification, it has spent the past two years working towards supporting its other businesses and clients to do the same. This effort has paid off, with the rest of Atkins' rail business becoming BS 11000 compliant in September 2014, and Atkins' entire UK business is aiming to get certification by the end of March 2015. Some of Atkins' major rail projects are being delivered in partnership and this is where the value of BS 11000 is being felt.

Take for example, the Stafford Area Improvements Programme, the first project to be delivered as a pure alliance by Network Rail. Now in its second phase, the project team is working to deliver this £250m infrastructure upgrade 12 months ahead of the December 2017 schedule set by the Department for Transport. This is due to the truly integrated approach taken by the project team, such as co-locating all four companies involved in one place so communication and problem solving is more effective. Setting the tone of the project from the beginning, by establishing a collaboration charter and a 'best person for the job' ethos, ensures that there is no duplication of effort and that staff have the power and support to make decisions. All of these aspects save time and money to deliver high quality projects to the travelling public sooner.

Likewise, East Kent Resignalling Phase 2 (EKR2) is achieving fantastic savings on the programme by working as one team with its partners: Balfour Beatty, C Spencer Ltd, Medway Council and Network Rail. Worth £145 million, the project will upgrade a 33-mile stretch of the region's network by 2016. This collaborative approach has achieved process and procedure efficiencies such as a combined project reporting dashboard, integrated project lifecycle, safety management and commercial management strategy. To deliver a project of this size in just three years, the project team have had to 'think outside the box'. This has seen around £7 million of value engineering savings made and allowed a possession and access strategy to be jointly developed between all parties. They have developed an innovative software package which allows all signal sighting work to be done by one person at their computer without the need to go on-site. This task can usually take up to nine months, but on EKR2 this was done in just four weeks. By working with partners Gioconda, the project route was filmed and then developed into the final software package, which means that the designer can do everything they could if they were on-site but allows the work to be completed in a fraction of the time.

As demonstrated by Atkins' rail projects, there are many benefits to be gained by working collaboratively. While the principles of this style of delivery aren't new to the UK rail industry, making partnerships official by moving to formal alliances and following the principles of BS 11000 is the way forward. Having worked successfully with its partners on alliances for projects such as the Stafford Area Improvements Programme, Atkins is looking to work in this way on more major projects in the future. ■

Having worked successfully with partners on alliances for projects such as the Stafford Area Improvements Programme, Atkins is looking to work in this way on more major projects.

IN ASSOCIATION WITH **DeltaRail** *Imagine the journey*

KEY PROJECTS

BORDERS RAILWAY

This project reinstates a 35 mile rail link from Edinburgh through Midlothian to Tweedbank in the Scottish Borders, the northern part of the Waverley route which was closed completely in January 1969. The line is to join the existing network at Newcraighall, and seven new stations are being built at Shawfair, Eskbank, Newtongrange, Gorebridge, Stow, Galashiels and Tweedbank. The mainly single track railway will have three dynamic passing loops.

Network Rail assumed management of the project in 2011, and passenger opening is scheduled for 6 September 2015.

The journey between Edinburgh Waverley and Tweedbank will take about 55min.

EDINBURGH-GLASGOW

The main element of the Edinburgh-Glasgow Improvements Programme is electrification of the Edinburgh-Falkirk High-Glasgow Queen Street line, expected to be ready for use in March 2017. In November 2014, Network Rail selected Costain and Morgan Sindall for the £250m contact to electrify the line, with infrastructure improvements.

This is associated with the reconstruction of Glasgow Queen Street as a transport hub: fastest journey times between there and Edinburgh will be reduced to 42min.

GREAT WESTERN MODERNISATION

The Great Western route modernisation now under way can be divided into electrification, resignalling, the rebuilding of the Reading station area, new trains, and preparation for Crossrail.

The new Thames Valley signalling centre by the end of 2015 will control an extended area including Oxford, Gloucester, Bristol and Newbury, associated with revision of track layouts for electrification.

Network Rail in conjunction with Reading Borough Council has enlarged and modernised Reading station, building two new entrances connected by a new footbridge. There are new lifts and escalators and five extra platforms to enhance station capacity. The new station was officially opened by HM The Queen on 17 July 2014.

Grade separation at the eastern end of the station allows trains to and from the Waterloo lines to reach the Relief Lines on the north side of the station.

By elevating the Main Lines with the construction of a new flyover west of the station, flows to and from the line to Basingstoke are enabled to cross to the Relief Lines towards Didcot without obstructing the Main Lines. This is a particular benefit for freight trains, but the scheme is aimed at removing one of the most restrictive bottlenecks on the whole railway system.

This has required the resiting of the Reading Traincare facility to the north side of the line and west of the station. It has also had its capacity enhanced. A new grade separated eastern chord from the Basingstoke direction will link with the north side of the station for the use of passenger services.

This massive project is due for completion in Summer 2015.

INTERCITY EXPRESS PROGRAMME

'The Intercity Express programme comprises the infrastructure, rolling stock and franchise changes needed to replace services operated by the ageing fleet of HST sets. The new trains will be faster, with higher capacity, more comfortable and more environmentally friendly services that will support growth on some of the busiest main line routes.' Thus the Department for Transport described its original contract with Agility Trains as part of the Intercity Express Programme.

Agility Trains is a consortium of Hitachi Rail (Europe) Ltd and John Laing plc. The company was appointed preferred bidder in 2009. The fleet will have some electric trains and some with a combination of electric

Construction work is due to begin in 2015 and complete in 2019 on the project to redevelop Glasgow Queen Street with extended platforms, improved facilities and a 500 sq m glass frontage as part of the Edinburgh-Glasgow Improvements Programme (EGIP). **NETWORK RAIL**

KEY PROJECTS AND CONSULTANTS

On the now doubled Lewisham Vale Junction-Tanners Hill Junction loop, Class 376 Electrostar No 376021 forms the 11.15 Dartford-Charing Cross via Woolwich Arsenal on 9 April 2013. This work was part of the Thameslink Programme, improving capacity between London Bridge and Lewisham. **BRIAN MORRISON**

Birmingham New Street station's new atrium roof covering - made from the same high-tech material as the Eden Project in Cornwall, ETFE – was installed in the summer of 2014. **NETWORK RAIL**

with diesel power under the floor (bi-modes). Part of DfT's interest in the bi-modes is in preserving through services away from the electrified network, without operating diesel traction under the wires for appreciable distances.

In the initial contract signed in July 2012, Agility Trains was responsible for the construction of 92 complete trains totaling 596 vehicles, together with maintenance depots in Bristol, Swansea, Old Oak Common and Doncaster. Agility is also responsible for maintaining the trains, with the train operating company (TOC) responsible for operations. The TOCs pay Agility a Set Availability Payment for each train that is presented for duty each day and remains reliable during the operational period.

The DfT is providing Agility Trains with a usage guarantee that there will be a franchised operator in place to make use of the trains.

Phase 1 trains will operate on the Great Western and will consist of 21 nine-car electric only trains and 36 five-car bi-mode trains (total 369 vehicles and 57 trains), due to start to enter passenger service in June 2017.

Phase 2 trains will operate on the East Coast franchise and will consist of 12 five-car electric only trains, 30 9-car electric trains, 10 five-car bi-mode trains, and 13 nine-car bi-mode trains, total 497 vehicles and 65 trains, with deliveries from 2018.

The contract to finance, supply and maintain the whole fleet takes the total value of the IEP programme to £5.8bn.

The bi-modes are electric multiple units with a number of diesel engines located beneath the floors. Driving vehicles are trailers and are equipped with pantographs specially developed by Brecknell-Willis.

The electric units have a single diesel engine to provide full hotel power in case of an overhead line fault, or offer limited traction power.

CROSSRAIL

The Crossrail project will deliver a new integrated railway through central London from Reading and Heathrow in the west through tunnels under central London with stations at Paddington, Bond Street, Tottenham Court Road, Farringdon, Liverpool Street and Whitechapel. It then divides into two routes, one to Stratford and Shenfield north of the Thames, and the other to Canary Wharf, Custom House, Woolwich and Abbey Wood to the south. The joint sponsors are the Department for Transport and Transport for London which set up a company, Crossrail Ltd, to act as the delivery agent.

Crossrail is the biggest transport project in Europe. Overall, the benefits of Crossrail are estimated to be worth at least £42bn to the national GDP over the next 60 years (current prices).

The twin bore tunnels for Crossrail trains under the centre of London will be completed in 2015. Tunnel portals and shafts will be completed in 2016 and other main civil works in 2017. Fitting out will continue to 2018, followed by testing.

Network Rail is responsible for the design, development and delivery of those parts of Crossrail on the existing network. This includes the upgrading of 70km of track, redeveloping 28 stations and renewing 15 bridges, as well as removing spoil from the tunnel excavations by rail.

All four tracks will be electrified west of Airport Junction, itself to be substantially rebuilt, and signalling renewed. There will be a new diveunder for freight at Acton yard. At Paddington, there will be a major reworking of platforms and interchange between the Crossrail station and main line platforms.

Crossrail is employing up to 14,000 people during the peak period of construction and an estimated 1,000 jobs directly when fully operational. The company's skills strategy supports the use of local labour.

Over 60% of Crossrail funding comes from Londoners and London-based

IN ASSOCIATION WITH **DeltaRail** Imagine the journey

business through direct contributions from the City of London, Heathrow Airport Ltd, Canary Wharf Group, a London Business Rates Supplement and a planning development levy. The government is providing about £5bn by means of a grant from the Department for Transport. The funding package is designed to strike a fair balance between businesses, passengers and taxpayers.

The trains to operate the Crossrail 1 service have been designated Class 345. These will be 9-car, 200 metre long lightweight sets, with air conditioning and inter-connected walk-through cars. They will be operated at 25kV AC, but with potential for third rail pick up. A contract to design, build and maintain the 65 train sets for 32 years, together with building a new depot at Old Oak Common has been let by Transport for London to Bombardier at Derby. There is an option to buy a further 18 trains. The new trains will be wholly publicly funded and the first is to be delivered in May 2017.

Crossrail's trains will operate in Automatic Train Operation mode with Automatic Train Protection in the central section, but will need to feature existing train protection systems until the European Train Control Systems (ETCS) is installed, separately, on the Network Rail sections of line.

Crossrail route control will be based at Liverpool Street in the first instance, and later at a new centre at Romford.

The operation of Crossrail services has been let as a £1.4bn concession to MTR Corporation (Crossrail) Ltd. This is for eight years, extendable to 10 years.

MTR will operate the existing Liverpool Street-Shenfield, Paddington-Maidenhead and Heathrow Connect services from dates related to franchise renewals. The new rolling stock fleet will be introduced first onto Great Eastern main line services in 2017 and then progressively elsewhere. Full Crossrail operation is due to start in December 2019.

At peak times, Crossrail will run 12 trains per hour between Shenfield and central London, calling at all stations, with an additional service of 6tph between Gidea Park and Liverpool Street main line station. A similar 12tph service will run from Abbey Wood.

The central section from Whitechapel westwards will thus carry 24tph at peak, of which 14tph will terminate at Paddington. During the off-peak, the service through the central area will be reduced to 12tph in total.

West of Paddington, Crossrail will provide 10tph on the GWML at peak; this will include 2tph from Reading, another 2tph from Maidenhead, 4tph from Heathrow (vice Heathrow Connect) and 2tph from West Drayton.

In August 2014, the government launched a study into a potential Crossrail extension from Old Oak Common to the West Coast main line. Diverting some West Coast services to Crossrail would make it easier to redevelop Euston station for HS2.

THAMESLINK

The Thameslink Programme is a £6bn project to deliver a high capacity, north-south spine railway through central London. With a scheduled completion of December 2018, Thameslink will provide greater capacity, higher frequencies, new services and improved access to central London from a range of destinations within London and across southeast England.

Major benefits from the works include a capacity increase in the core section between St Pancras Thameslink and Blackfriars to 24 trains per hour, mostly of 12-cars.

The Thameslink programme comprises three main elements. Major infrastructure works will provide platforms to accommodate trains of 12-car 20 metre vehicles and the removal of key capacity bottlenecks. Second is the specification and procurement of new rolling stock, and third refranchising of service operation.

The major works currently under way are centered on London Bridge, to remove bottlenecks, improve passenger facilities and capacity. Six high level through platforms and nine low-level terminal platforms are being converted to nine high level through platforms and six low-level terminal platforms. A new approach viaduct and two track bridge over Borough High Street, already in place, will feed the new high level station tracks. A new and very large station concourse, 70m wide and 150m deep, is being created underneath the tracks at street level, with new entrances both north and south.

Work started with the Brighton platforms, completed by the end of 2014. During 2015/16, Charing Cross services will not stop at London Bridge, and similarly for Cannon Street services in 2016/17.

New bi-directional signalling has been installed throughout between Kentish Town and Blackfriars. ETCS will be overlaid to provide automatic operation when infrastructure work in

The £59m Ipswich chord, completed in early 2014, removes the need for freight trains travelling to and from the Port of Felixstowe to use the sidings adjacent to Ipswich station as a turning point, eliminating a major bottleneck on the busy Great Eastern main line. **NETWORK RAIL**

KEY PROJECTS AND CONSULTANTS

The first train calls after the £19m upgrade of Gravesend station was completed over the Christmas and New Year period 2013-14. Improvements include a new platform and lengthened existing platforms for 12-car trains. **NETWORK RAIL**

the London Bridge area is completed.

The order for new Siemens trains for Thameslink was placed in June 2013. Delivery of the first of these Class 700 electric multiple-units is expected in 2015 and they will begin to enter service during 2016.

The Desiro City trains consist of 55 12-car and 60 8-car dual-voltage units. They have no intermediate cabs and cannot be split during normal operation. The contract is worth around £1.6bn. It includes the construction of new depots at both Three Bridges and Hornsey and maintenance of the fleet.

The merging of train services to access the central area between St Pancras International and Blackfriars will take place at Midland Road Junction (between the Midland and Great Northern lines north of St Pancras).

A new grade separated junction at Bermondsey will help keep Brighton and South Eastern services apart.

HIGH SPEED 2

High Speed 2 (HS2) is a planned new north-south railway promoted and built in two phases. HS2 Ltd, the company responsible for developing and promoting it, is wholly owned by the Department for Transport.

Phase One plans are for a new high-speed line from London Euston to north of Birmingham, where it will link with the existing West Coast main line allowing fast services direct to destinations further north. New high-speed trains are to serve Birmingham city centre (Curzon Street) and an interchange with Birmingham International and Birmingham Airport, designed to serve the wider West Midlands. At Old Oak Common in west London, a new interchange is to connect HS2 with Crossrail, the Great Western main line and the Heathrow Express.

The proposals for Phase Two would see the line extended north and east, to join the West Coast main line south of Wigan and the East Coast main line south of York. On a Manchester leg, the route for consultation had stations at Manchester Airport and Manchester Piccadilly (adjacent to existing station). A separate branch would serve an East Midlands station near Nottingham, Sheffield Meadowhall and Leeds New Lane. Passengers would be able to travel from central London to Birmingham in 49min

CONSULTANT FILES SUPPORTING RAIL DEVELOPMENTS

AECOM AND URS

AECOM is a global provider of professional technical and management support services, with international experience of a wide range of rail disciplines, such as systems enhancements, operations, infrastructure maintenance, rail engineering, and policy and strategy. AECOM is a 40% partner in the Transcend joint-venture, providing strategic management services for London Crossrail.

In July 2014 AECOM agreed to pay £2.3bn for rival URS Corporation. The combined company employs 95,000 people across 150 countries. URS in the UK offers consultancy services that cover all aspects of rail infrastructure planning, design, project management, construction supervision and asset maintenance. URS is the main design consultant for the Borders Railway, and has been awarded many Crossrail contracts.

ATKINS

Atkins is one of the world's leading design, engineering and project management consultancies, employing some 17,500 people across the UK, North America, Middle East, Asia Pacific and Europe. Atkins is a leader in rail engineering and systems design, providing expertise from experience and in-depth knowledge. From development and maintenance of existing systems to the implementation of new schemes, it helps clients through the entire project lifecycle to maximise value and outcomes.

Key rail projects include providing architectural and engineering design services on Crossrail. Atkins and Heriot-Watt University are collaborating on a Centre of Excellence for High Speed Rail.

ARUP

Arup is a global firm of designers, engineers, planners and business consultants which provides a full range of professional services. Arup's portfolio includes all modes of rail, ranging from high speed through to urban transport systems and freight.

Projects undertaken by Arup range in scope from master/strategic planning and total rail infrastructure improvement programmes requiring multi-disciplinary teams, to the application of singular, specialist skills such as operations, planning, permanent way, traction power, signalling, communications, acoustics, station design and tunnelling.

BECHTEL

Founded in 1898, Bechtel is a major engineering, construction, and project management company, active around the world. Major UK projects in which Bechtel has been involved include the West Coast route modernisation, and the Jubilee Line Extension. It was part of the Rail Link Engineering consortium creating High Speed 1; is involved in modernising the London Underground; and is part of the Project Delivery Partner team for the central tunnel section of Crossrail, and Network Rail's Delivery Partner for its Crossrail and Reading programmes.

CAPITA

Capita provides design, project and commercial management expertise supported by a range of railway specific skills. Services include permanent way and engineering design for guided transport systems, as well as commercial, cost, project and programme management, estimating, procurement and claims management for rail transport.

Capita also works as technical adviser for major railway schemes, providing comprehensive project monitoring, and carries out feasibility studies for new lines and infrastructure enhancements.

DELTARAIL

DeltaRail is a software and technology company dedicated to the needs of the rail industry, with its principal activity in signalling and traffic control technology, including the next generation signalling control system IECC Scalable, as well as operational planning software and management services.

rather than 1hr 24min today, and from London to Manchester in 1hr 8min (2hr 8min today).

HS2 is designed for a top speed of 250mph. Plans envisage services running at up to 225mph, seen as becoming the standard for new high speed trains. For future operation at 250mph, noise and other impacts would be considered first. New stations on the line would be built to accommodate 400m long trains, each capable of carrying up to 1,100 passengers. A 14 trains per hour capability in Phase One (12 in the initial specification), is expected to rise to 18 trains per hour in Phase Two. Network Rail estimates that over 100 cities and towns could benefit from new or improved services as a result of capacity released on the existing rail network.

The government announced in 2013 a potential funding requirement for HS2 of £42.6bn, at 2011 prices (£21.4bn for Phase One and £21.2bn for Phase Two – including a total contingency for both phases of £14.4bn). The target price for construction of Phase One is £17.16bn, with no spending above this without agreement of the DfT, working with the Treasury.

Permission for the scheme to go ahead is being sought through a 'hybrid' Bill process (combination of Public and Private Bill procedures). The Bill for Phase One received its Second Reading in the House of Commons in April 2014, approving it in principle, and then moved to the Select Committee stage, when petitions are heard.

HS2 Ltd Chairman, Sir David Higgins, in October 2014 proposed amendments to Phase Two plans, including consideration of a single redeveloped station for HS2 and existing railways at Leeds, and of a new site for the East Midlands station with better road and rail connections. While restating support for a Crewe HS2 station, with delivery accelerated to 2027 instead of 2033, he recommended consideration of through HS2 services via existing lines for Stoke on Trent.

NORTHERN HUB AND HS3

The Northern Hub upgrading of the rail network will see, alongside electrification of primary routes, improvements including two new platforms at Manchester Piccadilly to allow more trains to run through rather than terminate, and construction of the Ordsall Curve to provide a direct route between Manchester

Network Rail opened two new platforms at London Bridge station in September 2014 as part of the complex Thameslink Programme work. **NETWORK RAIL**

Asset management products include TracklineTwo for track geometry measurement, vehicle dynamics software Vampire Pro, and VIEW for automatic under-train inspection.

CH2M HILL AND HALCROW

Employee-owned CH2M HILL is one of the world's leading consulting, design, design-build, operations, and programme management companies serving government, civil, industrial and energy clients, employing over 26,000 people worldwide. Its work is concentrated in the areas of water, transportation, environmental, energy, facilities and resources.

Having operated in the UK for over 20 years, it acquired Halcrow in 2011 and now employs over 3,400 people in the UK. CH2M HILL provides infrastructure design, engineering and management services and specialised rolling stock services to the rail industry. It is working on some of the most iconic infrastructure programmes including High Speed 2 and Crossrail.

INTERFLEET TECHNOLOGY

A member of the SNC-Lavalin group of companies, Interfleet Technology is an international rail technology consultancy group. Founded in 1994, it delivers business benefits in the areas of rolling stock, railway systems and strategic railway management.

Interfleet's rolling-stock engineering expertise is established worldwide, with strength-in-depth across all areas from strategy to technical. It has significantly augmented its capabilities in rail infrastructure and train-control systems, to offer integrated cross-sector consultancy support. Capabilities in areas such as Track, Electrification & Power, the Built Environment and Signalling are being applied to major projects such as ERTMS.

JACOBS CONSULTANCY

Jacobs is one of the world's largest and most diverse providers of technical services. Jacobs UK provides a comprehensive passenger and freight consultancy service to the rail sector covering the full spectrum of infrastructure requirements, from project development, preliminary appraisal and feasibility studies through to detailed design, implementation and operational management advice.

Jacobs is the sponsors' Project Representative for Crossrail, designed the new Stockley flyover for Crossrail, and won an engineering design framework package for phase two of High Speed 2.

LLOYD'S REGISTER

A specialist team of railway experts within the Lloyd's Register Group provides a wide range of expert advisory and assurance services to improve the safety, performance, quality and management of rail systems.

Services offered include expert advice in rolling stock, signalling systems, safety engineering, human factors, energy efficiency, project management, software testing, power systems, civil engineering and asset management; plus independent assurance, training, and conditioning monitoring systems.

MOTT MACDONALD

In its global transport business Mott MacDonald has some 3,000 professional staff from a wide range of related disciplines. It provides rail engineering consultancy services through teams based in the UK and internationally. Its technical engineering disciplines cover all aspects of railway systems and infrastructure. It also specialises in applying advanced simulation techniques.

The project portfolio includes the Channel Tunnel, West Coast route modernisation, London Underground, high-speed rail including High Speed 1 and 2, Crossrail, the Thameslink Programme, the Northern Hub, and light rapid transit in cities such as London, Birmingham, and Manchester.

NETWORK RAIL CONSULTING

Network Rail's international rail consultancy business sets out to harness the range of skills and experience available within Network Rail to demonstrate British expertise overseas, and be an international

KEY PROJECTS AND CONSULTANTS

Crossrail's train tunnels in Docklands and southeast London were structurally complete, following the breakthrough by tunnel machine Ellie at Victoria Dock Portal in east London in October 2014. Tunnel machine Elizabeth had started the final push west from Whitechapel that was set to see her and sister machine Victoria complete all tunnelling at Farringdon in 2015. COPYRIGHT CROSSRAIL LTD

Piccadilly and Manchester Victoria. Selective track doubling is to increase capacity between Leeds and Liverpool and between Sheffield and Manchester, and Manchester Victoria is being rebuilt as a single transport interchange. More and faster trains will be able to run on key routes, with more direct rail services to Manchester Airport.

Proposals to improve east-west rail links on the Manchester-Leeds axis (dubbed 'High Speed 3' by the government) were set out by HS2 Ltd Chairman Sir David Higgins in his report, 'Rebalancing Britain', in October 2014. He said that the journey time between Leeds and Manchester could be cut to between 26 and 34min by improvements to rail infrastructure, rather than a major new line like HS1 or HS2, though Network Rail has been examining a wide range of options.

The government said that, working with the new Transport for the North organisation, it would produce a comprehensive transport strategy for the region, including options, costs and a delivery timetable for a HS3 east-west rail connection.

BIRMINGHAM NEW STREET

Birmingham New Street station is used by 140,000 passengers a day, more than twice the number for which it was designed.

The £600m New Street Gateway project project is to double passenger capacity with a much larger concourse, accessible platforms, and eight new entrances. Completion is expected in September 2015.

The project is funded by Network Rail, Birmingham City Council, Advantage West Midlands, Centro and the DfT.

EAST-WEST RAILWAY

Chiltern Railways' Evergreen 3 project is building a new chord from south of Bicester North station to Bicester Town and upgrading the line thence to Oxford, this will enable services to be offered from London Marylebone. A new station will be constructed at Oxford Parkway, to open in Summer 2015.

This scheme is linked with the East-West Railway scheme to restore local services between Oxford, Bletchley and beyond. They are being undertaken as a combined project with Network Rail. It is anticipated that Marylebone–Oxford services will commence in Spring 2016. New services which include a route from Aylesbury and to Milton Keynes Central are to start in 2017. ■

CONSULTANT FILES SUPPORTING RAIL DEVELOPMENTS

ambassador for Britain's rail industry. It also wants to help channel innovation back into Network Rail's core business.

It offers consultancy services across the full spectrum of Network Rail's expertise, including institutional and policy advice, strategic planning, asset management, operations and maintenance, and infrastructure projects.

NICHOLS GROUP

The Nichols Group is a UK consultancy specialising in areas including strategy, programme management and project management. The group has advised and assisted in implementing and restructuring major capital rail investment programmes, amongst them the West Coast Route Modernisation and Thameslink. Nichols has led capital programme reviews for the Office of Rail Regulation, and is a partner in the Transcend team working in programme management for the London Crossrail project.

ONYXRAIL

Onyxrail Ltd is an independent turnkey enhancement and maintenance provider to the rail traction and rolling stock industry, providing high quality managed solutions at its own facilities or client depots, enabling a complete service at the line of route.

Project management and procurement teams, with technology partners, provide comprehensive projects delivered locally at the point of need. Onyxrail also assists higher technology OEMs with route to market services in the UK, and through its sister company provides a range of castings, forgings, fabrications and machined components.

STEER DAVIES GLEAVE

Steer Davies Gleave is a leading independent transport consultancy providing services to government, operators, regulators, promoters, financiers and other interest groups.

Expertise includes rail demand and revenue forecasting, financial modelling, rail operations & costing, rail strategy development & implementation, business case preparation, public consultation, outreach & stakeholder engagement, rail project delivery & appraisal, procurement, rail franchise bidding, specification and evaluation.

VOSSLOH KIEPE UK

Vossloh Kiepe UK (formerly Transys Projects Limited) specialises in integration engineering and rolling stock enhancement.

Its wide range of capabiliites includes engineering, consultancy and design packages, turnkey solutions, technology enhancements, product support, refurbishment of rail vehicles, and traincare.

WSP AND PARSONS BRINCKERHOFF

WSP has 60 years experience in rail project delivery of all shapes and sizes. WSP works across all phases of a project - surveys, planning, design, construction and management. The design team working on London Bridge station includes a HyderWSP JV and architect Grimshaw.

Parsons Brinckerhoff is a global consulting firm assisting clients to plan, develop, design, construct, operate and maintain critical infrastructure. Its acquisition from Balfour Beatty by WSP Global was announced in September 2014.

Parsons Brinckerhoff offers skills and resources in strategic consulting, planning, engineering, programme/construction management, and operations for all modes of infrastructure. It has been involved in capacity building and electrification of the rail network, including Northern Hub, Crossrail and the Great Western electrification.

YORK EMC SERVICES

York EMC Services Ltd is an established market leader for the provision of EMC services to the railway industry.

York EMC Services offers a range of consultancy, testing and training services, specifically designed for the railway industry. The company has a solid track record of solving EMC problems and demonstrating EMC for major railway projects around the world.

INFRASTRUCTURE MAINTENANCE & RENEWAL

IN ASSOCIATION WITH

Lloyd's Register Rail

INFRASTRUCTURE MAINTENANCE AND RENEWAL

INTELLIGENT RAIL

LLOYD'S REGISTER RAIL'S 'ONE STOP SHOP' FOR COLLECTION, STORAGE AND ANALYSIS OF ASSET PERFORMANCE DATA

Real-time asset condition monitoring is not new to the rail industry. Yet its impact has frequently disappointed.

Often, this is down to projects losing sight of their original objectives as they progress along. Or because too much emphasis has been placed on the volume of data gathered, rather than the more important step of how the data will eventually be put to meaningful use.

Intelligent Rail is the term we use at Lloyd's Register for a range of services – originally developed for the Dutch rail market - that extend across the entire process, from the measurement technologies themselves through to the planning and delivery of operational improvements based on evidence found within the captured data.

And, as a 'One Stop Shop' for the collection, storage and analysis of asset performance data, Intelligent Rail has become a powerful tool for organisation-wide approaches to asset management.

WHAT CAN BE MEASURED?

The modular design of our measurement platform means we can provide measurements from both trackside and onboard sensors for a range of purposes; for example, the 'Gotcha' Wheel Impact Load Detection module is currently being installed at 36 locations on the UK network, and will soon be keeping a watchful eye on the wheel condition of around 80% of trains on the UK's tracks.

Network Rail is also trialling the 'PanMon' module, monitoring both uplift forces and pan head condition using a combination of radar, laser, optical and flash technology to capture high definition images of pantographs on passing trains, providing real-time measurement of the condition and wear of the carbon strip and the status of end-horns and aerofoils.

Other modules include 'Infra-monitoring' and 'Smartfleet'; these both use sensors and data-loggers installed onboard normal service trains to provide real-time monitoring of track and rolling-stock condition, providing a flexible and cost-effective alternative to dedicated measurement vehicles.

MAKE IT COUNT

But the real challenge for any monitoring project is finding the time and in-house expertise to analyse the volumes of data collected.

Once measurement programmes commence, project teams can quickly find themselves overwhelmed by complex, often irrelevant, diagnostic reports, and lacking the technical experience to spot the patterns and trends impacting on daily operations.

That is why data analysis and change management support both sit at the heart of Intelligent Rail. With teams of technical experts organising and prioritising the data as it is collected, we compile the diagnostic readings into meaningful and intuitive reports ready for integration directly into the organisation, whether for operational (advising train drivers and mechanics), tactical (e.g. performance analyses) or strategic (e.g. KPI management information) purposes.

TANGIBLE RESULTS

Regardless of whether the projects embarked upon are short or long-term in nature, the experiences of the Dutch market demonstrate there are considerable benefits to be gained from asset condition monitoring.

But tangible improvements can only be achieved as long as projects avoid the temptation of 'mission creep' and stay focused on their original business objectives.

The overarching principle of Intelligent Rail is that it is not the quantity of data captured that leads to a successful outcome, rather the presence of a consistent, methodical approach at every stage of the process. ∎

Intelligent Rail can provide measurements from both trackside and onboard sensors for a range of purposes.

Intelligent Rail

From the installation of discreet on-board and trackside measurement technologies to the roll-out of organisation-wide change programmes, Intelligent Rail is about turning real-time monitoring data into tangible operational benefits.

- A 'One Stop Shop' from data collection to operational change.
- Precise monitoring programmes designed around business objectives.
- Diagnostic data presented as coherent intelligence reports.
- Trend analysis and fault detection supported by expert technical advice.

For more information visit
www.lr.org/rail

Lloyd's Register Rail

Working together for a safer world

Lloyd's Register and variants of it are trading names of Lloyd's Register Group Limited, its subsidiaries and affiliates.
Copyright © Lloyd's Register Group Limited. 2014. A member of the Lloyd's Register group.

INFRASTRUCTURE MAINTENANCE AND RENEWAL

NR DRIVES TOWARDS RELIABLE ASSETS

The Office of Rail Regulation's (ORR's) assessment of Network Rail's performance during Control Period 4 (CP4), 2009-14, commends its success in the final year of CP4 in delivering a major programme of enhancements, working on over 300 projects at 1,300 worksites, and achieving key milestones over the Christmas and New Year period.

This was in the face of some exceptionally challenging weather conditions, says ORR, which extended over the winter of 2013-14, with incidences of flooding and numerous asset failures, notably the Dawlish coastal defence wall in Devon. Network Rail's reactive work to repair the assets, including failed earthworks at approximately 140 locations, was highly commendable, ORR added. For the future ORR says it is important to ensure lessons are learnt from these asset failures.

ORR says the company did not achieve the performance targets it was funded to deliver at the end of CP4 and as a result ORR determined that a package of 'balanced enforcement measures' was necessary, including financial penalties relating to train performance.

Network Rail played a key role in improving safety, achieving its CP4 regulated target, said ORR, and improved its capability and asset management systems. Renewals volumes for plain line track were 7% down on the levels planned for the whole of CP4, but ORR was satisfied that this would not adversely affect the long term sustainability of the network, provided Network Rail delivers the volume of renewal work planned for Control Period 5.

NEXT FIVE YEARS

ORR's Periodic Review 2013 (PR13) determined the outputs ORR expects Network Rail to deliver, the income the company will receive and the incentives it will face, in Control Period 5 (CP5), 1 April 2014 to 31 March 2019. The Secretary of State for Transport (for England & Wales) and the Scottish Ministers provided ORR with their requirements in terms of high level output specifications and statements of funds available.

ORR said its conclusions on PR13 were challenging but achievable for Network Rail in terms of efficiency, value for money and deliverability. ORR says they should also improve safety, and take account of long-term needs as well as short-term. ORR also believes it has incentivised Network Rail to efficiently manage costs it can control, providing appropriate protections against risk.

The starting point for the package is the outputs the company is required to deliver. Network Rail must continue to meet its legal safety

effectiveness of deployment of asset knowledge to make decisions. ORR also expects Network Rail to improve its approach to the environment.

ORR says it will be monitoring indicators such as asset condition and asset performance, to give early warning of possible problems in the future, and more of this monitoring will be at Network Rail route level. ORR will also monitor progress on 'enablers', which measure how Network Rail is building its long term capability in areas such as managing capital programmes.

ASSET MANAGEMENT INITIATIVES

Setting out its key current initiatives for asset management, Network Rail says it continues to run an overarching programme of asset management improvement. As well as accreditation to PAS55, the British Standards Institution's (BSI) publicly available specification for asset management, NR has been working towards accreditation under PAS55's successor, ISO 55000: NR contributed to its development as part of its role as patron with the Institute of Asset Management.

Key initiatives for CP5 include increasing the reliability of assets and reducing the number of failures, whether track, points or signals, through a process of continuous improvement using targeted maintenance, lean techniques of working, as well as the latest technology, to maintain the rail infrastructure.

The ORBIS programme (Offering Rail Better Information Services) is seen as key to a move from a 'find and fix' approach to 'predict and prevent'. This investment in asset information data and systems is aimed at making it easier to capture information through deployment of hand-held devices and advanced train-borne systems. NR also highlights its investment in the competency of its people.

Benchmarking against other asset-intensive industries around the world is continuing, aiming to identify appropriate best practice which can be implemented by Network Rail to further develop its plans.

NETWORK RAIL ORGANISATION

Network Rail's operation of the railway is organised by geographic zones or 'Routes'. The Kent and Sussex routes were merged in April 2014 to form a new South East route: the other routes are Anglia, London North Eastern and East Midlands, London North Western, Scotland, Wales, Wessex, and Western.

Each route managing director in effect runs their own infrastructure business with significant annual turnover and resources, with a supporting centre to help make the most of economies of scale. The railway still needs to be planned and operated as a network which operates seamlessly, Network Rail said, maintaining a focus on efficient and effective management of long-life railway assets.

The route MDs have responsibility for issues including: safety; all customer service matters; asset management outputs and spend; operations; planning and delivering maintenance; and delivery of some renewals and enhancements.

Network Rail has agreed with several train operating companies on new ways of working ever closer - 'alliances'

NETWORK RAIL TRACK DELIVERY PARTNERS 2014-19

PLAIN LINE (CONVENTIONAL), FIVE-YEAR DEALS:
Babcock: Western, Wales and Wessex / Scotland / LNW South – c.£200m.
Carillion: LNW North / LNE and East Midlands – c.£100m.
Colas: Kent and Sussex / Anglia – c.£75m.

SWITCHES & CROSSINGS, TEN-YEAR DEALS:
Amey Sersa: North alliance (Scotland / LNE and EM / LNW North) – up to £400m.
Colas URS: South alliance (Anglia / Kent and Sussex / Western, Wales and Wessex / LNW South) – up to £400m.

The high output track renewals programme is being taken in house from 2015.

An £81m project saw the junction layout improved and track renewed in the Watford Junction area over a series of bank holidays and weekends in 2014. **NETWORK RAIL**

obligations, improving safety where reasonably practicable. Maintenance efficiency savings are phased in to give Network Rail more time to introduce new ways of working. A major programme of improvement works is also included.

Although passenger and freight demand will be growing, Network Rail should deliver this programme while ensuring that 92.5% of trains arrive on time nationally by 2019 (by the Public Performance Measure). It should also reduce disruption to passengers (by 8%) and freight customers (by 17%) from engineering works over CP5, despite the major enhancements programme.

ORR also set outputs for Network Rail's management of the network infrastructure. There will be new outputs for the quality of asset data, for improvement of asset management capability, and for the delivery of the ORBIS (Offering Rail Better Information Services) programme to increase the

With new Switch & Crossing work delivered on tilting wagons, Network Rail engineers replaced Keymer Junction, near Wivelsfield in October 2014, as part of a campaign of improvement work on the railway between London and Brighton. **NETWORK RAIL**

139

INFRASTRUCTURE MAINTENANCE AND RENEWAL

in different forms, depending on the kind of railway in each area and the views of the operator.

A deep alliance with South West Trains (SWT) was the first to go further than other arrangements, enabled by a strong geographic overlap between the Network Rail management unit and the train operator. An alliance governance board has representatives from both SWT and Network Rail, and SWT's Managing Director is also MD of the alliance team. Train and infrastructure operations answer to one boss.

A new National Centre in Milton Keynes unites many of Network Rail's national teams and functions under one roof to support the new, more powerful business units.

INFRASTRUCTURE PROJECTS

Network Rail has also moved to a new, commercially focused, regionally based projects delivery business – Network Rail Infrastructure Projects – with four regional Directors and three programme Directors responsible for delivery of major renewal and enhancement work in their area. They manage their own profit and loss and will be charged with winning work under a proposed new competitive structure.

There is also a focus on developing the client capability within Network Rail to clearly define project outputs and work with delivery organisations much earlier in the project lifecycle. These changes should enable improved specification of output requirements, better integration of these into route plans, and greater discipline in the interface with the delivery team. This in turn should help to facilitate greater innovation, including through earlier engagement with the supply chain and through improved project-based partnerships with customers.

Where appropriate, says Network Rail, it will invite other organisations to tender for work in competition with Infrastructure Projects, enabling benchmarking of capital project delivery.

Network Rail Consulting was established in 2012, aimed at bringing further skills into the company, with further opportunities to benchmark against market competitors.

INFRASTRUCTURE CONTRACTORS

Network Rail carries out the bulk of maintenance work in-house, and is taking additional work in house during Control Period 5, but it has relied on contractors for track renewals and infrastructure projects work, and work on stations and structures, and aims to reinvigorate relationships with suppliers for CP5. Some of the main contractors are featured below.

AMEY

Amey's rail sector services include design, advisory and inspection services in signalling, electrification and power, track and civil engineering structures, as well as installation, renewals and enhancements services. Amey is part of Ferrovial, the major European services and construction group.

Amey secured a second consecutive term for Control Period 5 as Network Rail's sole supplier of civil examinations, (except London North Western, which Network Rail took in-house), and retained a major role in rail structures assessments. The new contracts are worth over £40m per annum.

In 2012 Amey won a £700m contract for electrification of the Great Western main line (Maidenhead to Bristol, Cardiff, Newbury and Oxford). In July 2014 a joint venture partnership with Keolis (30:70) won the franchise to operate and maintain the Docklands Light Railway for 6.5 years. Amey also has specialist skills in customer information and security.

BABCOCK RAIL

Babcock Rail - formerly First Engineering - is a leading player in the UK rail infrastructure market and a major track renewals company. It carries out a wide of range of rail infrastructure work, including track renewal, power and signalling contracts throughout Great Britain. Its Rail, Power and Communications businesses now work together as Network Engineering 'to leverage common skills and capabilities and provide value in a range of very competitive markets'.

The ABC Electrification joint venture of Alstom, Babcock and Costain secured two of Network Rail's National Electrification Programme framework contracts covering the Central (London North Western, South) and Wales and Western regions. These have an estimated value of £900m, shared equally by the partners. Babcock has had further success on the Edinburgh Glasgow Improvement Programme, winning a number of work packages both independently and with the ABC joint venture.

Babcock is also delivering conventional plain line track works across three regions, and the Rail business has also seen strong demand for overhead line and special project works.

The listed Chorley 'flying arches' were restored in summer 2014, with additional steel struts, during a blockade of the Chorley-Euxton Junction line for track lowering as part of the Northwest electrification project. **NETWORK RAIL**

BALFOUR BEATTY

Balfour Beatty Rail is one of the leading rail infrastructure suppliers in the UK, and Balfour Beatty's Construction and other businesses are involved in several major UK rail projects. From feasibility studies, planning and design through to implementation and asset management, Balfour Beatty Rail provides multi-disciplinary rail infrastructure services across the lifecycle of rail assets. Expertise covers electrification, track, power, signalling, civils, specialist rail plant, railway systems and technologies.

Balfour Beatty Construction in 2014 won a £70m contract to complete and fit-out the new Crossrail station at Woolwich. A contract in excess of £130 million to build two miles of the Crossrail route and Abbey Wood station was awarded to Balfour Beatty in 2013. Network Rail also awarded a contract to Balfour Beatty for the upgrade for Crossrail of a 12 mile section between West Drayton and Maidenhead.

Balfour Beatty in 2014 won a seven-year electrification framework with Network Rail, anticipated to be worth over £75m, covering design and installation of all electrification equipment for the Northern Hub electrification programme for routes between Manchester-Preston-Blackpool and Manchester-Stalybridge.

In July 2014, Balfour Beatty was awarded a £16m contract by Network Rail to deliver a series of Crossrail substations. Balfour Beatty is delivering the track remodelling for the London Bridge area as part of the Thameslink programme, a contract worth circa £50m. Track Partnership, a collaboration with London Underground, is working to transform track renewal delivery.

BAM NUTTALL

BAM Nuttall is Network Rail's main contractor for the delivery of the new Borders Railway. The £220m contract includes detailed design and construction works.

BAM Nuttall also won the Network Rail civils contract to build a dive under at Acton freight yard in Ealing for Crossrail. It was principal contractor for repairing the main breach of the Dawlish sea wall in 2014. Network Rail appointed BAM Nuttall as its Sussex region multifunctional framework contractor for CP5, a deal worth around £276m.

CARILLION

Carillion plc is one of the UK's leading support services and construction companies, recently awarded a share in a seven-year, £2bn electrification framework by Network Rail, in partnership with the Austrian firm SPL Powerlines. It covers the Central (East Midlands) and Scotland & North East regions. The partnership has opened training centres for rail engineers to develop skills needed to help deliver the electrification programme.

The £87m contract to design and construct Chiltern Railways' route between London Marylebone and Oxford and the western section of the East West Rail scheme was awarded in 2014 to a joint venture between Carillion and Buckingham Group Contracting.

A UK joint venture, Infrasig, combines Bombardier technology for both conventional and ETCS signalling solutions with the UK rail experience of Carillion to deliver signalling and multi-disciplinary projects. It received a framework contract for the development and design of the European Train Control System (ETCS).

Network Rail in 2013 awarded Carillion the contract to electrify the Cumbernauld-Glasgow Queen Street line, a £40m contract for over 50km of railway.

Carillion's £120m Key Output 2 contract for Thameslink involves fitting out of twin 650 metre tunnels and connecting the East Coast main line to Thameslink. It has also been awarded several Crossrail contracts, and won a £348m rail engineering framework for the London North Western and East Midlands routes in CP5.

COLAS RAIL

Colas Rail was created in 2007 after Amec Spie Rail was taken over by the French infrastructure company Colas, part of the Bouygues group. It combines the engineering skills of specialist businesses to provide total solutions in all aspects of railway infrastructure, from high speed rail systems to light and urban rail. It is also active in freight train operation (see 'Freight and Haulage' section).

Colas's on-track plant fleet includes modern S&C machines, which with additional compact and plain line

NETWORK RAIL'S TOP 20 SUPPLIERS, 2013-14

SUPPLIER	SPEND £M APPROX	SERVICE
EDF Energy	341	Electricity supply
Carillion Construction	281	Infrastructure contracting
Babcock Rail	220	Track infrastructure contracting
BAM Nuttall	209	Infrastructure contracting
Costain	203	Infrastructure contracting
Balfour Beatty Rail	183	Track infrastructure contracting
Amey-Colas	182	Track infrastructure contracting
Siemens Rail Automation	177	Signalling infrastructure contracting
Amalgamated Construction	160	Infrastructure contracting
J Murphy & Sons	150	Infrastructure contracting
Atkins	142	Signalling infrastructure contracting, consultancy
Signalling Solutions	139	Signalling infrastructure contracting
C Spencer	116	Infrastructure contracting
Tata Steel UK	113	Steel manufacturer
VolkerFitzpatrick	106	Infrastructure contracting
DB Schenker Rail (UK)	100	Rail logistics
Morgan Sindall	100	Construction services
Balfour Beatty Civil Engineering	89	Infrastructure contracting
Balfour Beatty Rail Infrastr Sers	86	Infrastructure contracting
Amey OWR	85	Structural inspection

INFRASTRUCTURE MAINTENANCE AND RENEWAL

machines provide Colas with what it believes to be the largest most advanced on-track plant fleet in the UK. In December 2013 it acquired Amey's on-track tamping machines business in a £5m deal.

Colas runs an extensive suite of courses for personnel who work on Network Rail infrastructure, including track safety and permanent way, electrification, safety training, and railway operations.

As part of a Multi Asset Framework Agreement, a joint venture between Colas Rail and Morgan Sindall has been awarded a £20m project by Network Rail to refurbish roof spans one to three at Paddington station. Other work the Colas Rail and Morgan Sindall joint venture has undertaken includes the circa £35m Swindon to Kemble Redoubling.

The Harlech-Pwllheli line now uses the new Pont Briwet viaduct, opened in September 2014, which replaced a 150 year-old wooden bridge over the Afon Dwyryd near Llandecwyn. **NETWORK RAIL**

COSTAIN

Costain is carrying out the major station redevelopment at London Bridge as part of the congestion-busting Thameslink programme, a contract worth circa £400m.

Costain, in the ATC joint venture with Alstom and TSO, has been awarded a contract worth approximately £300m to design, fit-out and commission the railway systems in Crossrail's tunnel network. Under the contract, ATC will design and install track, overhead lines and mechanical and electrical equipment to fit out the 21km of twin tunnels currently being bored under the streets of London. A joint venture with Alstom was awarded the £15m contract for the design, construction and commissioning of the system that will provide traction power for the trains in the central tunnelled section of the Crossrail scheme.

The ABC Electrification Joint Venture with Alstom and Babcock has won contracts for the electrification of the London North West (South) route (£435m), Edinburgh to Glasgow Improvement Programme (£75m) and Welsh Valley Lines (£450m).

Costain and Morgan Sindall were appointed to work with Network Rail to develop in-depth plans for the electrification of the main Glasgow-Edinburgh line and other major projects that form part of EGIP.

SPENCER

The £100m turnover Spencer Group employs 450 staff altogether, including 300 in its rail division. Spencer Rail Infrastructure provides quality multi-disciplinary engineering services to the UK and international markets - supporting and enhancing the operational infrastructure of heavy rail and light rail networks.

Recent projects include the design, construction and fit out of a new modular design building to house the Thames Valley Signalling Centre; a £30m project to extend station platforms on South West Trains routes; the design and build of an architecturally award winning station at St Helens Central; design and construction of a major new rail depot facility on behalf of East Midlands Trains; the major remodelling at Gravesend, and the new Ipswich chord project.

Spencer Rail was named as a principal contractor on the £150m Multi-Asset Framework Agreement for Scotland, covering upgrading and building platforms, bridges, crossings and signalboxes, as well as electrifying railways. Spencer is also delivering projects on a revised MAFA framework in East Anglia and Kent.

VOLKERRAIL

VolkerRail, part of the Netherlands-based Volker Wessels group, is a comprehensive multi-disciplinary rail infrastructure contractor. Capabilities include design, manufacture and construction; life time maintenance and asset inspection management; heavy rail rigid and ballasted track systems; light rail on-street track systems; signalling design, installation and testing; electrification, overhead line and line side civil engineering works; and high and low voltage power distribution systems. The overall railway capability is enhanced by the plant and welding division, with a large fleet of on-track plant, including Kirow rail mounted cranes.

VolkerRail, as part of the M-Pact Thales consortium with Laing O'Rourke and Thales UK, was awarded contracts to provide Manchester Metrolink Phase 3a and 3b extensions.

Sister company VolkerFitzpatrick carried out a Network Rail contract for a major enhancement of Gatwick Airport station, and has been constructing two Thameslink depots, three IEP depots, and Ilford Yard depot for Crossrail, and completed Siemens' Temple Mills depot, and Reading depot, as well as the third rail terminal at Felixstowe port.

A framework agreement covering enhancements, buildings and civils work on Network Rail's Anglia route in CP5 was also awarded to Volker Fitzpatrick (estimated value £480m). Volker Rail won the CP5 London North Western renewal and enhancement framework, plus a £61m electrification and plant framework. It was also awarded the second part of the Sheffield Supertram rail replacement project.

Rosehill Rail

NetworkRail Approved by Network Rail
Cert No. PA05/04429

THE NEW STANDARD · APPROVED BY NETWORK RAIL

ROAD CROSSING SYSTEMS

- High strength crossings designed for light or heavy traffic at all speeds as approved by Network Rail.
- Single panels are held securely by the Rosehill Connect system.
- Panels cannot become dislodged.
- Solid rubber panels can be individually removed or replaced without needing to dismantle the whole crossing.
- Developed from feedback at Network Rail & Rail Authorities worldwide.

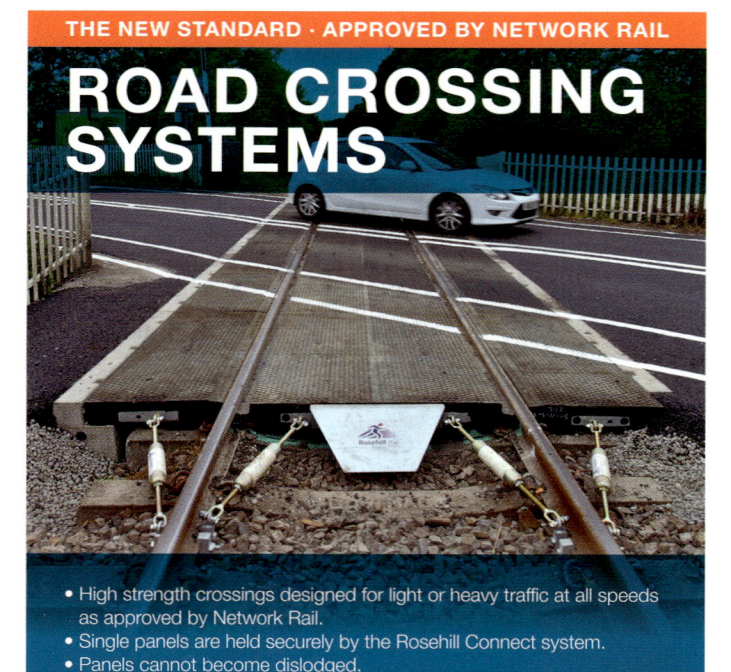

+44 (0)1422 317 482 · www.rosehillrail.com

SIGNALLING AND CONTROL

IN ASSOCIATION WITH

SIEMENS

SIGNALLING AND CONTROL

SIEMENS

A global leader in signalling and train control solutions, and with a proven track record in the successful delivery of both green and brownfield mainline and mass transit projects, Siemens Rail Automation has an extensive portfolio of track-side and train-borne systems. The company's range spans train control, computer-based interlockings, operations control systems, components, track vacancy detection, level-crossing protection and rail communications for mainline, light rail and mass transit applications.

Safety is at the heart of all Siemens' activities. With record levels of work across the UK's rail network, the company focuses on the safety of its people and systems - and the need to work closely with clients and contractor partners, ensuring that all activities are carried out in a manner that does not present harm.

In 2014, Siemens has been involved in some of the UK's most important rail infrastructure schemes, including the Thameslink, Crossrail, Northern Hub and Edinburgh Glasgow Improvement Programmes, as well as major projects including Watford, Birmingham New Street, Reading, Great Northern Great Eastern (GNGE), North Lincolnshire and Borders.

Work for the Thameslink Programme continues to be a major focus, with four new platforms brought into service during 2014 at London Bridge Station, together with a complete re-modelling of the adjacent Spa Road junction. The platforms have been progressively introduced since August, as the redevelopment of the station continued, and can now accommodate Siemens' new Thameslink 12-car trains.

With a series of major commissionings, the GNGE programme had a high profile in 2014, including the delivery of Phase 4 in August. Covering the re-signalling of 15 miles of railway, this saw 12 manually controlled barrier and three automatic half barrier level crossings brought into service after a 16 day blockade. Despite the scale of this work, the close relationship between Siemens, Network Rail and other GNGE Alliance partners enabled Phase 4 to be successfully delivered, ahead of time.

Siemens continues to support London Underground in maximising the capabilities delivered on the Victoria and Central Lines. The Victoria Line is now achieving a timetabled throughput of 34 trains per hour on a regular basis, putting it in the top league of European mass transit lines.

During 2014, at Network Rail's European Train Control System (ETCS) National Integration Facility (ENIF), Siemens successfully completed all planned demonstrations of ETCS functionality and capability on or ahead of schedule. Demonstrations included the UK's first ever on track RBC-to-RBC handover between two suppliers - a crucial demonstration of ETCS interoperability, proving that an ETCS Level 2 train can run seamlessly between areas signalled by different suppliers. Siemens also provided a full simulation of an ETCS 'overlay' (both ETCS L2 and conventionally signalled trains) running a representative timetable on the Reading final layout under the control of Siemens Trackguard Futur RBC and Westlock interlockings.

Away from mainline projects, Siemens' systems were also commissioned on the new Edinburgh Tram network. Having entered operational service in May (five weeks ahead of schedule), this was a major multi-discipline turn-key project for Siemens, with its RailCom Manager solution providing an integrated control and communications system, capable of further expansion as the network is likely to be extended in the future. At the control centre, two operators manage the entire network, with purpose-designed, fully-integrated work stations providing touch screen capability for all communications and systems monitoring.

Landmarks have also been reached in the development of Siemens' mobile communications technology. In September, the company released enhanced software for the British GSM-R cab radio fleet (approximately 8,000 Siemens-supplied units). The software, which is being rolled out by Network Rail, increases the resilience of the units' Disk on Module (DOM) memory to electrical interference, by detecting instability in the vehicle power supply and preventing concurrent writing to the module. Reliability of the units now exceeds all targets and expectations.

Alongside Siemens Rail Automation, Siemens Rail Systems division provides expertise and technology in a full range of rail vehicles – from heavy rail to metros and from trams to light-rail vehicles. In the UK alone the company employs around 700 people and maintains over 350 Siemens passenger trains which cover over 50 million miles a year. In 2013, the company was awarded the contract to deliver 1,140 new Desiro City carriages for the Thameslink Programme and to construct two new depots; this second-generation train combines the latest technology with the proven Siemens Desiro platform.

Building on Siemens' overall involvement in the Crossrail project, the company's Rail Electrification division has also now secured a contract to supply three auto transformer gas insulated substations for the programme. These traction power substations will be supplied to Network Rail, which is delivering the on-network Crossrail section.

With proven project experience, cutting-edge technology and some of the most talented signaling and control engineers in the rail industry, Siemens continues to set standards in efficiency, quality and reliability, enabling rail operators to realise operational and performance benefits from a wide range of integrated solutions.

The close relationship between Siemens, Network Rail and other GNGE Alliance partners enabled Phase 4 to be successfully delivered, ahead of time, in August 2014.

Station Equipment

Health & Safety

RAILTEX '15

12 – 14 MAY 2015 • NEC, BIRMINGHAM, UK
12th INTERNATIONAL EXHIBITION OF RAILWAY EQUIPMENT SYSTEMS & SERVICES

Rolling Stock

Electrification

Infrastructure

Signalling

Track

Railtex is the all-encompassing showcase for technological innovation across all sectors of

Tel + 44 (0) 1727 814400
info@railtex.co.uk

SIGNALLING AND CONTROL

The first live panel at Manchester ROC. **TONY MILES**

TRAFFIC MANAGEMENT DEVELOPS

Network Rail awarded contracts in 2014 for the first phase of a new nationwide traffic management system for Britain's railways.

The company has placed traffic management technology at the heart of its operating strategy, which is planned to consolidate control of Britain's rail network from more than 800 signal boxes into 12 state-of-the-art rail operating centres over the next 15-30 years. Once fully implemented, this strategy is expected to cut the cost of Britain's railways by £250m each year, improve industry efficiency, reduce delays and provide more accurate and timely information to staff and passengers.

Contracts worth a combined £28.8m were awarded to Thales UK to deploy traffic management technology at Network Rail's Cardiff and Romford operating centres by December 2015. Thales is one of three global suppliers who have been working with Network Rail since 2012 to develop and test a traffic management software prototype, using real-time information to mock up how the new system would control the railway in future.

Robin Gisby, Network Rail's managing director of network operations, said: 'As the number of people and businesses relying on rail continues to grow, it is vital we have the technology to make the best use of Britain's rail infrastructure. The traffic management which will be deployed on the network uses tried and tested technology used on railways around the world to help deliver a leaner, more efficient and reliable network.'

The new, highly automated system will allow larger areas of the network to be controlled from fewer locations and will help increase capacity and improve reliability through more effective handling of disruption.

Thales was chosen after an exhaustive process and rigorous testing, said Network Rail, while train operators will also be using common systems to maximise the benefits this new technology will bring. Network Rail has analysed and compared best practice from different systems used on a number of other rail networks to develop a reliable product which will suit the varied demands of Britain's complex rail network.

The value of the contracts for traffic management first deployment are worth a combined £28.8m to deploy traffic management technology at Network Rail's Cardiff and Romford rail operating centres (ROCs).

The contract for traffic management LINX (integration) development, delivery and support was awarded to Signalling Solutions Ltd at a value of £3.4m, with completion scheduled for December 2015.

The award of contracts for the national rollout of traffic management will be subject to future competitions and will involve all current traffic management framework holders: Thales UK, Signalling Solutions, and Hitachi Rail Europe.

Hitachi, Thales and SSL each developed a prototype traffic management system (TMS) which demonstrated specific functionality. These three systems were rigorously tested and evaluated by experienced frontline users for a three month period from July 2013.

Plans for further deployment of TMS across the network were being developed and will be subject to a separate commercial process.

Network Rail has over 800 operating locations, with aging and inconsistent equipment and different ways of working. Many of these locations already need replacing, but by upgrading signalling at faster than

Working in partnership delivers exceptional results

We think that collaboration starts with being open:
with our clients, to sharing ideas, to new ways of doing things.

ATKINS

STAFFORDSHIRE ALLIANCE
Staffordshire Alliance delivery partner

BSI
BS 11000 certification

Plan Design Enable

rail@atkinsglobal.com   www.atkinsglobal.com/rail

SIGNALLING AND CONTROL

ETCS provides train drivers with a target speed, including movement authority, on a screen in the cab. **ALSTOM**

The line between Huyton and Roby, near Liverpool, is the first section of railway being controlled from the new Manchester ROC following resignalling and upgrading work carried out in July 2014. **SIEMENS**

usual pace, Network Rail believes it can deliver savings sooner and for longer, and says similar approaches have already been proven internationally.

At the heart of the strategy are the rail operating centres – 12 centres which will become the central hub for all aspects of operating the railway, where Network Rail works with train and freight operators to deliver a better railway for Britain using leading technology. By 2015, Network Rail plans to have built six new operating centres, in addition to six existing locations.

Existing locations :
- Cardiff
- Derby
- Didcot
- Edinburgh
- Glasgow
- Gillingham

New buildings:
- Basingstoke
- Manchester
- Romford
- Rugby
- Three Bridges
- York

The development and implementation of traffic management technology adds the systems to complement the physical construction and investment taking place at these locations.

Significant benefits are anticipated for Network Rail and the broader industry, including passengers, freight users and train operators.

There should be less delay as better technology will help restore normal services much quicker following disruption; and there should also be more flexibility and capacity, as more reliable performance and better train regulation will allow for more flexiblility with train plans and can potentially put more services onto the network;

When complete, the programme is estimated to save £250m a year. Network Rail believes a more affordable railway with more passengers will help create a sustainable future for the network.

Whilst the ROCs bring big benefits for the future, they also mark the end of a remarkably long era for the 500+ mechanical signal boxes on the national network. Network Rail says it is keen to acknowledge this, and is working closely with heritage organisations to ensure the best examples of the signalling heritage are suitably preserved.

ERTMS INFRASTRUCTURE

The European Rail Traffic Management System and its signalling component ETCS (European Train Control System) will form the basis of future signalling schemes on the network.

Network Rail has the responsibility of co-ordinating and synchronising projects to commission ETCS on the East Coast and Great Western main lines.

According to an updated delivery plan in mid 2014, ETCS Level 2 (without signals) is planned to be deployed on the East Coast main line (ECML) in phases:
- King's Cross remodelling and relock, retaining signals (Phase 1, Stage 1);
- King's Cross to Wood Green overlay with signals, and Moorgate to Drayton Park Level 2 (Phase 1, Stage 2 – December 2018);
- King's Cross to South Peterborough Level 2, inclusive of Hertford Loop, Hitchin to Royston (Phase 1, Stage 3 – August 2020);
- South Peterborough to Doncaster South (Decoy) (Phase 2 December 2020).

ETCS for the Great Western route is initially planned as an overlay on the existing signalling system between London Paddington and Heathrow for the planned start of dynamic testing of Crossrail trains from April 2017. It is then to be installed as an overlay on Paddington-Bristol South, including Oxford and Newbury, by July 2019. The lineside signals will remain operational until all trains on the route have been fitted with ETCS, with the signals' removal currently planned for 2025.

Deployment on the Thameslink core route is managed by the Thameslink Programme.

ETCS provides train drivers with a target speed, including movement authority, on a screen in the cab. The train 'knows' where it is through a combination of trackside equipment and on-board sensors, while instructions from the control centre are conveyed through the GSM-R (Global System for Mobile - Railway) signal.

By signalling each train according to its braking and accelerating capabilities, it should allow more capacity to be squeezed out of the current network, and also bringing considerable cost savings over traditional lineside resignalling schemes.

Following an early deployment scheme on the Cambrian line in Wales, four companies' ETCS equipment has been tested by Network Rail – Signalling Solutions (Alstom and Balfour Beatty), Infrasig (Bombardier and Carillion), Siemens Rail Automation (formerly Invensys / Westinghouse), and Ansaldo STS (supplier of the pilot ERTMS project on the Cambrian route).

148

IMAGINE
THE JOURNEY

Transformed by our world-class digital technologies

DeltaRail
www.deltarail.com

SIGNALLING AND CONTROL

The ETCS National Integration Facility (ENIF) at Hitchin utilises a five-mile stretch of the down line on the Hertford Loop between Molewood tunnel and Langley South junction, controlled from a new structure in the former Hitchin goods yard. The test facility has been used by Network Rail for 18 months to examine four suppliers' trackside ETCS equipment, using a converted Class 313 laboratory train, and is also being used to test the new signalling systems for Thameslink.

ETCS CAB FITMENT FUND

Migration from conventional signalling to ETCS is to be a requirement in new train operating company franchises, but 'first-in-class' installation to each type of train cab is to be developed by Network Rail. It will work with freight and passenger operators to fund and co-ordinate the retro-fitment of ETCS on-board equipment to their fleets, as well as the consequential changes to their business to support operation with ETCS.

Network Rail also has to ensure sufficient ETCS-equipped on-track machines are available.

It is anticipated that up to 550 freight locomotives will need to be equipped with ETCS in Control Period 5 (2014-2019) to operate on the East Coast main line and prepare for subsequent route deployments.

SIGNALLING IN CP5

New Rail Operating Centres coming on stream in CP5 include a £50m centre in Basingstoke and a £23m centre at Three Bridges.

Meanwhile large resignalling projects under way include the Cardiff Area resignalling scheme, awarded to Atkins and begun in CP4, valued at £200m.

Atkins is also involved in the Stafford Area Improvements Programme, being delivered as a pure alliance by Atkins, Laing O'Rourke, Network Rail and Volker Rail.

Siemens (formerly Invensys) is the signalling contractor on the Reading redevelopment and remodelling, and is also at work on the Thameslink project, which will see the first implementation of Automatic Train Operation on Network Rail. It is also involved in resignalling projects at Watford, and as part of the GN-GE (Peterborough-Sleaford-Doncaster) route upgrading to provide an alternative to the East Coast main line, and has a Northern Hub project office in Manchester.

Other projects in the offing are:
- Birmingham New Street, possibly £100m of signalling work as part of the West Midlands resignalling;
- Edinburgh-Glasgow Improvements Programme (EGIP);
- a £140m signalling scheme between Richmond and Bracknell;
- a £26m scheme between Yeovil and Castle Cary;
- a £25m scheme on the Portsmouth line;
- East Kent resignalling Phase 2;
- Motherwell area signalling enhancements including bi-directional signalling on the West Coast main line;
- the Swansea area, Newport-Shrewsbury and Chester to Llandudno are also to be resignalled in CP5.

The rail operating centre in Manchester, opened in July 2014, is one of 12 which will eventually manage the entire rail network. **NETWORK RAIL**

The final stages of the GNGE route upgrading took place in 2014, with many level crossings modernised using obstacle detection technology. This is Rowston crossing, north of Sleaford. **NETWORK RAIL**

thalesgroup.com

Ground Transportation solutions

Everywhere it matters, we deliver

PASSENGER SATISFACTION
Offering real time information and ensuring security

OPERATIONAL EFFICIENCY
Ensure optimised network management with minimal investment

TRANSPORT SAFETY
Automate critical decisions to eliminate human errors

NETWORK CAPACITY
Improve flow with automated signalling for optimal train frequency

SEAMLESS JOURNEYS
Unique fare systems for all transport modes

REVENUE PROTECTION
Innovative solutions to collect revenues

Millions of critical decisions are made every day in transportation. The ability to run networks smoothly and efficiently is crucial to economic growth and quality of life. Thales is at the heart of this. We design, develop and deliver equipment, systems and services, providing end-to-end solutions. Our integrated smart technologies give decision makers the information and control they need to make more effective responses in critical environments. Everywhere, together with our customers, we are making a difference.

THALES
Together • Safer • Everywhere

SIGNALLING AND CONTROL

SIGNALLING RENEWALS AND ENHANCEMENTS

Network Rail awards the majority of signalling renewals and enhancements across England, Scotland and Wales through framework agreements of up to seven years that were established in 2012.

The frameworks were awarded to:
- Siemens Rail Automation (formerly Invensys Rail,
- Signalling Solutions,
- Atkins.

The framework agreements form the backbone of a programme to modernise and maintain safety-critical railway signalling systems and are designed to deliver efficiency savings across the company's signalling work bank over the next seven years, through further reductions in unit costs.

Network Rail said that the length of the agreements, coupled with a visible workload, would provide stability throughout the supply chain, and drive cost savings and innovation.

The frameworks incorporate collaborative working in order to deliver the necessary efficiencies. Integrated design teams and a reduction in man-marking will remove costly duplication of effort, while smoothing of peaks and troughs in Network Rail's work bank will allow better use of suppliers' resources.

The frameworks appointed both a primary and secondary supplier for each area. This provides the flexibility needed to meet the significant increase in volumes required over the life of the framework and provides an alternative in each area if the primary supplier does not have the capacity. The agreements also provide the option to competitively tender up to 20% of the predicted workload each year.

STAFFORD-CREWE SECOND PHASE

The second phase of the £250m Stafford Area Improvements Programme is seeing new signalling installed in and around Stafford station, and a new freight loop in the area, which will free space for additional passenger services.

The resignalling of Stafford is part of the wider package of investment in the West Coast main line between Stafford and Crewe which are aimed at helping to boost reliability and capacity and remove one of the last remaining bottlenecks on the route.

The third phase of the project is the construction of a flyover at Norton Bridge near Stafford which will replace a flat junction.

When complete, the upgraded section of line will be controlled by Network Rail's new rail operating centre in Rugby.

The signalling upgrade at Stafford includes installation of the new freight loop and the replacement of life expired signalling, telecoms and power supplies. Signalling control is being transferred from the existing Stafford No 4 and No 5 signalboxes to Rugby, with the installation of bi-directional signalling for platforms 1, 3, 4, 5 and 6, and an increase in the 'slow' line speeds (predominantly used by local passenger/freight services) from 75mph to 100mph between Great Bridgeford (near Norton Bridge) and Stafford. Running from spring 2014 to summer 2015, the majority of these works are being delivered during weekends and midweek nights.

The Stafford Area Improvements Programme is being delivered by the Staffordshire Alliance – a partnership of Atkins, Laing O'Rourke, Network Rail and VolkerRail, working as part of a new collaborative contract.

ETCS AWARD

Hitachi Rail Europe Ltd announced in August 2014 that it had signed a contract with Network Rail for implementation of the European Train Control System (ETCS) on two Class 37 locomotives. The project work includes the design, vehicle modification, ETCS installation, testing and commissioning of Hitachi's ETCS for West Coast Railways, for operational use on the Cambrian Line European Rail Traffic Management System (ERTMS) in Wales, for scheduled completion in August 2015.

This contract followed the successful proof of concept of Hitachi ETCS on a Class 97 Locomotive ('Verification-Train 3' trial) which tested interoperability with a separate supplier's groundside system in use on the Network Rail Cambrian Line infrastructure.

Also, Hitachi recently obtained certification from a Notified Body of the on-board system in accordance with the Control Command and Signalling TSI (Technical Specification for Interoperability) 2012/88/EU and 2012/696/E. This being achieved through a rigorous formal assessment process and demonstrating compliance with relevant TSI and EN norms to the highest Safety Integrity Level 4.

This is Hitachi's first formal order received for ETCS, which recognises the intensive development, testing and certification of the system over the last seven years to the European TSI and associated subsets. This in-cab radio based signalling system will also be implemented on the concurrent Intercity Express Programme Class 800/801 rolling stock for Great Western and East Coast main lines. ■

The ETCS National Integration Facility (ENIF) uses a five-mile stretch of the down line on the Hertford Loop, with this converted Class 313 laboratory train, testing four suppliers' ETCS equipment. **JOHN GLOVER**

LIGHT RAIL AND METRO

IN ASSOCIATION WITH

THALES

LIGHT RAIL AND METRO

New Alstom Citadis trams line up at Wilkinson Street depot in Nottingham. **ALSTOM**

LIGHT RAIL SPREADS ITS WINGS

The new Edinburgh tram system, opened in 2014, joins the eight main light-rail systems across the border in England, on which 227 million passenger journeys were made in the 2013/14 year. That represents a gain of 2% over 2012/13.

London's Docklands Light Railway accounts for 44.7% of the total and London Tramlink 13.7%. Other strong performers were Tyne & Wear Metro at 15.7%, and fast-growing Manchester Metrolink at 12.9%.

The remaining four systems carried 13.0% of all passengers between them: both Midland Metro and Nottingham Express Transit systems are currently being extended, and Sheffield Supertram is gearing up for its Tram-Train extension which will test the feasibility of mixing the operation of urban street trams with the general purpose railway. How many other locations are there in Britain for which this might be suitable?

The Stourbridge Town shuttle has Ultra-Light-Rail Parry People Mover vehicles of Class 139. Again, where else might such a system, or developments of it, be found suitable?

The much older Glasgow Subway is a wholly underground operation - and completely pointless (in the sense of not switching trains between tracks at points - the only rail connections are to and from the depot on the surface).

Those travelling the furthest by light rail were the riders on Midland Metro, at 10.5km average, followed very closely by Manchester Metrolink at 10.4km. Tyne & Wear Metro, with its lengthy system, came in at 8.3km, with the rest all at around 5km.

In the background are modern approaches such as driverless operation, a long term reality on the Docklands Light Railway, promised for the Glasgow Subway, and perhaps in the future for Tyne & Wear.

LIGHT RAIL AND METRO NETWORKS

Blackpool Transport

KEY STATISTICS	2012/13	2013/14
Passenger journeys (millions)	3.7	4.3
Passenger km (millions)	16.0	20.5
Passenger revenue (£m 2013/14 prices)	4.8	6.1

Blackpool's tramway, Britain's last surviving first generation tramway, has now been fully modernised. The single 18km route runs from Starr Gate in Blackpool to the Ferry Terminus in Fleetwood, mostly on reserved track along the seafront. Owned by Blackpool Borough Council, it is operated by the municipally-owned Blackpool Transport Services Ltd.

Government funded two thirds of the reconstruction costs of £102m, the rest equally from Blackpool and Lancashire councils. Of that, roughly £33m was required for the new trams.

A new depot was built at Starr Gate for the 16 Bombardier 'Flexity 2' trams, each with five articulated sections. They are a substantial 32.2m long and commenced fleet operation on 4 April 2012. Each has 74 seats and a standing capacity of 148; they are fully accessible. This required new level access platforms at stops, which were reduced in number to 37. Nine of the fleet of 1934-vintage double-deckers have been upgraded and retained for seasonal operations; there is also a heritage fleet.

Private/public body Transport for Lancashire (TfL) has made a new branch of the tramway to Blackpool North station a priority, with a £16m contribution anticipated from the Department for Transport.

IN ASSOCIATION WITH **THALES**

DLR

KEY STATISTICS	2012/13	2013/14
Passenger journeys (millions)	100.0	101.6
Passenger km (millions)	509.8	536.9
Passenger revenue (£m 2013/14 prices)	127.2	133.1

The original section of the Docklands Light Railway in London opened in 1987; successive extensions have taken it to its present length of 38km and 45 stations. Operation is by 149 cars built by Bombardier in Belgium, each 28.8m long. Most trains are now formed of three pairs of the two-section articulated vehicles. The main depot is at Beckton, with a subsidiary depot (the original) at Poplar.

The 750V DC third-rail electrification uses underside contact. The DLR has many grade separated junctions, keeping operational conflicts to the minimum. For signalling, the DLR uses the Thales Seltrac moving block system.

London 2012 resulted in passenger journeys growing by 16% in 2012/13 compared with 2011/12; in 2013/14 this reduced to less than 2%, but it was still positive. This trend is expected to continue until the opening of Crossrail, after which it is likely to level off.

From December 2014, the DLR is operated by Keolis/Amey on a franchise until April 2021, with a two year optional extension. It includes the sections to King George V and on to Woolwich Arsenal that were the responsibility of separate construction / operation concessions; these have been terminated by agreement. That leaves City Greenwich Lewisham (CGL) Rail, managing the Lewisham extension until 2021.

For the construction of Crossrail, Pudding Mill Lane station has been relocated and enlarged, opening in April 2014. Near Custom House the DLR has been realigned and the station will be alongside the new one for Crossrail.

Edinburgh Trams

The long-anticipated entry of Edinburgh Trams into public service took place on 31 May 2014. Trams run for 14km between the Airport, Edinburgh Park, Haymarket, St Andrew Square (for Waverley) and York Place. End-to-end journey times are about 30min. Project management was latterly overseen by Transport Scotland.

The revised overall project costs as approved by Edinburgh Council in 2011 were £776m. A report of 25 September 2014 showed that the target was met, consisting of £440m for infrastructure, £167m for project management, land etc, £104m for utilities and £65m for the trams themselves.

The twenty seven 42.8m seven-section trams built by CAF in Spain are the longest operating in Britain; they are based at Gogar depot. Ten or more trams, ordered when the system was to be much larger, are surplus to requirements, but they cannot be used easily on other British systems.

Fares are £1.50 for all single journeys except those using the Airport stop, when the price rises to £5.00. A new integrated organisation, Transport for Edinburgh, comprises local authority owned operators Lothian Buses and Edinburgh Trams.

SPT

KEY STATISTICS	2012/13	2013/14
Passenger journeys (millions)	12.6	12.7
Passenger km (millions)	40.2	40.6
Passenger revenue (£m 2013/14 prices)	14.8	16.0

The Glasgow Subway has 15 stations and runs for 10.6km in a complete circle. A round trip takes 24min to complete and trains run every four minutes at peak. Two separate running tunnels are to the restrictive diameter of 3.35 metres, and track gauge is set at the highly unusual 1,220mm (4ft 0in). The three car trains are a mere 38.3 metres long.

Often described as the world's third oldest underground railway, owners and operators Strathclyde Passenger Transport (SPT) add the word 'probably'. It opened on 14 December 1896, its predecessors being London on 10 January 1863 and Budapest in May 1896. On opening it was described officially as 'The first passenger-carrying underground cable-car system in the world.'

Last modernised in 1980, the Subway has a new improvement plan under way, focusing on modernisation of working practices; new smartcard ticketing; new automated trains and signalling; refurbished stations with platform edge doors and improved accessibility; and renewing track and improving the tunnel infrastructure.

The total cost of £290m is being funded with a grant of £246m from Transport Scotland, the balance by SPT. Completion is due in 2018/19.

TRAMLINK

KEY STATISTICS	2012/13	2013/14
Passenger journeys (millions)	30.1	31.2
Passenger km (millions)	156.4	162.4
Passenger revenue (£m 2013/14 prices)	22.9	23.5

TfL's London Tramlink is mostly a conversion to light rail of four under-used / disused rail lines around Croydon, with a central loop around the town centre. The system is 28km long and became fully operational in May 2000. Electrification is at 750V DC.

The original fleet consisted of 24 three-section trams, 30.1m long, and partly low-floor, built by Bombardier. An additional six Variobahn trams with five sections, 32.4m long, were delivered by Stadler in 2012, and a further four are on order.

Operation is by Tram Operations Ltd, a First Group subsidiary. In July 2014, TfL triggered a half-way break clause in Bombardier's 30-year fleet maintenance contract, and is bringing the work in-house.

A £30m project is set to enable a 12 trams/hr service between Wimbledon and Croydon. Work is under way on doubling single track from Beddington Lane to Mitcham Junction, and making a second platform available at Wimbledon. Completion is expected in 2016.

An extension from Morden to Sutton by about 2030 is outlined in the Mayor's London 2050 infrastructure plan, as well as further capacity improvements.

Metrolink

KEY STATISTICS	2012/13	2013/14
Passenger journeys (millions)	25.0	29.2
Passenger km (millions)	261.7	303.0
Passenger revenue (£m 2013/14 prices)	42.7	51.8

The first phase of Transport for Greater Manchester's Metrolink system created a city centre link between the former heavy rail lines to Bury and Altrincham. A 6km route to Eccles opened in 2000 and, after numerous issues over funding, work on the 'Big-Bang' expansion of the system began in 2009. This will see four new lines constructed, increasing the network from 37 to 95km by 2016, making Metrolink the largest light rail network in the UK, with 92 stops.

The expansion is being paid for from a special transport fund of £1.5bn,

Edinburgh Tram No 261 arrives at the airport on 5 June 2014, a few days after the tram line's long awaited opening. **TONY MILES**

LIGHT RAIL AND METRO

Alstom Citadis tram on trial in Nottingham in August 2014. **NOTTINGHAM EXPRESS TRANSIT**

drawn from an increase in council tax, contributions from Manchester Airport, increased fares revenue, and the early release of government allocations.

The first new section, the 400m spur to MediaCityUK, Salford Quays, opened in 2010, and in 2011, Trafford Bar to St Werburgh's Road opened.

In June 2012 the Oldham Mumps line opened, extended to Shaw & Crompton in December 2012 and Rochdale rail station in February 2013. The diversion through Oldham town centre opened in January 2014 and the rest of the route to Rochdale town centre opened in March 2014.

The East Manchester extension to Droylsden opened in February 2013, through key regeneration areas, and serving the Etihad Campus (Manchester City football stadium) and Velodrome. St Werburgh's Road to Didsbury carried its first passengers in May 2013, and the Droylsden to Ashton-under-Lyne section opened in October 2013.

Delivered by the MPT consortium (Laing O'Rourke, VolkerRail and Thales), the route from St Werburgh's Road to Manchester Airport, with several major structures, opened in November 2014, more than 12 months ahead of schedule.

To handle the increased flow of trams through the city centre, a 1.6km Second City Crossing is under construction from Deansgate-Castlefield via St Peters Square to Victoria station, due to open in 2017.

Plans for a line to the Trafford Centre retail complex are being progressed, with funding announced by government in November 2014. It could later continue to Port Salford.

The original 32-strong fleet of T68 and T68a trams was withdrawn by April 2014, replaced by new Bombardier M5000 vehicles. With further orders (for ten additional M5000s in December 2013, for the proposed Trafford Park line, and a further 16 in September 2014, to provide extra capacity), the Metrolink fleet will reach 120 trams, based at the Queens Road and Trafford depots.

The operator is Metrolink RATP Dev Ltd under a 10-year concession (from 2007, sold by Stagecoach in 2011.

KEY STATISTICS	2012/13	2013/14
Passenger journeys (millions)	4.8	4.7
Passenger km (millions)	50.4	49.1
Passenger revenue (£m 2013/14 prices)	7.9	7.9

Midland Metro's 20.4km Line 1 opened in 1999, mostly over the former Great Western Railway route between Birmingham Snow Hill and Wolverhampton. Services are operated by Travel West Midlands Ltd, part of the National Express Group. Electrification is 750V DC overhead.

A 1.4km extension, under construction by Balfour Beatty, runs from Snow Hill via a new £9m viaduct to a terminus in Stephenson Street (outside New Street station) in Birmingham. There will be four new stops, one of which replaces the existing Snow Hill station terminus. Opening is likely to coincide with the Gateway rebuild of New Street station in 2015.

Confirmed and funded further extensions are: Stephenson Street to Centenary Square, opening 2017; Centenary Square to Five Ways and Edgbaston (after 2017); to Wolverhampton railway station (2019). Funding for an Eastside line to Moor Street, Curzon Street (for HS2) and Digbeth was also announced in 2014.

A new tram fleet of 20 Urbos 3 trams (with options for five more) built by CAF is in the course of delivery. It is anticipated that they will be operating all services from spring 2015.

NET

KEY STATISTICS	2012/13	2013/14
Passenger journeys (millions)	7.4	7.9
Passenger km (millions)	32.9	35.7
Passenger revenue (£m 2013/14 prices)	8.6	8.3

Nottingham Express Transit's (NET's) Line 1 runs from the main line station to Hucknall via the city centre, with a branch to Phoenix Park. It opened in 1994. The original fleet consisted of 15 articulated five section cars of 33.0m, built in Derby by Bombardier. Electrification is at 750V DC and each car has 58 seats.

Patronage recovered slightly in 2013/14, reversing a trend which has been apparent for several years.

Phase 2 is expected to open in early 2015. Construction funding was by a grant of £480m by government; separately, Regional Funding Allocations included £7.8m for preparation work. Approval was linked to the introduction of a work place parking levy.

The Phase 2 route continues south across Nottingham station on a new bridge. It splits - Line 2 runs 7.6km to Clifton and Line 3 for 9.8km to Toton Lane. Both terminate at new Park & Ride facilities.

The 32km system will be more than double the length of the original Line 1. In December 2011, the PFI concession to finance, build, operate and maintain NET Phase 2, as well as operate and maintain Phase 1, for a period of 22 years, was awarded to Tramlink Nottingham. This is a consortium of tram builder Alstom, operators Keolis and Wellglade (parent of bus company

TrentBarton), Vinci, and Investors OFI InfraVia and Meridiam Infrastructure.

Delivery of 22 new five-section low floor Alstom Citadis 302 trams started in 2013 and is now complete.

Stagecoach SUPERTRAM

KEY STATISTICS	2012/13	2013/14
Passenger journeys (millions)	14.4	12.6
Passenger km (millions)	93.4	81.5
Passenger revenue (£m 2013/14 prices)	14.7	13.9

Roundly half of the 29km Sheffield Supertram network, completed in 1995, is fully segregated. The route incorporates some tight geometry, with a minimum horizontal curve radius of 25m and vertical curve of 100m. Maximum gradients are 10%.

Services are operated by Stagecoach from the City Centre to Middlewood in the north with a spur to Meadowhall Interchange. In the south the route is to Halfway, with a spur to Herdings Park. There are 25 Siemens/Duewag cars of 34.8m in the Supertram fleet.

Passenger numbers dropped noticeably in 2013/14, due in part perhaps to bus replacement during tram system re-railing.

The £60m Tram-Train Project is to test the operation of specialist tramway-type vehicles over conventional railway from Rotherham and then continuing on the Sheffield tram network. The trials are being led by South Yorkshire transport executive in conjunction with the Department for Transport, Northern Rail, Network Rail, and Stagecoach Supertram.

Services are to originate in Rotherham Parkgate Retail Park and use the freight only heavy rail route towards Sheffield. This is part single track. The tram-trains will then join the Supertram network via a 400 metre link in the Tinsley area at Meadowhall South. Network Rail is electrifying their part of the route at 750V DC overhead.

Tram-trains will use a new stop at Rotherham Parkgate, their own new section of platform at Rotherham Central and new dedicated island platform at Meadowhall South. Platform height will be 385mm above rail level.

The new tram-trains will make the eight mile journey non-stop to the Cathedral stop in Sheffield City Centre in about 25min.

Seven 37.2m Citylink tram-train vehicles are being built by Vossloh of Valencia, Spain. They will have 750V DC and 25kV AC capability, to accommodate future main line electrification. Three vehicles will provide the basic service, three will be available to strengthen existing tram services, with one maintenance spare. Delivery is expected from mid-2015.

Matters which will receive particular attention include the wheel/rail interface and profiles, variations in technical standards, vehicle detection for signalling purposes, the use of sanders for adhesion and the use of magnetic track brakes. It is anticipated that the tram-train services will be operational from early 2016.

M METRO
TYNE & WEAR METRO

KEY STATISTICS	2012/13	2013/14
Passenger journeys (millions)	37.0	35.7
Passenger km (millions)	299.3	295.4
Passenger revenue (£m 2013/14 prices)	44.4	45.2

Britain's first essay into modern light rail systems, the Tyne & Wear Metro, opened in stages from 1980 to 1983 between Newcastle, Gateshead, and North and South Tyneside. Using former British Rail lines plus new underground sections in the central area, it displays elements of light rail, heavy underground metro, and longer distance higher speed urban and interurban operation.

Its early popularity can be judged by a high of 59.1m passenger journeys in 1985 on a 56km system. Extensions to Newcastle Airport in 1991 and Sunderland/South Hylton in 2002 produced a system with 78km of route. Tracks between Pelaw and Sunderland are owned by Network Rail and there is mixed usage with National Rail operators. A low point came in 2000/01 with 32.1m passenger journeys; subsequent recovery to over 40 million journeys has not been sustained.

The 90 strong fleet of six-axle Metrocars was built by Metro-Cammell in 1980. As currently being refurbished, each seats 64 and they normally run in pairs. They are 27.8m long. Electrification is at 1,500V DC overhead and the single rolling stock depot is at Gosforth.

Since 2010, operations have been in the hands of Arriva group company DB Regio Tyne & Wear, under a concession that runs until 2017 and is extendable to 2019. Nexus Rail, owned by the Passenger Transport Executive, continues to own the Metro and sets fares and services. It pays DB Regio a performance-based fee, and has responsibility for infrastructure. Contracting-out of operations was a requirement of a £580m government funding package, providing £230m for operating subsidy over nine years from 2010 and £350m for the 11-year Metro 'All Change' renewal and modernisation.

In 2014, Nexus launched consultation on Metro Strategy 2030. 'Fleet renewal will require major capital investment, and depending on passenger demand and the availability of funding, there may be scope to extend the reach of Metro beyond its current sphere of operation and the boundaries of Tyne & Wear to more fully reflect travel pattern across the wider region.' A range of technical options is being considered.

The 'core' demand forecast for passenger journeys in 2030 is 60 million.

THE STOURBRIDGE SHUTTLE

Service provision on the 1,2km Network Rail branch between Stourbridge Junction and Stourbridge Town is by Pre-Metro Operations Ltd (PMOL). The company runs the four wheeled Parry People Mover railcars for franchise holder London Midland, employs the operating staff and maintains the trains.

This Ultra Light Rail operation commenced in 2009. The two Parry People Mover Class-139 units use flywheel stored energy charged by a small Ford engine. The 21 seat (and one wheelchair space) vehicles are 8.7m long and weigh a modest 12.5 tonnes. Carrying capacity is about 60 and they have a maximum speed of 45mph. With a running time of three minutes, one train can make six return trips in the hour. Reliability is better than 99%.

UKTRAM LTD

UKTram Ltd represents the industry in dealings with Government and statutory bodies. The aim is the development of a co-ordinated and structured approach to regulation, procurement and standardisation within the industry. The company is limited by guarantee and is owned in equal shares by PTEG Ltd (the Passenger Transport Executive Group), the Confederation of Passenger Transport UK, the Light Rapid Transit Forum and London Tramlink.

Guidance notes are readily available under the headings of General, Technical and those from the Office of Rail Regulation. They provide promoters with practical help in preparing schemes, reducing development costs and making the business case. In 2014 UKTram published research into the economic benefits for cities of light rail systems.

Manchester Metrolink - M5000 trams pass at Old Trafford. **TONY MILES**

LIGHT RAIL AND METRO

Jubilee Line - London Underground and Thales are working to provide more frequent and reliable trains. **BRIAN MORRISON**

LONDON UNDERGROUND AND THALES TEAMWORK BOOSTS CAPACITY

London's Underground handles more than 1.2 billion passenger journeys every year – and London Underground and Thales are working to provide more frequent and reliable trains for the growing number of people who need them.

The re-signalling of two of London's busiest Tube lines, the Jubilee and Northern, has been the biggest ever implementation of its kind anywhere in the world.

Thales's world-leading SelTrac Transmission Based Train Control (TBTC) system was commissioned into revenue service on the Jubilee Line in 2011, realising significant performance and capacity benefits.

The SelTrac system allows automatic control, timetabling and movement of trains, points and signals on the railway. It includes equipment on board the train, at the trackside and in the control centre.

The promised increased capacity (20%) has been delivered on the Jubilee Line, through new timetables being implemented - taking the number of planned trains from the previous maximum of 24 trains per hour to 30 trains per hour through central London.

With significant work undertaken to ensure the reliability of the TBTC signalling system, one of the biggest tests came over the summer of 2012 when London hosted the Olympic and Paralympic Games. During this 48-day period, the TBTC system achieved 37 days with zero delays and an average daily delay of less than two minutes.

The Jubilee Line has gone on to be one of London Underground's best performing lines, with record-breaking reliability. London Underground has been planning additional enhancements and upgrades as part of a World Class Capacity programme, to take Jubilee Line train frequencies to 34 or more trains per hour.

Meanwhile, on the Northern Line, the SelTrac TBTC system is now fully operational and in passenger service on the whole line, with the last section coming into revenue service in June 2014 - well ahead of the December 2014 TfL target that the contract required, and also under budget.

The TBTC system is designed to increase passenger capacity on the Northern Line by 20% and achieve a journey time improvement of 18%.

A team from London Underground and Thales won the Outstanding Teamwork Award at the 2014 National Rail Awards for their work on the modernisation of the Northern Line. A week later, the Jubilee & Northern Line Upgrade (JNUP) programme was awarded Bronze in the Mega Project category of the Project Excellence Award by the IPMA (International Project Management Association). Also, Andy Bell, Project Director at Thales UK for the JNUP program, was named Project Manager of the Year.

The National Rail Awards underlined that an integrated approach was central to the team's success in meeting the challenge. London Underground (LU) and Thales defined their working relationship as 'One Team', with project managers and engineers from both companies working side by side as a single team on everything from defining the user requirements and the design scope, to the detailed management of installation and testing works. The approach was followed throughout the entire project – from the senior LU and Thales executives who jointly oversaw the project and formed the 'One Team Board', to the combined teams of engineers working in the tunnels. This enabled the project to be delivered ahead of schedule with far fewer closures than on the Jubilee Line, under budget and with high reliability.

Again, for the Jubilee & Northern Line Upgrade (JNUP) program, the collaborative approach at the centre of the programme – building a trusted relationship between Thales and London Underground and co-creating the 'One Team' culture - was recognised by the IPMA.

IN ASSOCIATION WITH **THALES**

TRANSPORT for LONDON

Transport for London (TfL) is responsible for implementing the Mayor's transport strategy and managing transport by various modes across the capital.

Mayor Boris Johnson's main long term transport objectives are to support London and the UK's economy; serve a growing population; and make London more liveable.

London Underground is the principal rail operation, and in 2013/14 it carried a record 1,265 million people, up from 1,229m in 2012/13 – even though 2012 was the London Olympic and Paralympic year. In 1982 just 498m journeys were made.

London's population of 8.4m is forecast to grow to around 10m by 2030, with 800,000 or so new jobs. Something over four million passengers a day is thus likely to become the norm - giving urgency to the upgrade programme of replacing life-expired assets with modern technology, which in turn allows capacity to be increased.

TfL receives part of its income in government grant. The Chancellor of the Exchequer confirmed a six-year settlement in 2013. Investment grant of £925m in 2015/16 would rise to £1,007m in 2020/21, with annual borrowing of over £600m for capital investment.

The Mayor committed to efficiencies totalling £9.8bn to 2017/18. He said the grant settlement for 2015-16 represented a reduction of support for TfL of 8.5%.

The Chief Operating Officer is responsible for the running of the Underground and for nearly 12,000 operational and support staff across the 270-station network. Line General Managers are responsible for day-to-day management and performance; the Network Services division aims to deliver long-term improvements to the overall operating performance; and Operational Upgrades staff ensure that new assets and systems are fit for purpose and ready for acceptance into use.

Asset Performance team manages the upkeep and repair of the eight lines which were formerly part of the Public-Private Partnership consortium Metronet. This includes trains, stations, signalling, track, tunnels, bridges and structures, lifts and escalators, and other related assets. The Jubilee, Northern and Piccadilly are maintained by the wholly-owned Tube Lines subsidiary (a former PPP group).

London Underground's fundamental objective is to provide a safe and reliable service. This means properly and correctly trained staff, assets that consistently perform well, and an ability to recover swiftly from delays when they do occur.

This results in the challenge of delivering a safe service day-in, day-out, irrespective of the reliability of ageing

KEY STATISTICS
LONDON UNDERGROUND

	2012/13	2013/14
Passenger journeys (millions)	1,229	1,265
Passenger km (millions)	10,099	10,422
Passenger revenue (£m 2013/14 prices)	2,164	2,287

SENIOR PERSONNEL
TRANSPORT FOR LONDON

COMMISSIONER Sir Peter Hendy (in photo)
MANAGING DIRECTOR, LONDON UNDERGROUND AND LONDON RAIL Mike Brown
MANAGING DIRECTOR, FINANCE Steve Allen
MANAGING DIRECTOR, PLANNING Michele Dix

Impression of the 'New Tube for London', the next generation of Underground trains, being developed by Transport for London and transport design specialists PriestmanGoode. **TFL**

LIGHT RAIL AND METRO

In original 3-car form, London Overground's Class 378 No 378013 approaching West Hampstead on the North London Line. **KEITH FENDER**

and often obsolete assets; while also using the investment programme to make good deficiencies in asset quality, and to build in sufficient new capacity to meet future demand expectations; and also maintaining customer service during the biggest rebuilding programme that the Underground has ever seen.

To illustrate the scale of what the company achieves, Table 1 shows the 15 busiest stations on the system, in descending order. The figures represent the annual usage during 2013, being the summated totals of entry and exit counts taken on different days throughout the year (excluding interchange between lines).

In this group, Canary Wharf alone has a single Underground line (the DLR station of the same name and the forthcoming Crossrail station are separate). This, Stratford and Hammersmith are the stations featured here which are outside the central area.

Only 10 Underground stations have an annual entry/exit count of less than one million passengers a year. This is a story of sustained growth, as Table 2 shows.

HEATHROW

To what extent do air passengers and airport workers overwhelm the existing public transport providers? With an additional runway at Heathrow under discussion, it is instructive to examine the use made of the Piccadilly Line's Heathrow stations (Table 3). Usage of all four airport stations taken together at 17.73m is very similar to that of middle ranking stations such as Warren Street or Elephant & Castle. Hatton Cross, it might be added, is used mainly by airport workers.

London Underground operations are of course supplemented by Heathrow Express and Heathrow Connect services.

PEAK AND OFF PEAK

Table 4 sets out the maximum number of trains needed to maintain the service. Noticeable is the varying extent to which the numbers required reduce from the Monday to Friday peak to the midday period. Thus the Metropolitan and Northern lines both have fewer trains running, there is very little change on the Bakerloo or the Circle / Hammersmith & City. Overall, 83% of the trains in service at 09.00 are still running at 12.00. The Saturday service requires more trains again (87%), with rather fewer (78%) needed on Sundays.

Train loadings have thus become more constant, with variations between peak and off peak diminishing. Travelling during the off peak is no longer the solution to capacity problems.

MODERNISATION

The key elements of the 'Transforming the Tube' programme are to replace most trains to increase fleet reliability and capacity; to replace signalling assets to reduce service delays and increase network capacity by reducing headways; to reduce the backlog of track investment to reduce safety risks and increase capacity by removing speed restrictions; to renew infrastructure assets to maintain a safe service, reduce the risks of flooding, and service limitations caused by speed or weight restrictions; and to modernise

TABLE 1: LU STATION USAGE IN MILLIONS – TOP 15 IN 2013

Waterloo	89.40m
Oxford Circus	85.25m
King's Cross St Pancras	84.87m
Victoria	84.58m
London Bridge	69.88m
Liverpool Street	67.89m
Stratford	54.50m
Canary Wharf	50.05m
Paddington	49.71m
Bank & Monument	48.80m
Piccadilly Circus	41.70m
Bond Street	39.65m
Leicester Square	38.50m
Hammersmith (both stations)	38.25m
Tottenham Court Road	38.06m
TOTAL, TOP 15 STATIONS, 2013	**881.09M**

(LU annual station usage, entries and exits combined)

TABLE 2: USAGE OF TOP 15 STATIONS, 2010-2013

YEAR	USAGE, MILLIONS	AS INDEX
2010	768.71m	100
2011	821.78m	106.9
2012	851.76m	110.8
2013	881.09m	114.6

IN ASSOCIATION WITH **THALES**

TABLE 3: LU PASSENGERS AT HEATHROW

Heathrow Terminals 1,2,3	7.80m	8.14m
Heathrow Terminal 4	2.44m	2.43m
Heathrow Terminal 5	3.64m	4.08m
Hatton Cross	2.95m	3.08m
TOTAL, LU HEATHROW STATIONS	**16.83M**	**17.73M**

(LU annual station usage, entries and exits combined, 2013)

stations by replacing fire systems, public address, CCTV, and lifts and escalators.

A critical feature of line upgrades is to enable LU to provide capacity for future (or even present) demands. By the end of the current programme, the Underground will have delivered up to an additional 30% capacity.

From September 2015, all-night services are to be introduced on Friday and Saturday nights on much of the Northern, Piccadilly, Victoria, Central and Jubilee lines.

NEW TRAINS

Recent years have seen a much greater effort to standardise rolling stock types. The sub-surface lines are being completely re-equipped with the new walk-through S stock built in Derby by Bombardier, a total of 191 trains.

S stock is in either 8-car permanent formations (S8 stock for the Metropolitan Line, 58 trains) or S7 trains of 7-cars, for the Circle, Hammersmith & City and District lines (133 trains).

S8 trains have a mixture of longitudinal and transverse seating; the S7s are wholly longitudinal. The S8s have 306 seats in an 8-car train, of which 50 are 'tip-up'. Their A stock predecessors had 464 seats (16 tip-ups). The S8s have much greater standing capacity (perhaps of little comfort to those travelling to the end of the line).

New deep-level Tube trains are needed for the Piccadilly Line (currently 1973 stock) and Bakerloo Line (1972 stock); they will be followed by the Central/Waterloo & City lines (both currently 1992 stock). About 250 trains will be built, with roundly 100 trains for each of the Piccadilly and Central lines, 40 for the Bakerloo and 10 for the Waterloo & City.

These are to be to a common design and will feature walk-through cars and wider doors, air cooling, higher performance, and more overall line capacity. A train life of 'at least 40 years' is intended. Over time it is intended to introduce platform edge doors (where possible) and step free access between train and platform.

Automatic operation offers energy efficiency through optimisation of acceleration and regenerative braking, and driverless operation is envisaged eventually: cab space could be freed for passenger use, but that however would require careful plans to deal with incidents on crowded trains in deep tube tunnels. Fleet replacement will be accompanied by installation of moving block signalling.

A mock up of the 'New Tube for London', designed by PriestmanGoode, was exhibited in autumn 2014. A formal invitation to tender is expected to be issued in early 2015 to shortlisted bidders Alstom, Siemens, Hitachi, CAF and Bombardier, and a contract awarded in 2016. The first production train is expected to enter service on the Piccadilly Line in 2022.

FARES

The fares system on all TfL services is dominated by the Oyster smartcard. This acts as a prepaid credit card which can be topped up as necessary with additional payments made by the user to add credit. Oysters can be loaded with Travelcards, or they can be used on a pay-as-you-go basis. Since September 2014, contactless payment bank cards can be used in a similar manner. Cash fares remain available, but are priced to discourage usage. Ticket office use has been falling steadily and London Underground plans to revise staffing, with many stations having only ticket machines but with 'roving' staff to provide assistance.

STATIONS

Major projects to rebuild Vauxhall, Tottenham Court Road, Bond Street, Victoria and Finsbury Park stations will increase capacity and add step free access, while further projects to modernise the busy stations of Bank, Elephant & Castle, Holborn and Camden Town will be completed in the 2020s.

These can be major undertakings. That at Bank, for instance, includes boring a new southbound tunnel plus platform for the Northern Line, to tackle the chronic congestion that can occur in the present platform areas. Similar work has previously been carried out at that line's Euston, Angel and London Bridge stations.

For ventilation, shafts and fans at stations will mostly have to suffice at stations in deep level tunnels, though platform cooling systems have been tried out.

Balfour Beatty has a £220m contract lasting until 2016 to carry out track renewal work on the Bakerloo, Central and all sub-surface lines. The work covers replacement of ballasted track, points and crossings, including all ancillary signalling and drainage works.

NETWORK EXTENSIONS - CROXLEY

Among current network extension plans, the long-discussed Croxley rail link is to re-route the double track Watford branch of the Metropolitan Line via a new viaduct across the Grand Union Canal and a station at Cassiobridge. Here it will join the trackbed of the disused Croxley Green National Rail branch to join the existing 'DC lines' to Watford High Street and Watford Junction. This section will be shared with London Overground services originating from London Euston.

Presently under construction, the £117m scheme is funded by DfT (65%), Hertfordshire County Council (29%) and third parties (6%). Opening is now expected in 2017, when the present Watford (Metropolitan) station will close.

NORTHERN LINE

Northern Line Upgrade 1 is a 3.2km tunnelled extension from Kennington to Battersea with an intermediate station at Nine Elms. This would branch off from the terminal loop beyond the Charing Cross line platforms at Kennington. Given a Transport & Works Act order, construction could start in Spring 2015, with opening in 2020. The cost would be around £1bn, funded by developers. Ferrovial Agroman Laing O'Rourke is the preferred bidder for a design and build contract.

Northern Line Upgrade 2 is to include separation of the Charing Cross and City routes to increase capacity significantly from 24 trains per hour (tph) on each after the signalling upgrade to 28-32tph. Bids have been invited to supply additional trains to increase the Northern Line fleet, and also provide a more frequent service on the Jubilee Line.

BAKERLOO LINE

Public consultation began in September 2014 on a £3bn southern extension of the Bakerloo Line. There are two options for the tunnelled section from Elephant & Castle through Southwark to Lewisham, thence over Network Rail lines via Catford Bridge to Hayes and also to Beckenham Junction. Bromley town centre is also seen as a possible destination. Completion of this scheme is unlikely before the 2030s.

LONDON RAIL

Transport for London's London Rail deals with the National Rail network in London. Its main responsibilities are to oversee major new rail projects, including those relating to London Overground, to manage the

TABLE 4: UNDERGROUND LINES – TRAINS REQUIRED

LINE	MON-FRI (09.00)	MON-FRI (12.00)	SAT (MAX)	SUN (MAX)
Bakerloo	32	29	29	27
Central	79	66	72	61
Circle/Hammersmith & City	32	31	31	30
District	76	59	61	58
Jubilee	55	48	49	49
Metropolitan	48	34	34	34
Northern	92	77	77	77
Piccadilly	78	68	76	68
Victoria	39	29	32	29
Waterloo & City	5	3	3	no service
Total trains	536	444	464	433
As index	100	83	87	81

(Maximum number of trains required, October 2014)

LIGHT RAIL AND METRO

Overground concession and also the operation of the Docklands Light Railway and London Tramlink. It also supports and develops Crossrail, as well as the Thameslink Programme, and influences and supports National Rail's contribution to integrated public transport for London, liaising also with the freight industry to support the sustainable movement of goods.

A demonstration lift of an S stock train at Neasden depot using in-floor jacks supplied by Windhoff. As the S-stock bogies are not mechanically retained under the trains, synchronised 8-car lifting from under the wheels has been adopted. **KEN CORDNER**

LONDON OVERGROUND

Overground services are operated by London Overground Rail Operations Ltd (LOROL - a consortium of MTR Group and Arriva) and the company's concession (not a franchise) awarded by TfL has been extended until November 2016. Fares, procurement of rolling stock, and service levels are functions retained by TfL.

All Overground electric services are operated by four-car trains, but deliveries from Bombardier are under way so that all 57 trains can be increased to five cars - requiring attention to platform lengths, plus depot, maintenance, and stabling accommodation. 6-car trains are envisaged for the 2020s: meanwhile additional trains are to be ordered to increase North London line services.

Dual voltage AC/DC trains (Class 378/2) are used for Stratford-Richmond, plus Willesden Junction-Clapham Junction. DC-only units (Class 378/1) suffice between Highbury & Islington and New Cross / Clapham Junction / West Croydon / Crystal Palace; also Euston-Watford; while diesel trains (Class 172/0) run between Gospel Oak and Barking.

BARKING RIVERSIDE

Electrification of the Gospel Oak-Barking line has been confirmed, with a target completion date of Summer 2017 and new 4-car electric trains. There are further plans for an eastern extension to serve housing development at Barking Riverside. The Mayor has suggested a further extension from Barking Riverside across the Thames to Thamesmead and Abbey Wood.

OLD OAK COMMON

The proposed station for High Speed 2 at Old Oak Common will need access to and from local rail services. Besides platforms on the Great Western for Crossrail and perhaps Intercity type operations, TfL proposes a new London Overground interchange.

NATIONAL RAIL DEVOLUTION

The Mayor has argued for the devolution of decision making and on funding allocations on London's National Rail services to TfL. He argued that London Overground had demonstrated TfL's ability to leverage extra investment, increase service levels and make sizeable gains in passenger satisfaction.

London's political boundaries do not match railway geography – but two stations in Hertfordshire are involved in a government decision to devolve the Liverpool Street to Chingford, Enfield Town and Cheshunt (via Southbury) services to the Mayor, together with Romford-Upminster, from May 2015: these will be TfL services operated by London Overground, with new trains planned by 2018.

KEY STATISTICS
LONDON OVERGROUND

	2012-13	2013-14
Punctuality (0-5min)	96.6%	96.1%
Passenger journeys (millions)	125.3	136.2
Passenger km (millions)	959.5	805.6
Timetabled train km (millions)	7.6	8.1
Route km operated	124.0	124.0
Number of stations operated	57	57
Number of employees	1,211	1,129

CROSSRAIL 2 AND 3

A preferred route for a north-south Crossrail 2 railway was published by TfL and Network Rail in October 2014. Crossrail 3 was sketched out in the Mayor's draft Infrastructure Plan for 2050 on an east-west route.

For Crossrail 2, a tunnelled north-south route across London would link with the National Rail network near Tottenham Hale and Wimbledon. Stations on the tunnelled section are proposed at Dalston Junction, Angel, Euston St Pancras, Tottenham Court Road, Victoria, King's Road Chelsea, Clapham Junction and Tooting Brodway.

West of Wimbledon, route options over existing lines are to Epsom, Twickenham, Chessington and via Surbiton. In the north the route would continue towards Cheshunt, with a branch to Seven Sisters, Turnpike Lane, Alexandra Palace and New Southgate, mostly in tunnel, as a firm proposal. A branch from Angel to Hackney Central and beyond is an option. The project is estimated to cost around £20bn. The Mayor and TfL believe the wider UK economic and transport benefits support the case for a government contribution.

The DfT will consult on updating the previously safeguarded Chelsea–Hackney line. This dates back to 1991. An application to build could come in 2017. The railway could be operational by 2030.

LONDON TRAVELWATCH

This statutory consumer body, sponsored and funded by the London Assembly, promotes integrated transport policies and presses for higher standards of quality, performance and accessibility.

Chief Executive: Janet Cooke.

SENIOR PERSONNEL
LONDON OVERGROUND

MANAGING DIRECTOR Peter Austin (in photo)
OPERATIONS DIRECTOR Stuart Griffin
FLEET DIRECTOR Peter Daw
CUSTOMER SERVICE DIRECTOR David Wornham
CONCESSION DIRECTOR Mark Eaton

IN ASSOCIATION WITH **ATKINS**

The Railway Mission
Rugby Railway Station,
Rugby, CV21 3LA
T: 0845 269 1881
M: 07841 905768
E: office@railwaychaplain.net
W: www.railwaymission.org

Railway Projects Ltd
Lisbon House, 5-7 St Marys Gate,
Derby, DE1 3JA
T: 01332 349255
F: 01332 349261
E: enquiries@railwayprojects.co.uk
W: www.railwayprojects.co.uk

Railway Study Association (RSA)
PO Box 375, Burgess Hill,
West Sussex, RH15 5BX
T: 01444 246129
E: info@railwaystudy
association.org
W: www.railwaystudy
association.org

Railway Support Services
Montpellier House,
Montpellier Drive,
Cheltenham, GL50 1TY
T: 0870 803 4651
F: 0870 803 4652
E: info@railway
supportservices.co.uk
W: www.railway
supportservices.co.uk

Railway Systems Engineering & Integration Group
Birmingham Centre for Railway
Reasearch & Education College of
Engineering Sciences,
University of Birmingham,
Edgbaston,
Birmingham, B15 2TT
T: 0121 414 4342
F: 0121 414 4291
E: j.grey@bham.ac.uk
W: www.eng.bham.ac.uk/civil/
study/postgrad/railway.shtml

Railway Touring Company
14a Tuesday Market Place,
Kings Lynn, Norfolk, PE30 1JN
T: 01553 661500
F: 01553 661800
E: enquiries@railwaytouring.co.uk
W: www.railwaytouring.co.uk

Railway Vehicle Engineering Ltd (RVEL)
RTC Business Park, London Rd,
Derby, DE24 8UP
T: 01332 293035
F: 01332 331210
E: enquiries@rvel.co.uk
W: www.rvel.co.uk

Railways Pension Scheme
2nd Floor, Camomile Court, 23
Camomile St, London, EC3A 7LL
T: 0800 234 3434
E: csu@rpmi.co.uk
W: www.railwayspensions.co.uk

RVEL A LORAM COMPANY
Specialist rolling stock engineering - design, build, heavy overhaul and maintenance capabilities. Design, fitment and modification of ETCS, ERTMS & TPWS systems on passenger and freight vehicles. RVAR compliance work.
Railway Vehicle Engineering Ltd
RTC Business Park, London Road
Derby DE24 8UP
Phone: 01332 293035
Fax: 01332 331210
Email: enquiries@rvel.co.uk
www.rvel.co.uk

Railweight
Foundry Lane, Smethwick,
Birmingham, B66 2LP
T: 0121 568 1708
F: 0121 697 5655
E: sales@railweight.co.uk
W: www.averyweightronix.com/
railweight

Ramboll UK Ltd
Carlton House, Ringwood Rd,
Woodlands,
Southampton, SO40 7HT
T: 02380 817500
F: 02380 817600
E: tim.holmes@ramboll.co.uk
W: www.ramboll.co.uk

Rampart Carriage & Wagon Services Ltd
Brunel Gate, RTC Business Park,
London Rd, Derby, DE24 8UP
T: 01332 263261
F: 01332 263181
E: admin@rampartderby.co.uk
W: www.rampartderby.co.uk

Ramtech Electronics Ltd
Abbeyfield House,
Abbeyfield Rd,
Nottingham, NG7 2SZ
T: 0115 988 7090
F: 0115 970 5415
E: matt.sadler@ramtech.co.uk
W: www.ramtech.co.uk

Ransome Engineering Services Ltd
Clopton Commercial Park,
Clopton, Woodbridge,
Suffolk, IP13 6QT
T: 01473 737731
F: 01473 737398
E: info@ransomeengineering.co.uk
W: www.ransomeengineering.co.uk

Ranstad CPE
Forum 4, Parkway,
Solent Business Park,
Whiteley,
Fareham, PO15 7AD
T: 01489 560000
F: 01489 560001
E: railteam@ranstadcpe.co.uk
W: www.ranstadcpe.com/rail

Raspberry Software Ltd
9 Deben Mill Business Centre,
Old Maltings Approach,
Melton, Woodbridge,
Suffolk, IP12 1BL
T: 01394 387386
F: 01394 387386
E: info@raspberrysoftware.com
W: www.raspberrysoftware.com

Ratcliff Palfinger
Bessemer Rd,
Welwyn Garden City,
Herts, AL7 1ET
T: 01707 325571
F: 01707 327752
E: info@ratcliffpalfinger.co.uk
W: www.ratcliffpalfinger.com

Rayleigh Instruments
Raytel House, Brook Rd, Rayleigh,
Essex, SS6 7XH
T: 01268 749300
F: 01268 749309
E: sales@rayleigh.co.uk
W: www.rayleigh.co.uk

RE: wSystems
Systems House,
Deepdale Business Park, Bakewell,
Derbys, DE45 1FZ
T: 01629 815902
F: 01629 813349
E: steve.england@re-systems.co.uk
W: www.re-systems.co.uk

REACT Beyond Cleaning
Stanhope Rd, Swadlincote,
Derbys, DE11 9BE
T: 08707 510422
F: 08707 510417
E: info@ractbeyondcleaning.co.uk
W: www.reactbeyondcleaning.co.uk

React Engineering Ltd
Fleswick Court, Westlakes Science &
Tech. Park, Moor Row, Whitehaven,
Cumbria, CA24 3HZ
T: 01946 590511
F: 01946 591044
E: mail@react-engineering.co.uk
W: www.react-engineering.co.uk

Readypower
Readypower House, Molly Millars
Bridge, Wokingham,
Berks, RG41 2WY
T: 01189 774901
F: 01189 774902
E: info@readypower.co.uk
W: www.readypower.co.uk

Real Time Consultants Plc
118-120 Warwick St, Royal
Leamington Spa, Warks, CV32 4QY
T: 01926 313133
F: 01926 422165
E: contract@rtc.co.uk
W: www.rtc.co.uk

Record Electrical Associates Ltd
Unit C1, Longford Trading Est.,
Thomas St., Stretford,
Manchester, M32 0JT
T: 0161 864 3583
F: 0161 864 3603
E: alanj@reauk.com
W: www.record-electrical.com

Recruitrail (Recruit Engineers)
Bank Chambers,
36 Mount Pleasant Rd,
Tunbridge Wells,
Kent, TN1 1RA
T: 01909 540825
F: 0870 443 0453
W: www.recruitrail.com

Redman Fisher Engineering Ltd
Birmingham New Rd, Tipton,
West Midlands, DY4 9AQ
T: 01902 880880
F: 01902 880446
E: sales@redmanfisher.co.uk
W: www.redmanfisher.co.uk

Reg Harman Consultancy Services Ltd
2 Valley Close,
Hertford, SG13 8BD
T: 01992 415248
M: 07508 287514
E: reg.harman@ntlworld.com

Rehau Ltd
Hill Court, Walford,
Ross-on-Wye,
Herefordshire, HR9 5QN
T: 01989 762655
F: 01989 762601
E: anthonia.ifeany-okoro@
rehau.com
W: www.rehau.co.uk

Reid Lifting Ltd
Unit 1, Severnlink,
Newhouse Farm Ind. Est, Chepstow,
Monmouthshire, NP16 6UN
T: 01291 620796
F: 01291 626490
E: enquiries@reidlifting.com
W: www.reidlifting.com

Reinforced Earth Company
Innovation House, Euston Way,
Town Centre, Telford, TF3 4LT
T: 01952 201901
F: 01952 211523
E: info@reinforcedearth.com
W: www.reinforcedearth.com

Relec Electronics Ltd
Animal House, Justin Bus. Park,
Sandford Lane, Wareham,
Dorset, BH20 4DY
T: 01929 555700
F: 01929 555701
E: sales@relec.co.uk
W: www.relec.co.uk

Reliable Data Systems
March House, Lime Grove,
West Clandon, Surrey, GU4 7UH
T: 01483 225604
E: rdsintl@rdsintl.com
W: www.rdsintl.com

Renaissance Trains Ltd
4 Spinneyfield, Ellington,
Cambs, PE28 0AT
T: 07977 917148
E: peter.wilkinson@
renaissancetrains.com
W: www.renaissancetrains.com

Renown Training
Brookside House, Brookside
Business Park, Cold Meece,
Staffs, ST15 0RZ
T: 01785 764476
F: 01785 760896
E: enquiries@renownrailway.co.uk
W: www.renownrailway.co.uk

Replin Fabrics
March St Mills, Peebles, EH45 8ER
T: 01721 724311
F: 01721 721893
E: enquiries@replin-fabrics.co.uk
W: www.replin-fabrics.co.uk

REPTA (Railway Employees and Public Transport Association)
24 Foxglove Drive, Biggleswade,
Beds, SG18 8SP
T: 01767 317683
F: 01767 317683
E: 24foxglove@tiscali.co.uk
W: www.repta.co.uk

Resourcing Solutions
Vector House, 5 Ruscombe Park,
Ruscombe, Berks, RG10 9JW
T: 0118 932 0100
F: 0118 932 1818
E: info@resourcing-solutions.com
W: www.resourcing-solutions.com

Rethinking Transport
E: jon@rethinkingtransport.com
W: www.rethinkingtransport.com

Retro Railtours Ltd
2 Brookfield Grove,
Ashton-under-Lyne,
Lancashire, OL6 6TL
T: 0161 330 9055
E: info@retrorailtours.co.uk
W: www.retrorailtours.co.uk

Revitaglaze
Unit 9, Park Industrial Estate,
Frogmore, St Albans, Herts, AL2 2DR
T: 0843 289 3901
F: 01372 200881
E: marketing@revitaglaze.com
W: www.revitaglaze.com

Rexquote Ltd
Broadgauge Business Park,
Bishops Lydeard, Taunton,
Somerset, TA4 3RU
T: 01823 433398
F: 01823 433378
E: sales@rexquote.co.uk
W: www.rexquote.co.uk

RGB Integrated Services Ltd
Unit 3007, Access House,
Nestle Ave, Hayes,
Middlesex, UB3 4UZ
T: 020 8573 9882
F: 020 8711 3916
E: info@rgb-services.com
W: www.rgb-services.com

RGS Rail
6 Clarendon St,
Nottingham, NG1 5HQ
T: 0115 959 9687
M: 07973 676323
E: enquiries@rgsexecutive.co.uk
W: www.rgsexecutive.co.uk

RIB Software (UK) Ltd
12 Floor,
The Broadgate Tower,
20 Primrose St,
London, EC2A 2EW
T: 020 7596 2747
F: 020 7596 2701
W: www.rib-software.co.uk

Ricardo UK Ltd
Midlands Technical Centre,
Southam Rd,
Radford Semele,
Leamington Spa,
Warks, CV31 1FQ
T: 01926 319319
F: 01926 319352
E: jim.buchanan@ricardo.com
W: www.ricardo.com

Riello UPS Ltd
Unit 68, Clyvedog Rd North,
Wrexham Ind.Est.,
Wrexham, LL13 9XN
T: 01978 729297
F: 01978 729290
E: marketing@riello-ups.co.uk
W: www.riello-ups.co.uk

Riley & Son (E) Ltd
Baron St, Bury,
Lancs, BL9 0TY
T: 0161 764 2892
F: 0161 763 5191
E: ian.riley@btconnect.com

Ring Automotive
Gelderd Rd,
Leeds, LS12 6NA
T: 0113 213 2000
F: 0113 231 0266
E: autosales@ringautomotive.co.uk
W: www.ringautomotive.co.uk

RIQC Ltd
2 St Georges House, Vernon Gate,
Derby, DE1 1UQ
T: 01332 221421
F: 01332 221401
E: enquiries@riqc.co.uk
W: www.riqc.co.uk

RISC Ltd - Railway & Industrial Safety Consultants Ltd
Harlyn House,
3 Doveridge Rd, Stapenhill,
Burton Upon Trent, DE15 9GB
T: 0844 840 9420
F: 0871 247 2961
M: 07941 212568
E: enquiries@railwaysafety.co.uk
W: www.railwaysafety.co.uk

Risk Solutions
Dallam Court,
Dallam Lane,
Warrington, WA2 7LT
T: 01925 413984
E: enquiries@risksol.co.uk
W: www.risksol.co.uk

Risktec Solutions
Wilderspool Park,
Greenalls Ave,
Warrington, WA4 6HL
T: 01925 611200
F: 01925 611232
E: enquiries@risktec.co.uk
W: www.risktec.co.uk

Ritelite Systems Ltd
Meadow Park,
Bourne Rd,
Essendine,
Stamford, Lincs, PE9 4LT
T: 01780 765600
F: 01780 765700
E: sales@ritelite.co.uk
W: www.ritelite.co.uk

Rittal Ltd
Braithwell Way, Hellaby Ind Est,
Hellaby, Rotherham, S66 8QY
T: 01709 704000
F: 01709 701217
E: information@rittal.co.uk
W: www.rittal.co.uk

Riviera Trains
116 Ladbroke Grove,
London, W10 5NE
T: 020 7727 4036
F: 020 7727 2083
E: enquiries@riviera-trains.co.uk
W: www.riviera-trains.co.uk

RJ Power Ltd
Unit 1, Gaugemaster Ind. Est,
Gaugemaster Way, Ford,
West Sussex, BN18 0RX
T: 01903 868535
F: 01903 885932
E: info@rjpower.biz
W: www.rjpower.biz

RMS Locotec locomotive Hire
British American Railway Services,
Stanhope Station, Stanhope,
Bishop Auckland, DL13 2YS
T: 01388 526203
E: documentcontroller@
britamrail.com
W: www.rmslocotec.com

RMT
National Union of Rail, Maritime &
Transport Workers, Unity House,
39 Chalton St, London, NW1 1JD
T: 020 7387 4771
F: 020 7387 4123
E: info@rmt.org.uk
W: www.rmt.org.uk

RNA Recruitment Ltd
Mere House,
Brook St, Knutsford,
Cheshire, WA16 8GP
T: 01302 366003
W: www.rnarecruitment.com

Robel Bahnbaumaschmen GmbH
Industriestrasse 31,
D 83395, Freilassing,
Germany
T: 0049 8654 6090
F: 0049 8654 609100
E: info@robel.info
W: www.robel.info

Robert West Consulting
Delta House,
175-177 Borough High St,
London, SE1 1HR
T: 020 7939 9916
F: 020 7939 9909
E: london@robertwest.co.uk
W: www.robertwest.co.uk

Rock Mechanics Technology Ltd
Bretby Business Park,
Ashby Rd, Stanhope Bretby,
Burton on Trent, DE15 0QP
T: 01283 522201
F: 01283 522279
E: rmt@rmtltd.com
W: www.rmtltd.com

DIRECTORY

ROCOL Acme Panels
Rocol House, Wakefield Rd,
Swillington, Leeds, LS26 8BS
T: 0113 232 2800
F: 0113 232 2850
E: customer-service.safety@rocol.com
W: www.rocol.com

ROCOL Site Safety Systems
T: 0113 232 2800
F: 0113 232 2850
E: enquiries@rocol.com
W: www.rocol.com

Roechling Engineering Plastics (UK) Ltd
Waterwells Business Park,
Waterwells Drive,
Quedgeley,
Glos, GL2 2AA
T: 01452 727905
F: 01452 728056
E: david.ward@roechling-plastics.co.uk
W: www.roechling-plastics.co.uk

Roevin Engineering
4th Floor, Clydesdale Bank House,
33 Lower Regent St, Piccadilly,
London, WC1Y 4NB
T: 0845 643 0486
F: 0870 759 8443
E: rail@roevin.co.uk
W: www.roevin.co.uk

Rollalong Ltd
Woolsbridge Ind. Park,
Three Legged Cross, Wimborne,
Dorset, BH21 6SF
T: 01202 824541
F: 01202 826525
E: enquiries@rollalong.co.uk
W: www.rollalong.co.uk

Romag
Leadgate Ind. Est., Leadgate,
Consett, Co Durham, DH8 7RS
T: 01207 500000
F: 01207 591979
E: tiffany.sott@romag.co.uk
W: www.romag.co.uk

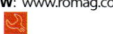

Romic House
A1/M1 Business Centre,
Kettering,
Northants, NN16 8TD
T: 01536 414244
F: 01536 414245
E: sales@romic.co.uk
W: www.romic.co.uk

Ronfell Ltd
Challenge House,
Pagefield industrial Est.,
Miry Lane,
Wigan, WN6 7LA
T: 01942 492200
F: 01942 492233
E: sales@ronfell.com
W: www.ronfell.com

Rose Hill P&OD Ltd
1a Queen St,
Rushden,
Northants, NN10 0AA
F: 01933 663846
M: 07771 612321
E: info@rose-hill.co.uk
W: www.rose-hill.co.uk

Rosehill Rail
Spring Bank Mills,
Watson Mill Lane,
Sowerby Bridge, HX6 3BW
T: 01422 839456
F: 01422 316952
E: peter.anderson@rosehillrail.com
W: www.rosehillrail.com

Rosenqvist Rail AB
Box 334, 82427 Hudiksvall, Sweden
T: 0046 650 16505
F: 0046 650 16501
E: info@rosenqvist-group.se
W: www.rosenqvistrail.se

Rotabroach Ltd
Imperial Works, Sheffield Rd, Tinsley,
Sheffield, S9 2YL
T: 0114 221 2510
F: 0114 221 2563
E: sales@rotabroach.co.uk
W: www.rotabroach.co.uk

Roughton Group
A2 Omega Park, Electron Way,
Chandlers Ford, Hants, SO53 4SE
T: 023 8027 8600
F: 023 8027 8601
E: hq@roughton.com
W: www.roughton.com

Rowe Hankins Ltd
Power House, Parker St,
Bury, BL9 0RJ
T: 0161 765 3000
F: 0161 705 2900
E: sales@rowehankins.com
W: www.rowehankins.com

Roxtec Ltd
Unit C1, Waterfold Business Park,
Bury, Lancs, BL9 7BQ
T: 0161 761 5280
F: 0161 763 6065
E: russell.holmes@uk.roxtec.com
W: www.roxtec.com

Royal British Legion Industries (RBLI)
Royal British Legion Village, Hall Rd,
Aylesford, Kent, ME20 7NL
T: 01622 795900
F: 01622 795978
E: sales.office@rbli.co.uk
W: www.rbli.co.uk/manufacturing/services/19/

Royal Haskoning Ltd
Rightwell House, Bretton,
Peterborough, PE3 8DW
T: 01733 334455
F: 01733 262243
E: info@peterborough.royalhaskoning.com
W: www.royalhaskoning.com

RPS Planning and Development
T: 01636 605700
F: 01636 610696
E: alan.skipper@rpsgroup.com
W: www.rpsgroup.com

RS Components Ltd
Birchington Rd, Corby,
Northants, NN17 9RS
T: 0845 602 5226
W: www.rswww.com/purchasing

RSK STATS Health & Safety Ltd
Spring Lodge,
172 Chester Rd, Helsby,
Cheshire, WA6 0AR
T: 01928 726006
F: 01928 725633
E: info@rsk.com
W: www.rsk.com

RSK Ltd
18 Frogmore Rd,
Hemel Hempstead,
Herts, HP3 9RT
T: 01442 437500
F: 01442 437550
E: info@rsk.co.uk
W: www.rsk.co.uk

RTC Group
The Derby Conference Centre,
London Rd, Derby, DE24 8UX
T: 01332 861336
F: 0870 890 0034
E: info@rtcgroupplc.co.uk
W: www.rtcgroupplc.co.uk

RTI UK
35 Old Queen St,
London, SW1H 9JD
T: 020 7340 0900
F: 020 7233 3411
E: rtiuk@rti.co.uk
W: www.rti.co.uk

RTS Infrastructure Services Ltd
The Rail Depot, B
ridge Rd,
Holbeck,
Leeds, LS11 9UG
T: 01132 344899
E: info@rtsinfrastructure.com
W: www.rtsinfrastructure.com

RTS Solutions Ltd
Atlantic House,
Imperial Way,
Reading, RG2 0TD
T: 0118 903 6045
F: 0118 903 6100
E: stuart@rts-solutions.net
W: www.rts-solutions.net

Rugged Com Inc. (UK)
InfoLab21,
Knowledge Business Centre,
Lancaster University,
Lancaster, LA1 4WA
T: 01524 510434
F: 01524 510433
E: ianpoulett@ruggedcom.com
W: www.ruggedcom.com

Rullion Engineering Personnel
2nd Floor,
Unit 5 Bath Court,
Islington Row,
Edgbaston,
Birmingham, B15 1NE
T: 0121 622 7720
F: 0121 622 7721
E: james.millward@rullion.co.uk
W: www.rullion.co.uk/rep

RWD Technologies UK Ltd
Furzeground Way,
First Floor,
Stockley Park,
Uxbridge, UB11 1AJ
T: 020 8569 2787
F: 020 8756 3625
E: info@gpstrategies.com
W: www.rwd.com

Rydon Signs
Unit 3, Peek House,
Pinhoe Trading Est, Exeter,
Devon, EX4 8JN
T: 01392 466653
F: 01392 466671
E: sales@rydonsigns.com
W: www.rydonsigns.com

S H Lighting
Salcmbe Rd, Meadow Lane Ind. Est,
Alfreton, Derbys, DE55 7RG
T: 01773 520390
F: 01773 520693
E: sales@shlighting.co.uk
W: www.shlighting.co.uk

S M Consult Ltd
3 High St, Stanford in the Vale,
Faringdon, Oxon, SN7 8LH
T: 01367 710150
F: 01367 710152
E: info@smcsolar.co.uk
W: www.smconsult.co.uk

S.E.T. Ltd
Atlas Works, Litchurch Lane,
Derby, DE24 8AQ
T: 01332 346035
F: 01332 346494
E: sales@set.gb.com
W: www.set.gb.com

SA Viewcom (now Axion Technologies)
Lokesvej 7-9, 3400 Hilleroed,
Denmark
T: 0045 721 93500
F: 0045 721 93501
E: info@axiontech.dk
W: www.axiontech.dk

Sabre Rail Services Ltd
Grindon Way,
Heighington Lane Business Park,
Newton Aycliffe,
Co Durham, DL5 6SH
T: 01325 300505
F: 01325 300485
M: 07768 533201
E: sales@sabre-rail.co.uk
W: www.sabre-rail.co.uk

Safeaid LLP
Signal House, 16 Arnside Rd,
Waterlooville, Hants, PO7 7UP
T: 02392 254442
F: 02392 257444
E: sales@safeaidsupplies.com
W: www.safeaidsupplies.com

Safeglass (Europe) Ltd
Nasmyth Building, Nasmyth Ave,
East Kilbride, G75 0QR
T: 01355 272828
F: 01355 272788
E: sales@safeglass.co.uk
W: www.safeglass.co.uk

Safeguard Pest Control Ltd
6 Churchill Bus. Park,
The Flyers Way,
Westerham,
Kent, TN16 1BT
T: 0800 195 7766
F: 01959 565888
E: info@safeguardpestcontrol.co.uk
W: www.safeguardpestcontrol.co.uk

Safeline Training Ltd
69-71 Haltwhistle Rd,
South Woodham Ferrers,
Essex, CM3 5ZA
T: 01245 426042
E: info@safelinetraining.co.uk
W: www.safelinetraining.co.uk

Safestyle Security Services
Exe. Suite 1,
Cardiff International Arena,
Mary Ann St,
Cardiff, CF10 2FQ
T: 02920 221711
F: 02920 234592
E: office@safestylesecurity.com
W: www.safestylesecurity.co.uk

Safetech Environmental Care
4 Upton St,
Hull, HU8 7DA
T: 01482 224165
F: 01482 214522
E: info@safetechenv.com
W: www.safetechenv.com

Safetell Ltd
Unit 46,
Fawkes Ave,
Dartford Trade Park,
Dartford, DA1 1JQ
T: 01322 223233
F: 01322 277751
E: sales@safetell.co.uk
W: www.safetell.co.uk

Safetrack Baavhammar AB
1 Moleberga,
S-245 93 Staffanstorp,
Sweden
T: 0046 4044 5300
F: 0046 4044 5553
E: sales@safetrack.se
W: www.safetrack.se

Safetykleen UK Ltd
Profile West,
950 Great West Rd,
Brentford,
Middx, TW8 9ES
T: 01909 519300
E: skuk@sk-europe.com
W: www.safetykleen.co.uk

SAFT Ltd
1st Floor, Unit 5,
Astra Centre,
Edinburgh Way,
Harlow, CM20 2BN
T: 01279 772550
F: 01279 420909
E: sarah.carter@saftbatteries.com
W: www.saftbatteries.com

SAFT Power Systems Ltd
See AEG Power Solutions Ltd

Saint Gobain Abrasives Ltd
Doxey Rd,
Stafford, ST16 1EA
T: 01785 279550
F: 01785 213487
E: sonia.uppal@saint-gobain.com
W: www.saint-gobain.com

Saltburn Railtours
16 Bristol Ave,
Saltburn, TS12 1BW
T: 01287 626572
E: r.dallara@btinternet.com
W: www.saltburnrailtours.co.uk

Samsung Electronics Hainan Fibreoptics
c/o Go Tel Communications Ltd,
4 Hicks Close, Wroughton,
Swindon, SN4 9AY
T: 01793 813600
F: 01793 529380
E: robindash@gtcom.co.uk
W: www.samsungfiberoptics.com

Santon Switchgear Ltd
Unit 9, Waterside Court,
Newport, NP20 5NT
T: 01633 854111
F: 01633 854999
E: sales@santonswitchgear.co.uk
W: www.santonswitchgear.com

Sartoria Corporatewear
Gosforth Rd,
Derby, DE24 8HU
T: 01332 342616
F: 01332 226940
W: www.sartorialtd.co.uk.co.uk

Savigny Oddie Ltd
Wallows Ind. Est, Wallows Rd,
Brierley Hill, West Midlands, DY5 1QA
T: 01384 481598
F: 01384 482383
E: keith@oddiefasteners.com
W: www.savigny-oddie.co.uk

SB Rail (Swietelsky Babcock)
Kintail House,
3 Lister Way,
Hamilton International Park,
Blantyre, G72 0FT
T: 01698 203005
F: 01698 203006
E: shona.jamieson@babcock.co.uk
W: www.babcock.co.uk/rail

SBC Rail Ltd
Littlewell Lane,
Stanton by Dale, Ilkeston,
Derbys, DE7 4QW
T: 0115 944 1448
F: 0115 944 1466
E: sbc@stanton-bonna.co.uk
W: www.stanton-bonna.co.uk

SCG Solutions
335 Shepcote Lane,
Sheffield, S9 1TG
T: 0114 221 1111
E: steve@scgsolutions.co.uk
W: www.scgsolutions.co.uk

Schaeffler (UK) Ltd
Forge Lane,
Minworth,
Sutton Coldfield,
West Midlands, B76 1AP
T: 0121 313 5870
F: 0121 313 0080
E: info.uk@schaeffler.com
W: www.schaeffler.co.uk

Schaltbau Machine Electrics
335/336 Springvale Industrial Estate,
Woodside Way,
Cwmbran, NP44 5BR
T: 01633 877555
F: 01633 873366
E: sales@schaltbau-me.com
W: www.schaltbau-me.com

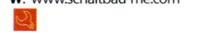

Scheidt & Bachmann (UK) Ltd
7 Silverglade Business Park,
Leatherhead Rd,
Chessington,
Surrey, KT9 2QL
T: 01372 230400
F: 01372 722053
E: info@scheidt-bachmann.de
W: www.scheidt-bachmann.de

Schenck Process UK
Carolina Court,
Lakeside,
Doncaster, DN4 5RA
T: 01302 321313
F: 01302 554400
E: enquiries@schenckprocess.co.uk
W: www.schenckprocess.co.uk

Schneider Electric Ltd
Stafford Park 5,
Telford,
Shropshire, TF3 3BL
T: 01952 209226
F: 01952 292238
W: www.schneider-electric.co.uk

Schofield Lothian Ltd
Temple Chambers,
3-7 Temple Ave,
London, EC4Y 0DT
T: 020 7842 0920
F: 020 7842 0921
E: enquiries@schofieldlothian.com
W: www.schofieldlothian.com

Schroff UK Ltd
Maylands Ave, Hemel Hempstead,
Herts, HP2 7DE
T: 01442 240471
F: 01442 213508
E: schroff.uk@pentair.com
W: www.schroff.co.uk

Schweerbau GmbH & Co KG
UK Branch Office, 20 Beattyville
Gardens, Ilford, IG6 1JN
F: 020 7681 3971
M: 07725 888933
E: verheijen@schweerbau.de
W: www.schweerbau.de

Rosehill Rail
ROAD CROSSING SYSTEMS
THE NEW STANDARD · APPROVED BY NETWORK RAIL
+44 (0)1422 839 456 · www.rosehillrail.com

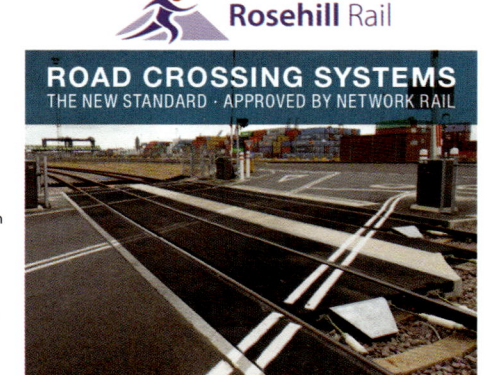

198

IN ASSOCIATION WITH **ATKINS**

Schweizer Electronic AG
Industriestrasse 3,
CH-6260 Reiden,
Switzerland
T: 0041 6274 90707
F: 0041 6274 90700
E: info@schweizer-electronic.ch
W: www.schweizer-electronic.ch

Schwihag AG
Lebernstrasse 3, PO Box 152,
CH-8274 Tagerwilen,
Switzerland
T: 0041 71 666 8800
F: 0041 71 666 8801
E: info@schwihag.com
W: www.schwihag.com

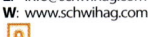

Scientifics
ESG House,
Bretby Business Park, Ashby Rd,
Burton upon Trent, DE15 0YZ
T: 0845 603 2112
F: 01283 554401
E: sales@esg.co.uk
W: www.esg.co.uk

Scisys
Methuen Park,
Chippenham,
Wilts, SN14 0GB
T: 01249 466466
F: 01249 466666
E: marketing@scisys.co.uk
W: www.scisys.co.uk

Scotrail
See First Scotrail

Scott Bader
Wollaston, Wellingborough,
Northants, NN29 7RL
T: 01933 663100
E: composites@scottbader.com
W: www.scottbader.com

Scott Brownrigg Design Research Unit
77 Endell St, London, WC2H 9DZ
T: 020 7240 7766
F: 020 7240 2454
E: enquiries@scottbrownrigg.com
W: www.scottbrownrigg.com

Scott White & Hookings
Fountain House, 26 St Johns St,
Bedford, MK42 0AQ
T: 01234 213111
F: 01234 213333
E: bed@swh.co.uk
W: www.swh.co.uk

Scott Wilson Railways
See URS

Scotweld Employment Services
See SW Global Resourcing

Screwfast Foundations Ltd
7-14 Smallford Works,
Smallford Way,
St. Albans,
Herts, AL4 0SA
T: 01727 821282
F: 01727 828098
E: info@screwfast.com
W: www.screwfast.com

SCT Europe Ltd
See Wabtec Rail Ltd

SEA (Group) Ltd
SEA House, PO Box 800,
Bristol, BS16 1SU
T: 01373 852000
F: 01373 831133
E: info@sea.co.uk
W: www.sea.co.uk

Search Consultancy
198 West George St,
Glasgow, G2 2NR
T: 0141 272 7777
F: 0141 272 7788
E: glasgow@search.co.uk
W: www.searchconsultancy.co.uk

Seaton Rail Ltd
Bridlington Business Centre,
Enterprise Way,
Bridlington, YO16 4SF
T: 01262 608313
F: 01262 604493
E: info@seaton-rail.com
W: www.seaton-rail.com

Secheron SA
Rue de pre-Bouvier 25, Zimeysa
1217 Meyrin, Geneva, Switzerland
T: 0041 22 739 4111
F: 0041 22 739 4811
E: info@secheron.com
W: www.secheron.com

Sefac UK Ltd
Unit C211, Barton Rd, Water Eaton,
Bletchley, MK2 3HU
T: 01908 821274
F: 01908 821275
E: info@sefac-lift.co.uk
W: www.sefac-lift.co.uk

Select Cables Ltd
Painter Close, Anchorage Park,
Portsmouth
T: 02392 652552
F: 02392 655277
E: sales@selectcables.com
W: www.selectcables.com

Selectequip Ltd
Unit 7, Britannia Way,
Britannia Enterprise Park,
Lichfield, Staffs, WS14 9UY
T: 01543 416641
F: 01543 416083
E: sales@selectequip.co.uk
W: www.selectequip.co.uk

Selex ES Ltd
8-10 Great George St,
London, SW1P 3AE
F: 0207 340 6199
M: 07500 813468
E: amanda.lachlan@selex-es.com
W: www.selex-es.com

Semikron Ltd
John Tate Rd,
Foxholes Business Park,
Hertford, SG13 7NW
T: 01992 584677
F: 01992 503847
E: sales.skuk@semikron.com
W: www.semikron.com

Semmco Ltd
9 Kestrel Way,
Goldsworth Park Trading Est,
Woking,
Surrey, GU21 3BA
T: 01483 757200
F: 01483 740795
E: sales@semmco.com
W: www.semmco.co.uk

Semperit Industrial Products
25 Cottesbrooke Park,
Heartlands, Daventry,
Northants, NN11 8YL
T: 01327 313144
F: 01327 313149
E: ian.rowlinson@semperit.co.uk
W: www.semperit.at

Senator Security Services Ltd
1 The Thorn Tree,
Elmhurst Business Park,
Lichfield,
Staffs, WS13 8EX
T: 01543 411811
F: 01543 411911
E: senatorgroup@
senatorsecurity.co.uk
W: www.senatorsecurity.co.uk

Senceive Ltd
Hurlingham Studios,
Ranelagh Gardens,
London, SW6 3PA
T: 020 7731 8269
E: info@senceive.com
W: www.senceive.com

Serco Transport services
Serco House, 16 Bartley Wood Bus.
Park, Bartley Way, Hook,
Hants, RG27 9XB
T: 01256 745900
F: 01256 744111
E: generalenquiries@serco.com
W: www.serco.com/markets/
transport

Serco Rail Technical Services
Derwent House, RTC Business Park,
London Rd, Derby, DE24 8UP
T: 01332 262672
F: 01332 264965
E: richard.hobson@serco.com
W: www.serco.com/srts

Rhomberg Sersa UK Ltd
Sersa House, Auster Rd, Clifton Moor,
York, YO30 4XA
T: 01904 479968
F: 01904 479970
E: carl.garrud@sersa-group.com
W: www.sersa-group.com

Setec Ltd
11 Mallard Way, Derby, DE24 8GX
M: 07748 328831
E: craig.king@setecltd.co.uk
W: www.setecltd.co.uk

Severn Lamb
Tything Rd, Alcester, B49 6ET
T: 01789 400140
F: 01789 400240
E: sales@severn-lamb.com
W: www.severn-lamb.com

The Severn Partnership Ltd
The Maltings, 59 Lythwood Rd,
Bayston Hill, Shrewsbury, SY3 0NA
T: 01743 874135
F: 01743 874716
E: mark.combes@severn-
partnership.co.uk
W: www.severnpartnership.co.uk

Severn Valley Railway
The Railway Station, Bewdley,
Worcs, DY12 1BG
T: 01299 403816
F: 01299 400839
E: mktg@svr.co.uk
W: www.svr.co.uk

Seymourpowell
The Factory, 265 Merton Rd,
London, SW18 5JS
T: 020 7381 6433
E: lucy.kirby@seymourpowell.com
W: www.seymourpowell.com

SGA (Stuart Gray Associates)
88 Spring Hill, Arley, Warks, CV7 8FE
T: 01676 541402
E: info@stuartgrayassociates.co.uk
W: www.stuartgrayassociates.co.uk

SGH Martineau LLP
No.1 Colmore,
Birmingham, B4 6AA
T: 0800 763 1000
F: 0800 763 1001
E: andrew.whitehead@
sghmartineau.com
W: www.sghmartineau.com

SGS Correl Rail Ltd
Gee House, Holborn Hill,
Birmingham, B7 5PA
T: 0121 326 3672
F: 0121 328 5343
E: gary.winstanley@sgs.com
W: www.sgs.com

SGS Engineering (UK) Ltd
Cranmer Rd,
West Meadows Ind. Est,
Derby, DE21 6JL
T: 01332 298126/01332 366552
F: 01332 366232
E: sales@sgs-engineering.com
W: www.sgs-engineering.com

SGS UK Ltd
Inward Way,
Rossmore Business Park,
Ellesmere Port, CH65 3EN
T: 0151 350 6666
F: 0151 350 6600
W: www.sgs.com

Shannon Rail Services Ltd
Orphanage Road Sidings,
Reeds Crescent,
Watford,
Herts, WD17 1PG
T: 01923 254567
F: 01923 255678
E: info@shannonrail.com
W: www.shannonrail.com

Shay Murtagh Precast Ltd
Raharney,
Mullingar,
Co Westmeath,
Republic of Ireland
T: 0844 202 0263
E: sales@shaymurtagh.co.uk
W: www.shaymurtagh.co.uk

Sheerspeed Shelters Ltd
Unit 3,
Diamond House,
Reme Drive,
Heath Park,
Honiton,
Devon, EX14 1SE
T: 01404 46006
F: 01404 45520
E: sales@sheerspeed.com
W: www.sheerspeed.com

Shell UK Oil Products Ltd
Brabazon House,
Concord Business Park,
Threapwood Rd,
Manchester, M22 0RR
T: 08708 500924
F: 0161 499 8930
E: lubesenquiries-uk@
shell.com
W: www.shell.co.uk/lubricants

Shere Ltd
See ATOS Origin

SIEMENS

Siemens Rail Automation is a global leader in the design, supply, installation and commissioning of track-side and train-borne signalling and train control solutions.

This is delivered by over 9,500 people across a network of offices worldwide, with 1,450 UK-based employees.

Siemens Rail Automation, PO Box 79,
Pew Hill, Chippenham, SN15 1JD
Tel: +44 (0) 1249 441441
Info.railautomation.gb@siemens.com
www.siemens.co.uk/rail

Siemens plc, Rail Systems Division provides expertise and technology in the full range of rail vehicles - from heavy rail to metros to trams and light-rail vehicles. In the UK, the Division employs around 700 people and maintains over 350 Siemens passenger trains for the First TransPennine Express, South West Trains, Heathrow Express, Great Anglia Franchise (Abellio), Northern Rail, London Midland and ScotRail. The company will also be supplying Eurostar with its new high speed fleet of trains.

Siemens plc, Rail Systems Division, Euston House, 24 Eversholt Street, London, NW1 1AD

info.railsystems.gb@siemens.com
www.siemens.co.uk/rail

SIEMENS

Sheridan Maine
Regus House,
George Curl Way,
Southampton, SO18 2RZ
T: 0871 218 0573
F: 0871 218 0173
E: southampton@
sheridanmaine.com
W: www.sheridanmaine.com

Shield Batteries
277 Stansted Rd,
Bishops Stortford,
Herts, CM23 2BT
T: 01279 652067
F: 01279 758041
M: 07900 403716
E: paul.bowles@
shieldbatteries.co.uk
W: www.shieldbatteries.co.uk

Shorterm Rail
The Barn,
Philpots Close,
Yiewsley,
Middx, UB7 7RY
T: 01895 427900
E: info@shortermgroup.co.uk
W: www.shorterm.co.uk

Shotcrete Services Ltd
Old Station Yard, Hawkhurst Rd,
Cranbrook, Kent, TN17 2SR
T: 01580 714747
E: stuart.manning@shotcrete.co.uk
W: www.shotcrete.co.uk

SICK (UK) Ltd
39 Hedley Rd,
St Albans, AL1 5DN
T: 01727 831121
E: info@sick.co.uk
W: www.sick.co.uk

Siegrist-Orel Ltd
Pysons Rd Ind. Est.,
Broadstairs,
Kent, CT10 2LQ
T: 01843 865241
F: 01843 867180
E: info@siegrist-orel.co.uk
W: www.siegrist-orel.co.uk

Siemens Rail Automation
PO Box 79, Pew Hill,
Chippenham, SN15 1JD
T: 01249 441441
E: info.railautomation.gb@
siemens.com
W: www.siemens.co.uk/rail

Siemens Rail Systems
Euston House,
24 Eversholt St,
London, NW1 1AD
T: 020 7227 0722
F: 020 7227 4435
E: info.railsystems.gb@
siemens.com
W: www.siemens.co.uk/rail

Sig Cyclone
Unit 16 Gerald House,
Sherwood Network Centre,
Sherwood Energy Village,
Newton Hill, Ollerton,
Notts, NG22 9FD
T: 07833 433404
E: liane.launders@sigcyclone.com
W: www.sig-ukgroup.com

SigAssure UK Ltd
Gerald House, Unit 4, Randall Park
Way, Retford, Notts, DN22 7WF
T: 01777 707809
E: info@sigassure-group.co.uk
W: www.sigassure-group.co.uk

Sigma Coachair Group UK Ltd
Unit 1, Queens Drive,
Newhall, Swadlincote,
Derbys, DE11 0EG
T: 01283 559140
F: 01283 225253
W: www.sigmacoachair.com

Signal House Ltd
Cherrycourt Way, Stanbridge Rd,
Leighton Buzzard, Beds, LU7 8UH
T: 01525 377477
F: 01525 850999
E: sales@signalhouse.co.uk
W: www.signalhousegroup.co.uk

signalling solutions

excellence in train control

Signalling Solutions offers turnkey solutions to the rail industry's train control and resignalling markets from conceptual design to full project delivery.

A Balfour Beatty and Alstom company.

Signalling Solutions Limited
Bridgefoot House, Watling Street,
Radlett, Herts WD7 7HT

Tel: 01923 635000
Email: info@signallingsolutions.com

www.signallingsolutions.com

199

DIRECTORY

Signalling Construction UK Ltd
Unit 12, Century Park, Garrison Lane, Bordesley, Birmingham, B9 4NZ
T: 0121 753 0060
F: 0121 772 7898
E: signallingconstruction@fsmail.com
W: www.scukltd.com

Signalling Solutions Ltd
Bridgefoot House, Watling St, Radlett, Herts, WD7 7HT
T: 01923 635000
E: info@signallingsolutions.com
W: www.signallingsolutions.com

Signature Aromas Ltd
Signature House, 65-67 Gospel End St, Sedgley, West Midlands, DY3 3LR
T: 01902 678822
F: 01902 672888
E: enquiries@signaturearomas.co.uk
W: www.signaturearomas.com

Signet Solutions
Kelvin House, RTC Business Park, London Rd, Derby, DE24 8UP
T: 01332 343585
F: 01332 367132
E: enquiries@signet-solutions.com
W: www.signet-solutions.com

Sill Lighting UK
3 Thame Park Bus. Centre, Wenman Rd, Thame, Oxon, OX9 3XA
T: 01844 260006
E: sales@sill-uk.com
W: www.sill-uk.com

Silver Atena
Cedar House, Riverside Business Park, Swindon Rd, Malmesbury, Wilts, SN16 9RS
T: 01666 580000
F: 01666 580001
E: info@silver-atena.com
W: www.silver-atena.com

Silver Software
See Silver Atena

Silver Track Training
Fleet House, Pye Close, Haydock, St Helens, WA11 9JT
T: 01942 728196
E: angela@silvertracktraining.co.uk
W: www.silvertracktraining.co.uk

Simmons & Simmons
City Point, One Ropemaker St, London, EC2Y 9SS
T: 020 7628 2020
F: 020 7628 2070
E: juliet.reingold@simmons-simmons.com
W: www.simmons-simmons.com

Simona UK
Telford Drive, Brookmead Ind. Park, Stafford, ST16 3ST
T: 01785 222444
F: 01785 222080
E: mail@simona-uk.com
W: www.simona.de

SIMS
Fourth Floor, Roman Wall House, 1-2 Crutched Friars, London, EC3N 2HT
T: 020 7481 9798
F: 020 7481 9657
E: inbox@sims-uk.com
W: www.simsrail.com

Simulation Systems Ltd
Unit 12, Market Ind.Est, Yatton, Bristol, BS49 4RF
T: 01934 838803
F: 01934 876202
W: www.simulation-systems.co.uk

Sinclair Knight Merz
Victoria House, Southampton Row, London, WC1B 4EA
T: 020 7759 2600
F: 020 7759 2601
E: enquiries@globalskm.com
W: www.skmconsulting.com

John Sisk & Sons Ltd
1 Caro Park, Frogmore, St Albans, Herts, AL2 2DD
T: 01727 875551
F: 01727 875642

Site Vision Surveys
19 Warwick St, Rugby, Warks, CV21 3DH
T: 01788 575036
F: 01788 576208
E: mail@svsltd.net
W: www.svsltd.net

Skanska UK
Maple Cross House, Denham Way, Maple Cross, Rickmansworth, Herts, WD3 9SW
T: 01923 423100
F: 01923 423111
W: www.cementationfoundations.skandka.co.uk

SKF UK Ltd
Railway Sales Unit, Sundon Park Rd, Luton, LU3 3BL
T: 01582 496490
F: 01582 496327
E: stewart.mclellan@skf.com
W: www.skf.com

Skills 4 Rail
35 Auckland Rd, Birmingham, B11 1RH
T: 01217714219
M: 01217714219
E: sales@sills4rail.co.uk
W: www.skills4rail.co.uk

SKM Colin Buchanan
The Metro Buiding, 33 Trafford Rd, Salford Quays, Manchester, M5 3NN
T: 0161 873 8500
F: 0161 873 8501
E: enquiries@globalskm.com
W: www.skmcolinbuchanan.com

Skymasts Antennas
Unit 2, Clayfield Close, Moulton Park Ind. Est, Northampton, NN3 6QF
T: 01604 494132
F: 01604 494133
E: info@skymasts.com
W: www.skymasts.com

Slender Winter Partnership
The Old School, London Rd, Westerham, Kent, TN11 1DN
T: 01959 564777
F: 01959 562802
E: swp@swpltd.co.uk
W: www.swpltd.co.uk

Smart Component Technologies Ltd
3M Buckley Innovation Centre, Firth St, Huddersfield, HD1 3BD
M: 07710 486888
E: r.bromley@hud.ac.uk
W: www.hud.ac.uk

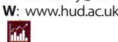

SMC Light & Power
Belchmire Lane, Spalding, Lincs, PE11 4HG
T: 01775 840020
F: 01775 843063
E: info@smclightandpower.com
W: www.smclightandpower.com

SMC Pneumatics Ltd
Vincent Ave, Crownhill, Milton Keynes, MK8 OAN
T: 0845 121 5122
F: 01908 555064
E: sales@smcpneumatics.co.uk
W: www.smcpneumatics.co.uk

SME Ltd
Unit 1, Lloyd St, Parkgate, Rotherham, S62 6JG
T: 08444 930666
F: 08444 930667
W: www.sme-ltd.co.uk

SMI Conferences
SMI Group Ltd, Unit 122, Great Guildford Business Square, 30 Great Guildford St, London, SE1 0HS
T: 020 7827 6000
F: 020 7827 6001
E: info@smi-online.com
W: www.smi-online.co.uk

Smith Bros & Webb Ltd
Britannia House, Arden Forest Ind.Est, Alcester, Warks, B49 6EX
T: 01789 400096
F: 01789 400231
E: sales@sbw-wash.com
W: www.sbw-wash.com

Smith Cooper
Wilmot House, St Helen's House, King St, Derby, DE1 3EE
T: 01332 332021
F: 01332 290439
E: janet.morgan@smithcooper.co.uk
W: www.smithcooper.co.uk

SML Resourcing
Unit 3.07, New Loom House, 101 Back Church Lane, London, E1 1LU
T: 020 7423 4390
F: 020 7702 1097
E: jobs@sml-resourcing.com
W: www.sml-resourcing.com

SMP Electronics
Unit 6, Border Farm, Station Rd, Chobham, Surrey, GU24 8AS
T: 01276 855166
F: 01276 855115
E: sales@smpelectronics.com
W: www.smpelectronics.com

Snap-On Rail Solutions
Distribution Centre, Telford Way, Kettering, Northants, NN16 8SN
T: 01536 413904
F: 01536 413874
E: rail@snapon.com
W: www.snapon.com/industrialuk

Society of Operations Engineers (SOE)
22 Greencoat Place, London, SW1P 1PR
T: 020 7630 1111
F: 020 7630 6677
E: soe@soe.org.uk
W: www.soe.org.uk

Socomec UPS (UK)
Units 7-9A, Lakeside Business Park, Broadway Lane, South Cerney, Cirencester, Glos, GL7 5XL
T: 01285 863300
F: 01285 862304
E: rail.ups.uk@socomec.com
W: www.socomec.co.uk/ups

Softech Global Ltd
Softech House, London Rd, Albourne, West Sussex, BN6 9BN
T: 01273 833844
F: 01273 833044
E: rail@softechglobal.com
W: www.softechglobal.com

SOLID Applications Ltd
Old Market Place, Market St, Oldbury, B69 4DH
T: 0121 544 1400
E: anton.plackowski@saplm.co.uk
W: www.saplm.co.uk/rail

Solo Fabrications
Landor St, Saltley, Birmingham, B8 1AE
T: 0121 327 3378
F: 0121 327 3757
E: sales@solorail.com
W: www.solofabs.com

Solution Rail
22 Somers Way, Bushey, Herts, WD23 4HR
F: 0871 989 5700
M: 07717 712272
E: enquiries@solutionrail.co.uk
W: www.solutionrail.co.uk

Solvay Speciality Polymers
Baronet Rd, Warrington, WA4 6HA
T: 01925 943546
F: 01925 943548
E: shayel.ahmed@solvay.com
W: www.solvayplastics.com

Somers Totalkare
15 Forge Trading Est., Mucklow Hill, Halesowen, B62 8TR
T: 0121 585 2700
F: 0121 501 1458
E: sales@somerstotalkare.co.uk
W: www.somerstotalkare.co.uk

Sonic Rail Service Ltd (SRS)
Unit 15, Springfield Ind. Est, Springfield Rd, Burnham-on-Crouch, Essex, CM0 8UA
T: 01621 784688
F: 01621 786594
E: stewart.robinson@sonicrail.co.uk
W: www.sonicrail.co.uk

Sonic Windows Ltd
Unit 14/15, Beeching Park Ind.Est., Wainwright Rd, Bexhill on Sea, E Sussex, TN39 3UR
T: 01424 223864
F: 01424 215859
E: enquiries@sonicwindows.co.uk
W: www.sonicwindows.co.uk

Sortimo International Ltd
Old Sarum Park, Salisbury, Wilts, SP4 6EB
T: 01722 411585
F: 01722 320831
E: vanrack1@sortimo.co.uk
W: www.sortimo.co.uk

Sotera Risk Solutions Ltd
22 Glanville Rd, Bromley, BR2 9LW
T: 01737 551203
M: 07946 638 424
E: chris.chapman@sotera.co.uk
W: www.sotera.co.uk

South West Trains
Stagecoach Group, 10 Dunkeld Rd, Perth, PH1 5TW
T: 01738 442111
F: 01738 643648
E: mail@stagecoachgroup.com
W: www.stagecoachgroup.com

South Yorkshire Passenger Trasport Executive
11 Broad St West, Sheffield, S1 2BQ
T: 0114 276 7575
F: 0114 275 9908
E: comments@sypte.co.uk
W: www.sypte.co.uk

Southco Manufacturing Ltd
Touch Point, Wainwright Rd, Warndon, Worcs, WR4 9FA
T: 01905 346722
F: 01905 346723
E: info@southco.com
W: www.southco.com

Southeastern
Friars Bridge Court, 41-45 Blackfriars Rd, London, SE1 8PG
T: 020 7620 5000
W: www.southeasternrailway.co.uk

Southern Electric Contracting
55 Vastern Rd, Reading, RG1 8BU
T: 0118 958 0100
F: 0118 953 4755
E: marketing@sec.eu.com
W: www.sec.eu.com

Southern/Gatwick Express
Go-Ahead House, 26-28 Addiscombe Rd, Croydon, CR9 5GA
T: 020 8929 8600
F: 020 8929 8687
E: communications@southernrailway.com
W: www.southernrailway.com / www.gatwickexpress.com

Sovereign Planned Services On Line Ltd
Unit 3d, Forge Way, Brown Lees Ind Est, Biddulph, Stoke on Trent, ST8 7DN
T: 01782 510600
F: 01782 510700
E: sales@sovonline.co.uk
W: www.sovonline.co.uk

Spartan Safety Ltd
Unit 3, Waltham Park Way, Walthamstow, London, E17 5DU
T: 020 8527 5888
F: 020 8527 5999
E: ryan@spartansafety.co.uk
W: www.spartansafety.co.uk

Specialist Engineering Services Ltd (SES)
SES House, Harworth Park, Doncaster, DN11 8DB
T: 01302 756800
E: info@ses-holdings.com
W: www.ses-holdings.com

Specialist Plant Associates
Airfield Rd, Hinwick, Wellingborough, Northants, NN29 7JG
T: 01234 781882
F: 01234 781992
E: info@specialistplant.co.uk
W: www.specialistplant.co.uk

Spectro
Palace Gate, Odiham, RG29 1NP
T: 01256 704000
F: 01256 704006
E: enquiries@spectro-oil.com
W: www.spectro-oil.com

Spectrum Freight Ltd
PO Box 105, Chesterfield, Derbys, S41 9XY
T: 01246 456677
F: 01246 456688
E: sales@spectrumfreight.co.uk
W: www.spectrumfreight.co.uk

Spectrum Technologies
Western Avenue, Bridgend, Mid Glamorgan, CF31 3RT
T: 01656 655437
F: 01656 655920
E: ehardy@spectrumtech.com
W: www.spectrumtech.com

Speedy Hire Plc
Chase House, 16 The Parks, Newton le Willows, Merseyside, WA12 0JQ
T: 01942 720000
F: 01942 720077
E: admin@speedyhire.co.uk
W: www.speedyhire.co.uk

Spence Ltd
Parcel Deck, Barnby St, Euston Station, London, NW1 2RS
T: 020 7387 1268
F: 020 7380 1255
E: info@spenceltd.co.uk
W: www.spenceltd.co.uk

C Spencer
Mill Lane, Barrow upon Humber, DN19 7DB
T: 01469 532266
F: 01469 532233
E: mailbox@cspencerltd.co.uk
W: www.cspencerltd.co.uk

Speno International SA
26 Parc Chateau-Banquet POB 16, 1211 Geneva 21, Switzerland
T: 0041 22906 4600
F: 0041 22906 4601
E: info@speno.ch
W: www.speno.ch

Sperry Rail International Ltd
Trent House, RTC Business Park, London Rd, Derby, DE24 8UP
T: 01332 262565
F: 01332 262541
E: jtansley@sperryrail.com
W: www.sperryrail.com

Spitfire Tours
PO Box 824, Taunton, TA1 9ET
T: 0870 879 3675
E: info@spitfirerailtours.co.uk
W: www.spitfirerailtours.co.uk

SPL Powerlines UK Ltd
Unit 3A, Hagmill Cres, East Shawhead Enterprise Park, Coatbridge, Lanarkshire, ML5 4NS
T: 01236 424666
F: 01236 426444
E: office@powerlines-group.com
W: www.powerlines-group.com

Spring Personnel
1 Canal Arm, Festival Park, Stoke on Trent, ST1 5UR
T: 01782 221500
F: 01782 221600
E: personnel@spring.com
W: www.spring.com

SPX Rail Systems
Unit 7, Thames Gateway Park, Choats Rd, Dagenham, Essex, RM9 6RH
T: 020 8526 7100
F: 020 8526 7151
E: brian.cannon@spx.com
W: www.spx.com

SRPS Railtours
3 South Cathkin Farm Cottages, Glasgow, G73 5RG
T: 01698 263814/457777
E: railtours@srps.org.uk
W: www.srps.org.uk

SRS Rail Systems Ltd
3 Riverside Way, Gateway Business Park, Bolsover, Chesterfield, S44 6GA
T: 01246 241312
F: 01246 825076
E: info@srsrailuk.co.uk
W: www.srsrailuk.com

SSDM
See Aura Graphics Ltd

SSP
169 Euston Rd, London, NW1 2AE
T: 020 7543 3300
F: 020 7543 3389
E: clare@templemerepr.co.uk
W: www.foodtravelexpert.com

St Leonards Railway Engineering Ltd
Bridgeway, St Leonards on Sea, E Sussex, TN38 8AP
T: 01233 617001

IN ASSOCIATION WITH **ATKINS**

Stadler Pankow GmbH
Lessingstrasse 102, D-13158 Berlin,
Germany
T: 0049 309191 1616
F: 0049 309191 2150
E: stadler.pankow@stadlerrail.de
W: www.stadlerrail.com

Stagecoach Group
10 Dunkeld Rd, Perth, PH1 5TW
T: 01738 442111
F: 01738 643648
E: info@stagecoachgroup.com
W: www.stagecoachgroup.com

Stagecoach Supertram
Nunnery Depot,
Woodbourn Rd,
Sheffield, S9 3LS
T: 0114 275 9888
F: 0114 279 8120
E: enquiries@supertram.com
W: www.supertram.com

Stahlwille Tools Ltd
Unit 2D, Albany Park Ind. Est,
Frimley Rd,
Camberley,
Surrey, GU16 7PD
T: 01276 24080
F: 01276 24696
E: scottsheldon@stahlwille.co.uk
W: www.stahlwille.co.uk

Stanley Tools
Sheffield Business Park,
Sheffield City Airport,
Europa Link,
Sheffield, S3 9PD
T: 0114 244 8883
F: 0114 273 9038

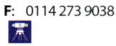

Stannah Lifts
Anton Mill, Andover,
Hants, SP10 2NX
T: 01264 339090
E: liftsales@stannah.co.uk
W: www.stannahlifts.co.uk

Stansted Express
Enterprise House,
Stansted Airport,
Essex, CM20 1QW
E: eleni.jordan@nationalexpress.com
W: www.stanstedexpress.com

Stanton Bonna Concrete Ltd
Littlewell Lane,
Stanton by Dale,
Ilkeston,
Derbys, DE7 4QW
T: 0115 944 1448
F: 0115 944 1466
E: sbc@stanton-bonna.co.uk
W: www.stanton-bonna.co.uk

Star Fasteners (UK) Ltd
Unit 3, Gallows Ind. Est, Furnace Rd,
Ilkeston, Derbys, DE7 5EP
T: 0115 932 4939
F: 0115 944 1278
E: sales@starfasteners.co.uk
W: www.starfasteners.co.uk

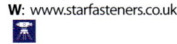

Statesman Rail Ltd
PO Box 83,
St Erth, Hayle,
Cornwall, TR27 9AD
T: 0845 310 2458
F: 0115 944 1278
W: www.statesmanrail.com

STATS
See RSK Ltd

Stauff Ltd
500 Carlisle St East,
Sheffield, S4 8BS
T: 01142 518518
F: 01141 518519
E: sales@stauff.co.uk
W: www.stauff.co.uk

Staytite Ltd
Staytite House,
Coronation Rd,
Cressex Bus.Park,
High Wycombe,
Bucks, HP12 3RP
T: 01494 462322
F: 01494 464747
E: fasteners@staytite.com
W: www.staytite.com

Steam Dreams
PO Box 169, Albury,
Guildford,
Surrey, GU5 9YS
T: 01483 209888
F: 01483 209889
E: info@steamdreams.co.uk
W: www.steamdreams.com

Steatite Ltd
Ravensbank Business Park,
Acanthus Rd, Redditch,
Worcs, B98 9EX
T: 01527 512400
F: 01527 512419
E: sales@steatite.co.uk
W: www.steatite.co.uk

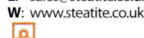

Steelteam Construction (UK) Ltd
46 Goods Station Rd,
Tunbridge Wells,
Kent, TN1 2DD
T: 01892 533677
F: 01892 511535
E: sales@steelteamconstruction.co.uk
W: www.steelteamconstruction.co.uk

Steelway Rail
Queensgate Works, Bilston Rd,
Wolverhampton,
West Midlands, WV2 2NJ
T: 01902 451733
F: 01902 452256
E: sales@steelway.co.uk
W: www.steelway.co.uk

Steer Davies Gleave
28-32 Upper Ground,
London, SE1 9PD
T: 020 7910 5000
F: 020 7910 5001
E: sdginfo@sdgworld.net
W: www.steerdaviesgleave.com

Stego UK Ltd
Unit 12, First Quarter Bus. Park,
Blenheim Rd, Epsom,
Surrey, KT19 9QN
T: 01372 747250
F: 01372 729854
E: info@stego.co.uk
W: www.stego.co.uk

Stent
Pavilion C2, Ashwood Park,
Ashwood Way, Basingstoke,
Hants, RG23 8BG
T: 01256 366000
F: 01256 366001
E: neil.beresford@stent.co.uk
W: www.stent.co.uk

Stephenson Harwood LLP
1 Finsbury Circus,
London, EC2M 7SH
T: 020 7809 2618
F: 020 7003 8220
M: 07976 363769
E: graeme.mclellan@shlegal.com
W: www.shlegal.com

Stewart Signs Rail
Trafalgar Close,
Chandlers Ford Ind. Est,
Eastleigh, Hants, SO53 4BW
T: 023 8025 4781
F: 023 8025 5620
E: sales@stewartsigns.com
W: www.stewartsigns.com

Stirling Maynard
Construction Consultants,
Stirling House, Rightwell, Bretton,
Peterborough, PE3 8DJ
T: 01733 262319
F: 01733 331527
E: enquiries@stirlingmaynard.com
W: www.stirlingmaynard.com

Stobart Rail
Solway Business Centre,
Carlisle,
Cumbria, CA6 4BY
T: 01228 882300
F: 01228 882301
E: grant.mcnab@stobartrail.com
W: www.stobartrail.com

Stock Redler Ltd
Redler House,
Dudbridge,
Stroud,
Glos, GL3 3EY
T: 01423 819461
F: 0049 6151 321043
E: r.illsley@schenckprocess.com
W: www.schenckprocess.com

Stocksigns Ltd/ Burnham Signs
43, Ormside Way,
Holmethorpe Ind Est,
Redhill,
Surrey, RH1 2LG
T: 01737 764764
F: 01737 763763
E: jgodden@stocksigns.com
W: www.stocksigns.com

Stockton Engineering Management Ltd
1 Warwick Row,
London, SW1E 5ER
T: 020 7808 7808
F: 020 7117 5253
E: info@stocktonlondon.com
W: www.stocktonlondon.com

Stored Energy Technology
See S.E.T. Ltd

Story Rail
Burgh Rd Ind Est,
Carlisle, CA2 7NA
T: 01228 640880
F: 01228 640881
E: info@storygroup.co.uk
W: www.storygroup.co.uk

STRAIL (UK) Ltd
Room 2, First Floor,
3 Tannery House,
Tannery Lane,
Send,
Woking,
Surrey, GU23 7EF
T: 01483 222090
F: 01483 222095
E: richard@srsrailuk.co.uk
W: www.strail.com

Strainstall UK Ltd
9-10, Mariners Way,
Cowes, IOW, PO31 8PD
T: 01983 203600
F: 01983 201335
E: enquiries@strainstall.com
W: www.strainstall.co.uk

Strataform
See TechnoRail (Technocover)

Strategic Team Group Ltd
Head Office,
Strategic Business Centre,
Blue Ridge Park,
Thunderhead Ridge,
Glasshoughton,
Castleford,
West Yorks, WF10 4UA
T: 01977 555550
E: contact@strategicteamgroup.com
W: www.strategicteamgroup.com

Strathclyde Partnership for Transport
Consort House,
12 West George St,
Glasgow, G2 1HN
T: 0141 332 6811
E: enquiry@spt.co.uk
W: www.spt.co.uk

Street Crane Co. Ltd
Chapel-en-le-Frith,
High Peak,
Derbys, SK23 0PH
T: 01298 812456
E: sales@streetcrane.co.uk
W: www.streetcrane.co.uk

STS Signals
See Mors Smitt

Stuart Group
Lancaster Approach, North
Killingholme, Immingham,
NE Lincs, DN40 3TZ
T: 0870 4141 400
F: 0870 4141 440
E: enquiries@stuartgroup.info
W: www.stuartgroup.info

Stuart Maher Ltd (SML)
Unit 3.07, New Loom House,
101 Back Church Lane,
London, SE1 1LU
T: 020 7423 4390
F: 07092 810 920
E: nick.stuart@stuart-maher.co.uk
W: www.stuart-maher.co.uk

Sulzer Dowding & Mills
Camp Hill, Bordesley,
Birmingham, B12 0JJ
T: 0121 766 6333
F: 0121 766 7247
E: engineering.birmingham@sulzer.com
W: www.sulzer.com

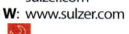

Superform Aluminium
Cosgrove Close,
Worcester, WR3 8UA
T: 01905 874300
F: 01905 874301
E: sales@superform-aluminium.com
W: www.superforming.com

Superjet London
Unit 5, Kennet Rd,
Dartford,
Kent, DA1 4QN
T: 01322 554595
F: 01322 557773
E: chris@superjet.co.uk
W: www.jetchem.com

Supersine Duramark
See Aura Graphics Ltd

Survey Inspection Systems Ltd (SIS)
Green Lane Ind. Est,
Enterprise House, Meadowfield Ave,
Spennymoor, Co Durham, DL16 6JF
T: 01388 810308
F: 01388 819260
E: sales@survey-inspection.com
W: www.survey-inspection.com

Survey Systems Ltd
Willow Bank House,
Old Road, Handforth,
Wilmslow, SK9 3AZ
T: 01625 533444
F: 01625 526815
E: enquiries@survsys.co.uk
W: www.survsys.co.uk/rail

SW Global Resourcing
270 Peters Hill Rd,
Glasgow, G21 4AY
T: 0141 557 6133
F: 0141 557 6143
E: admin@sw-gr.com
W: www.scotweld.com

Sweetnam & Bradley Ltd
Industrial Est,
Gloucester Rd, Malmesbury,
Wilts, SN16 0DY
T: 01666 823491
F: 01666 826010
E: sales@sweetnam-bradley.com
W: www.sweetnam-bradley.com

Swietelsky Babcock
See SB Rail (Swietelsky Babcock)

Swietelsky Construction Company Ltd
7 Clairmont Gardens,
Glasgow, G3 7LW
T: 0141 353 1915
E: office@swietelsky.at
W: www.swietelsky.com

Sydac Ltd
Derwent Business Centre,
Clarke St, Derby, DE1 2BU
T: 01332 299600
F: 01332 299624
E: paul.williamson@sydac.co.uk
W: www.sydac.co.uk

Sylmasta Ltd
Unit 1, Dales Yard,
Lewes Rd,
Scaynes Hill,
W Sussex, RH17 7PG
T: 01444 831459
F: 01444 831971
W: www.sylmasta.co.uk

Synectic Systems Group Ltd
32 Alexandra Way,
Tewkesbury,
Glos, GL20 8NB
T: 01684 295807
F: 01684 850011
E: sales@synx.com
W: www.synecticsystems.com

Synergy Health Plc
Gavenny Court,
Brecon Rd,
Abergavenny,
Monmouthshire, NP7 7RX
T: 01873 856688
F: 01873 585982
E: enquiries@synergyhealthplc.com
W: www.synergyhealthplc.com

Syntax Recruitment
1 College Place,
Derby, DE1 3DY
T: 01332 287720
F: 01332 296128
E: caroline.evans@syntaxconsulting.com
W: www.syntaxnet.com

Systecon (UK) Ltd
PO Box 4612,
Weymouth,
Dorset, DT4 9YY
T: 0871 641 2202
F: 01305 768480
E: phil.sturgess@systecon.co.uk
W: www.systecon.co.uk

Your online route to passenger transport's vital statistics

Our TAS Business Monitor on-line subscription service gives you instant access to essential data about the financial and market performance of our ground public transport operations - constantly updated. Give us a click!

TAS Business Monitor
Public Transport Intelligence, Statistics & Analysis

head for
www.tas.uk.net
and follow the links

Ross Holme, West End,
Long Preston, Skipton,
BD23 4QL.
Tel: 01729 840756
info@taspublications.co.uk

DIRECTORY

System Store Solutions Ltd
Ham Lane, Lenham, Maidstone,
Kent, ME17 2LH
T: 01622 859522
F: 01622 858746
E: sales@systemstoresolutions.com
W: www.system-store.com

Systra UK
Fourth Floor, Dukes Court, Duke St,
Woking, Surrey, GU21 5BH
T: 01483 742941
F: 01483 755207
E: jonions@systra.com
W: www.systra.com

T & R Williamson Ltd
36 Stonebridgegate, Ripon,
N Yorks, HG4 1TP
T: 01765 607711
F: 01765 607908
E: info@trwilliamson.co.uk
W: www.trwilliamson.co.uk

T & RS Engineering Ltd
Woodfield Business Centre,
Balby Carr Bank,
Doncaster, DN4 8DE
T: 01302 515390
E: mail@trsengineering.co.uk
W: www.trsengineering.co.uk

T J Thomson & Sons Ltd
Millfield Works, Grangefield Rd,
Stockton on Tees, TS18 4AE
T: 01642 672551
F: 01642 672556
E: postbox@tjthomson.co.uk
W: www.tjthomson.co.uk

TAC Europe
Matrix House, Basing View,
Basingstoke, Hants
T: 08700 600822
F: 01256 356371
E: enquiries@taceurope.com
W: www.taceurope.com

Talascend Ltd
First Floor, Broadway Chambers,
Hammersmith Broadway,
London, W6 7PW
T: 020 8600 1600
F: 020 8741 2001
E: info@talascend.com
W: www.talascend.com

Tanfield Engineering Systems
Tanfield Lea Ind. Est. North, Stanley,
Co Durham, DH9 9NX
T: 01207 521111
F: 01207 523318
E: enquiries@tanfieldgroup.co.uk
W: www.tanfieldgroup.co.uk

The TAS Partnership Ltd.
Ross Holme, West End, Long Preston,
Skipton, BD23 4QL
T: 01729 840756
E: info@taspublications.co.uk
W: www.tas.uk.net

Tasty Plant Sales
Copsham House,
53 Broad St,
Chesham,
Bucks, HP5 3EA
T: 0845 677 4444
E: info@tastyplant.co.uk
W: www.tastyplant.co.uk

Tata Steel Projects
Meridian House, The Crescent,
York, YO24 1AW
T: 01904 454600
F: 01904 454601
E: tatasteelprojects@tatasteel.com
W: www.tatasteeleurope.com

Tata Steel Rail
Rail Service Centre,
PO Box 1, Brigg Rd,
Scunthorpe, DN16 1BP
T: 01724 403398
E: rail@tatasteel.com
W: www.tatasteeleurope.com

Tate Rail Ltd
Station House, Station Hill,
Cookham, Berks, SL6 9BP
T: 0844 381 9956
F: 0844 381 9957
E: info@taterail.com
W: www.taterail.com

Taylor Precision Plastics / Commercial Vehicle Rollers Ltd
Mile Oak Ind. Est,
Maesbury Rd,
Oswestry,
Shropshire, SY10 8GA
T: 01691 679516
F: 01691 670538
E: sales@cvrollers.co.uk
W: www.cvrollers.co.uk

Taylor Woodrow
Astral House,
Imperial Way,
Watford, WD24 4WW
T: 01923 233433
F: 01923 800085
M: 07919 228399
E: david.booker@taylorwoodrow.com
W: www.taylorwoodrow.com

Taziker Industrial Ltd t/a TI Protective Coatings
Unit 6, Lodge Bank,
Crown Lane, Horwich,
Bolton, BL6 5HY
T: 01204 468080
F: 01204 695188
E: sales@ti-uk.com
W: www.ti-uk.com

TBM Consulting Group
Unit 8, H2O Business Complex,
Sherwood Business Park,
Annesley,
Nottingham, NG15 0HT
T: 01623 758298
F: 01623 755941
E: nfletcher@tbmcg.com
W: www.tbmcg.com

TDK-Lambda UK
Kingsley Ave, Ilfracombe,
Devon, EX34 8ES
T: 01271 856600
F: 01271 856741
E: powersolutions@emea.tdk-lambda.com
W: www.emea.tdk-lambda.com

TEAL Consulting Ltd
Deangate, Tuesley Lane, Godalming,
Surrey, GU7 1SG
T: 01483 420550
F: 01483 420550
E: info@tealconsulting.co.uk
W: www.tealconsulting.co.uk

Team Surveys Ltd
Team House,
St Austell Bay Business Park,
Par Moor Rd, St Austell, PL25 3RF
T: 01726 816069
F: 01726 814611
E: email@teamsurveys.com
W: www.teamsurveys.co.uk

Tecalemit Garage Equipment Co Ltd
Eagle Rd, Langage Business Park,
Plymouth, PL7 5JY
T: 01752 219111
F: 01752 219128
E: sales@tecalemit.co.uk
W: www.tecalemit.co.uk

Tecforce
Litchurch Lane, Derby, DE24 8AA
T: 01332 268000
F: 01332 268030
E: sales@tecforce.co.uk
W: www.tecforce.co.uk

Technical Cranes Ltd
Holmes Lock Works, Steel St,
Holmes, Rotherham, S61 1DF
T: 01709 561861
F: 01709 556516
E: info@technicalcranes.co.uk
W: www.technicalcranes.co.uk

Technical Cranes Ltd
Holmes Lock Works, Steel St,
Holmes, Rotherham, S61 1DF
T: 01709 561861
F: 01709 556516
E: info@technicalcranes.co.uk
W: www.technicalcranes.co.uk

Technical Programme Delivery
Systems House,
10 Heathfield Close,
Binfield Heath,
Henley on Thames, RG9 4DS
T: 01932 228710
F: 01932 228710
E: pac@tpd.uk.com
W: www.tpd.uk.com

Technical Resin Bonders
See TRB Lightweight Structures Ltd

Technocover
See TechnoRail (Technocover)

Technology Project Services Ltd
1 Warwick Row, London, SW1E 5LR
T: 020 7963 1234
F: 020 7963 1299
E: mail@tps.co.uk
W: www.tps.co.uk

Technology Resourcing Ltd
The Technology Centre, Surrey
Research Park, Guildford, GU2 7YG
T: 01483 302211
F: 01483 301222
E: railways@tech-res.co.uk
W: www.railwayengineeringjobs.co.uk

TechnoRail (Technocover)
Henfaes Lane, Welshpool,
Powys, SY21 7BE
T: 01938 555511
F: 01938 555527
E: admin@technocover.co.uk
W: www.technocover.co.uk

Tecnopali UK ltd
Unit 3, Headway Rd, Wobaston Rd,
Wolverhampton, WV10 6PZ
T: 01902 788588
F: 01902 788589
E: sales@tecnopali.co.uk
W: www.tecnopali.co.uk

TEK Personnel Consultants Ltd
Norwich Union House,
Irongate,
Derby, DE1 3GA
T: 01332 360055
F: 01332 363345
E: derby@tekpersonnel.co.uk
W: www.tekpersonnel.co.uk

Telent Technology Services Ltd
Point 3, Haywood Rd,
Warwick, CV34 5AH
T: 01926 693569
F: 01926 693023
E: services@telent.com
W: www.telent.com

Telerail Ltd
Royal Scot Suite,
Carnforth Station Heritage Centre,
Warton Rd, Carnforth,
Lancs, LA5 9TR
T: 01524 735774
F: 01524 736386
E: steve@telerail.com
W: www.telerail.co.uk

Televic Rail
Leo Bakaertlaan 1,
B-8870 Izegem,
Belgium
T: 0032 5130 3045
E: rail@televic.com
W: www.televic-rail.com

Temple Group Ltd
Tempus Wharf,
33A Bermondsey Wall West,
London, SE16 4TQ
T: 020 7394 3700
F: 020 7394 7871
E: enquiries@templegroup.co.uk
W: www.templegroup.co.uk

Ten 47 Ltd
Unit 2B, Frances Ind. Park,
Wemyss Rd, Dysart,
Kirkcaldy, KY1 2XZ
T: 01592 655725
F: 01592 651079
E: admin@ten47.com
W: www.ten47.com

TenBroeke Company Ltd
Dorset House, Refent Park,
Kingston Rd, Leatherhead,
Surrey, KT22 7PL
T: 01372 824722
F: 01372 824332
E: paul.tweedale@tenbroekco.com
W: www.tenbroekco.com

Tenmat Ltd (Railko Ltd)
Ashburton Road West, Trafford Park,
Manchester, M70 1RU
T: 0161 872 2181
F: 0161 872 7596
E: info@tenmat.com
W: www.tenmst.com

Tensar International
Cunningham Court,
Shadsworth Business Park,
Shadsworth, Blackburn, BB1 2QX
T: 01254 262431
F: 01254 266868
E: info@tensar-international.com
W: www.tensar.co.uk

Tension Control Bolts
Whitchurch Business Park,
Shakespeare Way, Whitchurch,
Shropshire, SY13 1LJ
T: 01948 667700
F: 01948 667744
E: info@tcbolts.co.uk
W: www.tcbolts.co.uk

Terram Ltd
Mamhilad Park Estate, Pontypool,
Gwent, NP4 0YR
T: 01495 757722
F: 01495 762383
E: info@terram.co.uk
W: www.terram.com

Terrawise Construction Ltd
104 The Court Yard,
Radway Green Business Centre,
Radway Green, Crewe,
CW2 5PR
T: 01270 879011
F: 01270 875079
E: info@terrawise.co.uk
W: www.terrawise.co.uk

TES 2000 Ltd
TES House,
Heath Industrial Park,
Grange Way, Colchester, CO2 8GU
T: 01206 799111
F: 01206 227910
E: info@tes2000.co.uk
W: www.tes2000.co.uk

Testo Ltd
Newman Lane, Alton,
Hants, GU34 2QJ
T: 01420 544433
E: info@testo.co.uk
W: www.testo.co.uk

Tevo Ltd
Maddison house, Thomas Rd,
Wooburn Green Ind Est,
Thomas Rd, Wooburn Green,
Bucks, HP10 0PE
T: 01628 528034
E: sales@tevo.eu.com
W: www.tevo.eu.com

Tew Engineering Ltd
Crocus St, Nottingham, NG2 3DR
T: 0115 935 4354
F: 0115 935 4355
E: sales@tew.co.uk
W: www.tew.co.uk

Thales UK
4 Thomas More Square,
Thomas More St,
London, E1W 1YW
T: 020 3300 6000
F: 020 3300 6994
E: uk.enquiries@thalesgroup.com
W: www.thalesgroup.com/uk

THALES
Together • Safer • Everywhere

As a pioneer in transportation technology, Thales is one of the world's top suppliers of systems, solutions, equipment and services for mobility on railways, roads and public networks.

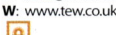

Thales UK
4 Thomas More Square,
Thomas More Street, London, E1W 1YW
0203 300 6000
www.thalesgroup.com/uk

TenBroeke Co

SPECIALISTS IN PROJECT DELIVERY
INTEGRATION, COORDINATION, COOPERATION

www.tenbroekeco.com

IN ASSOCIATION WITH **ATKINS**

ThermaCom Ltd
Farenheit House,
New Line Rd, Kirkby in Ashfield,
Notts, NG17 8JQ
T: 01623 758777
F: 01623 758444
E: sales@thermagroup.com
W: www.thermagroup.com

Thermal Economics Ltd
Thermal House, 8 Cardiff Rd,
Luton, Beds, LU1 1PP
T: 01582 450814
F: 01582 429305
E: info@thermal-economics.co.uk
W: www.thermal-economics.co.uk

Thermit Welding (GB) Ltd
87 Ferry Lane, Rainham,
Essex, RM13 9YH
T: 01708 522626
F: 01708 553806
E: rsj@thermitwelding.com
W: www.thermitwelding.co.uk

Thomas & Betts Ltd
See PMA UK Ltd
(Thomas & Betts Ltd)

Thomson Rail Equipment Ltd
Valley Rd, Cinderford,
Glos, GL14 2NZ
T: 01594 826611
F: 01594 825560
E: sales@thomsonrail.com
W: www.thomsonrail.com

Threeshires Ltd
Piper Hole Farm, Eastwell Rd,
Scalford, Leics, LE14 4SS
T: 01664 444604
F: 01664 444605
E: enquiries@threeshires.com
W: www.threeshires.com

Thurlow Countryside Management Ltd
2 Charterhouse Trading Est,
Sturmer Rd, Haverhill,
Suffolk, CB9 7UU
T: 01440 760170
F: 01440 760171
E: info@t-c-m.co.uk
W: www.t-c-m.co.uk

Thurrock Engineering Supplies Ltd
Unit 1, Tes House,
Motherwell Way,
West Thurrock,
Essex, RM20 3XD
T: 01708 861178
F: 01708 861158
E: info@thurrockengineering.com
W: www.thurrockengineering.com

Thursfield Smith Consultancy
25 Grange Rd,
Shrewsbury, SY3 9DG
T: 01743 246407
E: david@thursfieldsmith.co.uk
W: www.thursfieldsmith.co.uk

Thyssenkrupp GFT Gleistechnik GmbH
Altendorfstrasse 120,
45143 Essen,
Germany
T: 0049 201 188 3710
F: 0049 201 188 3714
E: gleistechnik@thyssenkrupp.com
W: www.tkgftgleistechnik.de

TI Protective Coatings
See Taziker Industrial Ltd t/a TI Protective Coatings

TICS Ltd
Oxford House,
Sixth Avenue,
Robin Hood Airport,
Doncaster, DN9 3GG
T: 01302 623074
F: 01302 623075
E: andrewmackenzie@tics-ltd.co.uk
W: www.tics-ltd.co.uk

Tidyco Ltd
Unit 2, Pentagon Island,
Nottingham B,
Derby, DE21 6BW
T: 01332 851300
F: 01332 290369
E: enquiries@tidyco.co.uk
W: www.tidyco.co.uk

tie Ltd (Transport Initiatives Edinburgh)
Citypoint,
65 Haymarket Terrace,
Edinburgh, EH12 5HD
T: 0131 622 8300
F: 0131 622 8301
E: comms@tie.ltd.uk
W: www.tie.ltd.uk

Tiflex Ltd
Tiflex House,
Liskeard,
Cornwall, PL14 4NB
T: 01579 320808
F: 01579 320802
E: sales@tiflex.co.uk
W: www.tiflex.co.uk

Time 24 Ltd
19 Victoria Gardens,
Burgess Hill,
West Sussex, RH15 9NB
T: 01444 257655
F: 01444 259000
E: sales@time24.co.uk
W: www.time24.co.uk

Timeplan Ltd
12 The Pines,
Broad St,
Guildford,
Surrey, GU3 3BH
T: 01483 462340
F: 01483 462349
E: dave@timeplansolutions.com
W: www.timeplansolutions.com

TMD Friction UK Ltd
PO Box 18 Hunsworth Lane,
Cleckheaton,
West Yorks, BD19 3UJ
T: 01274 854000
F: 01274 854001
E: info@tmdfriction.com
W: www.tmdfriction.com

TMP Worldwide
Chancery House,
Chancery Lane,
London, WC2A 1QS
T: 020 7406 5075
E: contactus@tmpw.co.uk
W: www.tmpw.co.uk

Tony Gee and Partners LLP
Hardy House,
140 High St, Esher,
Surrey, KT10 9QJ
T: 01372 461600
F: 01372 461601
E: enquiries@tonygee.com
W: www.tonygee.com

TopDeck Parking
Springvale Business & Industrial Pk,
Bilston, Wolverhampton, WV14 0QL
T: 01902 499400
F: 01902 494080
E: info@topdeckparking.co.uk
W: www.topdeckparking.co.uk

Topdrill
1 Seagrave Court,
Walton Park,
Milton Keynes, MK7 7HA
T: 01908 666606
E: info@topdrill.co.uk
W: www.topdrill.co.uk

Toray Textiles Europe Ltd
Crown Farm Way, Forest Town,
Mansfield, Notts, NG19 0FT
T: 01623 415050
F: 01623 415070
E: sales@ttel.co.uk
W: www.ttel.co.uk

Torrent Trackside Ltd
Network House,
Europa Way,
Britannia Enterprise Park,
Lichfield, Staffs, WS14 9TZ
T: 01543 421900
F: 01543 421931
E: richard.donald@torrent.co.uk
W: www.torrent.co.uk

Total Access (UK) Ltd
Unit 5,
Raleigh Hall Ind. Est,
Eccleshall,
Staffs, ST21 6JL
T: 01785 850333
F: 01785 850339
E: enquiries@totalaccess.co.uk
W: www.totalaccess.co.uk

Total Rail Solutions
Unit 1,
Hazeley Enterprise Park,
Twyford,
Winchester, SO21 1QA
T: 01962 711642
F: 01962 717330
E: info@totalrailsolutions.co.uk
W: www.totalrailsolutions.org

Total UK Ltd
Pottery Lane,
Ferrybridge,
West Yorks, WF11 8JY
T: 01977 636100
E: tom.hyde@total.co.uk
W: www.lubricants.total.com

Totectors (UK) Ltd
9 Pondwood Close,
Moulton Park Ind. Estate,
Northampton, NN3 6RT
T: 0870 600 5055
F: 0870 600 5056
E: sales@totectors.net
W: www.totectors.net

Touchstone Renard Ltd
120 Pall Mall, London, SW1Y 5EA
T: 020 7101 0788
E: paustin@touchstonerenard.com
W: www.touchstonerenard.com

Tower Surveys Ltd
Vivian House, Vivian Lane,
Nottingham, NG5 1AF
T: 0115 960 1212
F: 0115 962 1200
E: beverley.chiang@opusjoynespike.co.uk
W: www.towersurveys.co.uk

TPA Portable Roadways Ltd
Dukeries Mill, Claylands Ave,
Worksop, Notts, S81 7DJ
T: 0870 240 2381
F: 0870 240 2382
E: enquiries@tpa-ltd.co.uk
W: www.tpa-ltd.co.uk

TPK Consulting Ltd (RPS Group)
Centurion Court, 85, Milton Park,
Abingdon, Oxon, OX14 4RY
T: 01235 438151
F: 01235 438188
E: rpsab@rpsgroup.com
W: www.rpsplc.co.uk

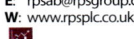

TQ Catalis
Garden Court,
Lockington Hall,
Main St, Lockington,
Derby, DE74 2SJ
T: 0845 880 8108
E: hotline@catalis.co.uk
W: www.catalis.com

TRAC Engineering Ltd
Dovecote Rd,
Eurocentral,
North Lanarkshire, ML1 4GP
T: 01698 831111
F: 01698 832222
E: engineering@trac.com
W: www.tracengineering.com

Track Maintenance Equipment Ltd
Witham Wood, Marley Lane,
Haslemere, Surrey, GU27 3PZ
T: 01428 651114
F: 01428 644727
E: info@tmeltd.co.uk
W: www.tmeltd.co.uk

Track Safe Telecom (TST)
See Centregreat Rail Ltd

Tracklink UK Ltd
Unit 5, Miltons Yard, Petworth Rd,
Witley, Surrey, GU8 5LH
T: 01428 685124
F: 01428 687788
E: enquiries@tklink.co.uk
W: www.tklink.co.uk

Tracksure Ltd
8 Woburn St, Ampthill,
Beds, MK45 2HP
T: 01525 840557
F: 01525 403918
E: sales@tracksure.co.uk
W: www.tracksure.co.uk

Trackwork Ltd
PO Box 139, Kirk Sandall Lane,
Kirk Sandall Ind. Est,
Doncaster, DN31WX
T: 01302 888666
F: 01302 888777
E: sales@trackwork.co.uk
W: www.trackwork.co.uk

Tracsis Plc
Unit 6, The Point, Pinnacle Way,
Pride Park, Derby, DE24 8ZS
T: 01332 226860
F: 01332 226862
E: info@tracsis.com
W: www.tracsis.com

Tractel UK Ltd
Old Lane, Halfway,
Sheffield, S20 3GA
T: 0114 248 2266
F: 0114 247 3350
E: tractel.info@tractel.com
W: www.tractel.com

TracTruc Bi-modal
See Truck Train Developments Ltd
(and TracTruc Bi-Modal)

Traffic Management Services Ltd
PO Box 10, Retford, Notts, DN22 7EE
T: 01777 705053
F: 01777 709878
E: info@traffic.org.uk
W: www.traffic.org.uk

The Train Chartering Company Ltd
Benwell House,
Preston,
Wilts, SN15 4DX
T: 01249 890176
E: info@trainchartering.com
W: www.trainchartering.com

TrainFX Ltd
Unit 15, Melbourne Business Court,
Millennium Way, Derby, DE24 8LZ
T: 01332 366175
E: enquiries@trainfx.com
W: www.trainfx.com

Train'd Up
Elmbank Mill,
Menstrie Business Centre,
Menstrie,
Clackmannanshire, FK11 7BU
T: 0845 602 9665
F: 0870 850 3397
E: enquiries@traindup.org
W: www.traindup.org

The Trainline
Trainline Holdings Ltd,
498 Gorgie Rd,
Edinburgh, EH11 3AF
T: 08704 111111
W: www.thetrainline.com

Trainpeople.co.uk Ltd
Arran House,
Arran Rd,
Perth, PH1 3DZ
T: 01738 446110
F: 01738 622055
E: info@trainpeople.co.uk
W: www.trainpeople.co.uk

Trakside Systems Ltd
See High Voltage Maintenance Services Ltd

TRAM Power Ltd
99 Stanley Rd, Bootle,
Merseyside, L20 7DA
T: 0151 547 1425
F: 0151 521 5509
M: 07976 949618
E: lewis.lesley@trampower.co.uk
W: www.trampower.co.uk

Tramlink (Croydon)
See Transport for London

Tranect Ltd
Unit 4, Carraway Rd,
Gilmoss Ind. Est, Liverpool, L11 0EE
T: 0151 548 7040
F: 0151 546 6066
E: sales@tranect.co.uk
W: www.tranect.co.uk

Trans Pennine Express (TPE)
See First Trans Pennine Express

Transaction Systems Ltd
See Vossloh Kiepe

Transcal Ltd
Firth Rd, Houstoun Ind. Est,
Livingston,
West Lothian, EH54 5DJ
T: 01506 440111
F: 01506 442333
E: info@transcal.co.uk
W: www.transcal.co.uk

Transdev Plc
401 King St,
London, W6 9NJ
T: 020 8600 5650
F: 020 8600 5651
E: information@transdevplc.co.uk
W: www.transdevplc.co.uk

Transec UK Ltd (Bowden Bros Ltd)
Brickworks House,
Spook Hill,
North Holmwood,
Dorking,
Surrey, RH5 4HR
T: 01306 743355
F: 01306 876768
E: ian.bowden@bowden-bros.com
W: www.bowden-bros.com

Translec Ltd
Saddleworth Business
Centre, Huddersfield Rd,
Delph, Oldham, OL3 5DF
T: 01457 878888
F: 01457 878887
E: mail@translec.co.uk
W: www.translec.co.uk

Translink NI Railways
Central Station,
East Bridge St,
Belfast, BT1 3PB
T: 02890 666630
F: 02890 899452
E: feedback@translink.co.uk
W: www.translink.co.uk

Transmitton
See Siemens Rail Systems

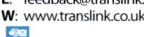

Transport & Travel Research Ltd (TTR)
Minster House,
Minster Pool Walk,
Lichfield, Staffs
T: 01543 416416
F: 01543 416681
E: enquiries@ttr-ltd.com
W: www.ttr-ltd.com

Transport 2000
See Campaign for Better Transport

Transport Benevolent Fund
New Loom House,
101 Back Church Lane,
London, E1 1LU
T: 0300 333 2000 (ETD 00 38571)
F: 0870 831 2882
E: help@tbf.org.uk
W: www.tbf.org.uk

Transport for London
55 Broadway,
London, SW1H 0BD
T: 020 7222 5600
E: enquire@tfl.gov.uk
W: www.tfl.gov.uk/rail

Transport iNet
SEIC, Holywell Business Park,
Loughborough University, LE11 3TU
T: 01509 635270
F: 01509 635231
E: a.m.wilkinson@lboro.ac.uk
W: www.eminnovation.org.uk/transport

Transport Interchange Consultants Ltd
1 Lochaline St, London, W6 9ST
T: 020 8563 0555
F: 020 8563 0555
E: mw@ticonsultants.co.uk
W: www.ticonsultants.co.uk

Transport Investigations Ltd
27-29 Margate Rd,
Ramsgate,
Kent, CT11 7SU
T: 01843 593595
F: 0845 280 2356
E: info@transportinvestigations.co.uk
W: www.transportinvestigations.co.uk

Transport Scotland
Buchanan House,
58 Port Dundas Rd,
Glasgow, G4 0HF
T: 0141 272 7100
E: info@transportscotland.gsi.gov.uk
W: www.transportscotland.gov.uk

Providing help and advice to public transport employees for over 90 years - and meeting the needs of today. Just **£1 a week** covers you, your partner and dependent children.

0300 333 2000
www.tbf.org.uk
help@tbf.org.uk

The Transport Benevolent Fund (known as TBF) is a registered charity in England and Wales (1058032) and in Scotland (SC040013)

tbf
Transport Benevolent Fund

DIRECTORY

Transportation Planning International
International Design Hub,
Colmore Plaza, 20 Colmore Circus,
Birmingham, B4 6AT
T: 0121 2125102
E: info@tpi-world.com
W: www.tpi-world.com

Transsol Ltd
32 Buxton Rd West, Disley,
Cheshire, SK12 2LY
F: 0870 052 5838
M: 07775 893620
E: enquiries@transsol.net
W: www.transsol.net

Trans-Tronic Ltd
Whitting Valley Rd,
Old Whittingham, Chesterfield,
Derbys, S41 9EY
T: 01246 264260
F: 01246 455281
E: sales@trans-tronic.co.uk
W: www.trans-tronic.co.uk

Transys Projects Ltd
See Vossloh Kiepe

Trapeze Group Rail Ltd
Middleham House,
6 St Mary's Court, Blossom St,
York, YO24 1AH
T: 01904 639091
F: 01904 639092
E: sales.railuk@trapezegroup.com
W: www.trapezegroup.com

Tratos Ltd
10 Eagle Court,
Britton St, Farringdon,
London, EC1M 5QD
T: 0845 413 9990
F: 020 3553 4815
E: john.light@tratos.co.uk
W: www.tratos.co.uk

Travel Info. Systems
Suite 1, Grand Union House,
20 Kentish Town Rd,
London, NW1 9NX
T: 020 7428 1288
F: 020 7267 2745
E: enquiries@travelinfosystems.com
W: www.travelinfosystems.com

Traxsydes Training
Room 11, E.L.O.C,
80-86 St Mary Rd,
Walthamstow,
London, E17 9RE
T: 020 8223 1257
F: 020 8223 1258
E: bookings@traxsydes.co.uk
W: www.traxsydes.co.uk

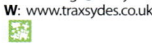

TRB Lightweight Structures Ltd
12 Clifton Rd, Huntingdon,
Cambs, PE29 7EN
T: 01480 447400
F: 01480 414992
E: sales@trbls.com
W: www.trbls.com

TRE Ltd
See The Railway Engineering Company Ltd

Treadmaster Flooring
See Tiflex Ltd

Trelleborg Industrial AVS
1 Hoods Close, Leicester, LE4 2BN
T: 0116 267 0300
F: 0116 267 0310
E: rail@trelleborg.com
W: www.trelleborg.com/industrialavs

Tremco Illbruck Limited
Coupland Rd, Hindley Green,
Wigan, WN2 4HT
T: 01942 251400
F: 01942 251410
E: uk.info@tremco-illbruck.com
W: www.tremco-illbruck.com

TTG Transportation Technology

The experts in driver advisory systems for traffic management and energy savings

The iD Centre,
Lathkill House,
The rtc Business Park,
London Road,
Derby, DE24 8UP

Tel: +44 (0) 133 225 8867
Email: enquiries@ttgeurope.com

www.ttgtransportationtechnology.com

Trent Instruments Ltd
Unit 39, Nottingham South and
Wilford Ind. Est, Ruddington Lane,
Nottingham, NG11 7EP
T: 0115 969 6188
F: 0115 945 5696
E: phillip@trentinstruments.co.uk
W: www.trentinstruments.co.uk

Tribo Rail
Unit 36,
Harpur Hill Business Park,
Buxton,
Derbys, SK17 9JL
T: 01298 214986
E: enquiries@triborail.com
W: www.triborail.com

Triforce Security Solutions Ltd
Westmead House,
Westmead,
Farnborough,
Hants, GU14 7LP
T: 01252 373496
E: enquiries@triforcesecurity.co.uk
W: www.triforcesecurity.co.uk

Trimble UK
Trimble House,
Meridian Office Park,
Osborn Way, Hook,
Hants, RG27 9HX
T: 01256 760150
F: 01256 760148
W: www.trimble.com

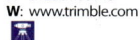

Tritech Rail/Tritech Rail Training
See AECOM

TRL
Crowthorne House,
Nine Mile Ride,
Wokingham,
Berks, RG40 3GA
T: 01344 773131
F: 01344 770356
E: rail@trl.co.uk
W: www.trl.co.uk

Trojan Services Ltd
PO Box 675,
Chichester,
West Sussex, PO19 9LG
T: 0845 074 0407
F: 01243 783654
E: info@trojan-services.com
W: www.trojan-services.com

Trolex Ltd
Newby Rd,
Hazel Grove,
Stockport, SK7 5DY
T: 0161 483 1435
F: 0161 483 5556
E: sales@trolex.com
W: www.trolex.com

Trough-Tec Systems Ltd (TTS)
Bennetthorpe, Doncaster, DN2 6AA
T: 01302 343633
E: info@ttsglobal.co.uk
W: www.ttsglobal.co.uk

TRS Staffing Solutions
8th Floor, York House,
Kingsway,
London, WC2B 6UJ
T: 020 7419 5800
F: 020 7419 5801
E: info-uk@trsstaffing.com
W: www.trsstaffing.com

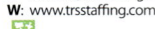

Truck Train Developments Ltd (and TracTruc Bi-Modal)
4 Elfin Grove, Bognor Regis,
W.Sussex, PO21 2RX
T: 01243 869118
E: pmtrucktrain@tiscali.co.uk
W: www.trucktrain.co.uk

Truflame Welding
Truflame House, 56 Newhall Rd,
Sheffield, S9 2QL
T: 0114 243 3020
F: 0114 243 5297
E: sales@truflame.co.uk
W: www.truflame.co.uk

TS Components Ltd
Ladywood House, Ladywood Works,
Lutterworth, Leics, LE17 4HD
T: 01455 553905
E: info@tscomponents.com
W: www.tscomponents.com

tsa Advet ltd
CAB-i-NET House, 7 Ellerbeck Court,
Stokesley Business Park,
Middlesbrough, TS9 5PT
T: 01642 714471
F: 01642 714451
E: andrew.frank@tsaadvet.co.uk
W: www.tsaadvet.co.uk

TSL Turton Ltd
Burton Rd, Sheffield, S3 8DA
T: 0114 270 1577
F: 0114 275 6947
E: sales@tslturton.com
W: www.tslturton.com

TSSA (Transport Salaried Staffs Association)
Walkden House, 10 Melton St,
London, NW1 2EJ
T: 020 7387 2101
F: 020 7383 0656
E: enquiries@tssa.org.uk
W: www.tssa.org.uk

TT Electronics plc
Clive House, 12-18 Queens Rd,
Weybridge, Surrey, KT13 9XB
T: 01932 825300
F: 01932 836450
E: info@ttelectronics.com
W: www.ttelectronics.com

TTCI UK
13 Fitzroy St, London, W1T 4BQ
T: 020 7755 4080
F: 020 7755 4203
E: michele_johnson@aar.com
W: www.ttc.aar.com

TTG Transportation Technology (Europe) Ltd
The iD Centre, Lathkill House, rtc
Business Park, London Rd,
Derby, DE24 8UP
T: 01332 258867
F: 01332 258823
E: enquiries@ttgeurope.com
W: www.ttgtransportationtechnology.com

TTR
See Transport & Travel Research Ltd (TTR)

Tubelines
15 Westferry Circus, Canary Wharf,
London, E14 4HD
T: 0845 660 5466
E: enquiries@tubelines.com
W: www.tubelines.com

Tuchschmid Constructa AG
Langdorfstrasse 26, CH-8501,
Frauenfeld, Switzerland
T: 0041 52 728 8111
F: 0041 52 728 8100
E: w.luessi@tuchschmid.ch
W: www.intermodallogistics.ch

Tufcoat
Fox House, 8-10 Whimple St,
Plymouth, PL1 2DH
T: 01752 227333
F: 0871 264 5801
E: info@tufcoat.co.uk
W: www.tufcoat.co.uk

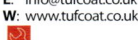

Tufnol Composites Ltd
Wellhead Lane, Perry Barr,
Birmingham, B42 2TB
T: 0121 356 9351
F: 0121 331 4235
E: sales@tufnol.co.uk
W: www.tufnol.com

Turbex Ltd
Unit 1, Riverwey Ind. Park,
Newman Lane, Alton,
Hants, GU34 2QL
T: 01420 544909
F: 01420 542264
E: sales@turbex.co.uk
W: www.turbex.co.uk

Turbo Power Systems Ltd
1 Queens Park, Queensway North,
Team Valley Trading Est, Gateshead,
Tyne & Wear, NE110NX
T: 0191 482 9200
F: 0191 482 9201
E: sales@turbopowersystems.com
W: www.turbopowersystems.com

Turkington Precast
James Park, Mahon Rd, Portadown,
Co. Armagh, BT62 3EH,
Northern Ireland
T: 028 38 332807
F: 028 38 361770
E: gary@turkington-precast.com
W: www.turkington-precast.com

Turner & Townsend
Low Hall, Calverley Lane, Horsforth,
Leeds, LS18 4GH
T: 0113 258 4400
F: 0113 258 2911
E: lee@turntown.com
W: www.turnerandtownsend.com

Turner Diesel Ltd
Unit 1A, Dyce Ind. Park, Dyce,
Aberdeen, AB21 7EZ
T: 01224 214200
F: 01224 723927
E: diesel.sales@turner.co.uk
W: www.turner-diesel.co.uk

tusp Ltd
Barrow Hill, Maidstone Rd, Ashford,
Kent, TN24 8TY
T: 01233 640257
E: enquiries@tusp.co.uk
W: www.tusp.co.uk

TUV Product Service Ltd
Octagon House,
Concorde Way,
Segensworth,
North Fareham,
Hants, PO15 5RL
T: 01489 558100
F: 01489 558101
E: info@tuvps.co.uk
W: www.tuvps.co.uk

TUV-SUD Rail GmbH
Ridlerstrasse 65,
D-80339, Munich,
Germany
T: 0049 89519 03537
F: 0049 89519 02933
W: www.tuv-sued.com

TXM Plant Ltd
TXM Plant House, Harbour Rd
Trading Est, Portishead,
Bristol, BS20 7AT
T: 01275 399400
F: 01275 399500
E: info@txmplant.co.uk
W: www.txmplant.co.uk

TXM Projects Ltd
1 St Peters Court,
Church Lane,
Bickenhill, B92 0DN
M: 07814 422589
E: simon.pitt@txmprojects.co.uk
W: www.txmprojects.co.uk

TXM Recruit Ltd
Blackhill Drive, Wolverton Mill,
Milton Keynes, Bucks, MK12 5TS
T: 0845 2263454
F: 0845 2262453
E: info@txmrecruit.co.uk

Tyne & Wear Metro
See Nexus (Tyne & Wear Metro)

Tyrone Fabrication Ltd (TFL)
Goland Rd, Ballygawley,
Co Tyrone, BT70 2LA
T: 028 8556 7200
F: 028 8556 7089
E: sales@tfl.eu.com
W: www.tfl.eu.com

UK Accreditation Service (UKAS)
21-47 High St, Feltham,
Middx, TW13 4UN
T: 020 8917 8400
E: info@ukas.com
W: info@ukas.com

UK Power Networks Services
237 Southwark Bridge Rd,
London, SE1 6NP
T: 0207 397 7695
E: rail@ukpowernetworks.co.uk
W: www.ukpowernetworks.co.uk/rail

UK Railtours
T: 01438 715050
E: john@ukrailtours.com
W: www.ukrailtours.com

UK Trade & Investment - Investment Services
1 Victoria St, London, SW1H 0ET
T: 0845 539 0419/020 7333 5442
E: enquiries@ukti-invest.com
W: www.ukti.gov.uk

UK Ultraspeed
Warksburn House, Wark, Hexham,
Northumberland, NE48 3LS
T: 020 7861 2497
F: 020 7861 2497
E: ncameron@bell-pottinger.co.uk
W: www.500kmh.com

UKDN Waterflow
12-16 David Rd, Poyle Trading Est,
Colnbrook, SL3 0DG
T: 01753 810999
F: 01753 681442
E: sales@waterflow.co.uk
W: www.waterflow.co.uk

UKRS Projects Ltd
See Bowen Projects Ltd

Ultra Electronics PMES Ltd
Towers Business Park,
Wheelhouse Rd, Rugeley,
Staffs, WS15 1UZ
T: 01889 503300
F: 01889 572929
E: enquiries@ultra-pmes.com
W: www.ultra-pmes.com

Ultra Electronics-Electrics
Kingsditch Lane, Cheltenham,
Glos, GL51 9PG
T: 01242 221166
F: 01242 221167
E: info@ultra-electrics.com
W: www.ultra-electrics.com

Underground Pipeline Services Ltd
See Integrated Water Services Ltd

Unic Cranes Europe
See GGR Group Ltd

UNIFE
Avenue Louise 221, B-1050 Brussels,
Belgium
T: 0032 2642 2328
F: 0032 2626 1261
E: judit.sandor@unife.org
W: www.unife.org

Unilokomotive Ltd
Dunmore Rd, Tuam, Co. Galway,
Republic of Ireland
T: 00353 93 52150
F: 00353 93 52227
E: omcconn@unilok.ie
W: www.unilok.ie

Unipart Dorman
Wennington Rd, Southport,
Merseyside, PR9 7TN
T: 01704 518000
F: 01704 518001
E: dorman.enquiries@unipartdorman.co.uk
W: www.unipartdorman.co.uk

The leading designer and supplier of innovative LED signalling and electronic solutions for the UK Rail infrastructure

Wennington Road, Southport
Merseyside, PR9 7TN

T: +44 (0) 1704 518000
F: +44 (0) 1704 518001
E: dorman.enquiries@unipartdorman.co.uk
W: www.unipartdorman.co.uk

UNIPART DORMAN

UNIPART RAIL

Unipart Rail serves the world's railways with:

- Products
- Supply Chain Services
- Technical Support Services
- Product Innovation & Technology
- Manufacturing Services
- Overhaul & Repair Services
- Consultancy

Unipart Rail (T&RS):
Jupiter Building, First Point
Balby Carr Bank, Doncaster
DN4 5JQ
T: +44 (0) 1302 731 400
trsenquiries@unipartrail.com

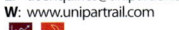

Unipart Rail (Infrastructure):
Gresty Road, Crewe,
Cheshire CW2 6EH
Tel: +44 (0) 1270 847 600
enquiries@unipartrail.com

SERVING THE WORLD'S RAILWAYS

Unipart Rail (infrastructure)
Gresty Rd, Crewe, CW2 6EH
T: 01270 847600
F: 01270 847601
E: enquiries@unipartrail.com
W: www.unipartrail.com

Unipart Rail (infrastructure)
Leeman Rd,
York, YO26 4ZD
T: 01904 544020
F: 01904 544021
E: enquiries@unipartrail.com
W: www.unipartrail.com

Unipart Rail (infrastructure)
Gresty Rd, Crewe, CW2 6EH
T: 01270 847600
F: 01270 847601
E: enquiries@unipartrail.com
W: www.unipartrail.com

Unipart Rail (T&RS) Ltd
Jupiter Building,
First Point,
Balby Carr Bank,
Doncaster, DN4 5JQ
T: 01302 731400
F: 01302 731401
E: trsenquiries@unipartrail.com
W: www.unipartrail.com

Unite - The Union
General Secretary,
35 King St,
Covent Garden,
London, WC2E 8JG
T: 020 7420 8900
F: 020 7420 8998
E: executive.council@unitetheunion.org
W: www.unitetheunion.org

United Kingdom Society for Trenchless Technology
38 Holly Walk,
Leamington Spa,
Warks, CV32 4LY
T: 01926 330935
E: admin@ukstt.org.uk
W: www.ukstt.org.uk

Universal Heat Transfer Ltd
Well Spring Close, Carlyon Rd,
Atherstone, Warks, CV9 1QZ
T: 01827 722171
F: 01827 722174
E: sales@uhtltd.com
W: www.universalheattransfer.co.uk

The Universal Improvement Company
17 Knowl Ave, Belper,
Derbys, DE56 2TL
T: 01773 826659
F: 01773 826659
E: info@theuic.com
W: www.theuic.com

Universal Railway Equipment Ltd
Princess Royal Buildings,
Whitecroft Rd, Bream, Lydney,
Glos, GL15 6LY
T: 01594 560555
E: unirail@btconnect.com
W: www.peeway.co.uk

University of Derby - Faculty of Arts, Design & Technology
Markeaton St,
Derby, DE22 3AW
T: 01332 593216
E: adtenquiry@derby.ac.uk
W: www.derby.ac.uk

Up & Cuming Consultancy Ltd (UCCL)
74 Chenies Mews,
London, WC1E 6HU
T: 020 7388 2232
F: 020 7388 3730
E: info@uccl.net
W: www.uccl.net

Urban Hygiene Ltd
Sky Business Park,
Robin Hood Airport,
Doncaster, DN9 3GA
T: 01302 623193
E: enquiries@urbanhygiene.com
W: www.urbanhygiene.co.uk

Urbis Lighting Ltd
See Urbis Schreder Ltd

Urbis Schreder Ltd
Sapphire House,
Lime Tree Way,
Hampshire International Business Pk,
Chineham,
Basingstoke, RG24 8GG
T: 01256 354446
F: 01256 841314
E: sales@urbis-schreder.com
W: www.urbis-schreder.com

Uretek UK Ltd
Unit 6, Peel Rd,
Skelmersdale,
Lancs, WN8 9PT
T: 01695 50525
F: 01695 555212
E: sales@uretek.co.uk
W: www.uretek.co.uk

URS
Scott House,
Alencon Link,
Basingstoke,
Hants, RG21 7PP
T: 01256 310200
F: 01256 310201
E: rail.marketing@scottwilson.com
W: www.urscorp.eu

URS Corporation Ltd
6-8 Greencoat Place,
London, SW1P 1PL
T: 0115 907 7086
F: 0115 907 7001
E: railways@scottwilson.com
W: www.urscorp.eu

VAE UK Ltd
Sir Harry Lauder Rd,
Portobello,
Edinburgh, EH15 1DJ
T: 0131 550 2297
F: 0131 550 2660
E: jim.gemmell@vae.co.uk
W: www.voestalpine.com/vae

Vaisala Ltd
351, Bristol Rd,
Birmingham, B5 7SW
T: 0121 683 1200
F: 0121 683 1299
E: liz.green@vaisala.com
W: www.vaisala.com

Van der Vlist UK Ltd
Burma Drive,
Kingston upon Hull, HU9 5SD
T: 01482 210100
F: 01482 216222
E: info@vandervlist.co.uk
W: www.vandervlist.co.uk

Van Elle
Kirkby Lane, Pinxton,
Notts, NG16 6JA
T: 01773 580580
F: 01773 862100
E: mark.williams@van-elle.co.uk
W: www.van-elle.co.uk

Variable Message Signs Ltd (VMS)
Unit 1,
Monkton Business Park North,
Mill Lane, Hebburn,
Tyne & Wear, NE31 2JZ
T: 0191 423 7070
F: 0191 423 7071
E: aisaacs@vmslimited.co.uk
W: www.vmslimited.co.uk

Vector Management Ltd
Strathclyde House,
Green Man Lane,
London Heathrow Airport, Feltham,
Middx, TW14 0NZ
T: 020 8844 0444
F: 020 8844 0666
E: ju-liang.trigg@vecman.com
W: www.vecman.com

Vectra Group Ltd
See Arcadis EC Harris

Verint Systems
241 Brooklands Rd, Weybridge,
Surrey, KT13 0RH
T: 01932 839500
F: 01932 839501
E: marketing.emea@verint.com
W: www.verint.com

Veritec Sonomatic Ltd
Ashton House, The Village,
Birchwood Bus.Park,
Warrington, WA3 6FZ
T: 01925 414000
F: 01925 655595
E: jl@vsonomatic.com
W: www.veritecltd.co.uk

Vertex Systems
See AMCL Systems Engineering Ltd

Veryards Opus
See Opus International Consultants Ltd

VGC Group
Cardinal House, Bury St, Ruislip,
Middx, HA4 7GD
T: 01895 671823
E: zena.wigram@vgcgroup.co.uk
W: www.vgcgroup.co.uk

Vi Distribution
Unit 7, Springvale Business Centre,
Millbuck Way, Sandbach, CW11 3HY
T: 01270 750520
F: 01270 750521
E: sales@vidistribution.co.uk
W: www.vidistribution.co.uk

Video 125 Ltd
Glade House, High St, Sunninghill,
Berks, SL5 9NP
T: 01344 628565
E: sales@video125.co.uk
W: www.video125.co.uk

VINCI Construction UK Ltd
See Taylor Woodrow

Vinci Park Services UK Ltd
Oak House, Reeds Cres, Watford,
Herts, WD24 4QP
T: 01908 223500
F: 01923 231914
E: info@vincipark.co.uk
W: www.vincipark.co.uk

Vintage Trains Ltd
670 Warwick Rd, Tyseley,
Birmingham, B11 2HL
T: 0121 708 4960
F: 0121 708 4963
E: vintagetrains@btconnect.com
W: www.vintagetrains.co.uk

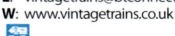

Virgin Trains (West Coast)
North Wing Offices. Euston Station,
London, NW1 2HS
T: 0845 000 8000
E: firstname.lastname@virgintrains.co.uk
W: www.virgin.com/trains

Vision Infrastructure Services Ltd
Unit 7, Durham Lane,
West Moor Park, Doncaster, DN1 3FE
T: 01302 831730
F: 01302 832671
E: ian@visioninfrastructureservices.com
W: www.visioninfrastructureservices.com

Vistorm Ltd
See HP Information Security

Visul Systems
Kingston House,
3 Walton Rd,
Pattinson North,
Washington,
Tyne & Wear, NE38 8QA
T: 0191 402 1960
F: 0191 402 1906
E: ross.carty@usluk.com
W: www.visulsystems.com

Vita Safety Ltd
1 Gillingham Rd,
Eccles,
Manchester, M30 8NA
T: 0161 789 1400
F: 0161 280 2528
E: ian.hutchings@vitasafety.com
W: www.vitasafety.com

Vital Rail
The Mill,
South Hall St,
Ordsall Lane,
Manchester, M5 4TP
T: 0161 836 7000
F: 0161 836 7001
E: info@vital-rail.com
W: www.vital-rail.com

Vitec
3 Cae Gwrydd,
Greenmeadow Springs Bus. Park,
Cardiff, CF15 7AB
T: 02920 620232
F: 02920 624837
E: cardiff@viteconsult.com
W: www.vitecwebberlenihan.com

Vix Technology
ACIS House,
168 Cowley Rd,
Cambridge, CB4 0DL
T: 01223 728700
F: 01223 506311
E: uk.marketing@vixtechnology.com
W: www.vixtechnology.com

Viztek Ltd
North East Business &
Innovation Centre,
Wearfield,
Enterprise Park East,
Sunderland, SR5 2TA
T: 0191 516 6606
E: info@viztekltd.co.uk
W: www.viztekltd.co.uk

VMS
See Variable Message Signs Ltd (VMS)

Voestalpine UK Ltd
Voestalpine House, Albion Place,
Hammersmith, London, W6 0QT
T: 020 8600 5800
E: catherine.crisp@voestalpine.com
W: www.voestalpine.com

Vogelsang Ltd
Crewe Gates Ind. Est, Crewe,
Cheshire, CW1 6YY
T: 01270 216600
F: 01270 216699
E: sales@vogelsang.co.uk
W: www.vogelsang.co.uk

Voith Turbo GmbH & Co.KG
Alexanderstrasse 2, 89522
Heidenheim, Germany
T: 0044 7321 37 4069
F: 0044 7321 37 7616
E: rail.uk@voith.com
W: www.voith.com

Voith Turbo Ltd
Unit 49, Metropolitan Park,
Bristol Rd, Greenford,
Middx, UB6 8UP
T: 020 8436 1051
F: 020 8578 4489
E: roger.everest@voith.com
W: www.uk.voithturbo.com

VolkerFitzpatrick Ltd
Hertford Rd,
Hoddesden,
Herts, EN11 9BX
T: 01992 305000
F: 01992 305001
E: volkerfitzpatrickrail@volkerfitzpatrick.co.uk
W: www.volkerfitzpatrick.co.uk

Volker Rail
Carolina Court,
Lakeside,
Doncaster, DN4 5RA
T: 01302 791100
F: 01302 791200
E: marketing@volkerrail.co.uk
W: www.volkerrail.co.uk

VolkerFitzpatrick

As an industry leader in rail engineering and construction work, we offer a fully integrated approach that delivers efficient and innovative solutions.

VolkerFitzpatrick Ltd
T 01992 305000
E volkerfitzpatrickrail@volkerfitzpatrick.co.uk
www.volkerfitzpatrick.co.uk

a VolkerWessels company

Vossloh COGIFER

VOSSLOH COGIFER UK Limited

Manufacturers of all types of Switch and Crossing Systems and ancillary components for the **Heavy Rail**, **High Speed** and **Light Rail** markets.

Vossloh Cogifer UK Ltd
80A Scotter Road,
Scunthorpe DN15 8EF
Tel: +44 0 1724 862131
Fax: +44 0 1724 295243
Web: www.vossloh-cogifer-uk.com

DIRECTORY

Vossloh Kiepe UK
Perfection in integration
Challenges overcome, projects delivered. With Vossloh Kiepe UK, success is sweet.

Vossloh Kiepe UK Ltd
2 Priestley Wharf, Holt St, Aston, Birmingham B7 4BN
T +44 (0)121 359 7777 E enquiries@vkb.vossloh.com
www.vossloh-kiepe.co.uk

Wabtec Group
- Vehicles
- Wheelsets and bogies
- Air Conditioning
- Door Systems
- Components
- Power Packs
- Cooler Groups
- Diesel Engines
- Transmissions
- Traction Motors

Now providing a wider than ever range of specialist skills, resources and techologies that are helping to make the country's railways better.

Wabtec Rail Ltd, PO Box 400, Doncaster DN1 1SL
T: 01302 340700
F: 01302 790058
E: wabtecrail@wabtec.com
W: www.wabtecgroup.com

Westinghouse platform screen doors

Westinghouse Platform Screen Doors, a business division of Knorr-Bremse, is a world leader in the design, manufacture and installation of platform screen systems.

To find out more contact us at:
wpsd.enquiries@knorr-bremse.com
+44 (0)1225 898700
www.platformscreendoors.com

KNORR-BREMSE

Volo TV & Media Ltd
Departure Side Offices, Platform 1, Paddington Station, Pread St, London, W2 1FT
T: 020 7706 4775
F: 020 7402 2498
E: findoutmore@volo.tv
W: www.volo.tv

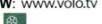

Vortok International
Innovation House, 3 Western Wood Way, Langage Science Park, Plymouth, PL7 5BG
T: 01752 349200
F: 01752 338855
E: gfermie@vortok.co.uk
W: www.vortok.co.uk

Vossloh AG
Vosslohstrasse 4, 58791 Werdohl, Germany
T: 0049 2392 520
F: 0049 2392 520
W: www.vossloh.com

Vossloh Cogifer UK Ltd
80a Scotter Rd, Scunthorpe, North Lincs, DN15 8EF
T: 01724 862131
F: 01724 295243
E: contact-uk@vossloh-cogifer.com
W: www.vossloh-cogifer-uk.com

Vossloh Fastening Systems GmbH
Am Schimmersfeld 7a, D-40880 Ratingen, Germany
T: 0049 2102 49090
F: 0049 2102 49094
W: www.vossloh-fastening-systems.de

Vossloh Kiepe
2 Priestley Wharf, Birmingham Science Park, Holt St, Aston, Birmingham, B7 4BN
T: 0121 359 7777
F: 0121 359 1811
E: enquiries@vkb.vossloh.com
W: www.vossloh-kiepe.co.uk

VTG Rail UK Ltd
Sir Stanley Clarke House, 7 Ridgeway, Quinton Business Park, Birmingham, B32 1AF
T: 0121 421 9180
F: 0121 421 9192
E: sales@vtg.com
W: www.vtg-rail.co.uk

VTS Track Technology Ltd
See Vossloh Cogifer UK Ltd

Vulcascot Cable Protectors Ltd
Unit 12, Norman-D-Gate, Bedford Rd, Northampton, NN1 5NT
T: 0800 035 2842
F: 01604 632344
E: sales@vulcascot cableprotectors.co.uk
W: www.vulcascot cableprotectors.com

W A Developments Ltd
See Stobart Rail

Wabtec Rail Ltd
PO Box 400, Doncaster Works, Hexthorpe Rd, Doncaster, DN1 1SL
T: 01302 340700
F: 01302 790058
E: wabtecrail@wabtec.com
W: www.wabtecgroup.com

Wacker Neuson (GB) Ltd
Lea Rd, Waltham Cross, Herts, EN9 1AW
T: 01992 707228
F: 01992 707201
E: chris.pearce@eu.wackerneuson.com
W: www.wackerneuson.com

Wagony Swidnica S.A.
UL. Strzelinska 35, 58-100 Swidnica, Poland
T: 0048 74 856 2000
F: 0048 853 0323
E: secretariat@gbrx.com
W: www.gbrx.com

A N Wallis & Co Ltd
Greasley St, Bulwell, Nottingham, NG6 8NG
T: 0115 927 1721
F: 0115 875 6630
E: mark.rimmington@an-wallis.com
W: www.an-wallis.com

Washroom Joinery Ltd
The Loughton Seedbed Centre, Langston Rd, Loughton, Essex, IG10 3TQ
T: 08700 111860
M: 0700 492 7476
E: info@washroomjoinery.co.uk
W: www.washroomjpinery.co.uk

Washtec UK Ltd
Unit 14A, Oak ind. Park, Great Dunmow, Essex, CM9 1XN
T: 01371 878800
F: 01371 878810
W: www.washtec-uk.com

Waterflow
See UKDN Waterflow

Waterman Transport & Development Ltd
Pickfords Wharf, Clink St, London, SE1 9DG
T: 020 7928 7888
F: 020 7902 0992
E: paul.worrall@watermangroup.com
W: www.waterman-group.co.uk

Waverley Rail Project
See Borders Railway Project

Wavesight Ltd
Talon House, Presley Way, Crownhill, Milton Keynes, MK8 0ES
T: 01908 265223
F: 01908 265143
E: sales@wavesight.com
W: www.wavesight.com

Webasto AG
Kraillinger Strasse 5, 82131 Stockdorf, Germany
T: 0049 89 857 948 444
F: 0049 89 899 217 433
E: tac3@webasto.com
W: www.rail.webasto.com

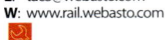

Webro Cable & Connectors Ltd
Vision House, Meadow Brooks Business Park, Meadow Lane, Long Eaton, Notts, NG10 2GD
T: 0115 972 4483
F: 0115 946 1230
E: info@webro.com
W: www.webro.com

WEC Group Ltd
Spring Vale House, Spring Vale Rd, Darwen, Lancs, BB3 2ES
T: 01254 773718
F: 01254 771109
E: stevecooke@wecl.co.uk
W: www.welding-eng.com

Weedfree
Holly Tree Farm, Park Lane, Balne, Goole, DN14 0EP
T: 01405 860022
F: 01405 862283
E: sales@weedfree.net
W: www.weedfree.net

Weidmuller Ltd
Klippon House, Centurion Court Office Park, Meridian East, Meridian Business Park, Leicester, LE19 1TP
T: 0116 282 3470
F: 0116 289 3582
E: marketing@weidmuller.co.uk
W: www.weidmuller.co.uk

Weightmans
High Holborn House, 52-54 High Holborn, London, WC1V 6RL
T: 020 7822 1900
F: 020 7822 1901
E: sarah.seddon@weightmans.com
W: www.weightmans.com

Weighwell Ltd
23 Orgreave Place, Sheffield, S13 9LU
T: 0114 269 9955
F: 0114 269 9256
E: rwood@weighwell.co.uk
W: www.weighwell.co.uk

Weld-A-Rail Ltd
Lockwood Close, Top Valley, Nottingham, NG5 9JM
T: 0115 926 8797
F: 0115 926 4818
E: admin@weldarail.co.uk
W: www.weldarail.co.uk

The Welding Institute
See Institute of Rail Welding

Welfare Cabins UK (WCUK)
See Garic Ltd

A J Wells & Sons Vitreous Enamellers
Bishops Way, Newport, IOW, PO30 5WS
T: 01983 537766
F: 01983 537788
E: enamel@ajwells.co.uk
W: www.ajwells.com

Wentworth House Rail Systems Ltd
Unit 4a, Avenue One, Crewe Hall Enterprise Park, Crewe, Cheshire, CW1 6UA
T: 01270 254176
E: enquiries@railelectrification.com
W: www.railelectrification.com

West Coast Railway Co.
Jesson Way, Carnforth, Lancs, LA5 9UR
T: 01524 732100
F: 01524 735518
E: info@wcrc.co.uk
W: www.wcrc.co.uk

West Midlands PTE
See Centro

West Yorkshire PTE (Metro)
Wellington House, 40-50 Wellington St, Leeds, LS1 2DE
T: 0113 251 7272
E: metroline@westyorks-ca.gov.uk
W: www.wypte.gov.uk

Westcode Semiconductors
Langley Park Way, Langley Park, Chippenham, Wilts, SN15 1GE
T: 01249 444524
F: 01249 659448
E: customer.services@westcode.com
W: www.westcode.com

Westermo Data Communications Ltd
Talisman Business Centre, Duncan Rd, Park Gate, Southampton, SO31 7GA
T: 01489 580585
F: 01489 580586
E: sales@westermo.co.uk
W: www.westermo.com

Westinghouse Platform Screen Doors
Knorr-Bremse Rail Systems (UK) Ltd, Westinghouse Way, Hampton Park East, Melksham, Wilts, SN12 6TL
T: 01225 898700
F: 01225 898705
E: wpsd.enquiries@knorr-bremse.com
W: www.platformscreendoors.com

Westinghouse Rail Systems
See Siemens Rail Automation

Westley Engineering Ltd
120 Pritchett St, Aston, Birmingham, B6 4EH
T: 0121 333 1925
F: 0121 333 1926
E: g.dunne@westleyengineering.co.uk
W: www.westleyengineering.co.uk

Weston Williamson
43 Tannner St, London, SE1 3PL
T: 020 7403 2665
F: 020 7403 2667
E: chris@westonwilliamson.com
W: www.westonwilliamson.com

Westquay Trading Co. Ltd
3F Lyncastle Way, Appleton Thorn, Warrington, WA4 4ST
T: 01925 265333
F: 01925 211700
E: enquiries@westquaytrading.co.uk
W: www.westquaytrading.co.uk

Westshield Ltd
Waldron House, Drury Lane, Chadderton, Oldham, OL9 8LU
T: 0161 682 6222
F: 0161 682 6333
E: mail@westshield.co.uk
W: www.westshield.co.uk

Wettons
Wetton House, 278-280 St Jamess Rd, London, SE1 5JX
T: 020 7237 2007
F: 020 7252 3277
E: mark.hammerton@wettons.co.uk
W: www.wettons.co.uk

WH Davis Ltd
Langwith Rd, Langwith Junction, Mansfield, Notts, NG20 9SA
T: 01623 741600
F: 01623 744474
W: www.whdavis.co.uk

Wheelsets (UK) Ltd
Unit 4B, Canklow Meadow Ind. Estate, West Bawtry Rd, Rotherham, S60 2XL
T: 01302 322266
F: 01302 322299
E: martin@wheelsets.co.uk
W: www.wheelsets.co.uk

White & Case LLP
5 Old Broad St, London, EC2N 1DW
T: 020 7532 2310
F: 020 7532 1001
E: twinsor@whitecase.com
W: www.whitecase.com

White Young Green
See Amey

Whiteley Electronics Ltd
See Gemma Lighting

Wicek Sosna Architects
Unit 15, 21 Plumbers Row, London, E1 1EQ
T: 020 7655 4430
E: office@sosnaarchitects.co.uk
W: www.sosnaarchitects.co.uk

Wilcomatic Ltd
Unit 5, Commerce Park, 19 Commerce Way, Croydon, CR0 4YL
T: 020 8649 5760
F: 020 8680 9791
E: sales@wilcomatic.co.uk
W: www.wilcomatic.co.uk

Wilkinson Star Ltd
Shield Drive, Wardsley Ind Est, Manchester, M28 2WD
T: 0161 793 8127
F: 0161 727 8538
E: steve.ross@wilkinsonstar.com
W: www.wilkinsonstar.com

WillB Brand Consultants
Studio 17, Royal Victoria Patriotic Building, John Archer Way, London, SW18 3SX
T: 020 7112 8911
M: 07815 056026
E: will@willbaxter.com
W: www.willbaxter.com

William Bain Fencing Ltd
Lochin Works, 7 Limekilns Rd, Blairlinn Ind. Est, Cumbernauld, G67 2RN
T: 01236 457333
F: 01236 451166
E: sales@lochrin-bain.co.uk
W: www.lochrin-bain.co.uk

William Cook Rail
Cross Green, Leeds, LS9 0SG
T: 0113 249 6363
F: 0113 249 1376
E: castproducts@william-cook.co.uk
W: www.william-cook.co.uk

Williamette Valley Company - WVCO Railroad Division
1075 Arrowsmith St, Eugene, OR 97402, United States
T: 001 541 484 9621
F: 001 541 284 2096
E: sales@wilvaco.com
W: www.wvcorailroad.com

206